GREAT BRITAIN AND CHINA
1833–1860

GREAT BRITAIN
AND CHINA
1833–1860

DS 740.5
G5
C65
1968

BY

W. C. COSTIN

Fellow of St. John's College,
Oxford

OXFORD
AT THE CLARENDON PRESS

FEB 28 '72

166951

Oxford University Press, Ely House, London W. 1

GLASGOW NEW YORK TORONTO MELBOURNE WELLINGTON
CAPE TOWN SALISBURY IBADAN NAIROBI LUSAKA ADDIS ABABA
BOMBAY CALCUTTA MADRAS KARACHI LAHORE DACCA
KUALA LUMPUR HONG KONG TOKYO

FIRST PUBLISHED 1937
REPRINTED LITHOGRAPHICALLY IN GREAT BRITAIN
FROM CORRECTED SHEETS OF THE FIRST EDITION
AT THE UNIVERSITY PRESS, OXFORD
BY VIVIAN RIDLER
PRINTER TO THE UNIVERSITY
1968

PREFACE

THIS study of British diplomacy in China, and of its efforts to open that great country more fully to Western influence, political, economic, and religious, suggested itself to me as a result of a visit paid to the Far East in the winter of 1931. I have to thank the generosity of the Rhodes Trustees which enabled me to leave Oxford for two terms and the kindness of Mr. Lionel Curtis, who, by arranging for me to be one of the British members at the Hangchow Conference of the Institute of Pacific Relations, put it in my power to travel as far as the capital of Szechuan Province. I was in particular stimulated to make this examination by the fresh and lively conversations which I was privileged to enjoy, in Shanghai, Nanking, and Peiping, with Mr. de Kat Angelino, the distinguished Adviser in Chinese Affairs to the Government of the Dutch East Indies.

The ground I have traversed has already been covered in detail by Mr. H. B. Morse; and the general aspect of the scene will be found very similar to that depicted by him. However, some of the materials I have used are different, and I venture to think that some new light is thrown upon the motives of the principal persons. I have relied mainly upon the dispatches between the Foreign Secretaries and the Crown's agents, to be found partly in the published *Parliamentary Papers*, partly in the original manuscript in the Public Record Office. These I have supplemented by the manuscript records in the archives of the Quai d'Orsay and the manuscript correspondence of the Catholic missionaries of Les Missions Étrangères in their Paris House. To these must be added the published American official papers in the Senate Executive Documents. Some published accounts of contemporary travellers such as Robert Fortune, works of British officers like T. T. Meadows, and eyewitness descriptions of military and naval commanders such as General Sir Hope Grant I have found interesting and for my purposes useful. It has been a matter of regret to me that I have not been given access to Lord Palmerston's papers at Broadlands, but the Peel and Auckland papers in the British Museum and the Granville and Russell papers in the Record Office have thrown light on events and more particularly on opinions when news from China arrived in England during a parliamentary recess.

Many Chinese documents in translation are among the dispatches of British officials. The publication of the Peiping archives which is being undertaken by Professor Tsiang may yield some fresh illustrations of the motives of the Chinese Court and its local officers, but it is probable that our knowledge of events will not thereby be greatly increased. The British agents were obliged to report as accurately as they could for the information and, if necessary, subsequent action of their principals in London. Their accounts and their opinions could be, and frequently were, checked and criticized by the direct and informed contact of the Chambers of Commerce, missionary societies, and other unofficial persons with the Foreign Office and members of Parliament. Unlike the British officers in China, the Chinese local Mandarins were left alone to manage affairs as best they might; the central authorities would only be interested if trouble arose whether from the Barbarians or from the native population in the trading ports. The Imperial officers were therefore under no necessity to report accurately to a Government which was in fact not governing; and they were directly interested in giving such reports as would be most pleasing to the Councils and the Emperor at Peking. This practice led to a misunderstanding of the nature and motives of the Western peoples which was undoubtedly one of the prime obstacles to a harmonious reconciliation of interests.

The romanization of Chinese proper names, which varies considerably in different documents, has been made uniform for each name. No attempt, however, has been made to standardize them: for example, I have employed the hyphen in Tung-chow but not in Tientsin. I have generally called Chinese or Manchu personages by their family names alone.

I would like to express my thanks to the personnel of the Record Office, the British Museum, and the Quai d'Orsay for their kindness and help; and to Père Sy of Les Missions Étrangères who so readily gave me access to the papers of that Society. I am deeply grateful to the Principal of Hertford and Professor H. A. Smith who have been good enough to read the book in manuscript and to give me invaluable criticism, and my thanks are also due to my colleague Mr. J. D. Mabbott. Finally, Mr. G. D. Bone, Fellow of St. John's, has very kindly read the book in proof and saved me from many a pitfall. For any errors whether of fact or judgement I am alone responsible.   W. C. C.

1936

CONTENTS

CONTENTS

VI. LORD ELGIN'S FIRST MISSION, 1857–9

VII. BRUCE'S MISSION, 1859

VIII. LORD ELGIN'S SECOND MISSION, 1860

MAPS

INTRODUCTION
GREAT BRITAIN AND CHINA BEFORE 1833
A. THE BRITISH TRADERS,[1] 1635–1833

FOLLOWING in the wake of Vasco da Gama, the Portuguese were the first Europeans to arrive by sea on the coasts of China, where, in the second decade of the sixteenth century, they established factories at various ports. But by the middle of the century these early enterprises had for the most part come to grief, and from 1580, in consequence of the conquest of Portugal by Spain, the Dutch became the dominant European race in the Far East, ousting their rivals from the control of the Malacca Straits—the gateway to the Pacific. It was their hostility in the reign of James I that frustrated the attempts of the 'Governor and Merchants of London trading into the East Indies' to secure a base at Hirado, a small island off the west coast of Japan, and thence to open negotiations for a direct trade with China. The Portuguese, however, threatened, like the English, by the Dutch supremacy and virtually cut off from their outlying factory at Macao, thought to improve their position by an agreement with the English. Their Viceroy at Goa agreed to allow the English to trade at Macao, but it was a vain understanding; for the local Portuguese Governor at Macao who opposed the scheme had sufficient interest with the Chinese authorities in Canton to bring it to naught. But in 1635 Captain Weddell, in command of four ships in which Charles I had an interest to the extent of £10,000, arrived off Canton. Though he got involved in hostilities with the Chinese, he was allowed to depart with a poor cargo after signing a declaration that his action was due to ignorance of Chinese customs, and that in future 'if we should act in any way contrary thereto, we will submit to any punishments the Mandarins and the City of Macao shall order'. Thus the first contact between English and Chinese ended in a failure—due very largely to the action of the nationals of another European power—the Portuguese.

During the latter part of the century conditions in southern China were very unsettled owing to the opposition offered by Ming supporters to the Manchu dynasty, an opposition which

[1] H. B. Morse, *Chronicles of the East India Company Trading to China*, contains full evidence of the activities of the Company and its agents in China before 1833.

persisted for thirty years after the establishment of the new government in Canton. Though in Charles II's reign the English obtained factories at Amoy and Taiwan on Formosa, trade was difficult owing especially to the exactions of the Manchu military officials. The ship *Delight*, for example, besides presents of guns and powder to the Emperor, had to pay exactions amounting to £2,000. But in 1687 the East India Company was investing £15,000, mainly in specie, in two ships trading at Amoy. English woollens did not find a ready market in the seventeenth or eighteenth century when the trade was with southern China, but lead, of which 40 to 60 tons was a usual quantity for one ship to carry, was a considerable export.

From early times the English noted the formation of a close corporation of Chinese merchants—'a set number of 8 or 10 exclusive of all others' who 'should buy our goods and contract for China cargo. This was oppressive to the merchants that had not liberty to trade, and indeed very prejudiciall to us, for we were forct to take what this knot of men wou'd give us.' On the other hand, when there were several ships in port, the super-cargoes of each would be competing against one another. But after 1715 the ships formed one fleet, all the supercargoes acted as a college, and the orders, accounts, and decisions were signed by all members of the Council. The supercargoes had to be not only commercial agents but men of diplomatic and linguistic ability, for a knowledge of Portuguese was almost necessary, as the early interpreters were mainly half-caste Portuguese. They had to know all the intricacies of exchange rates as nine-tenths of their imports consisted of silver, currencies of Spain, Mexico, France, or Venice. At the beginning they had low salaries—the chief in Amoy in 1681 received only £80 per annum. But, on the other hand, they were allowed a private trade of their own—in 1674 they with the ships' officers took out £135,000, nearly one-third of the Company's public venture. They were soon limited in their purchases, as the Company reserved the tea and spices for its own exclusive trade.

At Canton there were exactions and bribes to be paid, and it was difficult to deal with any merchant but the 'Great Mandarin's Merchants'. The Hoppo, or head of the Chinese Customs and Trade Department, went down to the outer anchorage and, on receipt of measurement dues and sundry presents, gave a pass, or 'chop', to proceed up the river to Whampoa. There another chop, a permit to trade, would be delivered before the hatches could be opened. The supercargoes soon came to prefer the Canton to the Amoy trade, owing to better facilities for their cargoes and the presence there of reliable and substantial Chinese merchants. By 1716 twenty foreign ships traded there. At first the Chinese merchants of Canton were frustrated in their attempt to maintain the organization of a close merchant gild or Hong by the passive resistance of the English, who refused to go up the river to Whampoa until the trade was resumed on its previous free trade basis. The Viceroy of the time, desirous of obtaining objects of curiosity for the Emperor, ordered the dissolution of this newly formed Hong. But by 1755 the English resistance had broken down and the trade was restricted to the limited number of Hong merchants and to such shopkeepers as entered into partnership of five persons for security of debts. This development led to an attempt to re-establish a direct trade with Ningpo which had failed in 1736, and now failed again. The influence of the Cantonese on the Peking Government was strong enough to induce the central authorities not indeed openly to forbid the trade at Ningpo, but effectively to kill it by charging greatly increased duties. From the middle of the eighteenth century, therefore, the trade was restricted both to certain persons and to the port of Canton. But it continued to increase most remarkably. The average annual tonnage, which was 7,500 in the forties, doubled in the next decade. In the period between the American and French revolutionary wars it averaged 56,000, at the end of the Napoleonic Wars, 97,000, until in the 1820's it exceeded 120,000 tons.

The trade, however, was subject to serious handicaps. The Hong system itself was open to grave criticism. These merchants became the channel of communication between the supercargoes or Select Committee of the Company and the local authorities. They were supported by the Hoppo and the Viceroy. The Company had to accept them as securities for the ships and for the good behaviour of the crews, and with them alone could trade in the staple articles be conducted. By 1779 two of the eight licensed Hong merchants were openly bankrupt, two were hopelessly involved, and one only was regarded as of unassailable credit. The total debts of the Chinese amounted in the aggregate to four and a quarter million dollars,[1] the accumulated interest on which, by Chinese law, could not be collected beyond an amount of twice the principal. As a result of the intervention of Admiral Vernon, the Imperial court ordered the property of two of the merchants to be seized; the balance of which, after Government debts had been met, was to be applied to the satisfaction of the English creditors. The Viceroy was instructed to draw up a body of rules which contained provisions for the re-establishment of the gild as a 'cohong', as it had existed between 1760 and 1771, in which all the Hong merchants became jointly responsible for the debts of an individual member.

The establishment of a guarantee pool called the Consoo Fund, into which was paid the produce of a special import tax, meant that foreign trade was taxed to provide an indemnity for bankrupt Hong merchants. But though difficulties of a financial character were not easily remedied, the Select Committee had a strong weapon at its command. Thus only four years before the lapse of the Company's monopoly of trade in 1833, they had held up the shipping at the mouth of the river until the Chinese authorities had increased the number of the Hong merchants and secured the return to Canton and to business of a Hong merchant who had absconded with his capital.

More serious was the occasional exercise of jurisdiction over foreigners by the Chinese authorities. In 1780 they carried out a sentence of strangulation upon a French seaman who had killed a Portuguese sailor. This the Select Committee thought a dangerous precedent.

'The late instance fully shews the nature of the Proceedings of a Chinese Tribunal. It condemned the unfortunate delinquent, although there were no witnesses they could examine, and the only circumstances on which a judgement could be formed tended to shew he was forced to it for self-defence. This act of the Chinese magistracy hath deprived us of the only Privilege we thought to possess in this Country.'

Four years later a Chinese was accidentally killed by an Englishman when a ceremonial salute was being fired. The Chinese demanded that the gunner should be handed over to them,

---

[1] The Carolus Dollar was worth approximately 4s. 6d. During the years 1853–6 its value increased and fluctuated violently round 6s. 6d.

held the captain of the ship concerned, the *Lady Hughes*, who happened to be in Canton, as a hostage, and threatened the English with a stoppage of trade and deprivation of food supplies. The Select Committee, understanding that an inquiry for form's sake only would be instituted, handed over the unfortunate gunner, who after reference to Peking was condemned and suffered death by strangulation. As a result the English chief outlined a project of extra-territoriality and reported to the directors in London that 'foreign nations have made similar representations to their superiors. They have considered this from the beginning a common cause.'

This incident gave rise in 1788 to the expedient of sending a mission to the court of Peking. There was already in existence a species of jurisdiction in the hands of the Company, for mutinous sailors could be tried by the captains of the ships, and, after confirmation of the sentence by the Select Committee, flogged with 18 to 100 lashes. But more was wanted—the recognition by the Chinese authorities of exclusive British jurisdiction over British subjects in all cases. Though the mission was never fulfilled, as its head, Lord Cathcart, died on his way out, the instructions prepared for his guidance were used when, five years later, Lord Macartney succeeded in gaining an Imperial audience. The British envoy was bidden to disabuse the Peking court of any idea it might have formed as the result of suggestions by other Western Powers that Great Britain was seeking to extend her sovereignty in every quarter. If he could persuade the Emperor to cede an establishment, he was to take it in the name of the King of Great Britain, and in that case he was instructed to seek the widest power of regulating the police and exercising jurisdiction over British subjects

'so as effectually to prevent or punish the Disorders of Our People, which the Company's supercargoes in their limited sphere of Action must see committed with impunity. Should it be required that no native Chinese be subject to be punished by our Jurisdiction, or should any particular modification of this Power be exacted, it is not material to insist upon it, provided British Subjects can be exempted from the Chinese Jurisdiction for crimes they may commit and that the British Chief be not held responsible if any culprit should escape the pursuit of justice, after search has been made by British and Chinese officials acting in conjunction.'

But though Lord Macartney was received at court in Peking,

in Jehol, and at the Summer Palace, no negotiations could be set on foot.

There were further incidents at the beginning of the next century. In 1807 riotous and drunken sailors of the ship *Neptune* killed a Chinese. The judicial officer demanded the culprit. Eventually the fifty-one sailors who were on shore in Canton at the time of the occurrence were brought up from the Whampoa anchorage to the city and examined in the presence of the British chiefs by Chinese officers. They all pleaded not guilty. On the following day the Chinese selected one man from among his companions to expiate the crime. The Company, however, were prepared to jeopardize their trade worth five million taels[1] rather than allow the surrender of the sailor. Finally, the security merchant of the man's ship, who had been cast into jail, paid an exorbitant bribe and the charge was altered to one of accidental killing. The matter was referred to Peking, and the alleged culprit, who all the time had been held a prisoner by the Company, was sentenced merely to pay a fine equivalent to £4. In 1820, when a Chinese was accidentally shot, by coincidence another sailor committed suicide. The death of the latter was accepted by the Chinese as adequate atonement. The real culprit got away from Whampoa to Lintin, took refuge in H.M.S. *Liverpool*, and ultimately returned to England on board a merchantman. The Chinese were, however, able to report that 'the chief of the English Residents having repaired to the ship and instituted an enquiry, which induced in the foreigner so great a dread of the crime he had committed, so that he killed himself, still showed a reverence for the Laws'. Such a subterfuge, however, was not at the disposal of the Americans when an Italian sailor named Terranova in one of their ships the *Emily*, in an attempt to chase away an importunate woman selling fruit, fatally struck her. When the captain of the ship refused to hand over to the Mandarins the man, who after a Chinese trial had been found by them guilty of homicide, the security merchant was put into chains and all American trade was stopped. Upon the assurance of the Hong merchants that another and fair trial should be held, the Americans produced the alleged culprit, who was tried by the

[1] The tael is a weight of silver (approx. 1⅓ oz. av.) varying in exact weight and fineness from city to city. During the period covered by this book it can be taken to be equivalent to 6s. 8d.

provincial judge and two days later strangled on the common execution ground. The whole foreign community, reported the Chief of the Select Committee, were surprised at the apathy and lack of exertion of the Americans in that affair. The American Consul, a merchant, apparently made not the slightest remonstrance.

The wonder is that with such diversity of customs the Chinese and foreigners managed to get along and prosper to the extent that they both did. The growth in the number of the country ships—as the individual traders, licensed by the East India Company, plying between India and China were called—added to the difficulties. If the Select Committee had had only their own Company ships and crews to control, things might have been easier. The directors in London were informed in 1781 that

'long Experience has shewn the Chinese that we must suffer almost anything to avoid an impediment to our Trade: but Country Ships are every day committing some irregularity, which sets aside their Decrees and mortifies their Pride. These they sometimes permit to pass unnoticed, and sometimes make it a pretence for oppressing the Hong Merchants; but when it becomes a matter of too great magnitude to be passed over, the Company are held responsible; they will not allow themselves to believe that every Englishman who comes here, is not under the Controul of the Chief; though every day Experience might have convinced them of the contrary.'

The danger to the Company increased with the growth of the importation of opium, which was by Chinese law a prohibited commodity. Already in 1771 the Select Committee at Canton had asked the Presidents of Bombay and Madras to prevent the importation of the drug, owing to the trouble that it was likely to cause to the general trade. Nevertheless, Warren Hastings in 1782 shipped three thousand chests in two ships, one of which eluded the French privateers and delivered her opium to a merchant, not of the Hong, who had already, by bribing the local officials, engaged in the trade. Such ventures were, however, uncommon. It was rather the country ships which were active in this trade which, though of importance in the financial economy of India, did not yet bulk sufficiently large in the China trade for the British Government at the time of Cathcart's mission to exclude the possibility of agreeing to a stipulation, in any commercial treaty which he might induce the

Emperor to make, against further British importations of opium. 'The sale of ophium in Bengal must be left to take its chance in the open market, or to find a consumption in the dispersed and circuitous traffic of the Eastern Seas.' At the end of the century, however, the Canton Council again asked the Indian authorities to forbid its being placed in any of the Company's ships, for although no new edict had been issued they apprehended possible trouble. The general belief, however, was that as this trade had produced great fees to the Hoppo, who clandestinely encouraged it, effectual preventive means were not to be expected. After 1800 the opium deliveries were entirely restricted to the country ships which delivered this cargo when sold at Whampoa direct from the ships to the Chinese purchasers, who made their own arrangements with the local authorities. In 1817 the British country ships imported over 600,000 dollars' worth at Whampoa. In addition, at Macao the Americans imported from Turkey close on half a million and Portugese and other ships three million dollars' worth of the drug. In 1819 J. P. Cushing, the head of the great American firm of Parkins, sold 300,000 dollars remitted from America to Calcutta for bills on mercantile houses in Canton, to meet which drafts opium and raw cotton were consigned to China.

Though after 1822 the opium trade at Whampoa was stopped and ships now sold the drug in the outer anchorages at Lintin, the 'facility that is now afforded in the disposal of this Commodity to regular Brokers in the vicinity of the River it is considered will render the alteration in the Traffic of no moment'. At Lintin the British and American opium ships anchored and delivered the drug to boats called 'fast crabs' manned by desperate people who could offer a violent but easy resistance to the Chinese war vessels, whose crews consisted of men hired at low wages and often ignorant of seamanship. This was not usually necessary, as the Hoppo's officers were frequently the agents by whose instrumentality the smuggling was undertaken. But this smuggling trade encouraged similar practices in other commodities, which could be and were easily disposed of in the same way, in order to escape payment of port and customs charges.

Restrictions of a personal character, galling to the foreigners residing in China, constituted another class of difficulties. They were not allowed inside the walls of the city of Canton, for the factories were situated in a small suburb between the city and the river. Theoretically they were only allowed to remain there during the shipping season, but in the summer months the Company's servants in fact frequently went up river and the agents of private firms trading with a licence from the Company habitually resided throughout the year at Canton instead of in Macao. The wives of the foreign merchants had to stay behind in Macao, and in 1830 the Viceroy threatened to invade the Canton factories by armed force to drive away the wife of a foreigner who was reported to be lodged there. Nor were the foreigners allowed to be carried in chairs unless they were ill or it was raining. The foreign community greatly resented the placarding of a proclamation calling attention to their depraved morals and enjoining on the Chinese merchants and linguists the duty of bringing them up to the level of Chinese civilization. The Select Committee pointed out that the supercargoes and writers in the Company's employ were sons and brothers of country gentlemen. In the following year there was a great dispute over a question of an improvement which the English had made in front of the factories, which had been destroyed while they were away at Macao during the summer. Feeling was rising high on both sides.

Meanwhile, the East India Company had lost its monopoly in trade to India, and though its stockholders received their dividends entirely on the profits of the Eastern tea trade, considerable criticism was aroused by the continuance of its monopoly in the direct trade between Great Britain and China. During the Napoleonic Wars when, except for the brief period 1812–14, the United States had been at peace with the world, American trade at Canton had prospered considerably. Part of this trade consisted in importing teas to Europe, some of which found their way illegitimately to England. American citizens could ship British goods at Liverpool and sell them in Canton. Naturally, the private, 'country' traders argued that it were better that they should satisfy a demand if the Company were unable or unwilling to do so. There were also cogent reasons against opening the China trade. The existence of the powerful unified commercial interest of the Company's supercargoes, who were regarded as the heads of all the foreigners by the Chinese, gave a considerable prestige and safety to all

the foreign community. Yet the position of the country traders
was anomalous. James Innes, who had refused, unlike some of
his British contemporaries, to shield himself under a commission
as consul from a continental Power, alleged that he had received
free merchant's indentures from the court of directors. Nevertheless, though the Select Committee thought it their duty to
attempt to expel him as unauthorized to tarry in Canton, they
reported that he was a man of excellent character, and they
could not but express their conviction that the residence in
China of respectable individuals who were British subjects was
more desirable from the standpoint of the Company than that
of foreigners over whom they had no control, and into whose
hands the conduct of the very important trade in opium and
other branches of the commerce with India would necessarily
fall, if British subjects were prohibited from forming commercial
establishments for that purpose in China.

In 1830 a Select Committee of the House of Commons published a mass of evidence on the trade with Canton; and the
free traders had their way in the non-renewal of the monopoly
of the Company, whose charter expired in April 1833. The
local Chinese authorities in Canton were anxious at the prospect
of the British merchants being left unorganized and uncon-
trolled, perhaps especially as the country traders had in the
past been the chief smugglers. Accordingly, the Viceroy in 1831
ordered the Co-Hong to inform the Company's Select Committee in Canton that in the event of the dissolution of the
Company it would be incumbent on the directors 'to appoint
a chief who understands the business, to come to Canton for
the general management of commercial dealings'. The Select
Committee were aware that the opening of the trade might
lead to an increase of smuggling and therefore to a diminution of the revenues of the Government, as well as to more frequent collisions between Europeans and Chinese. In either
case the trade might be stopped. It might have been desirable to obtain a commercial treaty at the time of the expiration of the monopoly. But it was rightly thought that only
by coercion could the Chinese be induced to enter into such a
treaty.

B. CHINESE SOCIETY AND GOVERNMENT IN 1833

The China with which the British Foreign Office was to come into direct contact through the triumph of the free trade movement was little understood in the circles of Lord Palmerston or Sir Robert Peel. Indeed, those most familiar with life in China had inevitably looked upon her with the myopic eyes of the merchant in the market-place. It was no doubt unfortunate that in the Chinese scheme of things the merchant was a member of a despised class. First in honour came the scholar, who alone was fitted for administration, then the farmer, after him the craftsman, and only in the fourth place the merchant. No doubt in the England of William IV the governing class would regard the merchant as somewhat on a lower social plane, but of all the Western Powers the English aristocracy had been most ready to intermarry with wealthy traders. Nearly four hundred years before 1833 the Hull merchant family de la Pole had made marriage connexions with the royal family, while the increase in the wealth of the nation by fostering and extending its commerce had been of primary concern to the landed gentry of the eighteenth century. The Chinese Emperor could observe with scorn in 1849: 'It is plain that these Barbarians always look on trade as their chief occupation and are wanting in any high purpose of striving for territorial acquisitions', to which his interlocutor replied: 'At bottom they belong to the class of brutes; it is impossible they should have any high purpose.' It was, perhaps, unfortunate too, that the British Government, so much influenced by the great trading cities, should select as the title of their representative in the East, 'Superintendent of Trade'. From the beginning a false note was struck.

But it would have been impossible for the governing class in China to have looked upon the British or other Western peoples in any other light than as barbarians. For hundreds of years they had known but the nomadic Mongols, the miserably poor Thibetans, the enervated Annamites, and the slavish Coreans or Japanese. Compared with these peoples the Chinese were without exaggeration the dwellers in the central flowery kingdom, enjoying the special favour and enlightenment of Heaven. A Chinese ruler must have regarded the border races of his known world much as a Roman emperor surveyed the backward tribes beyond the Wall, the Rhine, or the Danube: proud of the achievements, intellectual, aesthetic, and spiritual of his own folk, disdainful of the degradation and barbarism which surrounded them on all sides. Just as Claudius Lysias, refusing to try Paul 'whom I perceived to be accused of questions of their law', and Festus, finding that the Jews 'had certain questions against him of their own superstition', regarded the local customs of the Jews, though valid in the Jewish community and enforceable by Jewish authorities, as of no concern to the Roman Government, so the Chinese, except in cases of homicide, were quite prepared to allow foreigners to decide things among themselves. It was not according to reason that the outer barbarians should be able to live according to the law of reason, a law fit only for the enlightened children of the central kingdom. This claim of the Chinese to a monopoly of civilization was naturally regarded by the British as a mark of oriental arrogance, as stupid as it was unwarranted. While they were prepared and expected to treat the 'Emperor' on terms of equality with their own sovereign, it was impossible for the Son of Heaven to regard George III or Queen Victoria as other than a dependent ruler, differing only in turbulence and martial ability from the tributary potentates of Siam or the Loochow Islands. There could be but one Son of Heaven, and to him as mediator between the Almighty above and the people below all other sentient creatures owed reverence and obedience.[1] It was this unbridgeable difference in attitude towards each other that made impossible the harmonious development of international relations between China and Great Britain—by the beginning of the nineteenth century incomparably the most important Western State in Chinese waters. And this was the fundamental cause of the antagonism which manifested itself in two wars popularly called from the incidents which were their occasions the Opium and the Lorcha *Arrow* Wars. Not until after the second of these was finally brought to an end in 1860 were foreign ministers allowed to have direct intercourse with the supreme authorities in Peking; even then another thirteen years had to elapse before they were admitted to an audience with the Emperor, and only in 1894—seventeen years before the Empire collapsed—was equality of status fully recognized.

Indeed the Western Powers were long in understanding that they were not dealing with anything comparable to a sovereign

---

[1] De Kat Angelino, *Colonial Policy*, to which I am much indebted.

State in their sense of the word. They were deluded by a knowledge of the existence of an integrated hierarchy of officials, whose titles were translated into Western terminology, into thinking that they recognized a State such as those with which they were familiar in Europe. China had, it is true, a wonderfully organized administrative system dependent upon the Emperor, whose will alone appeared to direct the subordinate officers of the Government. There was no feudalism interposing an autonomous authority, such as had existed in medieval Europe or as still prevailed in contemporary Japan. In the eighteen provinces the viceroys or governors exercised their functions as representatives of the Peking throne and were frequently recalled or dismissed by an act of the Imperial will. They had never established hereditary fiefs, for at regular intervals they were summoned to the capital to give an account of their stewardship. These provinces contained an average of 80 Hsien or districts, within which in a walled city resided the Magistrate who bore the familiar name of 'Father and Mother of the People' and who to its inhabitants was the Emperor in miniature. He was connected with the throne by three grades of officials (called by the Westerners Mandarins)—the Prefect of the Department, and above him the Intendant or Taoutai of the Circuit, through whom the Provincial Governor or Viceroy, who alone had the right of direct communication with the court, was reached.

In Peking there was an elaborate series of councils, and though there was nothing in the nature of a parliamentary control of the Emperor, the Board of Censors checked all ministers central and local, and even enjoyed the duty of remonstrating with the Emperor himself. The translation of the title of the supreme ruler, 'Teen-tze', as 'Emperor' was unfortunate. It would have been far more in consonance with realities if he had always been designated the 'Son of Heaven', for he was in fact rather a spiritual head than a political potentate. He was the supreme mediator, the representative on earth of the Heavenly Power. It was by good government alone, or, in other words, by acting in accordance with divine principles laid down in the sacred books, that he or his house could establish a claim to divine right. Hence the Board of Rites at Peking was the most important department of State, and the most characteristic function of the Son of Heaven was the due performance of the sacrifices, and especially those of the winter solstice when, after a night of abstinence, he mounted the Altar of Heaven to obtain the favour of the Supreme Being, whom he alone could invoke, for himself and his people during the ensuing year. Failure to observe the traditional code of behaviour, the non-removal of extortionate and evil ministers or governors or the occurrence of earthquakes, war, pestilence, and famine were sure signs of the removal of Heaven's mandate. The famous historical novel *San Kuo* opens with the downfall of the Han dynasty. There were evil councillors, a monstrous black serpent coiled itself on the very seat of majesty, a terrific tempest with thunder, hail, and torrents of rain worked havoc on all sides, two years later the earth quaked in Loyang, while a tidal wave swept away all the dwellers by the sea, a mountain fell in, and certain hens developed male characteristics. 'So the Government went quickly from bad to worse, till the country was ripe for rebellion and buzzed with brigandage.' On occasions such as these the Emperor would issue an abjectly humiliating decree, publicly accusing himself of unworthiness and announcing his repentance in a trembling effort to avert the execution of divine justice. The Chinese Government therefore rested on an ethico-religious basis and was far from being a military despotism. Though each province had its Manchu garrison, which numbered 800 men in Anhwei and 68,000 in Kwantung, there were but some 600,000 Manchu troops and Chinese militiamen in the whole Empire. It was a force which could deal with factious risings, but if the people as a whole grew dissatisfied, nothing could stop a rebellion. When a rebellion had so far succeeded, it would of itself be proof of the lack of divine support of the ruler, and its successful leader could become the new Emperor. In this way, for example, the Ming dynasty had been founded, and in this way the Taipings in the middle of the nineteenth century bade fair to assume control of China. For while the Chinese are the least revolutionary of peoples they are the most rebellious. Indeed, the right of rebellion would appear to be the chief right they possessed.

From this standpoint, from a consideration of the hierarchy of officials, all theoretically owing their places to success in the democratic literary examination system, it might appear that China was a highly centralized theocracy: perhaps more akin to the Papacy than to any other institution of western Europe. One would only have to laicize it for China to become a State.

But this is only one side of the picture. For this wonderfully compact governmental system was essentially not governmental at all. It was in fact the expression of the cultural and ethical unity of a vast population of varied races and speech. China of the Imperial days was far more like medieval Europe than the England of Lord Palmerston. Just as in medieval Europe there was, in Latin, a common language for the men of learning, so that a scholar of Oxford would be at home in Paris, or a Lanfranc educated at Pavia could live in the court of the Conqueror and administer the Province of Canterbury; just as in medieval Europe there were common institutions, rooted in a common ethic of which the Church and her Pontiff, the vicar of Christ on Earth, were the guardians and interpreters moulding the Canon Law, not *ex arbitrio*, but in accordance with received and revealed moral standards—so too China had its common literature and its ideographic script, intelligible alike to a Cantonese, to a Pekinese, or to a Szechuanese, and the Son of Heaven developed the Law of China in accordance with the accepted fitness of things and sought in every way to bring about harmony between Heaven and Earth.[1] And too, just as within this cultural and religious unity of western Europe of the Middle Ages, the real bond of human association, the real πόλις, was not the State but the simple township, gild, or manor, so China consisted of myriads of petty republics—of families, clans, gilds, and villages.

Family life in China was exceedingly strong and found its deepest expression in a veneration of common ancestors which bound the members together in a common religious act.[2] Under one roof several generations might live, for the family would not break up so long as either parent was alive, and often not even then. It was customary for the children to be married at an early age, that they might beget male grandchildren to satisfy the elders that acts of honour would be duly performed for them after their demise. The property was in common stock, administered by the father or on his death by the eldest son. Collectively the family was responsible for the crimes of its members, as it was held that the moral turpitude of the individual could be traced to his bad education. Corrupt fruit

[1] De Kat Angelino, op. cit.
[2] Y. K. Leong and L. K. Tao, *Village and Town Life in China*; A. H. Smith, *Village Life in China*.

suggests a corrupt tree, and in extreme cases the whole family might be exterminated. The Chinese family, therefore, entailed a subordination of the individual economically and morally, a phenomenon characteristically medieval rather than modern. The institution of adoption was a necessary corollary to this close conception of the family. A rich man would take a concubine or secondary wife and so continue his line, but most men could not afford such a luxury. An Imperial law laid down that 'a man having no male issue shall choose the continuator of his line from among those who are of the same clan, beginning with his father's issue, next relatives of the first and third degrees, lastly the fourth degree. If these all are impossible he may take any one of the same clan. Unlawful appointment is to be punished with 80 blows.' It is interesting to observe that in this most important matter the Imperial law was in fact not obeyed. Different customs of adoption prevailed in the various clans: there were different rules in the same village. In some clans it was not necessary to select a member of the same clan, and where clan custom did prescribe such selection, the Imperial degrees might not be obligatory. There was no effective 'national' law on this subject.

All the members of a clan bore the same surname, and the various families which constituted it were themselves bound together by the common veneration of the clan spirits on their birthdays, and by common gatherings for social purposes, in the ancestral hall. In south and central China it appears that great clans have lived together for centuries and have given their names to the villages. The clan owned joint property, out of which were met the expenses of the upkeep of the temple and graveyards. A clansman was bound to observe the customs and moral code of his group, to aid his fellows whose rights were infringed by outsiders or who had fallen on evil days. There was a tribunal of elders and an executive of, perhaps, twelve, nominated by the annually retiring committee and approved by the whole clan. The twelve controlled the ancestral hall, looked after the common property, paid taxes and collected rents. They could not, without the approval of three-quarters of the members, alienate the common land from the corporate revenues of which the members received money, feasts, fowls, and meat. To partake of one's share was an act of sacramental nature—a linking up of one's family with the wider organization of the clan.

The wealthy felt called upon to give free education to poorer clansmen, while every member would help a promising boy to prepare for the various Civil Service examinations for the honour which success in those competitions conferred on the clan as a whole. In addition the clan provided maternity benefits, old age and widows' pensions, free medical treatment and burial. Hence normally there was no occasion for the village and still less for the Imperial authorities to provide organized relief.

The centre of the life of the village (which might contain families of more than one clan) was the village temple, an institution more resembling a town-hall than a parish church. To it the superstitious would resort to have their luck forecast by a priest drawing lots, or to invoke individually the war-god Kwanti, Peh-ti the culture god, or maybe Wen-Chang the patron of schoolboys and literature. But the village elders and literati, successful candidates in the examinations who, not being absorbed in the Civil Service, were often disgruntled men, rather than the priests, were *par excellence* the temple officers, men holding their position on a more or less permanent footing with the sanction of popular feeling and recognized by the officers of the Government. They were the true leaders and mouthpiece of the community, to whom strangers would repair to make complaint or seek redress against a member of the village and who would conduct the foreign relations by entering into treaties of alliance with neighbouring villages, and by deciding whether strangers could reside in their area. They controlled the arrangements for the annual patronal festival, made provision for the decorations, illuminations, and general merrymaking for that occasion, which was not so much a religious act as a sort of annual carnival. Their police duties entailed the supply by each householder of a man to watch for so many days and nights, or in case of danger from large gangs of robbers the mobilization of the whole male population over sixteen years old. They also supervised public lighting, the repair of roads and canals, and provided schooling when this was not done by the clan hall. They exercised judicial functions and arbitrated in disputes. This and all their other public work was done, significantly enough, not as agents of the Central Government, but in the name of the temple. Indeed, one of the most characteristic functions of the elders and literati was to voice popular opposition to the measures of the governmental officers.

'Seen from the distance and judged by some isolated acts which now and then are recorded in the newspapers', reported the British Plenipotentiary in 1852, 'it might seem as if the Emperor of China was the depository of unlimited power. . . . Yet nothing can be further from the truth. The Sovereignty of the Emperor is constantly receiving severe checks—engaged in public controversies with public opinion or with the more violent outbreaks of armed malcontents— it often surrenders and succumbs to an opposition which it cannot subdue. In a word, it governs as much as it can, and when it is unable to govern it negotiates or bribes, and in thus acting it merely perpetuates the habits and the traditions of its ancient history, and gives effect to the teaching of a succession of sages who are the moralists and the lawgivers alike of the Ruler and the People.'[1]

The Magistrates were always extremely sensitive to popular outbursts, led by the elders and literati. In 1857 a violent protest was made by nineteen villages of the silk districts near Hangchow. The soldiery was repulsed by the people who imagined themselves to be overtaxed, and the Magistrates fled.[2]

There was, therefore, a considerable amount of self-government and voluntarily imposed organization in the Chinese village, which was extremely jealous of external interference. At best the central authorities could indicate a policy: reform or change had to come from within and not from without. If the Imperial authority attempted to interfere with the government of the village it would immediately find itself involved in a sea of difficulties. As Sir Robert Hart observed in 1871, 'the Chinese idea is for the locality to initiate and for the central authority to (i) wink at, (ii) tacitly permit, (iii) openly allow, (iv) officially recognize, and (v) crystallize. It is useless to attempt—except where outside force does it—to get the central offices to *order* the adoption of *novelties.*'

To complete the picture of the self-governing social organization mention should be made of the gilds—gilds of co-provincials safeguarding the interests of their members in a foreign province, merchant gilds such as the bankers, rice dealers, or tea-men. Such bodies had a strong sense of corporate duty which found its sanction in the threat of expulsion and casting the friendless individual out of society. Like the gilds of medieval Europe they had a common worship and observed the birthday

---

[1] Bowring to Clarendon, 5 May 1852 (F.O. 17/189).
[2] Bowring to Clarendon, 5 Oct. 1857 (F.O. 17/272).

festival of the patron deity. These bodies existed naturally in towns, and their organization ran side by side with the village system, since China never developed a municipal government. Each city was composed of chia or wards of a hundred families and was in fact a collection of villages destitute of a unifying urban organization.

Such was the loosely knit collection of societies with which the British Government in 1834 came for the first time into direct relations. Much of the misunderstanding and many of the difficulties with which it was faced were due to a failure to appreciate this curious and to them anomalous situation. It had been much easier in the past when Anglo-Chinese relations were on the plane of relations between two merchant gilds—the monopolistic Hong and the monopolistic East India Company, acting normally in commercial competitive co-operation, and occasionally in economic conflict. But now William IV and his niece were to attempt to enter into discussions on the basis of equality with men whom they regarded as fellow sovereigns. They expected the Emperor of China to make agreements with them and to enforce such agreements upon his own subjects as they in their turn would fulfil their part in any stipulations which they had contracted. But the Peking Government, based on a wholly different conception of society, could not but look at the foreigners at Canton as tribes bordering on the southern extremity of the Celestial Kingdom, which had to be pacified by a wise officer entrusted to arrange local matters with the reasonable people of the Empire as well as with the irrational barbarians to whom force and not reason appeared to be the ultimate sanction. This attitude was well expressed in an Imperial edict issued shortly after the Treaty of Nanking: 'These foreigners having but newly been brought back to peace, a border quarrel must not be suffered again to break out.'[1]

Nor were the Emperor and his officers in a position to control the Chinese as was ultimately the London Government able, by law, to curb the turbulent British merchants. Thus in 1855 the elders and literati of Foochow came to the rescue of the people of that city, who were suffering from an influx of base coins, by compelling 'the Mandarins to exchange the bad for good money at the cost of the Imperial Treasury. Similar influences', reported Sir John Bowring, 'are constantly in action

[1] Pottinger to Aberdeen, 19 Apr. 1843 (F.O. 17/67).

—it is in the same spirit that leaders of revolts and insurrections are frequently recompensed by being admitted to high offices in the government service. No government is more arbitrary and cruel where opinion comes to its aid—nor more feeble and surrendering where there is any apprehension from popular clamour.'[1]

Before relations between Great Britain and China could be put on a satisfactory basis, the Chinese rulers would have to regard themselves as sovereigns, endowed with the prerogative of foreign relations and able to recognize in the British, French, Russian, or American Governments entities such as they were themselves. But the process could not be complete until the Chinese people also could lift their horizon beyond the narrow bounds of the societies which alone had a positive attraction and cohesive power, and achieve a conception of a national State which might well comprehend but must also transcend the closer and more palpable organizations of the family, clan, village, and gild. How far during the century which has followed the arrival of the first representative of the British State and Sovereign this result has been attained by the impact of the Western States with their doctrine of international law, which premises a condition of sovereign States, is a question for the publicist. Let us turn now to the story which will take us in a generation from the exclusive merchant society of Canton to the legally founded international society of Peking.

[1] Bowring to Clarendon, 5 Nov. 1855 (F.O. 17/234).

I

FIRST OFFICIAL CONTACTS, 1834–9

A. NAPIER TO ROBINSON, 1834–6

IN consequence of the abolition of the trading monopoly of the East India Company, a new era began in the relations between the Western Powers, notably Great Britain, and the Celestial Empire. Apart from the special missions of Macartney and Amherst, there was to be for the first time an attempt made to found an establishment on a wider and more secure basis than could be provided by a mere commercial connexion between two monopolistic bodies of merchants—the East India Company's Select Committee and the Hong merchants at Canton. For now His Britannic Majesty sent a commissioned officer not only as a protector of his subjects and an overseer of their commercial activities, but as a political and diplomatic representative at the Yamen of the Viceroy at Canton. The commission, which was dated 10th December 1833, was followed by instructions issued to Lord Napier, who was given the style of First Superintendent of Trade. He was to have as colleagues Davis and Robinson, former supercargoes, now Second and Third Superintendents, with Captain Elliot, R.N., as 'Master Attendant'. It is significant that the Government chose a person of the rank of Napier, the eighth baron, and that he was under the direction of the Secretary of State for Foreign Affairs. Clearly, as the bearer of a royal commission, a Scottish peer of ancient lineage, and a Foreign Office servant he was something more than a mere superintendent of trade. He was to forward to the Secretary of State an account of the trade, both British and foreign, to assist British subjects in the prosecution of their lawful pursuits, and to enjoin them to conform to the laws of the Chinese Empire so long as these were fairly and equally administered. He was to ascertain whether it were possible to extend foreign trade to other parts of China and to Japan, but he was warned against jeopardizing the existing trade by a precipitate attempt to secure wider channels of commerce. He was not to call for armed assistance 'unless, in extreme cases, the most evident necessity shall require it'. At the same time Palmerston instructed him that 'the establishment of direct communications with the Imperial court at Peking would be desirable'. He was informed that it was the Government's intention to set up a Court of Justice for British subjects in China; and finally Palmerston placed prominently in the instructions the injunction, 'Your Lordship will announce your arrival by letter to the Vice-roy'[1].

On the 15th July 1834 Napier arrived in Macao, which though a Portuguese settlement, ruled over by a governor, was not in the sovereignty of Portugal. There, however, were the English church and graveyard and the residences of the wives and families of the foreign community. It was the advanced base of foreign activities in the Far East, though as the sequel will show, under but very inadequate European control, if ever a conflict should arise between the foreign element and the Chinese. Thence, after a stay of eight days, Napier went up to the Boca Tigris, the entrance to the Canton River, where he was received with a salute of guns from a war junk. On his arrival in Canton his troubles began. He sent his secretary to one of the city gates with a letter informing the Viceroy of his appointment. The Mandarins there refused to receive it on two grounds—it should have been presented through the close monopolistic corporation of Hong merchants, the sole avenue of communication between foreigners and the Chinese authorities, and it was described as a letter, whereas it should have been endorsed, as a humble petition, with the character 'Pin'. Even after consultation with the Viceroy, so that they alone should not bear the responsibility of refusing to accept the letter, the Mandarins remained obstinate. The senior Hong merchant tried in vain to prevail upon Napier to change the mode of his address. The truth was that the Viceroy was annoyed that Napier had come to Canton without permission. He had tried to stop him at Macao, but Napier had eluded the messengers. It had been the custom of the senior merchant of the East India Company to wait at Macao until the pleasure of the Emperor had been taken on his humble request to proceed up river to Canton. Napier confessed to Palmerston that he wished

'to open and maintain a direct personal communication with the vice-roy, so that I may be enabled to get redress from him in all commercial grievances connected with the Hong Merchants, and in criminal proceedings connected with the office of Kwang-chow-

---

[1] Palmerston to Napier, 25 Jan. 1834 (P.P. 1840, xxxvi, nos. 1–3).

foo, or Criminal Judge, instead of leaving myself at the mercy of those Hong Merchants who in fact, exercise no official powers whatever, and can never be depended upon for the transmission of complaints to the different heads of departments when circumstances require.' Napier thought he was acting both in accordance with his instructions and with the practice, 'so often exercised in times past by the President of the Select Committee, of enjoying direct communication with the Viceroy'[1].

Napier called down upon his head four edicts and the assembly in Canton of 40,000 troops. But contemptuous of this display of force—for he regarded the soldiery as so ridden with vice that their value as fighting men was negligible—he remained on in the suburbs of Canton. If the British Government wished to extend trade with a high hand, he gave it as his opinion that they could do so 'with a facility unknown even in the capture of a paltry West Indian island', and that, in fact, was the only way in which it could be done. The Chinese authorities, unlike the people, did not care for trade and commerce so long as they received their pay and plunder. 'The Viceroy is a presumptuous savage', 'the Government of utter imbecility', 'our first object should be to get a settlement on the same terms that every Chinaman, Pagan, Turk or Christian, sits down in England.'

Napier was demanding equality between himself as representative of the British Crown and the Viceroy at Canton. This latter officer, however, could only regard Napier as 'Barbarian Eye', whose object was solely commercial. 'The Celestial Empire appoints officers—civil ones to rule the people, military ones to intimidate the wicked. The petty affairs of commerce are to be directed by the merchants themselves.' If any changes were to be made in foreign trade, the Hong merchants should consult together and make a joint statement to the Viceroy, and his reply to their suggestions must be awaited. The great ministers of the Empire were not allowed to have private intercourse by letter with outside barbarians, and the Viceroy[2] Loo refused to receive any dispatches from Napier.[3]

[1] Between 1731 and 1816 the supercargoes visited the Viceroy on seven occasions. The last visit had been paid in 1816. Napier to Palmerston, 9 Aug. 1834 (recd. 31 Jan. 1835) (ibid., no. 6).
[2] Napier styles Loo 'Governor' but the title should be translated 'Viceroy', as he was in charge of the two 'Kwang' Provinces of Kwangtung (Canton) and Kwangsi. Each of these two provinces was headed by an officer whose title is generally given as 'Governor'.
[3] Napier to Palmerston, 14/17 Aug. 1834 (ibid., no. 7).

Loo held the Hong merchants responsible for the conduct of Napier and ordered them to contrive his removal from Canton immediately.[1] Napier offered to drop the demand for the reception by the Viceroy of a letter if Loo would send a high officer to conduct him to a personal interview, but this suggestion was declined by the Viceroy. The Hong merchants accordingly stopped British trade, and their action was enforced by the Kwang-chow-foo. Napier thought that, as the greater part was already carried on by smuggling, the rest could wait without hardship until he heard whether the British Government would allow him, backed by force, to negotiate a treaty.[2] But he was also certain that 'if after a fair trial of all justifiable means, I find the merchants likely to suffer, I must retire to Macao, rather than bring the cities of London, Liverpool, and Glasgow upon your Lordship's shoulders; many of whose merchants care not one straw about the dignity of the Crown or the presence of a Superintendent'[1].

It looked, however, as though the Chinese authorities were beginning to vacillate, for on the 22nd August the two senior Hong merchants brought a request that Napier should receive three officers of high rank, two civil and one military.[3] The conference took place on the following day and was marked, on the part of Napier, by an insistence on his due position which caused the dismissal from office of the senior Chinese negotiator. For in the reception room at the English factory where the interview was to take place the chairs were arranged by the Chinese to give their officers the seats of honour. Indeed, the British commissioners were to be placed in seats inferior in honour to those allotted to the Hong merchants. Napier had the seating rearranged so as to assert his equality. In answer to Chinese inquiries Napier stated that he had come in accordance with the Viceroy's order of 1831 to the Hong merchants and in virtue of his royal commission. The nature of his business was contained in his letter to the Viceroy, which the officers could open and read if they would promise to deliver it, and lastly he informed them that he would return to Macao when it suited his convenience. This ended the conference.

This meeting was to have been followed by another on the

[1] Napier to Palmerston, 14/17 Aug. 1834 (P.P. 1840, xxxvi, no. 7).
[2] Napier to Lord Grey, 21 Aug. 1834 (ibid., no. 11).
[3] Napier to Palmerston, 27 Aug. 1834 (recd. 24 Feb. 1835) (ibid., no. 12).

30th, but this never took place owing to the insistence of the Mandarins on a new arrangement of chairs. Both sides issued public proclamations maintaining their points of view and the trade stoppage was declared absolute on the 4th September, the Superintendent's house was surrounded by soldiers, and orders were issued to prevent Chinese serving the English either at Canton or Macao and selling them provisions. Napier ordered up two frigates to Whampoa (in which three men were lost in a clash with the forts at the Boca Tigris) and a guard for the Superintendent's office. He announced that if trouble resulted it would be due to the Hong and the Viceroy, that he would take steps to inform the Emperor of his officer's proceedings, that the King of Great Britain with immense territories obeyed no one—he had fierce soldiers and great warships.[1] There could be no negotiations between such diametrically opposed points of view. War might have broken out if Lord Napier, bound by his instructions to do nothing which might cause a grievous loss to the British merchant community, some of whom were apparently already disturbed at the turn of events,[2] had not fallen seriously ill, and decided on the 14th September to ask leave to return to Macao. He was conveyed by the Chinese thither, 'sous bonne garde à peu près comme on conduit les criminels', wrote an unsympathetic Catholic missionary.[3] They took a circuitous route and delayed the journey to make certain that the frigates had left Whampoa according to Napier's instructions given as a condition of his leaving the factories. It was asserted that this delay was partly responsible for Napier's death. He arrived in Macao on the 26th September, and died there on the 11th October. Trade was opened up on the 29th September.

Davis, the Second Superintendent, then took over the management of the commission, and decided upon a policy of 'absolute silence and quiescence on our part until further orders are received from home'. In reviewing recent events he was led to regret that a letter had not been sent through the Viceroy from the King to the Emperor together with a few presents.

'It seems to me', he wrote to the Foreign Office, 'that the native government had some right to it, and that it was an eligible and

[1] F.O. Memorandum, Feb. 1840 (ibid., no. 14).
[2] Agents of E. India Coy. to Directors, 29 Sept. 1834 (ibid., no. 16).
[3] Legrégeois to Dubois, 28 Sept. 1834 (M.E., vol. 321, f. 167).

inexpensive way of dispelling or allaying their characteristic suspicion. The next best thing might have been a discretionary power
vested in Lord Napier in the event of the provincial authority being
found hostile or impracticable (an event quite within the range of
possibility) to send up a respectful address to the Emperor by the
Yellow Sea, announcing the change and praying for just and liberal
treatment from the Canton Government.'

But the First Superintendent was precluded from following this
line of action by the express instruction to avoid communication
with the central government without reference to London.

'I would have wished that, at so great a distance as 15,000 miles,
a larger latitude of discretion had been allowed. My own moderation and love of peace . . . have always made me lean to the maxim
of "quieta non movere" but should the foolish unfriendliness or
misconduct of the provincial government give us trouble in spite
of a uniform conciliation and forbearance on our part, a quiet
appeal to Peking (without any Embassy whatever) seems a very
easy and unobjectionable remedy.'[1]

And he was convinced that not until such an appeal to the
capital had been shown to be fruitless would it be proper either
in point of policy or justice to adopt coercive measures. As
things were, he foresaw

'no expectation of any voluntary advances from the Chinese authorities towards the recognition of His Majesty's commission. The
government of foreigners, through the medium of the Hong Merchants, is a system too valuable to the Canton officers, in diminishing
their responsibility, and enabling them to practise their heavy
exactions with impunity, to be readily abandoned by them'[2].

Point was added to this opinion by the Hong merchants requesting the local British merchants to elect a taepan, or senior
merchant, from among their number.[3] The object of this move,
which was unsuccessful,[4] was clearly to sidetrack the commission.
Meanwhile, the Melbourne Ministry had fallen and the Duke
of Wellington had taken Palmerston's place as Foreign Secretary. He deprecated force and violence. It was by 'conciliatory measures so strongly inculcated in all the instructions
which you have received' that the Government sought to
establish a commercial intercourse between British subjects and

[1] Davis to Foreign Office, 7 Aug. 1834 (F.O. 17/6).
[2] Elliot to Backhouse, 1 Nov. 1834 (P.P. 1840, xxxvi, no. 20).
[3] Davis to Palmerston, 2 Nov. 1834 (recd. 12 Mar. 1835) (ibid., no. 21).
[4] Davis to Palmerston, 11 Nov. 1834 (ibid., no. 24).

China.[1] Wellington was quite certain that Lord Napier's high-sounding titles[2] were but the pretext for the jealousy of the Chinese towards him; the true cause of it was his pretension in fixing himself at Canton, without previous permission, and insisting upon direct communication with the Viceroy. The Superintendent must not go to Canton without permission. He must not depart from the accustomed mode of communication.[3] The Duke thought it necessary for the sake of trade that the First Superintendent should be a person of official rank and reputation, and that he must be enabled to control and keep in order British subjects. He recommended that a Chief Superintendent should be appointed who would fulfil these requirements and that he should be assisted by a Secretary-Treasurer as his deputy. The Second Superintendent should be a lawyer to preside over the court which it was proposed to erect for the control of British subjects.

The reaction to the Napier affair was, however, very different in the case of sixty-four British merchants headed by members of the Jardine and Matheson families. They deprecated strongly a quiet submission to insult. They asked for the appointment of a plenipotentiary backed by three warships and empowered to demand from the Peking court the dismissal of Loo and redress for the trade stoppage, and expressed the opinion that there would be no difficulty in intercepting the greater part of the internal and external trade of China and the capture of all the armed vessels of the Empire. 'Voilà donc Mrs. les Anglais convaincus qu'on ne fait pas trembler je ne dirai pas l'Empereur de Chine mais le Vice-Roy de Canton avec de la jactance et quelques coups de canon.'[4] They desired also the restoration of trade which had been carried on previously with Amoy, Ningpo, and Chusan. They objected to the limited number of Chinese merchants with whom they could have dealings, and summed up the position by stating 'we have laboured under disabilities because of our acquiescence in the theory of Chinese superiority'[5].

[1] Wellington to Napier, 2 Feb. 1835 (ibid., no. 10).
[2] This point was stressed by a Catholic missionary who criticized Napier for making 'Un long numéraire de ses titres sans oublier celui de sa noblesse, moins encore sa qualité de Representant de Sa Majesté très puissante le Roi de la Grande Bretagne' (Legrégeois to Dubois, 28 Sept. 1834 (M.E., vol. 321, f. 167)).
[3] Wellington Memorandum, 24 Mar. 1835 (P.P. 1840, xxxvi, no. 23).
[4] Legrégeois to Dubois, 28 Sept. 1834 (M.E., vol. 321, f. 167).
[5] British Merchants in Canton, Petition to King in Council, 9 Dec. 1834 (P.P. 1840, xxxvi, no. 27).

Davis criticized the petition of the British merchants as crude and ill-digested, and stated that some of the most respectable houses refused to sign it.[1] But the Glasgow Chamber of Commerce also pressed for direct access to Peking and the opening of the whole coast to trade, while the Foreign Office received a well-reasoned memorandum from a British merchant who had traded in Canton and intended to return there,[2] in which he argued that, had the monopoly of the East India Company remained, the two sets of monopolistic traders could well have settled disputes between themselves. Now, however, the 'British traders are broken into numerous fractions without any bond or community of interest'. 'That Lord Napier acted in some respects injudiciously I will not attempt to deny, that the Chinese were predetermined to insult him and that no moderation on his part would have procured for him a fitting reception.' No one else of character should be exposed to such treatment, nor was it sensible to keep up at Macao an establishment costing £20,000 a year. Either a policy of armed interference for the redress of past grievances and future security should be pursued or the attempt to establish political relations should be abandoned. If the second alternative was adopted, a minor customs official should be appointed to give clearances to shipping. If trouble arose and the Chinese asked who the chief British officer was, they could be told that their conduct had precluded the appointment of such a person. On what grounds, the writer asked, could war be justified? Obedience is owed to the laws of a foreign country. 'But, on the other hand, it always presupposes that our intercourse is with a civilized nation, that the laws and regulations to which your compliance is required are clear and defined and that they give a reasonable protection to Life and Property.' Now in China, the argument ran, this was not the case. There were no defined laws for the guidance of foreigners; but they varied according to the whim and caprice of the local authorities, and neither life nor property could be considered secure, 'specially in regard to the barbarous regulations they endeavour to enforce respecting Homicides, which are equally at variance with Chinese Law, Humanity and Reason'. He was certain that negotiations would be fruitless, but thought that a demand should be made

---

[1] Davis to Palmerston, 19 Jan. 1835 (recd. 18 May) (ibid., no. 31).
[2] H. H. Lindsay, Berkeley Square, Jan. 1836 (F.O. 17/16).

for a commercial treaty on terms of equality and liberty of trade
at two or more northern ports. The use of expressions such as
barbarian and devils must be stopped. 'So long as this superiority
continues there is no hope.' The writer then discussed, on the
assumption that coercion was justified, the best methods of coercion. He was of opinion that a small naval force assembling in
the Straits of Malacca in March and sailing up the Chinese
coast with the monsoon would so vex their great coastal trade
as to cause the Imperial Government to grant these terms.
And he cast an interesting glance at the other Western Powers
at the end of his memorandum. 'I feel satisfied that the French,
Dutch, and Americans would gladly see us adopt such a line
of conduct towards the Chinese, for the simple reason that they
would participate equally with ourselves in all the advantages
to be acquired therefrom.'

Meanwhile the commissioners had again experienced difficulties with the Chinese authorities in Canton. Sir George Best
Robinson took over the first place on the commission when
Davis retired on the 21st January 1835. Sailors of a British ship
who had been sent ashore by their captain for provisions fifty
miles west of Macao had been seized and held to ransom by
pirates who demanded 500 dollars. Captain Charles Elliot, the
new Third Superintendent, sent to the Water Gate near the
Viceroy's Palace in Canton with a letter from the superintendents requesting help in releasing these sailors, was roughly
handled and knocked down by the Chinese soldiers. Two
general officers appeared after some delay, but refused to
receive the letter as it was not in the form of a petition.[1]
Robinson thereafter adopted a *laissez-faire* policy. 'I have
never, in the slightest degree', he reported to the Foreign
Secretary, 'perceived a disposition on the part of the Chinese
authorities to enter into communication, or even permit an
intercourse, with the officers of this Commission'[2]. Yet
though the mercantile marine service was in a very disorderly
state, it was surprising that so few difficulties had occurred,[3]
and that commercial activity was unabated. Robinson, who
regretted the bitter feeling which reigned in the foreign com-

[1] Extracts from 'Records of Proceedings', 29 Jan. 1 835 (P.P. 1840, xxvi,
no. 35).
[2] Robinson to Palmerston, 16 Oct. 1835 (ibid., no. 42).
[3] Robinson to Palmerston, 11 Nov. 1835 (ibid., no. 43).

munity at Canton,[1] pointed out that he possessed no civil jurisdiction whereby their disputes could be adjusted.[2] He was still more alarmed at his lack of power to prevent British subjects from committing excesses and taking, by arbitrary means, direct personal action against Chinese for alleged or substantial wrongs. The case of an irascible and strong-willed merchant, Innes, was an illustration of this difficulty. Innes was aggrieved at the action of the Chinese authorities and, had it not been for his respect for the commissioners, he would have sought by his own power what he considered his justifiable redress. Unless the British Government acted firmly a state of anarchy would result.[3]

At the end of the year Robinson transferred himself from Macao, where the commission had resided since Lord Napier's withdrawal, to the cutter *Louise*, stationed off Lintin.[4] There he was in a position to deal with difficulties masters might have with their crews on their arrival from England, and to give port clearances to ships coming from Canton, thereby saving them a visit to Macao. Moreover, Robinson was of opinion that the commissioners, as far as their purely commercial character was concerned, could never carry so much weight with the Hong merchants as did the traders. For they were of no advantage to the Hong merchants, unlike the late Select Committee of the East India Company, 'who with so powerful an engine in their hands as the Company's trade, were regarded by the Hong merchants with extreme deference and consideration; to which may be added, their having at their disposal, during the period when difficulties were likely to occur, a well-ordered and disciplined fleet'[5]. Robinson was convinced that

'the principal object of maintaining a British authority in this country, is to exercise a salutary control over the safety, conduct and perhaps property of the King's subjects in China: to arbitrate and assist in the adjustments of disputes and differences, and to prevent the occurrence of actions or proceedings whereby the natives of China may be wronged or aggrieved. To these ends a full and efficient control over the shipping is the main point. Little else seems requisite.'

[1] Robinson to Palmerston, 13 April 1835 (P.P. 1840, xxxvi. no. 39).
[2] Robinson to Palmerston, 1 July 1835 (ibid., no. 40).
[3] Robinson to Palmerston, 20 Nov. 1835 (ibid., no. 44).
[4] Robinson to Palmerston, 1 Dec. 1835 (recd. 25 Mar. 1836) (ibid., no. 46).
[5] Robinson to Palmerston, 10 Dec. 1835 (ibid., no. 47).

In his opinion by staying in Lintin he was efficiently achieving these ends. In Macao the Portuguese authorities did not recognize the commission. The Chinese authorities of Canton, he reported, were 'perfectly willing tacitly to permit our controul and superintendence of British subjects, provided we do not repair to Canton'[1]. It was true that the 'establishment of the commission at Canton was most desirable in itself, and likely to be attended with the greatest advantages and benefits'. Yet if the commission went to Canton, a step which could never be taken except by force of arms, it must be established in a proper and becoming position. He urged, if force were to be applied, that the 'occupation of one of the islands in this neighbourhood, so singularly adapted by nature, in every respect, for commercial purposes, would promptly produce upon this barbarous nation, arrogant in proportion to their ignorance, every effect we could desire'. The Government would have to make a decision on this question, though from the mere point of view of the control of the trade there was no necessity to take any active measures. In the meantime, until fresh instructions arrived he meant to act on the motto 'Letting that which is well alone'[2].

B. ELLIOT, 1836-9

Lord Palmerston, now back in the Foreign Office, had, however, other sources of information and other opinions than Sir George Robinson's before him in making a decision on the future of British relations with China. For Charles Elliot had undertaken, by request, a private correspondence with Lennox Conyngham of the Foreign Office, in which he developed his views of the situation.[3] Davis had already highly commended this colleague of his, reporting to the Government that 'the talents, information and temper of that gentleman would render him eminently suited to the chief station in this country'[4]. He had served with distinction under the Colonial Office as Protector of Slaves and a member of the Government in British Guiana. He had been ordered home in 1833 to put his know-

[1] Robinson to Palmerston, 29 Jan. 1836 (recd. 6 June) (ibid., no. 55).
[2] Robinson to Palmerston, 29 Jan. 1836 (recd. 14 June), (ibid., no. 57).
[3] Elliot to Lennox Conyngham, 11, 25, 28 Jan. 1836 (last recd. 6 June) (F.O. 17/15).
[4] Davis to Foreign Office, 9 Dec. 1834 (F.O. 17/6).

ledge at the disposal of the Imperial Government at the time
when the great measure for the abolition of slavery was being
prepared. For his helpful advice he had won the approval of
the Secretary of State, the Lord Chancellor, Sir Robert Peel,
and others. Though he had accepted at the age of 33 the minor
office of Master Attendant in Lord Napier's Commission, he
was dissatisfied, as he desired a position of greater authority and
responsibility.[1]

The correspondence of Elliot with Lennox Conyngham is
of prime importance as evidence of that officer's policy and
also of the attitude of the British Government, since Elliot was
selected by Palmerston for the office of Superintendent one week
after he had received the most important of these letters. Elliot
complained of the 'very heedless spirit in active operation at
Canton'. The conciliatory policy of the King's Government is
'not very generally approved amongst the fifty or sixty resident
Merchants at Canton'.

'The plain truth is that we have "two Houses" here, and they are
so desperately angry with each other that their feuds colour their
opinions upon every subject under the sun. One set of gentlemen
are *absolutely in a passion* with the whole Chinese government and
people because they are very ill-inclined to another set of gentlemen
who, they imagine, are willing to conciliate the Chinese and go on
smuggling quietly. I wish I could add that the moderate party were
the stronger, but that is not at all the case. The ardent gentlemen
have it hollow in point of numbers.'

Elliot informed the Foreign Office that Sir George Robinson
'has virtually suspended the functions of his colleagues. The
Chief Superintendent has only informed me of what he is going
to do or not to do'—And 'to be perfectly frank, I will not
conceal my own feelings of sincere regret that the strong necessity of taking up the cautious and conciliatory instructions of
the Government with an earnest spirit to give them effect, is less
apparent or palatable to my colleague Sir George Robinson than
it is to be wished it were'. Elliot hoped that there would be a
plain and strong expression of the determination of the Government to discountenance the temper shown by the majority of
the merchants.

'It is entirely our own fault that we have not long since renewed
our communications with the Provincial Government and I have a

---

[1] Elliot to Foreign Office, 13 Aug. 1834 (F.O. 17/6).

pretty strong conviction that this *standing out* upon the point of direct official intercourse with the Viceroy, without the intervention of the Hong Merchants, is not warranted by our Instructions. If poor Lord Napier could have carried the point without incurring serious risks, he was right at least to try, but be that as it may, I am sure we are wrong most needlessly and hazardously to protract a very unhappy experiment.'

He thought that the Chinese had been ready to receive the commission and that it was due to Napier's pretensions to exalted official rank and subsequent unhappy proceedings that the wishes of the Chinese had been defeated. As a result the commission would be exposed for some time

'to suspicion, and an assumed disregardfulness. But the pervading principle of the Chinese policy in respect to the European governments, and pre-eminently our own, is to keep the peace. . . . I believe then, that as soon as the Provincial Authorities at Canton were reassured in respect to the real feelings of the English officers there, and felt convinced that these last were hearty in their desire to conciliate, and to prevent difficulties, they would by the very force of circumstances come to exercise a daily increasing and most beneficial influence.'

He deprecated sending any one to China with high official rank until the Chinese themselves asked for such a personage. It would be mischievous to think of sending an ambassador, for as Sir Thomas Roe had advised the Company in 1614, 'an ambassador lives not in fit honour here'. And like Roe, Elliot was averse to the policy of annexing Chinese territory, partly on the ground of expense to the Home Government of large and growing establishments and partly from a doubt whether the present commercial and financial advantages would continue.

'My own strong opinion is that the Govern^t would do wisely to abstain from sending a High political officer to this country to exhibit any thing like a demonstration of force till there be some *specific* grievance, something to be redressed which calm expostulation has failed to accomplish. If any man be robbed by this Govern^t or unjustifiably killed or detained in captivity, there will be an *obvious cause* for earnest interference.'

He minimized the value of a commercial treaty as, owing to our inadequate knowledge of the language, the Chinese might well irritate and injure us by the most faithless and perplexing construction of its terms. Moreover, there was not much advantage to be gained from such a treaty, for

'practically speaking the aggregate of our trade with China is less burdened than it is in any other country with which we have commerce to an analogous extent. It is perfectly obvious that the officers of the Customs themselves *openly* adapt it to the necessities of the case. Articles charged with preposterous duties are entered by the officials themselves under other names, and thus the difficulty is avoided.'

One party indeed of the British merchants thought it scandalous that the Emperor should be defrauded and that they should have to resort to smuggling. But in Elliot's view it was foolish to run a very serious risk of disturbing a most prosperous commerce just 'to let them try their hands at the social, commercial, political, and religious regeneration of this Empire'. Elliot was sure that with caution, conciliatory conduct, and a very watchful attention to improve opportunities, the King's officers in China would soon win their way into the confidence of the Chinese Government. But they must possess some means of repressing rashness upon the part of the King's subjects, and thus convincing the provincial authorities that the British Government was in earnest in its 'expressions of deference and good will'. There was, in Elliot's judgement, nothing wrong with the instructions that had been given to the commissioners, though he agreed with Robinson in thinking that the establishment might require remodelling and reduction.

Elliot therefore offered the Government a line of conduct midway between Robinson's dilemma of staying at Lintin as a mere registrar of shipping or of entering Canton by armed force to make good an immediate footing of equality with the Viceroy. He was prepared to start all over again and endeavour by conciliatory proceedings to win the respect and confidence of the local provincial authorities. Palmerston, like Wellington, was naturally attracted by the possibility opened up by such suggestions, and by a dispatch of June 1836 placed Elliot in a position to carry his policy into effect. However, Elliot was enjoined to communicate directly with the Viceroy or Chinese officials on public matters to the exclusion of the Hong merchants, and he was to refrain from using the character 'Pin' in his communications to the Viceroy.[1] In other words, his

[1] Palmerston to Elliot, 22 July 1836 (P.P. 1840, xxxvi, no. 66).

communications were not to be in the form of a petition from
an officer of lower to one of higher grade, but of a letter to an
equal. This dispatch was received by Elliot in the middle of
January 1837. By that time he had been the responsible British
officer for one month.[1] The commission had been reduced to
one Superintendent, a Deputy, and a Secretary-Treasurer, so
that responsibility rested with one man.

On announcing his assumption of office on the 14th December
Elliot wrote that he entertained 'a strong persuasion that a conciliatory disposition to respect the usages, and above all to refrain from shocking the prejudices of this government, is the
course at once most consonant with the magnanimity, of the
British nation, and with the substantial interests at stake'[2].
The same day he sent a 'letter' to the Viceroy endorsed with the
character 'Pin'. This 'petition' was sealed and placed in an
envelope directed to the Hong merchants and forwarded from
Macao by the agents of the East India Company. The Viceroy
was in receipt of the letter on the 20th and he replied three days
later. As Elliot said in a private letter to the Foreign Office,

'it needed adherence to the bye gone forms of the Select Committee
as respected the *address* of the communication, together with some
cautious but formal means of showing that it was not from a mere
commercial chief. I was so fortunate as to reconcile these difficulties
by using the Chinese character which the committee were wont to
do in description of the *nature* of the address, and I added a few words
to the effect that it came *from an officer*. . . . By very great good luck
no doubt, but perhaps not without something of good management,
we hit the Governor in the right place at the right moment, and *He
broke the seals*. From the moment I knew that result, I felt I could
safely assure Lord Palmerston that there was a peaceful end to all
the risks and the mischief of the interruption of responsible communication.'[3]

To the Foreign Secretary he pointed out that 'the Hong Merchants indeed, are already merely messengers, for they unquestionably convey the paper to his Excellency's hands, sealed up.
. . . But in the passage of the papers from the Governor to us,
in a sealed shape, or at least through a respectable officer of the
Government, there remains a substantial point to be gained.'[4]

[1] Robinson to Palmerston, 14 Dec. 1836 (ibid., no. 79).
[2] Elliot to Palmerston, 14 Dec. 1836 (recd. 1 May 1837) (ibid., no. 84).
[3] Elliot to Lennox Conyngham, 2 Jan. 1837 (F.O. 17/19).
[4] Elliot to Palmerston, 27 Jan. 1837 (recd. 17 July) (P.P. 1840, xxxvi, no. 89).

In the middle of March an edict arrived from Peking, for the new Viceroy, Tang, had reported Elliot's letter of December to the Emperor, authorizing the grant of a passport to the Superintendent. Elliot congratulated himself that 'for the first time in the history of our intercourse with Canton the principle is most formally admitted, that an officer of a foreign Sovereign, whose functions are purely public, should reside in a city of the Empire'. Yet this view of his position was hardly warranted by the terms of the edict which, although indeed it stated that the 'said foreigner has received a public official commission for the control of the Merchants and Sailors', went on to minimize the change by adding 'Though his title and rank are not the same as that of the Taepan, the business of controlling does not differ'[1]. In consequence of the permission thus granted, Elliot duly arrived in Canton on the 12th April 1837. However, he soon had reason to modify his view 'that it is easier, much easier in this country to get on than to get in'[2]. For just before his arrival in the city he sent a direct letter to the Viceroy acquainting him with the rescue by a British ship of some Chinese sailors wrecked in a junk off Malaya. The Viceroy protested, in a letter to the senior Hong merchant, against the Superintendent's failure to conform to the old rules. He had omitted the respectful expression 'Celestial Empire', and had absurdly used such words and expressions as 'Your honourable country' and 'peace and goodwill between the two nations', 'giving utterance to his own puffed-up imaginations'. In consequence, the senior Hong merchants were ordered to peruse any communication before it was sealed by Elliot. No longer were they to be merely messengers bearing a direct communication.

Upon Elliot threatening to leave Canton, the Viceroy, however, allowed him to write directly, though he refused to do so himself. The Superintendent indeed had to be firm, for since his original letter subscribed with the 'Pin' character he had received Palmerston's dispatch of the 22nd July. Even before that he seems to have had doubts whether the British Government would approve his course of conduct, for in a private letter to the Foreign Office he asked for 'one line by the overland mail to Bombay just to tell me whether my movements are to be fatal to me or not'. He defended his actions by stating

[1] Elliot to Palmerston, 18 Mar. 1837 (recd. 2 Dec.) (P.P. 1840, xxxvi, no. 96).
[2] Elliot to Lennox Conyngham, private, 1 Jan. 1837 (F.O. 17/19).

that it was the fixed principle of Chinese policy never to make
any formal concessions to demands for relaxation, and that
negotiation supported by the appearance of an armed force
would result in the 'subversion of this Trade, if not for ever,
at all events for many years to come'[1]. After his passports for
Canton had finally arrived, Elliot expressed the hope, in a
private letter to the Foreign Office, that the British Government
would upon the whole be satisfied with the result of his proceedings, and

'to speak plainly, though I cannot bandy arguments with them, I
should be sorry you felt that I had any doubt of the perfect reasonableness of my own conduct. If Lord Palmerston finds fault with
me, I have had a quarter-deck education, and I know how to duck
my head to the storm, and hope for fairer weather. But I must
permit myself to say, that I do not think it would be easy to *persuade*
me I have done wrong. I believe I could show strong grounds to
support another view, if it were decent or respectful to debate with
your office.'[2]

As soon as Palmerston learned that Elliot had addressed his
letter to the Viceroy through the medium of the Hong merchants he had in fact instructed the Superintendent to state to
the Chinese officer that 'His Majesty's government will not allow
you to address the Chinese officers through the intervention of
private and irresponsible individuals'. And he again ordered
Elliot not to endorse his letters with a character used by an
inferior to a superior—a mode of communication which was
contrary 'to the established usages of England'[3]. Yet Palmerston
was glad to notice that in April the Viceroy had sanctioned
direct communications to himself and hoped that Elliot would
soon receive the Viceroy's letters direct.[4] Elliot seems, however,
to have thought that there might be some advantage in the
Viceroy's communicating to him through the channel of the
Hong merchants, as he could then argue that such communications could be regarded as at best highly credible but certainly
not as authoritative.[5] By June he was able to report that: 'I
am getting on; and with time, and caution and some degree

---

[1] Elliot to Backhouse, 23 Jan. 1837 (F.O. 17/19).
[2] Elliot to Lennox Conyngham, private, 18 Mar. 1837 (F.O. 17/19).
[3] Palmerston to Elliot, 12 June 1837 (P.P. 1840, xxxvi, no. 88).
[4] Palmerston to Elliot, 2 Nov. 1837 (ibid., no. 94).
[5] Elliot to Palmerston, 1 April 1837 (recd. 13 Nov.) (ibid., no. 99).

of countenance from Home, I think I should soon mend the aspect of circumstances here. Be assured that I have got hold of the right clue.'[1] The Viceroy had given him permission freely to pass up and down the river between Macao and Canton so that he could control the merchantmen.[2] In his opinion

'this establishment may now be declared to have taken root in the country; and the first shoot of its class which has ever been planted in the soil, I would hope that its early nurture will be encouraged. We were wont to hear on the spot (but that note has died away) and we have frequently seen it suggested in European publications that the entire removal of the King's officers from China would be a sound measure. I do believe that no course would be more unfortunate whether considered merely commercially or with some regard to those higher motives that certainly make it an object of vast moment to disabuse a remarkable government and people of their stiff-necked prejudices.'

He deprecated the further reduction of his staff, as their duties were rapidly increasing, and the necessity of a 'respectable attitude' together with the high cost of living made a financial reduction dangerous. The presence of an official British resident was greatly to the advantage of other foreigners, who would share in any relaxations which Britain, through her representative, might gain for his countrymen. 'The force of all those circumstances that have placed us in the station we occupy amongst the Nations of the Earth' committed the British Government to the 'task of peacefully subjecting the anti-social spirit of the Chinese, with many another hard but great work'. To make one of the British merchants a consul would entail, in spite of all their virtues, the 'complete sacrifice of respect in the Estimation of these people'[3].

Elliot was indeed soon able to make an inroad on the position hitherto maintained by the local authorities in regard to the method of correspondence. The Peking Government had instructed the Viceroy to have the opium ships removed from Lintin and the outer port. When this request was sent to Elliot through the Hong merchants, the British Superintendent, while

---

[1] Elliot to Lennox Conyngham, private, 12 June 1837 (F.O. 17/19).
[2] Elliot to Backhouse, 2 June 1837 (P.P. 1840, xxxvi, no. 102).
[3] Elliot to Lennox Conyngham, private, 28 July 1837 (recd. 8 Jan. 1838) (F.O. 17/19).

acknowledging that he was well aware of these irregularities, refused to transmit to his Sovereign a communication directed to him through such a channel. In consequence, the Viceroy ordered the prefect of the city and the chief military officer to authenticate his 'commands'. Thereupon Elliot promised to forward the dispatch by steam from Bombay.[1] But Palmerston's definite orders that Elliot should stop using the character 'Pin' brought the correspondence between the British and Chinese authorities to an end, for the Viceroy refused to recognize any other superscription. At the same time he ordered the Hong merchants 'to inform me that he entertained a respect for me, and that he had reported in that sense to the Emperor'[2]. Elliot appears to have resided in Macao from December 1837 until the following August, when he went up to Canton to explain to the provincial authorities the friendly nature of a visit about to be paid to Canton by Rear Admiral Sir Frederick Maitland, but as they still insisted on the use of 'Pin' he was unable to make any communication.[3] Palmerston fully approved of Elliot's conduct and ordered him to press for the dropping of the objectionable character.[4] He again issued similar orders in June 1839, though he gave general approval of Elliot's handling of the dangerous crisis that arose in the previous December during a phase in the opium dispute. The foreign factories were for two hours in the hands of an immense and excited mob. The Chinese authorities determined to search British boats suspected of this traffic. Elliot wished to accompany them himself to the boat station to prevent 'the well disposed' from being involved in the same consequences as the perverse, whom the British Government had no desire to protect. He thought it of such importance to gain this permission that, contrary to his instructions, he used the character 'Pin' in order to request it of the Viceroy. But at the same time the Viceroy agreed on this and future serious occasions to send his 'commands' to the Superintendent through the Prefect and the Commandant.[5] Elliot pointed out to Palmerston that the principle of direct official intercourse between British officers and

---

[1] Elliot to Palmerston, 18 Nov. 1837 (recd. 15 May 1838) (P.P. 1840, xxxvi, no. 109).
[2] Elliot to Palmerston, 29 Nov. 1837 (ibid., no. 111).
[3] Elliot to Palmerston, 7 Aug. 1838 (recd. 19 Feb. 1839) (ibid., no. 124).
[4] Palmerston to Elliot, 30 March 1839 (ibid., no. 129).
[5] Elliot to Palmerston, 2 Jan. 1839 (ibid., no. 137).

the Chinese Government in both directions had been granted.[1] He had ceded a point of form to win a point of substance and thus had prevented innocent British property and persons from falling into Chinese hands. Elliot might congratulate himself on having 'got in' without trouble, but he had not 'got on' very far by the beginning of 1839 when the long-threatened breaking-point in the strained relations of the British and Chinese at length was reached with the coming of the High Commissioner Lin to Canton.

C. THE QUESTION OF JURISDICTION, 1833–9

The difficulties that Elliot had to face were not by any means confined to the delicate task of establishing communications in a manner regarded by the British Government as sufficiently dignified. He had to contend also with the local British community. When he took over the commission he had no legal position which would give him or his colleagues any real control, and at the same time he had an unruly and intractable crowd of sailors and merchants with whom to deal. Before 1833 the Select Committee had been able in case of trouble from Chinese quarters to suspend trade, and in case of refractory behaviour by an individual British trader to refuse him a licence to trade. The abolition of the Company's monopoly had weakened the authority of the British chief by removing both these sanctions. Elliot could exert no pressure on the Chinese, nor had he, until later on, any jurisdiction by which he could enforce British law upon his countrymen. At the same time he felt it was impossible to hand over alleged malefactors for trial by the Chinese owing to the lack of a system of jurisprudence which could commend itself to Western ideas of justice. The Chinese doctrine of the responsibility of an association for the homicides committed by any one of its members led to a demand for the execution of any of its members in expiation of a crime attributed to an unascertained individual. There was general agreement that it would be impossible to allow British subjects to be tried by Chinese methods. The East India and China Association in London agreed that the British officer at Canton should have judicial functions.[2] The Duke of Wellington had stated that our 'officer must have great powers to enable him to control

[1] Elliot to Palmerston, 2 Jan. 1839 (P.P. 1840, xxxvi, no. 138).
[2] Larpent and others to Palmerston, 29 June 1836 (F.O. 17/16).

and keep in order the King's subjects'[1], while Sir George
Robinson had urged the necessity of the Superintendent being
able to control British subjects and to adjudicate in civil cases
arising between them.[2] In the summer of 1837 Elliot was still
emphasizing the necessity

'for the early establishment of official controlling regulations. It is
my bounden duty to press that subject upon the consideration of
His Majesty's Government. The altered state of this trade has filled
Canton with a class of people who can never be left to their own
devices amongst the natives of this country, without the utmost risk
to the safety of this trade, and to the respectability of the national
character. I never put my foot out of doors that I do not observe
evidence of a growing dislike upon the part of the common people
to our countrymen. It is the fashion of the young men particularly
to treat the Chinese with the most wanton insult and contumely, and
if this folly be not checked we shall have ugly matter to deal with.
We want police regulations to which Chinese could resort.'[3]

In the autumn of that year, indeed, Elliot was faced with a
kind of difficulty well known to the British Government, but
to meet which as yet no adequate steps had been taken. There
had been a fray between some British subjects, Lascar seamen,
and local Chinese, one of whom, it was alleged, had been
stabbed. The Chinese authorities seized the Lascars. To
Elliot's demand that they be handed over to him, Howqua,
the senior Hong merchant, replied that in France these men
would be tried by French law. Elliot answered that he would
agree to the analogy as soon as there was that equality before
the law between foreigners and Chinese in China which there
was between foreigners and Frenchmen in France. He urged
the

'utter impossibility to concede their right to try British subjects for
a breach of Chinese laws by Chinese officers, whilst those laws were
only partially administered towards them, and whilst appeal to
the higher Chinese tribunals is entirely shut out from them. All
that could be justly expected from my Government, under such
circumstances, was to provide means for the fair trial of British
offenders against Chinese life and property by British laws and
British officers.'

[1] Wellington (Memorandum), 24 March 1835 (P.P. 1840, xxxvi, no. 23).
[2] Robinson to Palmerston, 1 July 1835 (recd. 28 Jan. 1836) (ibid., no. 40).
[3] Elliot to Lennox Conyngham, private, 12 June 1837 (F.O. 17/20).

Elliot threatened to leave Canton where there were then about two thousand British subjects, of whom he thought something like a thousand might rush to the city gates to demand the release of their comrades. In order to prevent such a breach of peace the Lascars were eventually handed over.[1]

To meet such difficulties the British Government had had before them, in 1837, a draft of a Bill[2] for creating a British Court in China. On the 8th May 1838 the East India and China Association asked Palmerston to inform them of the date on which the committee stage would be taken in the House of Commons, as they intended to prepare opposition to it. Some days later their chairman, Larpent, indicated to Palmerston the main lines of their opposition. The Bill, they said, gave the Superintendent unlimited legislative power to determine offences; no power existed to compel Chinese and non-British foreigners to submit to the judgement of the court. It was proposed to give the court jurisdiction for one hundred miles from Canton, and this would bring the Lintin opium trade within its purview. The Association while welcoming the disciplining of the crews, which could, they thought, be adequately done by stationing a man-of-war in Chinese waters, were afraid that the Bill as it stood would lead to disputes between the Governments. Palmerston in reply stated that it was in the interests of British commerce and due to the maintenance of the national character that British merchants should pay their debts to the Chinese, even if it meant that British subjects had to have recourse to Chinese courts for theirs. On the general political point the Foreign Secretary was emphatic. 'It appears', he replied, 'to Lord Palmerston that far from the establishment of the proposed Courts being likely to lead to disputes between the two Governments the probable effect of the measure would on the contrary be to prevent disputes, by averting causes that might give rise to them'[3]. But the China Courts Bill was never passed. It sought to give the Superintendent civil jurisdiction in cases between British subjects, and the power after due trial to expel a British subject beyond the limits of its jurisdiction. Peel in the Commons opposed

[1] Elliot to Palmerston, 26 Sept. 1837 (F.O. 17/23).
[2] Palmerston to Treasury, 8 Nov. 1836 (F.O. 17/17).
[3] Larpent to Palmerston, 8 and 17 May 1838 (F.O. 17/28); Palmerston to Larpent, 21 May 1838 (F.O. 17/28).

such arbitrary powers, and the opposition of Lord Ellenborough on behalf of the Tories in the Lords finally influenced the Government to withdraw the measure.

In any case, Palmerston had not meant to bring the Bill into force until the British Government had secured the assent of the Chinese authorities, as the exercise of the powers contained in it would be a derogation from the sovereignty of China.[1] When that assent had been granted, the Queen would have enacted regulations drawn up by Elliot for the policing of the seamen which were not inconsistent with British law. The Foreign Secretary showed by this attitude his consistency. He regarded the Chinese Empire as a sovereign State, the equal in international law of Great Britain. Though an equal in status it was capable of a species of legal servitude, such as would be involved by the grant of extraterritoriality. The Chinese, however, held very different views. Regarding the Celestial Emperor as the only Sovereign in the world and peoples other than the Chinese as tributary or dependent, they could have no conception of international law. But in fact they were not averse to granting recognition of the claim of the British Government to try British nationals by English law, for only Chinese could be expected to be so civilized as to be amenable to Chinese law. Other folk, such as Thibetans or British, had different ideas, different (and a lower) morality and law. In much the same way none but the citizens of the Roman Republic were amenable to the *Jus Civile*, though Rome through the praetor peregrinus evolved a system of Law Merchant in the *Jus Gentium* which could be applied to foreigners residing in Rome. Such a development did not occur to the Chinese, partly, no doubt, because of the much greater difference in customs and manners between Europeans and Chinese than between Romans and members of other contemporary Mediterranean cities. Urging again the grant of disciplinary powers over British subjects, Elliot had in fact stated that 'the assent of the Chinese Government to institutions of this kind is beyond all doubt'. In a recent conversation with Howqua, the Chinese merchant had 'entreated me to remind my Nation's Great Minister that his government never interfered except in cases of extreme urgency, upon the principle that they were ignorant of our laws and customs and that it was unjust to subject us to

[1] Palmerston to Elliot, 23 March 1839 (P.P. 1840, xxxvi, no. 127).

rules made for people of totally different habits'[1]. Nevertheless, Elliot meant to continue to demand the release of a British subject, 'be his crime what it may', until he was instructed to the contrary. No doubt the simplest way of putting Elliot in control at least of the seafaring men would have been to have commissioned his cutter and given him the 'same powers over British vessels visiting these ports as may be lawfully exercised by the commodore over a Fleet of Merchant Ships'[2]. The British seamen of the cutter could have been sworn as constables.[3]

As a result of the great crisis in the spring of 1839 it became still clearer that it would be the height of folly to allow the Chinese authorities any jurisdiction over foreigners. The High Commissioner proscribed a list of persons doubtless drawn up by Chinese merchants and compradors, some of whom Elliot was certain had never been engaged in the pursuits for which they were condemned. 'It places the lives and liberty of the whole foreign community at the disposal of the Hong merchants, linguists, and compradors, and their retainers. And the situation and liabilities of these Chinese make them very unsafe reporters, and yet it is mainly upon their reports that the judgement of the Government will be taken.' Another pertinent example occurred in the summer of 1839. There was a riot in which foreign sailors were engaged on the east shore anchorage in Hong Kong Bay, when a Chinese named Lin Weihe was killed. As the result of the issue by the Superintendent of a notice offering a reward for the apprehension of the murderers,[4] six men were placed on trial according to English law, were found guilty of riot and assault, and sentenced to fines and imprisonment for periods varying from three to six months.[5] In October they were sent to Singapore. But the Chinese wanted to keep one of the convicted men to be executed for the death of the Chinese.[6] Elliot's refusal to surrender a single British subject was primarily responsible for a naval action on the 3rd November 1839.[7] Had the British community been inside the Boca Tigris instead of at Macao at the time, Elliot

[1] Elliot to Palmerston, private, 2 Jan. 1839 (F.O. 17/30).
[2] Elliot to Palmerston, 2 March 1838 (F.O. 17/26).
[3] Elliot to Palmerston, 4 July 1837 (F.O. 17/21).
[4] Elliot to Palmerston, 18 July 1839 (P.P. 1840, xxxvi, no. 154).
[5] Elliot to Palmerston, 14 Oct. 1839 (F.O. 17/33).
[6] Elliot to Palmerston, 21 Oct. 1839 (recd. 13 Mar. 1840) (P.P. 1840, xxxvi, Add. Corr. no. 1).   [7] Elliot to Palmerston, 5 Nov. 1839 (ibid., Add. Corr. no. 2).

was certain that the trade would have been stopped until the Hong merchants had purchased a slave in Macao or inveigled some wretched Lascar and delivered him up as the murderer. Indeed the Mandarins had suggested that he should report a man, who by chance was found drowned at Hong Kong at the time, to be the murderer. They held out strong assurances that it would then be in their power to satisfy the Imperial Commissioner and the Governor,

'so anxious were their Excellencies at that time to adjust affairs, at every sacrifice of truth, decency or reason; always saving the principle that they had a right to a man. The monstrous proposition that I should deliver to his Excellency's hands, five men convicted of the offence of rioting, to the end that he might detain and execute one in satisfaction for Lin Weihe, furnishes a remarkable practical comment upon the insecurity of Chinese judicial proceedings against foreigners, shut out from all appeal to the higher tribunals of the Empire.'[1]

The two cases of riots had concerned sailors over whom Elliot could exercise his powers. But in order to preserve due discipline it was highly necessary for him to be given control over all British subjects. These last, however, greatly resented the illegal assumption of powers by the Superintendent, who was more than once reprimanded by Lord Palmerston. For the merchants had in their China Association an easy and powerful means of putting pressure on the Government. Indeed, nowhere does the contrast between England and China appear greater than in the immense influence exercised by the commercial classes over the Government in the one, and the avowed indifference to the 'petty matters of trade' by the Government, local and central, of the other. This independence of the merchants from the officer of the British Government had been commented upon by Sir George Robinson. 'I perceive', said he, 'on the part of . . . the British community an anxious wish to avoid any reference to the officers appointed by His Majesty's Government to superintend the trade'[2]. The attitude and activities of James Innes,[3] a 'licensed' trader in the old East India Company days, were typical of the most lawless and

[1] Elliot to Palmerston, 16 Nov. 1839 (recd. 27 Mar. 1840) (ibid., Add. Pap. no. 1).   [2] Robinson to Palmerston, 16 Oct. 1835 (ibid., no. 42).
[3] In 1833 he set fire to the Hoppo's house for the non-execution of an order from that official. In consequence redress had at once been accorded. The Select Committee considered that he had acted most unjustifiably.

individualistic members of the merchant community. Innes
threatened to seek his own private redress against what he regarded as unfair activities of the Chinese authorities.[1] Palmerston replied definitely that such an action would be tantamount
to piracy.[2] And it was Innes who was the ostensible cause of a
serious crisis in December 1838. Two of his coolies, who confessed that they were his servants, were apprehended carrying
opium. Innes and his ship were ordered to leave Canton, and
one of the Hong merchants who was security to the Chinese
Government for her underwent the indignity of being punished
by the wooden collar. Elliot was, in fact, certain that the ship
in question did not belong to Innes, but was American owned.
Other British merchants made common cause with their fellow-
countryman and threatened to prevent the destruction ordered
by the Viceroy of the house rented by Innes from one of the
Hongs.[3] And in the final struggle with the Imperial Commissioner Lin, Elliot's task was complicated by this trader, who,
residing at Macao while his fellow-subjects were incarcerated
in Canton, had been trafficking in opium and 'so painfully
increased the risks and embarrassments of the whole foreign
community'. The Imperial Commissioner demanded and Elliot,
no doubt exasperated, agreed to, Innes's expulsion.[4] For his
agreement Elliot was censured by the Foreign Secretary,[5] who
pointed out that however much Innes had crossed the Superintendent's policy, he had not acted contrary to English law,
and that the Superintendent's action was therefore arbitrary.
On another occasion Elliot had asked, in a memorandum of
December 1835, for authority to forbid a steamship of Jardine's
plying up river to Canton. As the Chinese authorities had
issued an edict against her, he feared that if she were not prevented, the whole British trade might be jeopardized. But
Palmerston replied that he ought not to interfere with the
undertakings of British subjects nor 'assume a greater degree of
authority over British subjects in China than that which you in
reality possess'[6]. He was similarly reprimanded in 1840 for

[1] Robinson to Palmerston, 20 Nov. 1835 (recd. 28 Mar. 1836) (P.P. 1840, xxxvi,
no. 44).
[2] Palmerston to Robinson, 6 June 1836 (ibid., no. 53).
[3] Elliot to Palmerston, 8 Dec. 1838 (ibid., no. 133).
[4] Elliot to Palmerston, 18 May 1839 (ibid., no. 150).
[5] Palmerston to Elliot, 4 March 1840 (F.O. 17/37).
[6] Palmerston to Elliot, 22 July 1836 (P.P. 1840, xxxvi, no. 66).

having ordered a Liverpool ship not to go to Canton and for promising, on behalf of the British Government, to indemnify the owners against any loss consequent upon obeying his order.

Elliot had been adamant in refusing to comply with Commissioner Lin's request that all foreign merchants should sign a bond whereby the signatory merchant should acknowledge that he would willingly suffer capital punishment if again he were found by the Chinese authorities to be importing opium. He was naturally incensed that Americans, for whom he thought he had done much, were willing to sign it.[1] Still more was he incensed at the signing of the bond by one Warner of the British ship *Thomas Coutts*. 'This selfish and stupid and reckless action', as Elliot characterized it, destroyed his negotiations with Lin who demanded similar signatures from the masters of all ships.[2] Palmerston, however, would not hear of preventing people from signing such bonds, 'because it would not be expedient to give to the Superintendent such extensive and arbitrary powers as would be requisite for the purpose'[3]. Elliot had before asked to be invested 'with adequate powers for the reasonable control of men whose rash conduct cannot be left to the operation of Chinese laws, without the utmost inconvenience and risk, and whose impunity is alike injurious to British character and dangerous to British interests'. 'It was a source of great support to him, that the general body of the whole community, settled at Canton, strongly concur with him' in deprecating and in resolving to put an end to the dangerous irregularity of the smuggling of opium in Canton.[4] Palmerston's attitude was purely negative. The Chinese authorities could not expect the British Government to assist in putting down smuggling. That would have meant arming the Superintendent with very great powers. On the other hand, he was equally certain that British merchants, engaged in such illegal operations, could not reasonably expect their own Government to give them any protection.

'Her Majesty's Government cannot interfere for the purpose of enabling British subjects to violate the laws of the country to which they trade. Any loss, therefore, which such persons may suffer in

---

[1] Elliot to Palmerston, 8 Sept. 1839 (ibid., no. 158).
[2] Elliot to Palmerston, 5 Nov. 1839 (ibid., Add. Corr. no. 2).
[3] Palmerston to Elliot, 4 July 1840 (F.O. 17/37). The words 'extensive and arbitrary' were added in Palmerston's own hand to the draft dispatch drawn up in the Foreign Office.
[4] Elliot to Palmerston, 2 Jan. 1839 (recd. 13 May) (P.P. 1840, xxxvi, no. 138).

consequence of the more effectual execution of the Chinese laws on this subject, must be borne by the parties who have brought that loss on themselves by their own acts.'[1]

Elliot indeed had a high conception of his office. He seems to have wished to be something like a colonial Governor *vis-à-vis* the British community and an ambassador of the British Government to the Cantonese authorities. He would have failed to make good the first position had it not been that the attack of the Commissioner Lin welded together to a considerable degree, but even then not wholly, the discordant, competitive instincts of the British merchants. And in the stress of the conflict the Chinese, who had been so apprehensive at the coming of the superintendents, appear to have considered and treated him as an all-powerful representative of the British Government, indeed as a kind of Governor over the whole foreign community, not only British, but also American, French, and Dutch.

Palmerston, on the other hand, took less of a political than a juridical view of affairs. In default of legal powers, which the opposition in Parliament prevented him from conferring upon the Superintendent, he was prepared to protect the British merchants, so long as they did not contravene the law, alike from the illegal or arbitrary action of his own officer and from the Chinese authorities. This in effect meant the triumph in Canton of a chaos of individualism modified on the British side by the vague fear of a charge of piracy and the stoppage of trade, and on the Chinese side by the threat of the enforcement of the *Jus belli* upon a people which had no conception of that international legal system of Europe from which such a right was derived. While he hated the disorders as a sign of the absence of law, it must be confessed that Palmerston and the British Government did not make very strenuous efforts to end them in the only legal way possible, for he and they accepted almost without a protest the criticisms of the parliamentary opposition, backed by the influential opinion of the merchant community organized in the China Association. But it was not long before an arbitrary action of a sensational kind on the part of the Chinese authorities gave the British Government the means of defining and strengthening by legislation the position of their representative in relation to his fellow-subjects, and of regulariz-

---

[1] Palmerston to Elliot, 15 June 1838 (P.P. 1840, xxxvi, no. 116).

ing by treaty in a Western and European sense his relations with the Imperial authorities.

D. THE OPIUM TRADE, 1833–9

When Lord Napier landed in Canton in 1834 there was already a very considerable opium trade, which in recent years had shown a prodigious increase. The import of 4,100 chests[1] in 1796 had risen in 1837 to 30,000. This remarkable result had been made possible by 'the open and undisguised connivance of the local mandarins'. It is noteworthy that neither Napier, Davis, nor Robinson had been troubled with the question of opium, as this drug hardly figures in their correspondence with the Foreign Office. Not until July 1836 did dispatches of the Superintendent deal at all with the problem of the opium trade, and then Elliot reported that it seemed probable that the trade in that commodity at Canton was to be legalized. 'This stroke', he wrote, 'is aimed at the overthrow of the Lintin and outside trade, and the limitation of our commercial sphere to Canton and the Hong merchants'. As at that time it cost the smuggler $40 a chest to land, Elliot was doubtless right in thinking that the proposed scheme of a fixed duty of $7 would successfully kill the trade in the outer waters. 'Smuggling there may be at Canton, as there is now of all sorts of merchandise to an immense extent, but there will be smuggling nowhere else than at Canton.' Elliot thought that it was due less to the Lintin or coast trade in opium that the proposed change was apparently to be brought about 'than the tea and tract Missions to the coasts, of last year. The opium ships might have continued to visit the coasts with little more than former notice, but the books alarmed the Court seriously.'[2] It is curious that, in the judgement of the Superintendent, the early activities of missionary societies were to result in the legalization of the opium trade. By the new year of 1837, though he noticed the 'protracted interruption of the opium trade'[3], he was still expecting, as he had been in October 1836,[4] the Government of Peking to end its consideration of the opium trade by legalizing it. The Chinese authorities, he thought, were afraid

[1] A chest contained 135 or 160 lbs., according to provenance: H. B. Morse, *The Trade and Administration of China*, p. 355.
[2] Elliot to Foreign Office, 27 July 1836 (P.P. 1840, xxxvi, no. 82).
[3] Elliot to Lennox Conyngham, private, 24 Jan. 1837 (F.O. 17/19).
[4] Elliot to Foreign Office, 10 Oct. 1836 (P.P. 1840, xxxvi, no. 83).

partly of the extension of this illicit, smuggled trade on the coast of the north-east of China, and partly of the export of silver in exchange for the opium. Apparently, if opium were legalized it was expected that it would exchange for Chinese exports and so prevent the drain of precious metal. The drain of silver, though substantial, was not so serious as it appeared, for it was to a certain extent used later in Canton for the purchase of commodities. The temporary interruption of the trade, Elliot reported, 'has considerably aggravated the embarrassment of the merchants, by crippling their means of forcing down the high rates of export staples'. In 1836 the value of the imported opium was eighteen million dollars, or one million in excess of the combined value of the two staple exports of tea and silk. Elliot was able to forward memoranda from Chinese sources both for and against the legalization,[1] and finally on the 21st February 1837 he came into possession of what he regarded as the decree of legalization. In future opium was only to be exchanged for merchandise and so the export of sycee silver[2] would be stopped. Elliot was obviously worried on economic, to say nothing of other, grounds at the vast growth and importance of this trade.

'The fact', he reflected, 'that such an article should have grown to be by far the most important part of our import trade, is of itself a source of painful reflection. And the widespreading public mischief which the manner of its pursuit has necessarily entailed . . . aggravates the discomfort of the whole subject. . . . It cannot be good that the conduct of a great trade should be so dependent upon the steady continuance of a vast prohibited traffic in an article of vicious luxury, high in price, and liable to frequent and prodigious fluctuations. In a mere commercial point of view, therefore, I believe it is susceptible of proof, that the gradual diversion of British capital into other channels of employment than this, would be attended with advantageous consequences. I hope your Lordship will let me say that there are many urgent reasons for regretting the extent to which the Indian revenue is dependent upon such a source of revenue.'

He hoped that the legalization of the growth of the poppy in China would gradually lessen the imports. Yet a sudden interruption of the trade would entirely paralyse commerce, as the

---

[1] Elliot to Palmerston, 2 Feb. 1837 (recd. 17 July 1837) (P.P. 1840, xxxvi, no. 90).
[2] Silver contained in a bar of the shape of a Chinese shoe, theoretically of chemically pure silver.

movement of money at Canton depended upon it.[1] Elliot was,
however, rather premature in thinking in February 1837 that
legalization was determined upon by the Imperial Court. For
he wrote in July: 'The opium legalization is still to come; but
it may be depended upon that the measure is resolved: the time
when, and the manner how, are certainly not points of easy
solution to us, in our state of information of the motives and
springs at work in such a Court as this.'[2] In August and
September, however, in consequence of orders from Peking,
the local authorities through the Hong merchants asked Elliot
to send away the opium ships from the outer port and Lintin.
It was asserted that since 1833 ten British warehousing vessels
had been stationed at Kumsingmoon on which the opium and
sycee trade was carried on. When Elliot had authentic requests
forwarded to him by the Prefect and chief military officer he
agreed to inform his Sovereign,[3] while the local authorities for
the moment confined their attentions to native smugglers. This
action increased the number of ships off the east coasts, and
European passenger boats, belonging to British owners, manned
by small crews of Lascars and scantily armed, were carrying
opium directly to Canton. As yet the higher officers were not
opposing this change in the method of distribution.

'But the continuance of their inertness is not to be depended upon.
Disputes among themselves for the shares of the emoluments, private
reports against each other at Court, and, lastly, their ordinary practice of permitting abuse to grow to ripeness, and to rest in false
security, are all considerations which forbid the hope that these
things can endure.'

Blood had already been spilt, and the temptation to robbery
and violence on the way up to Whampoa was considerable
owing to the value of the cargo.[4] In April Elliot reported a
great increase in the smuggling trade. 'I was sensible', he wrote,
'that the present state of things at Canton could only subsist
as long as the Governor could venture to appropriate a large
share of the bribes, by which the system is upheld; and therefore
I looked for no other result at his hands', but it was impossible
to foresee how soon his position in that respect might be changed

---

[1] Elliot to Palmerston, 21 Feb. 1837 (recd. 22 Aug.) (ibid., no. 93).
[2] Elliot to Lennox Conyngham, private, 28 July 1837 (recd. 8 Jan. 1838)
(F.O. 17/21).
[3] Elliot to Palmerston, 18 Nov. 1837 (F.O. 17/22).
[4] Elliot to Palmerston, 19 Nov. 1837 (P.P. 1840, xxxvi, no. 110).

by the wavering policy at the court.[1] In December an incident occurred in connexion with the alleged finding of opium on two of Innes's coolies. A week later preparations were made for executing a Chinese opium-seller in the square immediately in front of the factories. The foreigners were incensed at what they regarded as a provocative indecency and removed the apparatus of execution without resistance. A large crowd then gathered in the early afternoon and the foreigners began to assail with sticks the Chinese, who replied by throwing stones and driving their opponents inside the gates of the factories. Not until the crowd had increased to some six thousand persons did the Chinese authorities disperse them by using the military, and executed the prisoner in the usual place.[2] The foreigners wrongly thought that this activity was solely directed against them. The prisons were full of opium smokers. Nothing went through the customs without the minutest inspection. The trousers of the Chinese were searched—a procedure hitherto unheard of.[3] Palmerston, indignant at the conduct of the foreign community, wanted to know whether they were British. 'I also want to know upon what alleged ground of right these persons considered themselves entitled to interfere with the arrangements made by the Chinese officers of Justice for carrying out in Chinese form the orders of their superior authorities.'[4] The smuggling of opium by British and other foreign subjects had placed the lives and property of the whole community in jeopardy. It had been long clear to the Superintendent that 'the opium trade must grow to be more and more mischievous to every branch of trade, and certainly to none more than to that of opium itself'. It was obvious that it would fall by rapid degrees into the hands of more and more desperate men, that it would 'stain the foreign character to the great peril of vast public and private interests'. Until recently China had been a safe place for life and property. This safety had been imperilled for the sake of 'comparatively speaking insignificant gains of a few reckless individuals, unquestionably founding their conduct upon the belief, that they were exempt from the operation of all law, British or Chinese'. Some of the opium was actually sold from

---

[1] Elliot to Palmerston, 20 Apr. 1838 (recd. 1 Dec.) (P.P. 1840, xxxvi, no. 120).
[2] Elliot to Palmerston, 13 Dec. 1838 (recd. 13 Apr. 1839) (ibid., no. 134).
[3] Legrégeois to Directeurs, 12 Dec. 1838 (M.E., vol. 323, f. 1).
[4] Palmerston to Elliot, 15 Apr. 1839 (P.P. 1840, xxxvi, no. 135).

the factories themselves, for the good conduct of which the Hong merchants as proprietors were responsible to the Government. They naturally protested at the prospect of the ruin of their legitimate trade, and with the concurrence of the Provincial Government refused to do business until the opium traffic in Canton was suppressed. Elliot, who was in Whampoa when the fracas started, rushed to Canton in an attempt to keep the peace,[1] and called a meeting of all foreign residents. He counselled Innes, who was the proximate cause of the trouble, to ask the Governor for a stay of all proceedings, to state his willingness to abide by the decision of the officers of his nation, and to withdraw in time 'from a very unsuitable position'. This Innes on the 13th December refused to do. At the general meeting, held on the 17th December, Elliot adopted a firm attitude. He announced that

'he should forthwith serve a notice upon the boats in the river, to the effect that, if they were British owned, and were either actually or occasionally engaged in the traffic, they must proceed outside within three days and cease to return with any similar pursuits; that failing their conformity with these injunctions, he should place himself in communication with the Provincial Government, and frankly and fully express these views of his own upon the necessary and perfectly admissible treatment of so serious an evil.'

On the 23rd, though there were still some smuggling boats at Whampoa, Elliot wrote to the Viceroy Tang that the British Government regarded illegal practices with severity, that he had requested the opium boats to leave the river, that Her Majesty would not interpose for the protection of illegal British property, but he asked that he might accompany Chinese officers to the anchorages so that innocent persons and property might not be involved in the same consequences as the perverse. He also asked that the two coolies of Innes might be pardoned as they were ignorant of the contents of the boxes they were carrying. The Viceroy refused the last request on the ground that Chinese justice was so perfect, but he agreed to Elliot going with the Chinese officers to inspect the boats. In this way a settlement satisfactory to the local authorities was arranged, and on the 1st January 1839 lawful trade was again established. Elliot, in a second address to the British community on the eve of the reopening, stated that he had 'resolved to shrink from

[1] Elliot to Palmerston, 8 Dec. 1838 (P.P. 1840, xxxvi, no. 133).

no responsibility in drawing this dangerous irregularity to a conclusion, and he will as firmly use all lawful means in his power to prevent its recurrence'[1].

The lawful trade continued briskly all that January, and at the same time the Chinese authorities persevered with an active drive, not only against the introduction, but also against the consumption of opium.[2] Indeed, the stagnation of the opium trade for the last four months had been complete.

E. LIN'S ACTION

It was at this moment, when the opium trade in the river was at an end, that it became known that a very high official from Peking was on his way, with powers equal to those of the Viceroy, to continue and complete the suppression. Elliot, fearing that there might be an embargo on the legal trade until the opium trade was entirely suppressed, warned Howqua that the British Government would regard such a proceeding as hostile. The 'inside' trade in opium, which had been induced by the venality of the highest officers of the province, had in fact been put down by the Superintendent's efforts.[3] Elliot's fears were well founded. Every foreign merchant was issued with a translation of an edict which threatened an entire stoppage of trade unless the warehouse ships in the outer seas were sent away, and there was a complete cessation of the opium trade, not only in the river, but on the coasts. However, the trading season was nearly over and Elliot comforted himself with the thought that by the time the Imperial Commissioner arrived an embargo on the lawful trade would be immaterial. The Imperial Commissioner Lin issued his edict on the 18th March 1839.[4] He ordered that every particle of opium owned by foreigners should be delivered to the Government, that the Hongs should draw up a list of the parties concerned and the number of chests in their possession, and that foreigners should give a bond that their vessels would never again bring in opium and that if any were found after search, the parties were willing to suffer the supreme penalty of death. The Hongs were accused of participation in the traffic and were threatened with death if the foreigners refused to deliver the opium or to sign

[1] Elliot to Palmerston, 2 Jan. 1839 (recd. 13 May) (P.P. 1840, xxxvi, no. 137).
[2] Elliot to Palmerston, 21 Jan. 1839 (ibid., no. 140).
[3] Elliot to Palmerston, 30 Jan. 1839 (ibid., no. 141).
[4] Elliot to Palmerston, 8 Feb. 1839 (recd. 26 June) (ibid., no. 143).

the bond. Elliot had gone to Macao on the 10th March, as warlike preparations were taking place there: tents had been pitched, a number of Chinese soldiers were assembled, while some old native vessels were fitted out as fire ships to force the opium ships at the entrance of the Bay of Hong Kong to concentrate at Macao.[1] But the storm broke at Canton on the 22nd. Elliot immediately left for the factories and, arriving at Whampoa at 4 o'clock on the 24th, learnt that communications between that place and Canton had been severed for the previous forty-eight hours. He donned his uniform and proceeded in the gig of H.M. sloop *Larne*, with ensign and pennant hoisted and, with the Chinese passport for the cutter *Louise* in his hand, went to the chief local Mandarin who attempted in vain to dissuade the Superintendent from continuing his journey. Although armed Chinese boats approached the gig, the admirable steadiness of the sailors and a favourable breeze brought him to the stairs of the factories, to the great relief not only of his fellow countrymen, but of the whole foreign community. He ordered the ensign to be flown from the flagstaff, and found 'a sense of support in that honoured flag'. The European merchants had offered the Imperial Commissioner to surrender 1,030 cases of opium which belonged to them. This would have been perhaps a sacrifice 'assez facile à faire car ces 1,030 caisses sont tellement avariées qu'elles valaient à peine à ce qu'on dit chacune 50 pts. Le Délégué qui connaît parfaitement toutes les affaires de ces Mrs. a refusé d'accepter la proposition.'[2]

Obstinate demands had been made that Dent, a leading merchant, should attend the Imperial Commissioner's tribunal, but Elliot, who brought him from his house to the former hall of the East India Company (since become the head-quarters of the Superintendents), told the Hongs that Dent could go to the city only if accompanied by himself and provided he was never out of his sight. He urged the community to be firm, moderate, and united. That night the native servants were called out, and all supplies cut off. The foreign community was thus straitly imprisoned. All vessels were removed from before the factories and an immense barrage of boats cut them off from Whampoa.[2] On the 22nd March, while still at Macao, Elliot had ordered all the

---

[1] Legrégeois to Directeurs, 13 Mar. 1839 (M.E., vol. 323, f. 73).
[2] Legrégeois to Directeurs, 3 Apr. 1839 (M.E., vol. 323, f. 85). 50 piastres = approximately £10.

British ships in the outer anchorages to go to Hong Kong and be prepared to resist acts of aggression as he was 'without con-fidence in the just and moderate dispositions of the provincial government'. On the 25th he asked the Viceroy for passports and boats for the English at Canton and safe conduct for British ships, and declared himself free from responsibility for any consequences that might arise. He guaranteed that the ships then at Whampoa would not go up to Canton if he could get into touch with them. He also asked for the return of the servants, for provisions, and the removal of the barriers before the factories. While professing a desire never to show disrespect to the Governor and the high officers, he also requested that an officer should be deputed to arrange all things peacefully. Lin answered through the Prefect and Commandant of Canton that Elliot must hand over all the opium in the store ships of the outer waters, when permission would be given to the British community to depart and passports would be issued to them. The next day the Commissioner added that he held Elliot responsible, as on the eve of his arrival at Canton the foreigners were prepared to hand over their opium and he had but stiffened their resistance. On the 27th at 6 a.m. Elliot, bowing to *force majeure*, issued in the name of Her Britannic Majesty's Government a public notice ordering the British merchants to surrender to him all their opium for Her Majesty's service before 6 p.m. Proof of British ownership and the value were to be determined by the British Government subsequently. On the 28th he informed the Commissioner that he held himself in a position to hand over 20,283 chests.[1] But they were not all at hand in the port of Canton, and he expressly stated that he could deal only with British-owned opium. Lin ordered Elliot to ascertain the amount in the factories, which his officers would collect on the morrow; the amount at Whampoa, which would be collected on the 30th; and the amount in the twenty-two store ships which would be subsequently collected at the Boca Tigris by himself and the Governor. Elliot was also to hand over any-thing there might be in other ports, even if the total thereby exceeded the 20,283 chests. Lin issued similar orders to the American, Dutch, and French merchant-consuls and bade Elliot persuade them to hand over their opium. The Imperial Commissioner wished the foreigners to write orders to the

---

[1] Some three million pounds weight.

masters of the ships in the outer anchorages to hand over the opium to the officers of the Government. On the 2nd April, however, he agreed that Elliot's Deputy Superintendent should proceed outside and deliver up to the officers the agreed amount. When a quarter had been surrendered, the compradors and servants would be restored; when a half, the passage boats could go freely; when three-quarters, the embargo on foreign trade would be raised; and when all was accounted for, conditions should return to normal. To these conditions Elliot agreed on the 3rd April. The British in Canton were then allowed to purchase food and to have the use of coolies to wash their linen, but otherwise the blockade there continued. All was quiet apparently at Whampoa and Macao,[1] though the Mandarin at Casabranca had ordered the Governor of the Portuguese settlement to hand over all the opium in the city. To be on the safe side with the Chinese the Governor had refused to allow British ships to purchase provisions at Macao.[2] Elliot closed his dispatch to the Foreign Office, which he sent out by Johnston, the Deputy Superintendent, with the reflection that that was the first time the Government

'has taken unprovoked initiative in aggressive measures against British life and property and against the dignity of the British Crown. I say *unprovoked* advisedly, because. . . . I offered to adjust all things peacefully, by the fulfilment of the Emperor's will, as soon as it was made known to me'[1]. 'All sense of security has been broken to pieces. . . . 'The movement of a few hours has placed the lives, liberty and property of the foreign community in China, with all the vast interests, commercial and financial, contingent upon our security, at the mercy of this government.'[3]

The British merchants, still straitly blockaded in Canton after Johnston had left to supervise the handing over of the opium from the ships below river, were asked to sign the bond. Elliot was of opinion that 'if we are ever free, the more practical and fit reply will be the withdrawal of all the Queen's subjects from the grasp of this government. Trade with China at any point remote from the station of our ships is no longer a possible state of circumstances.' One of the major causes of the troubles had been the complete uncertainty 'to the very day before the Commissioner's first edicts appeared, whether the avowed pur-

[1] Elliot to Palmerston, 30 Mar. 1839 (recd. 29 Aug.) (P.P. 1840, xxxvi, no. 146).
[2] Legrégeois to Directeurs, 3 Apr. 1839 (M.E., vol. 323, f. 85).
[3] Elliot to Palmerston, 3 Apr. 1839 (P.P. 1840, xxxvi, no. 147).

poses were to be depended upon or not, or whether the object
was merely the extensive check of the trade by subjecting it to
heightened temporary inconvenience, and exacting some considerable fees for the price of its future relaxation'. The chief
mischief which was likely to arise was, thought Elliot, that the
traders in opium, men like Innes, would feel justified in any
species of retaliation. The only way to avoid such anarchical
proceedings and

'of saving the coasts of the Empire from a shocking character of war-
fare, both foreign and domestic, will be the very prompt and powerful
interference of Her Majesty's government for the just vindication of
all wrongs, and the effectual prevention of crime and wretchedness
by permanent settlement. Comprehensively considered, this measure
has become of high obligation towards the Chinese government, as
well as to the public interests and character of the British Nation.
There can be neither safety nor honour for either government until
Her Majesty's flag flies on these coasts in a secure position.'

In other words, confidence had been so shattered that there
could be no decent trade unless to Great Britain, as a result of
regular war, which would in itself satisfy the desire for revenge
of the reckless and angry opium traders, were ceded a base for
trade, a colonial possession where British protection and English law would alike shelter and discipline the merchant and
seafaring community.[1] Foreign merchants had signed an undertaking in very wide terms to abjure the opium trade, but they
refused to bind themselves to submit to Chinese justice.[2] This,
however, did not satisfy Lin. The confinement continued,
though Elliot reported on the 17th April that the native servants
were gradually coming back.[3] On the 21st Elliot tore up the
bond again brought for his signature by the Hong merchants,
saying that he would sooner give his life than sign it. The
Chinese authorities, Johnston informed him on the 17th, were
making at the Boca Tigris an elaborate examination and classi-
fication of the opium and then carefully repacking it, all which,
Elliot thought, erroneously in fact, did not seem to portend its
destruction. By the 4th May 15,501 chests had been accounted
for and handed over. All the British but sixteen persons were then
allowed to leave Canton.[4] It was not until the 24th May that

[1] Elliot to Palmerston, 6 Apr. 1839 (P.P. 1840, xxxvi, no. 148).
[2] Elliot to Palmerston, 11 Apr. 1839 (ibid.).
[3] Elliot to Palmerston, 17 Apr. 1839 (ibid.).
[4] Elliot to Palmerston, 4 May 1839 (ibid.).

all the opium was finally checked and delivered and the remaining sixteen persons, after signing at Lin's commands and on the advice of Elliot an undertaking, without a penal clause, never to return to Canton, left in company with the Superintendent for Macao. They had been under restraint for just over two months.[1] Shortly afterwards the Imperial Commissioner offered Elliot 1,000 cases of tea: an offer which finds no mention in the British dispatches and which was naturally promptly refused. His conduct had won general approval. One not very friendly to the English wrote: 'Le cher Mr. Elliot s'est parfaitement conduit dans toute cette affaire d'après l'aveu général sans cependant rien faire pour disculper un commerce qu'il a toujours regardé comme illégal.'[2]

Elliot reviewed the motives that lay behind his conduct in a private letter to the Under Secretary of State:

'I have returned from Canton much shaken by recent severe indisposition, and have need of rest. Nine weeks of more wearing anxiety have rarely ever been passed by a public officer. It was my duty to preserve a temperate tone, and to avert mischief from the Merchants, most of them exceedingly delicately situated on this opium question; but I can assure you, Sir, it has not been an easy task to refrain from letting this government understand that its hour of reckoning was at hand. I feel, however, I cannot depart from the line of patience and discretion without the utmost public inconvenience, and I know how incumbent it is upon me to leave the unembarrassed treatment of these most serious affairs to Her Majesty's Government. Moderate ulterior purposes, and prompt and vigorous proceedings, cannot fail to turn them to great and lasting advantage.'

He suggested besides a money indemnity the extension of the trade, its establishment 'on a firm and honourable footing', and ended with the suggestion that 'it should never be forgotten, however, that communication with the Court from Canton is hopeless; nothing can reach the Emperor from this quarter in an ungarbled form'[3].

F. HOSTILITIES BEGIN

The British Government learnt of these affairs finally on the 21st September. Palmerston sent Elliot a secret dispatch on the 18th October which informed him that Her Majesty's Govern-

---

[1] Elliot to Palmerston, 24 May 1839 (ibid., no. 150).
[2] Legrégeois to Directeurs, 5 June 1839 (M.E., f. 134).
[3] Elliot to Backhouse, private, 30 May 1839 (F.O. 17/31).

ment meant to place the relations between Great Britain and China on a proper footing. A naval and a small military force would be sent out to blockade Canton and the Peiho—the river which gives access to Peking. The expedition should arrive in Chinese waters in March. The particular operations were to be determined upon by the Governor-General of India, the Admiral in command, and the Superintendent. One of the Chusan islands was to be occupied to act, during the hostilities, as a secure base, and thereafter as a British commercial establishment. Chinese ships should be seized and the Admiral was to send a letter from the mouth of the Peiho to Peking to secure that a proper officer of the Chinese Emperor should be sent to treat and accede to the British demands on board his flagship. Elliot was to warn the British community near the time of the arrival of the expedition to remove their persons and property.[1] Secret instructions were sent to Elliot on the 23rd November regulating his conduct in the negotiations to follow the British show of force. It is unfortunate that the dispatch in the Foreign Office files is incomplete. Alone there remain the pages on which Palmerston made his correction of the first draft. But these show unmistakably that the war which was about to be undertaken was not one, as has been sometimes said, to force the Chinese to trade with the British in opium. Palmerston stated categorically that

'Therefore H.M. govt. by no means dispute the right of the Government of China to prohibit the importation of opium into China, and to seize and confiscate any opium which, in defiance of prohibition duly made, should be brought by Foreigners or by Chinese subjects into the Territories of the Empire. But these fiscal prohibitions ought to be impartially and steadily enforced; and traps ought not to be laid for Foreigners by at one time letting the prohibition remain . . .'[2]

Here the manuscript ends. It is not difficult to continue Palmerston's thought. He was not objecting to the fact of prohibition, or to seizure of opium, but to the methods that had been used in carrying out the prohibition. The law against opium had for so long been a dead letter, and the local authorities had tacitly allowed the trade, with great gain to themselves. Then suddenly arrived Commissioner Lin, with the normal Chinese

---

[1] Palmerston to Elliot, secret, 18 Oct. 1839 (F.O. 17/37).
[2] Palmerston to Elliot (no. 16 encl. in no. 19. The original no. 16 was recalled), 4 Nov. 1839 (F.O. 17/37).

views on collective criminal responsibility, and in a manner that any Englishman, used to the rule of law, must have thought highly arbitrary, he virtually imprisoned a whole community in order to impose upon some members of it the will of the Imperial court. But as well as redress for this specific wrong, the British Government would seek to prevent the recurrence of such incidents by claiming an island in which British justice could give security for the future. At the same time it meant to put the relations of its accredited agents on a basis more in consonance with recognized Western international law.

Not until February of the following year were definite orders to leave London.[1] Before, however, any instructions had reached Elliot, the situation had become more and more strained. A great smuggling trade developed along the Fukien coast, which threatened to become tantamount to buccaneering.[2] The Commissioner Lin remained at Canton exposed to a good deal of criticism on the part of the Chinese, both merchants and officials, and dared not leave it until the trade was open. Elliot hoped to establish the foreign trade at Macao, where it could be under proper protection. But the Imperial Commissioner was inflexible. Such proceeding, he declared, was contrary to custom: if the Europeans desired to carry on their commerce they should bring their ships up to Whampoa: if not let them return to Europe. Trade at Macao was to be restricted in the future as in the past to the Portuguese. He threatened with death any Chinese who traded with other Europeans elsewhere than at Whampoa. For the rest he preserved an ominous silence which astonished every one.

There was always a fear that some unfortunate incident would arise to obscure the real point at issue between Elliot and Lin. One such nearly occurred on the 24th May, the day the Superintendent left Canton, an affair well illustrating the lawless actions of many British subjects in the Far East at the time. After a dinner to celebrate the Queen's Birthday an English captain who had not observed the rules of sobriety 'thought fit solely for his amusement to fire ball shot on a Chinese frigate moored near his ship. He fired 9 shots one after the other, and hit only once without however doing any damage.' A French missionary in describing this incident comments: 'Cette action

---

[1] See p. 74.
[2] Elliot to Palmerston, 18 July 1839 (recd. 2 Dec.) (P.P. 1840, xxxvi, no. 154).

qu'il est impossible de qualifier a mis tout le monde en effroi sur le sort des Européens qui se trouvent encore à Canton. . . .'[1] In the first week of July the fatal affray took place in Hong Kong,[2] in which a party of drunken sailors, including Americans, killed the Chinese Lin Weihe. In spite of great precautions being taken to prevent the knowledge of this outrage from reaching the ears of Lin, the Imperial Commissioner heard of the affair in mid-August. He was able to use the death of Lin Weihe, unavenged by the execution of one of his murderers, as an excuse for the interruption of the trade and for throwing the blame for the state of commercial stagnation upon the foreigner rather than on himself. Lin threatened to move down with two thousand troops towards Macao, and on the 16th August servants were again taken from the British. Elliot therefore transferred himself to the ship *Fort William* in order to relieve pressure on the Portuguese Government of Macao. By the beginning of September all British subjects went from that town to Hong Kong, and the merchant fleet, strengthened by the arrival of H.M.S. *Volage*, was put in a state of defence.[3] Into Macao Lin made a triumphal entry: Portuguese soldiers led him into the town to the accompaniment of a fanfare of trumpets, while guns from the chief fortress saluted his entry and departure. The Governor was ordered to keep a sharp eye on opium contrabandists and never to permit the English to set foot in the town.[4]

Meanwhile in Hong Kong itself there were attempts to poison the fresh water, and orders were given to prevent the Chinese from selling provisions to the British. Elliot issued a warning to the Chinese officers at Kowloon, a village on the mainland opposite to Hong Kong, that if the English were deprived of regular food supplies there were bound to be frequent conflicts. Going across in his cutter, accompanied by the pinnace of the *Volage* and a small armed vessel, Elliot sent his European interpreter on board one of the three war junks stationed there to ask for permission to buy supplies. After a delay of five or six hours a boat was sent on shore. The natives agreed to sell, but on the approach of runners from the Mandarins they felt them-

---

[1] Legrégois to Directeurs, postscript 10 May 1839 (M.E., vol. 323, f. 122).
[2] See p. 44.
[3] Elliot to Palmerston, 27 Aug. 1839 (recd. 9 Jan. 1840) (P.P. 1840, xxxvi, no. 155).
[4] Legrégeois to Directeurs, 7 Sept. 1839 (M.E., vol. 323, f. 205).

selves obliged to refuse. Elliot thereupon opened fire, which
was returned by the war junks and land batteries. But the
British ammunition having run out, he was obliged temporarily
to withdraw until more cartridges had been made. The British
then forced back the Chinese junks which had been making
use of the lull to break away from an action in which they had
lost several killed.[1] The British had three or four men wounded,
and Elliot had had a narrow escape: one ball had shot off his
hat band.[2] By the third week of September Elliot was able to
report that the notices ordering the poisoning of the wells had
been removed,[3] while from the 9th food and supplies had been
coming in from Kowloon without difficulty.[4]

A month later the British community was returning to Macao.
In the hopes of a temporary arrangement Elliot agreed to confiscate the cargo of any ship found by the Chinese officers and
himself to be carrying opium and also to expel opium traders
from the Empire. Consequently, on the 20th October British
trade was to be opened outside the Boca Tigris without any
bond being exacted, and detailed arrangements were made
between the Hong and the British merchants for carrying this
plan into effect.[5] Elliot believed, as he told a Catholic missionary, that 'les affaires s'arrangeront au moins temporairement'[6].
But he was too sanguine. There is little doubt that the action
of other foreigners and of the British subject, Warner, of the
ship *Thomas Coutts*[7] who had signed the bond, led Lin to believe
that trade might be opened again at the factories on his conditions, and that there was therefore no need to adopt the expedient of permitting it at the Boca Tigris. When on the
2nd November Elliot arrived in H.M.S. *Volage* to assist in the
negotiations he found an imposing array of war junks. There
was some exchange of notes between the captain of the *Volage*
and the Chinese admiral. The following morning 'the Chinese
squadron, under the command of the Admiral, broke ground
and stood out towards H.M.'s ships which were immediately
got under weigh and directed towards the approaching force'.
The squadron of twenty-nine sail then anchored and H.M.'s ships

[1] Elliot to Palmerston, 5 Sept. 1839 (P.P. 1840, xxxvi, no. 157).
[2] Legrégeois to Directeurs, 7 Sept. 1839 (M.E., vol. 323, f. 205).
[3] Elliot to Palmerston, 23 Sept. 1839 (P.P. 1840, xxxvi, no. 159).
[4] Elliot to Palmerston, private, 9 Sept. 1839 (F.O. 17/32).
[5] Elliot to Palmerston, 21 Oct. 1839 (P.P. 1840, xxxvi, Add. Corr. no. 1).
[6] Legrégeois to Directeurs, 21 Oct. 1839 (M.E., vol. 323, f. 231).   [7] See p. 47.

hove to and the Chinese were requested to withdraw. Their Admiral replied by demanding from Elliot the murderer of Lin Weihe. Captain Smith was afraid the Chinese squadron would pass inside him during the night and carry into effect the menaces made against the merchant vessels, which were at anchor a mile below the first battery. He felt it incompatible with the honour of the flag to retire and at noon gave the signal to engage. The Chinese answered with their accustomed spirit, but in less than an hour, having suffered the loss of four junks with several water-logged in addition, the admiral with the rest of the Chinese squadron retired. Smith offered no opposition to this and sailed to Macao. Elliot asked the merchant vessels to rendezvous at Tong Koo, which he deemed a safer anchorage.[1]

In spite of these acts of hostility, however, British trade was flourishing. This was due to the action of American and other foreign shipping. Their ships came to Chinese waters in ballast, and the American buyer paid for his purchases not in China but in London. 'When there is no British import trade there can be little or no trade with this empire; because at least eleven-twelfths of all that is exchanged with China is British property.' British trade was, in fact, only formally cut off. And owing to the political uncertainty the native purchaser was paying considerably higher prices as well as the additional freightage charges. Moreover, the confiscation of the 20,000 chests of opium had the effect of raising the price of opium so that its importation was more profitable at the end of 1839 than for some previous time. Elliot foresaw, therefore, that the Indian production of the current year would find a ready market.[2] Merchants in England, however, were alarmed at this development of American commerce. Petitions came to Palmerston from Leeds and Liverpool stating that 'some portion of the trade with China, formerly in the hands of British subjects, has already passed over to the merchants of other nations . . . at least one extensive shipper of British goods has directed his property at Canton to be placed in the charge of an American house'[3]. Though British manufacturers might not lose, there was an evident loss to the commercial community. Elliot,

---

[1] Elliot to Palmerston, 5 Nov. 1839 (P.P. 1840, xxxvi, Add. Corr. no. 2). Elliot's account is corroborated in Rev. E. B. Squire to Rev. W. Jowett, 16 Nov. 1839 (C.M.S. Parcel 325).

[2] Elliot to Palmerston, 28 Nov. 1839 (recd. 27 Mar. 1840) (ibid., Add. Pap. no. 4).   [3] Petition from Liverpool, 4 Oct. 1839 (F.O. 17/35).

however, had criticisms of a political order to make against the
Americans in Canton. In 1836 he had reported that an American merchant had been furnished with a consular commission
for about a year and that he had 'full instructions to insist upon
the distinction between the views of Americans and Englishmen, in the event of any interruption of the trade arising out
of our disputes and pretensions'[1]. The British Superintendent
emphasized this point in criticism of the forward policy advocated by Larpent and the China Association in London.

'Did Mr. Larpent', he asked, 'never hear of a two-legged creature
called a Yankee? Let him look through the whole cloud of American
papers and My life for it, he never saw such drivel advocated *there*.
The Americans are just in the situation to take advantage of the first
blunder Mr. Larpent persuades our Government to commit. They
will show the Chinese how to wound us, and then laugh at us for our
simplicity and we should richly deserve their derision.'[2]

But, in the meantime,

'the Americans and all other foreigners at Canton derive the most
direct advantage from that sense of great respect for His Majesty's
power which undoubtedly influences this Government. They . . .
would all enjoy any extent of relaxation which may be gradually
secured.'[3]

The troubles which arose under Lin's rule in Canton affected
all foreigners alike. All were ordered to deliver up opium[4] and
to sign the bond.[5] In spite of the fact that two American
frigates had arrived at Macao,[6] the Chinese Commissioner
refused to accept the assertions of the American consul that his
nationals had delivered up all their opium. The general confidence in the word of Her Majesty's officer and the recognition
of Elliot's authority by the Emperor afforded Lin sufficient
ground for founding his report to the Throne upon the Superintendent's declaration. Elliot accordingly gave Lin a certificate that the American Consul's assertions were accurate and
from that time the Americans were not further worried.[7] It
was, therefore, with great annoyance that Elliot saw them

[1] Elliot to Palmerston, 16 Oct. 1836 (F.O. 17/15).
[2] Elliot to Lennox Conyngham, private, 12 June 1837 (F.O. 17/20).
[3] Elliot to Lennox Conyngham, private, 28 July 1837 (F.O. 17/21).
[4] Elliot to Palmerston, 30 Mar. 1839 (P.P. 1840, xxxvi, no. 146).
[5] Elliot to Palmerston, 6 Apr. 1839 (ibid., no. 148).
[6] Elliot to Palmerston, 6 May 1839 (ibid., no. 149).
[7] Elliot to Palmerston, 27 May 1839 (ibid., no. 150).

remain behind in Canton after he and the last British merchants had left. In their common difficulties he had acted as beneficially as he possibly could for them, 'not only because of the friendship between Her Majesty's and the American Governments, but because I know that union amongst foreigners for all honourable objects is the best defence against the encroaching spirit of the Chinese authorities'. They had signed the bond 'at the formal sacrifice of the most important principles of policy, which Her Majesty's, their own, and all the Western Governments hitherto firmly repudiated in their intercourse with China'. There was no doubt in Elliot's mind that trade would long since have been temporarily re-established on a respectable footing if the Americans had left Canton with the British. As it was, 'their submission to the inadmissible pretensions of this government, and to the practical reduction of the foreigners at Canton almost to the condition of the Dutch at Japan, is excessively inconvenient to the interests of the Western Nations holding intercourse with China'. Elliot therefore proposed that the British Government should stop the importation of Chinese produce into England by American ships if the manifests were not signed by him, or until the normal trade was again open. He also suggested 'the expediency of a representation to the American government concerning proceedings for which their citizens here have never pretended to put forward any other excuse than the perfectly unfounded and unbecoming declaration, that they having nothing to expect from the protection of their own Government, and must therefore look to their immediate interests at the sacrifice of all general considerations.'[1]

The other power whose activities in the Far East were of great interest to the British was Portugal, owing to her occupation of Macao. After the establishment of Robinson in Macao, the authority of the Superintendents had been extended to embrace that town. But the Portuguese Governor, who at first had refused to recognize the public character of the commissioners, ultimately agreed to the issue by Elliot of a public notice extending the limit of his powers on condition that he inserted a clause to the effect that 'no acts done by us at Macao are to be taken to be in prejudice of the just rights, authority and Sovereignty of Her Most Faithful Majesty'. Elliot confessed that he did not know exactly what those rights were.

[1] Elliot to Palmerston, 8 Sept. 1839 (P.P. 1840, xxxvi, no. 158).

'I wish they were better understood by foreigners and more consistently asserted as respects the Chinese.'[1] The difficulties in the way of correspondence between the Portuguese authorities and the British commissioners were, however, removed through the intervention of the Foreign Office with the Lisbon Government.[2] Yet Elliot was, in fact, powerless in Macao. He was unable, for example, to have arrested an alleged buccaneer charged with murder and piracy.[3] And there were also difficulties of another character. He had occasion to protest at the vexatious treatment suffered by British subjects in the management of customs affairs by the Portuguese.[4] But the difficulties in the way of regarding Macao as an adequately secure base for British commerce became glaringly apparent in the crisis of 1839. For when the Chinese threatened Macao, 'an object of secondary moment to the Portuguese government; but to that of Her Majesty it may be of indispensable necessity, and most particularly at this moment', Elliot instructed Captain Blake of the *Larne* to give the Governor every assistance. The city was defended by four hundred poor Indian troops and five hundred Caffre slaves. The Governor, who intended to preserve his neutrality as long as possible, declined the proferred aid on the ground that he had enough rice and ammunition and thought that the forts were efficient against a Chinese attack. Elliot wondered whether the British Government could persuade the Portuguese to give them the right to fortify Macao, for he was of opinion that it was in a 'wretched state'[5]. When therefore Lin moved troops down against the place, Elliot, as we have seen,[6] in order to relieve the pressure on the Portuguese, removed himself and British subjects to Hong Kong. After Lin had left Macao Elliot asked the Governor that he and his fellow countrymen might be allowed to return, promising if any fears of the safety of the city were entertained to supply a force of 1,000 men. Elliot's letter was laid before the Senate, but contrary to the Governor's recommendations every senator spoke and voted strongly for a negative answer. The British Superintendent was informed that though the Macao Government had not turned the English

---

[1] Elliot to Palmerston, 31 Dec. 1836 (F.O. 17/15).
[2] Elliot to Palmerston, 5 July 1837 (P.P. 1840, xxxvi, no. 104).
[3] Elliot to Palmerston, 15 Aug. 1838 (F.O. 17/27).
[4] Elliot to Palmerston, 12 Sept. 1838 (F.O. 17/27).
[5] Elliot to Palmerston, 6 May 1839 (P.P. 1840, xxxvi, no. 149).   [6] p. 62.

out of the city, it no longer had the power, after the promises
Lin had demanded, to allow them to return. Though it was
true that the British had not been expelled, the Governor, by
informing Elliot that for a stated time the Portuguese soldiery
would guard their embarkation, had in substance warned him
that at its expiration he could no longer guarantee their safety.
Macao was therefore incapable in such hands of serving as a
haven to the foreign community.[1] And this was again made
clear in February 1840, when the British, who had returned
during a quieter interval, again brought down on the Portuguese settlement the angry threats of the Chinese authorities.
On this occasion Elliot decided that he would not leave the
city without a written order to that effect from the Governor.
Several hundred Chinese troops arrived with the object of
seizing Elliot and certain other British subjects designated by
Lin. Whereupon, after giving forty-eight hours' notice, H.M.S.
Hyacinth entered the inner harbour. Her commander, Captain
Smith, notified the Governor that his sole object was to prevent
the execution of the atrocious decree ordering the seizure of
Elliot and others which had been placarded by the Chinese
authorities, but received in reply a protest against the entry
of the frigate, as a hostile act, 'contre tous les droits et sans
exemple'[2]. Smith asked whether the Governor would protect
British subjects or whether they were to be harassed as they had
been for the last six months. The Governor and Senate, which
deliberated anxiously for ten hours, replied that if the frigate
departed they would protect British subjects 'as much as possible'. The appearance of the *Hyacinth* had thrown the city into
a state of panic.

'It would be difficult for me to portray', wrote the Procureur des
Missions Étrangères, 'the alarm caused by the appearance of this
frigate in the port and what hatred she drew upon the English.
Every one laid in a stock of provisions and the Chinese profiting
by these circumstances sold everything at exorbitant prices. Well,
the English are now assured of protection at Macao. I am not sure
whether they would not rather have received the opposite declaration. On the other side Lin threatens to cut off the food supplies
and to call off the Chinese from Macao if the Portuguese do not
drive the English away. On the 13th Mr. Elliot made as though to

---

[1] Elliot to Palmerston, 27 Aug. and 5 Nov. 1839 (P.P. 1840, xxxvi, no. 155
and Add. Corr. no. 2).

[2] Legrégeois to Directeurs, 9 Feb. 1840 (M.E., vol. 323, f. 315).

depart with some of his fellow countrymen and has secretly returned home. . . . The future looks very black.'[1]

'We shall have to hold it, if possible with Portuguese concurrence, but if not, without', wrote Elliot.[2] That might be all very well for the moment, but clearly Macao in such an equivocal position was of little use to the British merchants. Out of the need for some sea base where British ships could afford protection and out of the impossible situation in regard to Macao, was born the necessity for the acquisition of Hong Kong in British sovereignty. The utter lack of confidence now engendered in the minds of the British community caused both Elliot and the British Government to go back on the opinion of Sir Thomas Roe, quoted by the elder Mill.

'If the Emperor of China were to make a present of one of the islands at the mouth of His River, with a good and easily defended Harbour, perhaps it might be of some service to us, but if we were to place ourselves in the silly condition of being obliged to take one, or ten, or ten times ten, I should be very much of Sir Thomas' mind', wrote Elliot in 1836, 'and say "They will increase charges but not recompense it. If Sir Thomas had lived to the present day", says Mr. Mill, in his own strong way. . . ."he might have urged the trade with China as proof by experiment of the proposition he advanced".'[3]

But, in 1839, the situation was far different from what it had been in 1836 or when Mill wrote in 1817.

[1] Legrégeois to Directeurs, 9 Feb. 1840 (M.E., vol. 323, f. 315).
[2] Elliot to Palmerston, secret, 11 Feb. 1840 (F.O. 17/38).
[3] Elliot to Lennox Conyngham, 28 Jan. 1836 (F.O. 17/15).

II

WAR AND SETTLEMENT, 1840-4

A. THE FIRST PHASE, 1840-1

1. *Diplomatic and Military Preparations*

THE aim of Elliot's policy during the winter of 1839-40 was to keep trade going as far as was possible and to refrain from action until the wishes of the British Government were known. By the time that he had received advance information from Palmerston that the Government was sending out an expedition to demand redress from the Chinese he was able to report that the trade was over for the season and not a single British ship or subject was inside the Boca Tigris. It was fortunate that the Chinese had demanded the bond, for 'nothing short of such extremities would have induced the merchants to leave Canton'[1]. The exports of the British to Europe would amount to thirty million pounds weight of tea, which was a normal amount, regard being had to the stocks at home.[2] This had been achieved in spite of the fact that the trade had been officially closed since the previous August. The plain truth was that the local government could not stop British trade without disturbing the peace of the southern provinces, as millions of Chinese depended upon it for their daily bread. 'The Hongs are literally swept out and I do hope', Elliot wrote in June 1840 to Lennox Conyngham, 'that this plain exhibition of figures will be a sufficient answer to all charges of my gross mismanagement'[3].

In March the Provincial Government had declared the trade at Macao open because of the respectful obedience of the Portuguese in driving forth the English and because they had actually departed.

'The English however are here in greater numbers than they have been for the last eight months, but being officially gone, there is nothing further said about them. This is a significant and at this moment a really interesting comment upon the Chinese system of arranging difficulties. When they are not to be levelled in point of fact, the next course is to solve them by proclamation.'[4]

[1] Elliot to Palmerston, private, 16 Feb. 1840 (recd. 9 July) (F.O. 17/38).
[2] Elliot to Palmerston, 9 Mar. 1840 (F.O. 17/38).
[3] Elliot to Lennox Conyngham, 25 June 1840 (F.O. 17/39).
[4] Elliot to Palmerston, 23 Mar. 1840 (F.O. 17/38).

But though Macao offered a temporary retreat it was still in a highly unsatisfactory condition. There was daily encroachment by the Chinese on Portuguese rights in the territory, the place was filled with thieves, and, though the Governor was a man of the best will, he was powerless to do anything himself and fearful of calling upon the British to help him. If the trade was to be carried on from that point, Macao must 'be placed in a situation to afford efficient protection'[1]. 'Whether the Portuguese flag flew over these buildings or the British has always seemed to me to be a matter of indifference provided the whole of the island and the inner navigation towards Canton was ceded by the Chinese.'[2]

During this time Elliot had been considering what steps the British Government ought to adopt. He was of opinion that 'we shall never advance one step in China till we have proved to the Chinese government that Canton is very vulnerable in a three days' campaign'[3]. The trade, he thought, had been confined to Canton in the past both because it was at an extremity of the Empire, far away from the court of Peking, and because of its assumed impregnability. Hence Elliot looked forward to the immediate destruction of the forts guarding the Boca Tigris and an armed advance to within shelling distance of Canton. Amoy would be a very eligible situation, but its possession would bring us 'into complicated political relations and possibly territorial expansion'. The best outpost would be one of the Chusan group, off the mouth of the Yangtse Kiang.

'From that point, My lord, British manufactures would soon find their way to millions and millions of the most trading people on the face of the earth, from whom they are entirely shut out by the present close and expensive system. And in less than ten years I have a firm belief that that station would be the seat of a flourishing trade with Japan.'[2]

While Elliot was sending these suggestions home, the British Government had laid its policy before Parliament. The bulk of the correspondence between the Superintendents and the Foreign Office from Napier's appointment to the end of 1839 was printed in order to inform members of the facts. In reply to a question in the Commons on 19th March 1840 Palmerston stated that the

[1] Elliot to Lord Auckland, 22 Mar. 1840 (F.O. 17/38).
[2] Elliot to Palmerston, private, 16 Feb. 1840 (F.O. 17/38).
[3] Elliot to Palmerston, 20 May 1840 (F.O. 17/39).

object of the warlike preparations was threefold: to obtain reparation for the insults given to the Superintendent and the other
subjects of Her Majesty, an indemnity for the loss of the merchants' property, and future security for British traders. On the
7th April a motion of censure on the Government was moved
and after a very lengthy debate defeated by the narrow majority
of 9 in a house of 533 members.[1] The debate, which was on
party lines, ranged over the whole period from 1833 to 1840.
Sir James Graham pointed out the disastrous effect which the
war would have on the finances both of Great Britain and of
India. He assessed the value of the China trade to India at
twenty millions, and to the British Exchequer at over four
millions sterling. The Chinese were particularly jealous of the
British as they knew that our political control over India was
the result of the extension of commercial activities. It was
therefore especially unfortunate that Palmerston had instructed
Lord Napier to go to Canton and to announce his arrival there
to the Viceroy without a previous consultation with the court
of Peking. What a contrast between Wellington's wise insistence upon the accustomed mode of communication and Lord
Palmerston with his 'Pin-point'. The Government was highly
to blame for not providing Elliot with adequate police powers,
their non-interference had encouraged piratical proceedings.
Elliot was to be censured for merely preventing the opium
traffic in the inner waters while ordering the opium ships to
defend themselves in the Hong Kong anchorage. Gladstone's
speech was much more extreme in tone.

'Was it not mere mockery to affect—to pretend—indignation as
to the pernicious consequences of the opium trade, and yet exhaust
all the armoury of ingenuity and eloquence to prove that the Chinese
government were not justified in taking effectual means for crushing
that trade? The circumstances being so notorious, the Chinese
government were justified in acting against the entire community,
the more especially as there was no possibility of fixing the guilt
upon the individuals.'

Though the British Government could not have organized a
preventive system on the Chinese coasts, they might at least
have prevented the sailing of the opium ships from Bombay and
other Indian ports and have broken up the depot at Lintin.
Indeed in the opinion of some of his hearers, Gladstone even

---

[1] Hansard, Third Series, vol. liii; cols. 669–836, 845–955.   [2] Ibid., col. 821.

went as far as giving a qualified approval of the poisoning of the wells in Hong Kong. Mr. G. Palmer, who had commanded a vessel himself in Chinese waters, criticized the Superintendent for doing too much. 'I believe that no commander of a single vessel was unwilling to sign the bond. They looked upon it merely as an acknowledgement and declaration that they were not smugglers, and that they were ready to abide by the Chinese laws and restrictions in the event of their turning out otherwise.' He praised the good faith of the Chinese and made much of the safety of life in Canton where it was possible to sleep with windows open. The war was a menace to the valuable trade, forty thousand tons to Britain and between fifty and sixty thousand between China and India. Though Sir Robert Peel, the Leader of the Opposition, regarded the war, as things were, as necessary, he nevertheless laid the blame for its necessity upon the Government mainly for the inadequacy of the powers of discipline enjoyed by the Superintendent.

Palmerston began his defence by eulogizing his servant. Elliot had in fact discouraged the opium trade even at the cost of losing much social enjoyment. Did the Opposition suggest that 'the powers you ought to have given were to expel from China, by your authority, every man who was engaged in the opium trade, and to drive away every ship by which that trade was carried on?' That would have been a monstrous and arbitrary power open to great abuse, one which the Legislature never meant to give nor the Government to ask for. A court of criminal and admiralty jurisdiction existed and had been called into action. The China Courts Bill which was dropped was intended to give a civil jurisdiction between British parties. He had wished in the China Courts Bill to enable the criminal court to sentence British subjects to expulsion from the limits of the court's jurisdiction. It was not enacted owing to the opposition in the Lords of Lord Ellenborough. Peel himself had stated that he objected 'to the absolute power which is given for the deportation of British subjects'. And now the Leader of the Opposition was saying that the Government should have given Elliot powers of deportation. It would have been impossible to have prevented British subjects from engaging in the opium trade unless we had kept an army and a navy in Chinese waters. Even then the trade would have been conducted in a clandestine way up the coast.

'He wondered what the House would have said to Her Majesty's Ministers if they had come down to it with a large naval estimate for a number of revenue cruisers to be employed in the preventive service from the river at Canton to the Yellow Sea for the purpose of preserving the morals of the Chinese people, who were disposed to buy what other people were disposed to sell them?'

The result would have been a largely increased trade under the American flag. The Foreign Secretary ended by reading a dispatch from Washington which contained a memorial from American merchants in Canton soliciting the co-operation of the United States and Great Britain in establishing commercial relations on a secure and extended basis. 'The memorialists avow their opinion that the course pursued by the Chinese Commissioner was unjust, and no better than robbery and that if satisfaction is not yielded to the demand of the British government the chief ports and rivers of China ought to be blockaded.' And to cap this neutral opinion he read a letter from thirty London firms which requested the Government to use strong measures.

On the 20th February the Foreign Secretary had sent his instructions to the Superintendent and to that officer's cousin, Admiral Elliot, the naval commander-in-chief, as joint plenipotentiaries.[1] They were ordered immediately to occupy one of the Chusan group of islands, to communicate to some officer of the Chinese Government a letter from Palmerston to 'the Minister of the Emperor of China', and then to proceed to the mouth of the Peiho to sign a treaty with an accredited plenipotentiary of the Chinese Emperor. If, however, satisfaction were not given, pressure was to be applied by blockading the chief ports and the two great rivers, the Yangtse Kiang and the Yellow River, until the demands of the British Government were conceded. In his letter to the Chinese Government Palmerston complained of the violent outrages which had been committed against the British residents and the Queen's officer. 'It seems that the cause assigned for these proceedings was the contraband trade in opium, carried on by some British subjects.' 'Her Majesty does not wish to protect them from the just consequences of any offences which they commit in foreign ports; but she cannot permit her subjects to be treated with violence

---

[1] The Admiral had won high praise from Nelson, and after serving as one of the Lords Commissioners, had been for the last two and a half years Commander-in-Chief of the Cape of Good Hope.

and exposed to insult and injustice.' He made a great point of the necessity of an impartial administration of the law, and maintained that it was highly improper suddenly and without sufficient warning to enforce a law which had been so dormant or dead that from the Governor downwards a considerable profit had been annually derived from the opium trade. The first persons who should have been punished were these very officials. Still the British Government would not have complained if after due notice opium had been confiscated which had been brought into the country in violation of the law. 'The Chinese government had a right to do so by means of its own officers and within its own territory.' But, instead of seizing the opium, it had laid hands on the persons of the Superintendent and British merchants, innocent as well as guilty, and in effect through the practice of virtual starvation had compelled the British officer to become an instrument in the hands of the Chinese authorities for carrying out Chinese law. He demanded the repayment of the ransom, that the British officer should be communicated with 'in a manner consistent with usages of civilized nations', repayment by the Chinese Government of the debts owed by the Hong merchants, as it had granted exclusive rights to this monopolist body, and finally future security. For this last purpose 'one or more sufficiently large and properly situated Islands on the coast was to be fixed on by the British Plenipotentiaries to be permanently given up to the British government as a place of residence and commerce for its subjects'. The Indian Government agreed that if the time should come when questions of mutual concessions should be discussed, and the abandonment by the Indian Government of a direct interest in the production of opium should be a point of policy or honour insisted upon, it could be said without hesitancy that the

'government would be disposed fairly to weigh such a proposition as the price of full reparation for injuries received and of our commerce with China being placed upon a more liberal and satisfactory footing than it has yet been. Foreseeing the possibilities of such a result, I have been desirous even under present circumstances of discouraging on the part of our agents, any extension of the cultivation of the Poppy. But I would not immediately go further.'[1]

A draft treaty was sent to the Plenipotentiaries. In Article I

[1] Auckland (Minute), 7 Apr. 1840 (Add. MSS. 37715, f. 1 ff.).

it was stipulated that British subjects of both sexes with the persons of their establishments should be allowed freely to reside without molestation at the five ports of Canton, Amoy, Foochow, Shanghai, and Ningpo. The second article contained the provision that British consuls or superintendents were to reside there, to be treated with respect, and to enjoy direct communication with Peking. Article IV stipulated that a money equivalent for the destroyed opium, the ransom paid to preserve the lives of British hostages, was to be repaid. Article V arranged for the abolition of the monopolistic Hong system and for the payment of the Hong debts. Article VI contained an agreement for the reimbursement of the expenses of the expedition. Article VII dealt with the method and times of payment of the sums demanded in the three preceding articles. Article VIII arranged the successive stages of the relaxation of the British hold on Chinese territory and shipping. Article IX laid down that the treaty was to be drawn up in both languages, though the English text was to be authoritative. The tenth and last article provided for ratification by the Chinese Emperor and by Queen Victoria. All the foregoing articles, Palmerston expressly instructed the two Plenipotentiaries, 'are articles which Her Majesty's government regard as conditions *sine qua non*, without the conclusion of which or of articles substantially equivalent thereto, hostilities are not to cease'.

In the third article, as a satisfaction for the proceedings against Her Majesty's officer and subjects, the Queen was to receive the cession of islands or an island to be designated by the British Plenipotentiaries. But Palmerston instructed the Plenipotentiaries in the event of an unwillingness on the part of the Chinese to cede any territory, to secure instead the grant of factories and permanent arrangements for carrying on a trade on the mainland. These constituted in fact a commercial treaty designed, as was the cession of an island, to ensure security against such treatment as had been experienced in 1839. In these areas British subjects were to be free to build warehouses, factories, and houses, and to buy and sell, subject to the payment of duties according to a tariff to be drawn up within ten months and only to be changed after a year's notice had been given. Any prohibited articles were to be prohibited to all foreigners, and the Chinese Government was to grant

British subjects any rights which it gave to any other foreigners. The Chinese authorities were expressly authorized to confiscate any prohibited goods, or lawful goods which had been smuggled into the country, but the persons of British subjects were to be immune from molestation. Finally, the British Government was to be allowed to erect courts to try alleged British criminals and civil cases in which British subjects were the defendants. Palmerston gave the Plenipotentiaries liberty to agree to one restriction on the otherwise absolute freedom of commercial activities. If the Chinese Government strongly objected to the exportation of precious metals, British subjects might be debarred from receiving coin or bullion for the sale of their commodities.[1]

The British negotiators were therefore very narrowly restricted in their powers. And it should have been still more obvious how definite the Government was in its demands, when a dispatch written a few days afterwards arrived in China. It occurred to the Under-Secretary of State that Elliot might have made some arrangement with the Chinese authorities before the instructions of the 20th February and the expedition reached the Far East. Palmerston minuted the comment: 'I don't however think it likely that Captn Elliot would do such a thing without Instructions'. Nevertheless Elliot was ordered, in case any such thing had happened, 'immediately to announce to the Chinese government that such arrangement will not be ratified, and that the questions which have arisen between the two governments shall be arranged according to the terms the Plenipotentiaries of Her Majesty have been instructed to propose to the Plenipotentiaries of the Emperor of China'[2]. That Palmerston had a clear view of what to him were essentials is shown by an additional demand to press for, but not insist upon as a *sine qua non*, some regulation of internal transit duties.[3]

Meanwhile, the Indian Government had been preparing the armament which was to be placed at the disposal of the Plenipotentiaries. The military force, under the command of General Burrell, was to consist of three regiments of infantry, a volunteer regiment of Indian troops, two companies of European artillery, and two companies of sappers and miners. The naval armament consisted of 3 ships of 72 guns, 2 of over

---

[1] Palmerston to Elliot, 20 Feb. 1840 (F.O. 17/37).
[2] Palmerston to Elliot, 4 Mar. 1840 (F.O. 17/37).
[3] Palmerston to Elliot, 25 Apr. 1840 (F.O. 17/37).

40, 5 of 20 or over, 6 smaller vessels, and 4 steamers. The whole expedition was to be expected at Singapore before the end of May. The Governor-General's view was that the 'first blow in this campaign would be powerless if the blockade of Canton were not made complete and if our power should not be felt there, where we have been most injured'. He argued strongly for the occupation of Chusan or one of its sister islands, and for an attack upon the Government junks, ports, and other property, while taking care not to damage the civilian population and their trade.[1]

2. *Elliot's Action and Negotiations*

How did Charles Elliot fulfil these instructions? He had no doubts on the utter incapacity of the Chinese to resist British arms. 'The effect of systematic and vigorous attack by organized European forces against the Chinese Empire would be to the full as remarkable as that of Cortez against Mexico.'[2] But as he thought the Chinese Government was 'dependent upon feeling, and the whole fabric would probably fall to pieces under the effect of a blow, notorious to the people', he looked with misgivings at his orders to proceed to the Peiho. He was afraid that the Plenipotentiaries would be insulted there and that 'then a far more critical blow' than the blockade of the coast, 'would come almost immediately to be necessary, and . . . the effect of that blow might probably overthrow the actual Dynasty. I can't conceive a more unfortunate consequence to ourselves than extensive political convulsion in China.'[3] He had wished, like the Governor-General of India, the initial move to be the occupation of the channel to Canton, but with the arrival of the fleet in the middle of June the blockade of the coast was established and a detachment sent off to occupy Chusan. He was entirely in favour of establishing a stronghold on the mouth of the Yangtse, especially at Chin-kiang, where that great river is crossed by the Grand Canal, along which passed the important grain trade upon which the capital and the court subsisted. 'The Yangtse Kiang is the main artery and if we can but occupy a favourable station at the mouth of the Grand Canal on that river, the Emperor is checkmated.'[4]

[1] Auckland (Minute), 7 Apr. 1840 (Add. MSS. 37715, f. 1 ff.).
[2] Elliot to Palmerston, 12 Apr. 1840 (F.O. 17/39).
[3] Elliot to Palmerston, 20 May 1840 (F.O. 17/39).
[4] Elliot to Lennox Conyngham, private, 25 June 1840 (F.O. 17/39).

When he arrived in July at the island of Chusan with his coadjutor the admiral, he was already contemplating throwing overboard his explicit instructions. 'In my judgement Her Majesty's Government will do well to keep and improve what they have got, and to leave all details of indemnity, all expenses of the expedition to be made good out of the growing advantage of extending trade.' He was of opinion that within three months of taking the coast forts and interruption of the native trade he would be discussing modes of adjustment. 'Not that I think we shall be able to settle permanently on the basis laid down by our own government, but I do believe we shall have the option of arranging upon some footing involving the resumption of the trade in a very extended manner, deferring all questions about the abandonment of the Island, indemnity, etc., etc., upon the plea that we need further instructions from England.' Hence he actually 'proposed to the Admiral that we should transmit a communication to the Governor of Chekiang Province requesting him to move his court to appoint Plenipotentiaries to meet us'. Quite correctly the admiral was of opinion that they ought not to disregard their instructions to such an extent,[1] and insisted on a move to the Peiho. Like Captain Elliot, Lord Auckland certainly did not share the views of the Home Government. He wished that the instructions from England had not ordered the seizure of private junks. But the naval commander would have to obey his orders.

'I have always looked forward to the possibility of being able to secure no better end to the war than the establishment of a secure rendezvous for Chinese and European Commerce under the protection of the British Flag at a station apart from the mainland of China—after such punishment for past misdeeds shall have been administered, as shall prevent any wanton recurrence of them.'[2]

But the First Lord of the Admiralty wrote to the Governor-General: 'After all it is neither more nor less than the conquest of China that we have undertaken.' If this or anything more than the maintenance of a blockade or the occupation of one or two islands was expected, Auckland, who was afraid that ministers expected more to be done than the land forces he had been able to send could possibly effect, urged Admiral Elliot

[1] Elliot to Lennox Conyngham, private, 20 July 1840 (recd. 9 Dec.) (F.O. 17/39).
[2] Auckland to Bremer, private, 30 Apr. 1840 (Add. MSS. 37715, f. 47).

either to do the best he could with his available forces or to send back the transports for another regiment or two.[1]

A vain attempt had been made at Amoy to induce the local officers to receive and forward Palmerston's letter. It had ended in fact in the Chinese firing on the flag of truce, under which it had been sought to make the communication. But at Ningpo they did receive the letter, although they declined to forward the original English version. The British Plenipotentiaries were considerably encouraged by the decent tone of the correspondence which ensued. The Ningpo officers omitted the usual word 'command' and made no protest at the use of the phrase 'our two countries'. They admitted that Lin had mismanaged affairs in Canton.[2] On the 8th August the British Plenipotentiaries arrived off the Peiho and received courteous treatment when three days later they got into communication with the shore. The Provincial Governor Keshen stated that though he had heard something of the Canton affair, the Emperor, whose aim had been the suppression of the opium traffic, was unaware that any injuries had been done to the English. The Governor, however, promised to communicate with the court at Peking, and to forward Lord Palmerston's letter. After an interval, during which the squadron visited Shantung Province for supplies, Keshen and the Plenipotentiaries foregathered at Takoo. The Chinese officer received Elliot with great courtesy. He agreed that the Emperor ought to punish his officers responsible for the molestation of British subjects, but refused to recognize the justice of the demand for repayment of the value of the surrendered opium. Elliot pointed out that though Palmerston had no objection to the seizure of opium whenever and wherever it was taken by Chinese officers on the coast of China, he did strongly resent the seizure of the subjects and the officer of the British Crown under threats of the privation of food, water, and even of life. The opium in question had not been confiscated by Chinese officers but paid as a ransom by the British officer. Upon being asked definitely by Elliot whether the demand for indemnity for this opium was rejected, Keshen replied that he was but one of six in the Cabinet and that more mature deliberation was necessary.

After being rebuked by Elliot for stating that English sove-

[1] Auckland to Elliot, 20 May 1840 (Add. MSS. 37715, f. 50).
[2] The Plenipotentiaries to Palmerston, 17 July 1840 (F.O. 17/40).

reigns had twice sent tribute bearers to Peking, he finally agreed
that it would not be difficult to adjust satisfactorily the question
of equality in official intercourse. He vigorously opposed the
cession of an island, and asked whether Great Britain was prepared to stop the export of opium from her dominions. Elliot
argued that such a proposal would not be of much advantage,
owing to the fact that quite as much opium was grown outside
dominions in British control—such as the Indian native States
and Persia—from which it would be brought by persons of
other nationalities. He pointed out the great evil of smuggling
and the consequent lack of order on the coasts of China, and
suggested that extensive smoking of opium was a lesser evil than
extensive smuggling. But though the account of the interview
did not show much approach to the demands of the British
Foreign Secretary, Elliot reported: 'The general impression
which this interview has left upon me is the existence of an
anxious desire to avert a rupture.' The Plenipotentiaries indeed
saw and stated to Keshen that their demands were apparently
rejected and yet they had been recommended to negotiate in
Canton. If the Emperor had promised to repay the ransom money
they would have acquiesced in removing the seat of the negotiations to the south. Keshen asked for a delay of ten days to
make a further report to the Peking court. On the 13th September he gave his final reply. As the opium was a contraband
commodity and had been banned, 'the principle can by no
means be admitted of paying indemnity for it'. When Keshen
arrived in Canton 'he may perhaps upon the said Honourable
Nation soliciting again the favour of commercial intercourse,
lay before the throne a memorial humbly requesting that the
favour may be granted'. During the last two years British goods
had found no opening for their disposal, 'and to the purchase
of tea and rhubarb no channel had been discovered'. He suggested that it was much easier for China with everything on the
spot to defend herself than for the British coming from afar to
attack her. If the admiral failed to get a settlement and a
resumption of trade, his Sovereign would recall him. Some one
else would be sent out who could 'surely pay respectful obedience
to the declared pleasure of the Great Emperor by returning to
Canton there to await arrangements being made'. But finally
the Imperial negotiator urged the admiral to return to Canton,
'there to await the speedy arrival of an Imperially deputed

High Minister to manage the affair. Although the value of the opium does not amount to much, it will be sought by all means to enable the Honourable Admiral to have that wherewith to respond to his Honourable Nation's Sovereign', and the Superintendent could then also receive amends and satisfaction for past grievances and injuries.

This reply was regarded as adequate by the British officers. Doubtless the fact that it was now mid-September and the season for operations in the north was drawing to a close and that they had not with them a sufficient force on the spot for a striking military success influenced their decision to comply with Keshen's request. They were laying the greatest stress on repayment of the ransom money, and although Keshen plainly suggested that no compensation as such could be made, he hinted that at least a sum of money would be forthcoming which might satisfy the British Government. At the same time it is apparent that the Chinese Government was blind to realities. During the last two years trade had been very brisk in spite of the theoretical prohibition. Elliot was no doubt unduly solicitous for the continued prosperity of the trade and therefore anxious to prevent extreme measures. Keshen had gained by his skilful, delaying diplomacy, what was for the Imperial court an immense relief—the withdrawal of an armed force from the mouth of the river which led to the capital, and the consignment of the Barbarians to the further extremity of the Empire. In announcing their agreement to remove to Canton the Plenipotentiaries stated that 'notwithstanding what has passed it will be a hearty satisfaction to them on their arrival at Canton on the 15th October, to receive a plain declaration that the value of the property lawlessly and insultingly wrung from the British superintendent shall, as satisfaction for the wrong done, be restored'[1].

Auckland was disappointed in reading the dispatches from the Peiho. He thought that the declaration of the Chinese authorities was tantamount to a 'general and substantial rejection of the demands of the British government', and that there was little hope of a favourable result in further negotiations at Canton. He warned Elliot against being entangled in the south in dilatory and delusive negotiations, and suggested that he should at once act vigorously so as to protect to the utmost the

[1] The Plenipotentiaries to Palmerston, 22 Sept. 1840 (F.O. 17/40).

interests of Her Majesty's Crown and subjects without waste
of the means which had been collected with vast expense and
difficulty. The Bogue Forts should be destroyed and an island
depot seized at the mouth of the Canton River. Such island
or islands which might upon careful consideration be thought
suitable as naval or military stations or as British settlements
for trade should be declared permanently annexed to the
British Dominions and placed under the protection of the
British Crown.[1]

On their way back south the Plenipotentiaries were much
impressed by the considerable sickness and indeed heavy mortality which had fallen upon the troops in Chusan, and which
they attributed in part at least to the incompetence[2] of General
Burrell. They came to the conclusion that it was desirable to
obtain a settlement on terms much less exacting than those laid
down in Palmerston's instructions of February.

'Carefully considering the extensive demands of Her Majesty's
government and the whole body of circumstances we feel it incumbent upon ourselves to express the opinion that they are doubtful
of complete achievement without a protraction of hostilities. Upon the
other hand we believe that there would be no great difficulty in an
early and temporary settlement involving an indemnity for the opium,
probably of gaining an insular station near Canton, and of opening
out the trade at that point upon an extended solid and improving
footing, on the condition that we consent to evacuate Chusan.'[3]

They asked for instructions—but before any answer was received
Captain Elliot, left alone on his cousin's withdrawal owing to
illness, had accepted a settlement upon that basis. This change
of policy decided upon by Elliot was perhaps made easier by
the receipt of a private letter from the Governor-General, and
some responsibility must undoubtedly be borne by Lord Auckland. He reported that Sir Charles Hobhouse, the President
of the Board of Control, had written 'We have no doubt that
no detriment will happen to the public service, in consequence
of the difference of views entertained by the Home Authorities
and the Governor-General in regard to the operations in the
China Seas.' In a private letter to Auckland Hobhouse had
said: 'I have only to repeat that all you have done and written

[1] Auckland to Elliot, 20 Nov. 1840 (Add. MSS. 37715, f. 69).
[2] Auckland to Hobhouse (confidential), 7 July 1841 (Add. MSS. 37715, f. 136).
[3] Elliot to Palmerston, 29 Sept. 1840 (F.O. 17/40).

is perfectly satisfactory and has been approved.' Lord Palmerston had written to the Governor-General: 'We shall be anxious to hear the result of our China Expedition but the arrangements you have made are so perfect that we have no doubt of success.' Doubtless this referred to the means to be used—the amount of force and the action to be taken in regard to private Chinese junks. These had in accordance with instructions been seized by the British naval forces but had afterwards been released. Auckland was glad that interference with private trade had been abandoned, and was ready to take his share of responsibility in disregarding the London Government's orders in this matter.[1] But it was at least misleading when he commented on Sir John Hobhouse's letter: 'All this shows that you may do pretty much as you like and I trust that you will do so.'[2]

By the middle of December Keshen was ready with his answer to Palmerston's demands. He refused an indemnity, but promised a payment of five million dollars for British losses during the last ten years. Official intercourse would be put on a basis of equality. No island could be ceded, Chusan was to be evacuated, but the trade for the future, though restricted to Canton, was to be placed on a better footing. The Chinese negotiator was already corresponding on terms of equality, and Elliot noted that the tone of his reply was good and free from all bravado. He determined to demand trade at other ports—Amoy and Chusan for example, and if possible a greater sum of money.

'If I can secure so much without a blow, it will better become me to incur the responsibility of departing from the letter of my instructions than to cast upon the country the burden of a distant war for the sake of a balance of concessions pretty surely within our grasp in no long lapse of time by a quiet improvement of our opportunities. I shall indeed have stopped far short of the demands of the government.'[3]

Auckland was glad to think that there were better hopes of successful negotiations than he had imagined, though the result apparently would not come up 'to the high scale of demand which was originally made', but 'I have never expected', he wrote, 'unqualified compliance with the first demands. I will not attempt to define the limits of compensation and of com-

---

[1] Auckland to Adm. Elliot, 17 July 1840 (Add. MSS. 37715, f. 58).
[2] Auckland to Adm. Elliot, 20 Sept. 1840 (Add. MSS. 37715, f. 63)
[3] Elliot to Auckland, 13 Dec. 1840 (F.O. 17/40).

mercial freedom with which I should feel contented but I earnestly hope that you may be able to accomplish the object of at least a modest and eligible factory and suitable trading arrangements on the Eastern Coast.' If this were impossible, he fully agreed that hostilities should be pushed forward on the Canton River, for he deeply regretted 'that such an effort was not made at the very outset of the expedition'[1].

At the beginning of January 1841 Elliot was writing that his principles were 'to require as little in satisfaction of the past as I could venture to do', and to evince the utmost moderation, if only Chusan could be retained. As he thought the Imperial Commissioner was a man of 'yielding spirit', he had indeed gone 'greatly beyond the letter of his instructions'. After bargaining on the amount to be paid and the period within which the money was to be handed over both sides finally agreed on six millions, one to be paid immediately and the balance in seven years. Keshen refused to cede Chusan. Elliot agreed to drop this demand on consideration that Amoy, Canton, and Chusan should be open for trade and that the merchants should be allowed to reside there. The Imperial Commissioner retorted that trade might be allowed at one port other than Canton, but that at such second port dealings were to be on board ship, and no residence was to be allowed on shore. Elliot stated that the British Government had instructed him to arrange for the opening of five ports. If Keshen agreed on two besides Canton and memorialized the Emperor to ratify that arrangement, he would immediately begin to evacuate Chusan, which would be cleared of British troops one month after the Imperial ratification was received, while the two new ports need not be opened for trade until after the Imperial ratification. Keshen explained that the Emperor desired the restitution of Tinghai—the principal town in Chusan—not for its importance to him who has 'under his benign sway ten thousand realms, and rules over a multudinous people and a wide spreading territory —but as a substantial mark of a respectful and dutiful spirit'. In spite of that revival of what Palmerston regarded as Chinese arrogance, Elliot suggested that a personal meeting with the Imperial Commissioner might lead him to agree on one extra port. Surely the British would be given some place 'where the British flag may fly as the Portuguese does at Macao'. He

[1] Auckland to Adm. Elliot, 1 Jan. 1841 (Add. MSS. 37715, f. 78).

pointed out that if the Imperial Commissioner incurred responsibility so too did the British Plenipotentiary for 'so vastly diminishing the demands of his government'[1]. When finally Keshen informed Elliot that no Imperial signet could be placed on a document which gave such terms to the British, the Superintendent was clear that the Imperial court had no sincere disposition to adjust the difficulties of the situation. On the 8th January Elliot ordered the fleet into action.

After three hours the forts on Chuenpi and Tycocktow Islands at the mouth of the Boca Tigris were taken. There was a heavy loss of Chinese life but few British casualties. The following day, as a result of the release of the prisoners taken on the 8th, there was no resistance at the Boca Tigris forts. On the 11th, after a suspension of hostilities, Elliot agreed to accept Hong Kong in lieu of Chuenpi. But, having secured an insular station, he waived his demand for the other ports and promised to surrender Tinghai. The Canton trade was immediately to be opened.[2]

The suspension of hostilities and the acceptance of these terms caused great disappointment to the Indian Government.[3] For the immediate evacuation of Chusan Elliot had obtained no equivalent commercial position in eastern China, no improvement in the relations of British merchants with the Canton authorities. The payments were inadequate and spread over too long a period—the collection of duties by or for the Chinese Government in a British possession and the whole dependent on the condescension of Peking 'fail very far short of the expectations with which this powerful expedition was fitted out'[4]. Auckland thought from the tone of the British comments on the Peiho negotiations that the London Government were certain to disapprove the terms of the Chuenpi agreement.[5]

Before the formal treaty was even signed by Keshen, Elliot announced the terms he had arranged to the British community, whom he adjured to implement the political peace by a

<hr/>

[1] Elliot to Palmerston, 5 Jan. 1841 (F.O. 17/47).
[2] Elliot had done a little deed of mercy in securing from Keshen the release of an imprisoned French missionary: 'tout autre que lui dans sa position aurait-il pensé à un pauvre M^{re}?' asked the Procureur in referring to this act of 'notre cher ami M^r. Elliot.' Legrégeois to Directeurs, 20 Jan. 1841 (M.E. vol. 323, f. 496).
[3] Auckland to Bremer, 25 Feb. 1841 (Add. MSS. 37715, f. 88).
[4] Auckland to Elliot, 16 Feb. 1841 (Add. MSS. 37715, f. 91).
[5] Auckland to Bremer, 16 Feb. 1841 (Add. MSS. 37715, f. 92).

conciliatory treatment of the people and a becoming deference
to the constitution and government of the country. And he
stated publicly the doctrine of the Open Door, about which so
much was to be heard in future years. 'Her Majesty's government has sought for no privilege in China exclusively for the
advantage of British subjects and merchants, and he is only
performing his duty in offering the protection of the British
Flag to the subjects and citizens and ships of foreign Powers
that may resort to Her Majesty's Possession.'[1] To Palmerston
he wrote that the cession of Hong Kong meant that the whole
foreign commerce of China would be under the British flag, but
that for the present, owing to lack of facilities there, the trade
was to be carried on at Whampoa.

With great ceremony the Plenipotentiary and the High Commissioner met on the 26th January, but upon Elliot's presenting
a draft treaty to Keshen embodying their agreement the Chinese
officer remarked that, difficult as were the questions of substance, those of form might be insuperable. He criticized the
articles dealing with the indemnity, the cession of Hong Kong,
and trade regulation. The first could not appear in any treaty
which was to be reported to the throne—the payment was a
private arrangement of the High Commissioner's. He did not
mean to cede the whole island of Hong Kong, but only to grant
as much as was necessary for the purposes of residence. The
proposed method of changing the trade was impracticable,
'without breaking up the whole political system of the Empire,
so far as it regarded foreign intercourse'. Most strongly he disapproved of the article dealing with the Imperial ratification,
which would be 'a violation of the most ancient and respected
customs of the Empire'. Elliot admitted no compromise on the
subject of Hong Kong, but both were desirous of postponing
the signing of the agreement until it should be known that
Chusan was evacuated. Keshen was suspicious of Elliot's good
faith, and the latter was anxious to hear that the rearguard had
safely embarked. All was finally arranged on the 12th February, but the actual signatures were deferred until it was known
three days later that Chusan would be fully restored on the
1st March. The treaty provided in Article I for free access to
Canton on possession of a passport. Dwellings and persons were
to be immune from molestation. All British vessels which had

[1] Elliot to Palmerston, 21 Jan. 1841 (F.O. 17/47).

not contraband on board were to be admitted and no bond was to be exacted. Article II secured equality of intercourse. The third article ceded Hong Kong, but a Chinese custom-house was to be established on the island at Tsien Shatsung. The fourth article arranged for the trial of accused British persons at Hong Kong by British officers, and the delivery of Chinese criminals escaping to Hong Kong to their own authorities. The fifth article stipulated that trade regulations should be drawn up by three British and three Hong merchants. The sixth article recognized the right of the Chinese authorities to seize and confiscate contraband cargo and the ship in which it was introduced. But British persons engaged in contraband trade were to be freed or handed over to British authorities. And, lastly, ratifications were to be exchanged by a High Officer for each country.

But Keshen never set his seal to this treaty. Orders were given by the Imperial court for the resumption of the war, and three new High Commissioners were sent from Peking 'to take charge of the affair'. Elliot had with him in Hong Kong the whole Chusan force. He therefore immediately resumed hostilities. The forts up the river were occupied, and on the 6th March General Gough, who had been sent out by Auckland in November to supersede Burrell (whom the Governor-General accused of 'insufficiency on every side'[1],) seized one of the gates of the city of Canton. On the 20th an armistice was agreed upon and temporary arrangements were made to carry on the season's trade. Elliot now determined, as he was unable to get a moderate peace without serious military measures, considerably to increase his terms. He decided to demand the payment of six million dollars within three days and a further six payable the following year. Until then the British forces would keep all that they held. The Chinese customs-house was to be established not in Hong Kong Island but on the mainland at Kowloon. He would also arrange for the discharge of the Hong merchants' debts—of which nothing had been stated in the Chuenpi agreement—within three years, after which the Hong monopoly would be abolished. But nothing came of these demands and Keshen was sent in chains to Peking.[2] And before the news of these events arrived in London Elliot had been ordered home.

[1] Auckland to Adm. Elliot, 27 Nov. 1840 (Add. MSS. 37715, f. 71).
[2] Elliot to Palmerston, 10 Mar. 1841 (F.O. 17/47).

3. Recall of Elliot

Palmerston was already disturbed, as Auckland had been,[1] at Elliot's account of the meeting with Keshen at the Peiho. He pointed out how often the old tone of superiority was assumed. Phrases like 'the pleasure of the Great Emperor' or 'respectfully obey the declared Imperial pleasure' were galling to the Foreign Secretary. He would have been more pleased if, when the British Plenipotentiaries were asked to go to Canton at the Emperor's command, they had replied that they were in China to obey the commands and fulfil the orders of their own Sovereign. 'It seems to me that Captain Elliot is disposed to act upon an erroneous principle in his dealings with the Chinese and to use too much refinement in submitting to their pretensions.' That might have been all very well in the days when the British agent at Canton had no force to back his views. Palmerston pointed out that it did not appear, from the Peiho conversations, that the Chinese were willing to cede an island and there was no mention of war expenses.[2] Elliot had asked in September whether the British Government would modify their instructions. Palmerston refused. 'Those instructions were founded upon a great variety of communications received from many Persons well acquainted with China and who, without concert or communication with each other, gave to Her Majesty's government opinions tending very nearly to the same conclusions.' Though it might be convenient to have also some station at the mouth of the Canton River, the main point to be gained was a position off the east coast. It might be that Chusan was insalubrious. But at least all the money demands should have been met. 'After all our naval power is so strong that we can tell the Emperor what *we* mean to hold, rather than that *he* should say what he would cede.'[3] It is not surprising therefore that, on receipt of the arrangement made at Chuenpi, Palmerston in no measured terms censured his

[1] 'I should be wanting in all sincerity if I did not say that I have read those reports with much pain and disappointment. . . . In high, almost haughty, terms you are told to return Southwards, there to await the management of the affair, and that not to obey the imperial command and pleasure would be greatly in contradiction of the principle of deference and duty and in compliance with the pleasure of the Emperor you agree so to return to the South.' Auckland to Adm. Elliot, 27 Nov. 1840 (F.O. 17/47).

[2] Palmerston to Elliot, 9 Jan. 1841 (F.O. 17/45).

[3] Palmerston to Elliot, 3 Feb. 1841 (F.O. 17/45).

subordinate. He began by stating his disappointment at the result of the negotiations and his disapproval of the manner in which they had been conducted. 'I gave you specific demands, and furnished you with the means for obtaining them.' 'You have disobeyed and neglected your instructions.' Elliot had abstained from employing his force, and accepted terms which could have been justified only after considerable military reverses. Indeed, even then he ought to have asked for further instructions. But in fact everywhere the British forces had been successful. Had this refusal to use force resulted in all the demands being granted well and good. But as it was 'throughout the whole course of your proceedings, you seem to have considered that my Instructions were waste Paper, which you might treat with entire disregard, and that you were at full liberty to deal with the interests of your Country according to your own Fancy'. He pointed out that he had not obtained enough compensation for the surrendered opium, and that the payment of it was to be spread over such a long period of years that it would in fact fall on British trade. There was not a penny for the expenses of the expedition, or for the Hong debts. Chusan was to have been held until everything was paid, and in fact it had been restored. Hong Kong, thought Palmerston, was but a barren island with hardly a house upon it, and it was not ceded to Britain in sovereignty, but would be just another Macao. Elliot had failed to obtain an opening for the trade to the north, and had allowed Keshen to assume a tone of superiority, while Elliot had addressed the High Commissioner in the style of an inferior. Therefore he would be relieved.[1] Palmerston's political opponents shared his views. Though Stanley was himself disposed to recommend an address praying that the treaty Elliot had negotiated be not ratified, he was 'much inclined to think that a motion condemning the conduct of the affair and the terms obtained would meet with pretty general support'[2].

There seems little doubt that ever since Elliot had assumed the position of Superintendent he had had a definite policy of quiet penetration, which although rudely shaken by the events of 1839 he was still maintaining. His eyes were rather on the past than on the future, on Canton and the improvement of

[1] Palmerston to Elliot (Draft), 21 Apr. 1841 (F.O. 17/45).
[2] Stanley to Peel, 18 Apr. 1841 (Add. MSS. 40467, f. 27).

the position of the British representative and British trading interests there, than on the length of the coast up to the Yangtse and the extension of British trade to the north. To Palmerston there was not only the problem of the righting of past wrongs, but of the development of the intercourse of the West with the Chinese Empire. Elliot sought to get as much improvement as he could short of engaging in long hostilities; Palmerston was prepared for the use of force, at no ultimate financial loss, and at negligible cost in British lives, in order to settle as far as could be seen the future relations of Great Britain and China. Palmerston too was in touch with opinion at home, which meant very largely mercantile opinion, while Elliot, like his successors, was not wholly in sympathy with a large body of the trading community. Above all, Elliot was by the summer of 1840 under instructions. Stationed far from home by a Government which had only just assumed responsibility for Anglo-Chinese relations, he had in the past been left to manage affairs with but meagre orders and advice. In the days before the telegraph, when steam shipping was in its infancy, a far-flung representative who was militarily dependent, not on Great Britain, but on the Governor-General of India, he assumed a responsibility which it was not his to assume. It may be that Palmerston confined him too closely by the Draft Treaty, but yet it is significant that Elliot's successor won all the terms, both political and financial, laid down by the Foreign Secretary, and that when Palmerston gave way to Aberdeen, the Foreign Secretary of the Peel Administration, the new Government did not give the new Plenipotentiary any substantial freedom.

It remains to be seen how Elliot dealt with the situation before he received news of his recall and Sir Henry Pottinger relieved him of his duties.

We left Elliot on the 20th March 1841 in a position to hold the city of Canton and with arrangements made to carry on the trade. A week later he held a conference with the naval and military commanders and came to the decision to establish the British position firmly at Hong Kong, to be ready to assume complete military and political control of Canton, and to attack Amoy as soon as the monsoon had set in from the south-west, when operations in the north could be undertaken. In the meanwhile the commodore was to go to Calcutta to fetch more steamships, an extra regiment, and drafts to fill up the gaps caused by the deaths at Chusan during the previous summer. On the 18th April Elliot reported that the trade was going on briskly, and on the arrival of the last two of the three new Imperial Commissioners, numerous petitions were presented to them by the Chinese praying them not to disturb the trade of the province. Though 'the ancient forms of foreign control and intercourse continued to subsist at Canton, essentially considered, there has been an entire overthrow of the whole system', reported Elliot to Lord Auckland.[1] On the 18th May, however, things were changing for the worse, for Chinese troops were massing in the city. He asked the authorities for proof of their faithful adherence to the armistice of the 20th March. The natives were departing from the city in increasing numbers and Elliot recommended the foreign merchants gradually and unostentatiously to withdraw from Canton. Finally, the gathering storm broke on the 21st May, by sunset of which day the loading of the British merchant vessels was complete and but one Englishman, a clerk in an American firm, remained in the factories. At 11 p.m. that night the Chinese set fire-ships loose on the shipping and began a cannonade from a battery on the flats of Shameen. By daylight this fort was silenced, and two days later the factories were occupied by British troops. On the 25th the British general moved to the heights at the north-west of the city, destroying the forts that guarded the entrance, while the British naval forces had silenced all the forts on the river. The Chinese capitulated. Elliot refused to allow the armed forces of the Crown to occupy the city. He had said to General Gough before the operations started that 'the protection of the people of Canton and the encouragement of their good will towards us are perhaps our chief political duties in this country'. In this clement policy he was supported by Auckland, who thought 'it was right and wise to spare that city; as it was proper to preserve the friendly feeling towards the English which the populace evinced'[2]. His basic idea was to compel the Cantonese to remain quiet so that British traders, who between March and May had exported 28 million pounds weight of tea, might carry on when the main British forces, on the commodore's return from India, concentrated on the

[1] Elliot to Auckland, 1 May 1841 (F.O. 17/48).
[2] Auckland to the Plenipotentiaries, 10 May 1841 (Add. MSS. 37715, f. 100).

Yangtse. Though there was little to be gained, thought Auckland, in a blockade of the Great Rivers, yet he observed with some apprehension the many instances in which Elliot had attempted to connect his measures of war and diplomacy with general and even particular commercial interests. The Governor-General was of opinion that it would be more prudent and perhaps for all parties the more profitable course for the Superintendent to fix his own measures and act on them firmly, consistently leaving the merchants to take care of themselves.[1] It was undoubtedly with an eye on the commercial position that on the 27th May Elliot agreed that the British forces should retire below the Boca Tigris if the Chinese troops collected from other provinces and the three Imperial Commissioners departed within one week at least sixty miles from Canton. By that time, too, six million dollars was to be paid over as a ransom for the city, in addition to reparation for the losses in the factories, and for the destruction in 1839 of the Spanish ship *Bilbaino*. By the 2nd June five millions had been paid in cash and one million in securities. Elliot extended the time-limit for the departure of two of the Commissioners to the 7th June. The third he decided to allow to remain, as he had been satisfied that this officer had opposed the late breach of the truce. Canton was thus pacified or reduced to impotence when on the 5th July Commodore Bremer arrived back in Macao from India. As Elliot had arranged for Chinese freely to trade with Hong Kong all was ready for an advance on Amoy and the Yangtse to start between the 15th and 20th of July. The departure, however, was postponed for a short while owing to serious damage done to the ships by a typhoon. Hence Sir Henry Pottinger, who arrived on the 10th August, after a journey of ten weeks from Falmouth, found everything prepared for an immediate advance.

On his return home Elliot wrote a memorandum[2] reviewing his conduct, which was circulated to the members of the new Conservative Cabinet. He began by justifying his taking over the opium in 1839 by quoting the Duke of Wellington's approval of that act. He thought he had acted rightly in not blockading the Canton River when he moved up to the Peiho on the ground that the Chinese knew that the trade was more important

[1] Auckland to Elliot, 23 May 1841 (Add. MSS. 37715, f. 116).
[2] Elliot to Lord Aberdeen, 53 Cadogan Place, 25 Jan. 1842 (F.O. 17/61).

to foreigners than to themselves, and to have stopped it would in effect have been doing their work. Had it been necessary for the proper prosecution of the war to neglect commercial interests he would have regarded them as a secondary consideration, but that was not so. His policy had resulted, during the last two years, in a clearance of fifty thousand tons of British shipping and a trade to the value of ten million pounds sterling.

After the Chusan Island had been occupied he had not had enough ships both to blockade the Yangtse and to go to the Peiho. Personally he wished to concentrate on the Yangtse and to negotiate there, but the Admiral had overruled him. Similarly the Plenipotentiaries had been unable to effect any military pressure at the Peiho, where Keshen had not wittingly deceived him but rather, as his subsequent punishment showed, had seriously overestimated the strength of the peace party in Peking. By November 1840, when he was back in Canton, there were only 2,500 British effectives, owing to disease and death at Chusan. It was that diminution of his force that seemed to him to fall within the proviso in his instructions— 'circumstances may happen and questions may arise, which have not been foreseen by Her Majesty's government, in such case you will use your discretion, guiding yourself according to the spirit of your instructions'. He was of opinion that he had got everything essential except one thing—the money payments for the expedition, but at that time the expedition had cost little more than half a million. It was true also that the time limit for payment of the ransom money had been extended from three to five years. With regard to the debts owed by the Hong merchants to the British, Elliot had informed the Governor-General in June 1841 that the two parties concerned had come to an arrangement, which was being carried out. The Hong system was bound to die a natural death if the right which he had acquired of individual Chinese to trade with the British in Hong Kong had been maintained. Anyhow, the question was solving itself, as the Hong merchants had become little else than brokers. He defended his arrangement whereby a committee of British and Hong merchants were to settle the terms of the commercial treaty, on the ground that these Chinese were very much under the influence of the more powerful British. And in any case the duties paid in Canton were moderate if compared with the duties levied on Chinese produce, especially tea, in British ports. This joint committee was to have been instructed by Elliot to sanction the abolition of the Consoo Fund as soon as the Hong debts were paid.

He contended further that to secure additional authorized ports of trade while the opium question was not settled was to place so many more hostages in the power of the Chinese. Chusan was not as good a settlement as Hong Kong, owing to its unhealthy climate and the hostility of the peasantry, without whose good will no place was worth keeping. It was quite a mistake to suppose that Hong Kong would be a British Macao. His underlying principles he clearly stated when he said:

'It has been popularly objected to me, that I have cared too much for the Chinese. But I submit that it has been caring more for lasting British honour and substantial British interests to protect a helpless and friendly people. . . . They love both their country and their profit, and I believe we shall do better by continuing to enlist the latter motive on our side, than by raising up the other against us.'

He thought that, given time to explain his motives more fully between the 7th January 1841 and the resumption of hostilities in May, he could have satisfied Palmerston.

It is certain that, contrary to his own hopes and expectations, when he was relieved Elliot was about to do what Pottinger did—to blockade the Yangtse. There is no doubt that he might there have won the very terms which were secured in 1842. But it would appear that it was essential to the carrying out of the British Government's views to get a fresh man without the experiences of Elliot. The Superintendent had in the past more than once been obliged to use the character 'Pin'. There was more likelihood of a stronger stand being made by one who had not thus humiliated himself. A moderate achievement to a man who had been in Elliot's position naturally seemed a great improvement. But the British Government was intent on a radical alteration of the unfortunate position in which, as the whole story of the last seven years had shown, the Queen's representative and her subjects had been placed. 'I am sorry for Charles Elliot,' wrote Auckland on hearing of his recall, 'for I am satisfied that he has acted zealously and as he thought for the best. But I have never agreed with him in his view. He has been greatly misled.'[1] Auckland had never approved of the

---

[1] Auckland to Bremer, 20 June 1841 (Add. MSS. 37715, f. 118).

policy by which from the beginning the expedition had been directed. 'There must be definite demands and no admission of any but categorical and authorized answers.'[1] That comment might well have been made by Palmerston, but did not come with very good grace from one who had written that he never expected all the demands of the British Government to be granted, who had been prepared to discuss the question of the Indian Government's opium monopoly, and who had himself written 'you may do pretty much as you like and I trust that you will do so'.

B. THE SECOND PHASE, 1841–4

1. *Pottinger and the Treaty of Nanking*

The new British Plenipotentiary, an Irishman born in 1789, had already had many years of successful service in India to his credit. He had shown enterprise and energy during a perilous journey into Persia in 1810. As political agent in Sind, from which he had retired owing to ill health in 1840, his diplomatic handling of the ameers had won him a baronetcy. In later years he was to show as Governor successively of the Cape of Good Hope and of Madras that he was better fitted to deal firmly with a crisis than to conduct ordinary administrative duties. 'He is a most popular character with the army and navy', wrote a field officer of him in 1842, 'his penchant for energetic measures, even of somewhat an indiscriminable nature, finding much greater favour than the vacillations of his predecessor'[2].

Upon his arrival at Macao Sir Henry Pottinger sent his secretary Malcolm up to Canton to announce his appointment to the Prefect of the city and to inform that officer in outline of the British demands and of his decision not to enter into communication with any representative of the Emperor not accredited with full powers. When the Canton authorities maintained that there was no necessity to go to the north, and suggested that the truce at Canton might in that case be broken, Malcolm answered in a definite tone that the British would be well able

---

[1] Auckland to Elliot, 23 May 1841 (Add. MSS. 37715, f. 116).
[2] *The Last Year in China*, by a Field Officer, letter xv, 28 Jan. 1842.

to take care of themselves.[1] Leaving in Hong Kong 1,350 men,
the expedition proceeded to Amoy in August 2,500 strong.[2]
On the 26th the batteries of that city were silenced and Sir
Hugh Gough took possession of the walled town the following
day. The Chinese had thought, reported Pottinger, that the
defences were impregnable, for not until the afternoon did the
Viceroy and other high officers take to flight.[2] Leaving a small
force to hold the island of Koolangsoo the troops re-embarked
at the beginning of September, and on 1st October Tinghai, the
chief town in the island of Chusan, some twenty-five miles long
by an average of seven broad, was captured. By the middle of
the month Chinhai on the sea and Ningpo some miles up-
river were in British hands, whence the forces penetrated in a
raid about forty miles inland, and somewhat dramatically
planted the British flag on the summit of a hill while three
cheers for the Queen were given.[3] Ningpo was in a state of
anarchy with the removal of the Chinese authorities, for the
British forces were too small effectively to stop the nightly
excesses of native bands of robbers. The situation in Chusan
was far better than during the previous occupation: the health
of the troops was excellent, the inhabitants soon returned and
supplies were plentiful. Pottinger summed up his impressions
of these few months of active operations with the words 'either
Peking must give in, or the Maritime provinces will be at our
disposal'. It might rest 'with the Queen of England to pronounce what ports, or portions of the sea coast of China shall
be added to Her Majesty's Dominions'[4].

But winter was arriving and active operations had to be
temporarily arrested. This was not unexpected, as Auckland
foresaw the inevitability of a campaign in 1842 for which he
had made arrangements to send reinforcements to Hong Kong
in March,[5] though trouble with the King of Ava made it difficult for the Indian Government to find the troops.[6] The force
was finally to be brought up to 4 European and 4 to 8 native regiments with 750 gunners and sappers.[7] Pottinger had acted with

[1] Pottinger to Palmerston, 14 and 19 Aug. 1841 (F.O. 17/54).
[2] Pottinger to Palmerston, 30 and 31 Aug. 1841 (F.O. 17/54).
[3] Pottinger to Palmerston, 19 and 23 Oct. 1841 (F.O. 17/54).
[4] Pottinger to Palmerston, 30 Oct. 1841 (F.O. 17/54).
[5] Auckland to Palmerston, 8 July 1841 (Add. MSS. 37715, f. 131).
[6] Auckland to Pottinger, 10 Oct. 1841 (Add. MSS. 37171, f. 3).
[7] Auckland to Elphinstone, 26 Nov. 1841 (Add. MSS. 37171, f. 17).

firmness. He had on one occasion at least somewhat disturbed the British Government. After the capture of Ningpo, at a conference with Admiral Sir William Parker and the General, he gave in a memorandum in which he stated that he had looked forward to plundering the city, but as the General and Admiral objected that the method in which it had been handed over made that impossible, he agreed to confine himself to the destruction of public property. The Foreign Office thought this 'the worst proposal that I have seen from Mr. [sic] Pottinger and that it ought not to pass unnoticed'[1].

In November Aberdeen, Foreign Secretary in the new Administration, wrote that it was the intention of the Tory 'government to prosecute the war with vigour and effect'. But there were some important modifications which they had determined to make to Palmerston's instructions 'principally with the view of extending your discretionary powers, and thus, as they hope, facilitating the success of your endeavours'. Pottinger had been ordered not to cease operations until he had received from a duly authorized officer of the Chinese Government a full and unconditional compliance with all the demands which he had made in the name of the British Government. As this might place an unsurmountable obstacle in the way of his negotiations at a moment when they might be renewed with the best prospect of success, he was now authorized to resume them at any time when in conjunction with the commanders he should be of opinion that the warlike operations had produced a sufficient impression upon the Chinese to enable him to do so with the hope of a favourable issue. While there was to be no diminution of the payment for the opium ransom or for the Hong debts, Pottinger was given greater latitude in estimating the cost of the expedition. The Government desired four or five new ports to be opened for trade, but they were not prepared to regard any such acquisition as Hong Kong 'in the light of a permanent conquest'.

'The permanent retention of possessions under the dominion of the Crown would be attended with great and certain expence; while the extent of commerce which their occupation would enable us to carry on, in defiance of the Chinese government, appears somewhat doubtful. It would also tend to bring us more in contact politically with the Chinese than is at all desirable, and might ultimately lead, perhaps unavoidably, to our taking part in the

[1] Pottinger to Palmerston, 30 Oct. 1841 (F.O. 17/54).

contests and changes which at no distant period may occur among this singular people. A secure and well regulated trade is all we desire; and you will instantly bear in mind that we seek no exclusive advantages and demand nothing that we shall not willingly see enjoyed by the subjects of all other states.'[1]

Auckland, however, attached great importance to the possession of such an island, provided one could be found accessible to shipping, healthy in climate, and militarily defensible. 'I can contemplate', he wrote home, 'but little security to commercial privileges extorted and held by sufferance under a government so tenacious of its usages and forms and so void of faith as we know that of China to be'[2].

Pottinger had left the scene of operations in mid-December and after staying some time in Macao went subsequently to Hong Kong, to which latter place he moved the office of Superintendent of Trade. This change of head-quarters gave a great impetus to the development of the island where the population had grown to 25,000 souls and 'highly respectable Chinese merchants are flocking from Canton and Macao to settle here, or at least to form branches of their trading firms'[3]. This was written about a week before Aberdeen's amended instructions arrived. Pottinger clearly disagreed with the policy of non-acquisition. He wrote to the Foreign Secretary in May that warehouses of a solid and lasting description were being built. 'Within six months of Hong Kong being declared to have become a permanent colony, it will be a vast Emporium of Commerce and wealth.' If Tinghai and Amoy were also to be annexed, 'we shall be able to hold them with a very small comparative force, and they will repay England for all her present heavy expenses and trouble in a very few years, by placing the whole sea-going trade of this vast Empire in our hands, with, of course, the competition we may anticipate from other States of Europe and America'[4].

In March 1842 active operations were begun by a Chinese counter-attack near Ningpo. Ten to twelve thousand Chinese took part and were repulsed with great slaughter, for field guns opened fire on dense masses at less than 100 yards range. The English losses were nil. On the 18th May the British took

[1] Aberdeen to Pottinger, 4 Nov. 1841 (F.O. 17/53).
[2] Auckland to Hobhouse, 11 Aug. 1841 (Add. MSS. 37715, f. 148).
[3] Pottinger to Aberdeen, 8 Mar. 1842 (F.O. 17/56).
[4] Pottinger to Aberdeen, 3 May 1842 (F.O. 17/56).

Chapoo, defeating for the first time Manchu soldiers, in an engagement in which the Chinese lost between 1,200 and 1,500 men, the British only 9. On the 14th June Pottinger was at the mouth of the Yangtse Kiang at Woosung, the forts of which had been captured a week earlier. On the fall of Shanghai after a feeble resistance a request came from Keying, the 'great minister', and Elepoo, the Governor-General of Chekiang, asking for a place to be designated at which negotiations could be begun. Pottinger replied that he was willing to negotiate with any one in possession of full powers. By the 26th July, after a delay due to heavy rains, the whole fleet was at Chin-kiang and the Grand Canal was blockaded. In reply to a further request for a place for negotiations, Pottinger named Nanking, the provincial capital, informing Keying that operations would cease as soon as he could show that he was in a position to conclude arrangements agreeable to the demands.

Nanking was reached on the 5th August. On the way up Pottinger received an offer of 600,000 dollars as a ransom for the city. On the 8th a million was sent 'to reward the toil of the Forces'. On the 10th Elepoo announced that he had received from Peking the seals of office as Imperial Commissioner, and forwarded a transcript of the instructions which had come from the Emperor. On the 12th and 13th August Pottinger's secretary and interpreters met emissaries of the high Chinese officers Elepoo and Keying who had arrived the previous day. Upon being asked to suspend further operations of British troops, some of whom had been landed, Malcolm complained to the Tartar General that the British officers had secret intelligence that fresh Chinese troops were moving on Nanking. As a result their further progress was stayed by the Governor-General. On the 19th Pottinger's terms were accepted and on the 20th the Imperial Commissioners paid a visit of courtesy to him in H.M.S. *Cornwallis*, to express their great satisfaction that a settlement had finally been arranged. In return Pottinger, with the admiral and general, paid a visit of state to the Chinese Plenipotentiaries on the 24th and were well entertained. Pottinger reported most favourably upon 'the total abandonment of that tone of exclusiveness and arrogance, which has in all ages marked the Government of this Empire, and has hitherto rendered anything like cordial or equal intercourse with it, a matter of positive impracticability'. The Chinese officers were ready to sign the treaty then, but Pottinger preferred to visit them again in a quieter and unofficial form. This he did on the 26th, being met at the landing-stage by Mandarins, and at the city gate by others of higher rank. As he dismounted at the Yamen the Imperial Commissioners welcomed him, and 'a very elegant repast was immediately served up and occupied nearly two hours from the Chinese custom of bringing in a variety of courses in succession'. They then discussed the meaning of the various points in the treaty. On the 27th the Emperor's assent to the terms was received, though at this last moment the Commissioners asked Pottinger to allow one modification, much desired by Peking—the abandonment of the demand for trade at Foochow. The British Plenipotentiary thinking however that 'it was a mere scheme of the "clique" connected with Canton to force us to continue to carry on the Black Tea Trade at that port', refused, and the request was readily dropped.

The treaty was finally signed on the 29th August 1842. The Chinese agreed to pay twenty-one million dollars, to the credit of which was carried ransom money received from various cities. Canton, Amoy, Foochow, Ningpo, and Shanghai were to be open for trade, where Consular offices were to be established and a regular tariff was to be arranged. Hong Kong was ceded in perpetuity. Captured British subjects were to be unconditionally released and an amnesty granted to all Chinese who had helped the British forces. Officers of the two governments of equal status were to have the right of corresponding as equals. The Hong system was abolished, and a promise given of moderate transit duties on British goods. When six millions had been paid and the Emperor's agreement had been received, the British forces would retire from Nanking, the Grand Canal would be open, and Chinhai evacuated. But Chusan and Koolangsoo were to be retained until the whole indemnity was paid and until arrangements for opening the five ports were complete.

In transmitting the terms of the treaty Pottinger remarked that

'the retention of Hong Kong is the only single point in which I intentionally exceeded my modified instructions, but every hour I have passed in this superb country has convinced me of the necessity and desirability of our possessing such a settlement as an

Emporium for our trade and a place from which Her Majesty's subjects in China may be alike protected and controlled.'[1]

Peel's Government were overjoyed when the news of the Treaty of Nanking arrived in London.

'I think', wrote the Prime Minister, 'that there can be no doubt of the propriety of a feu de joie. There was never better reason for one and I do heartily participate in your feelings of satisfaction on the apparent termination with Honour and credit of our Difficulties in India and China. I hope the Emperor of China . . . may be able to ratify and fulfill the Treaty he has signed.'[2]

Auckland, now retired by Peel, must have been pleased to see falsified the doubts of full success which he had expressed to his successor Ellenborough in December 1841. He had always been sceptical whether Great Britain would obtain a direct compensation in money for her injuries and expenses, and had been afraid that city after city might be deserted by all authority as the British troops advanced and that so the Emperor might escape the humiliation of direct concession.[3]

2. *The Supplementary Treaty and Retirement of Pottinger, 1842–4*

Pottinger was as aware as had been Elliot that the difficulties in his way would not all be from the side of the Chinese. 'I am convinced', he wrote to Lord Ellenborough in India, 'that it will be a far more difficult undertaking to control than to protect British subjects'. He urged the necessity of the choice of a good man to succeed him, invested with strong powers, who should have the right to deport British subjects, to seize and confiscate British ships visiting places outside the legally opened ports, and to assist the Chinese authorities in the prevention of smuggling.[4] 'A new era is opening in this quarter of the world, and I am apprehensive, that unless the Head British Authority in China is vested with extraordinary powers, he will find so many turbulent spirits to control, that his best exertions towards carrying out the Treaty will fail.' Indeed, he had hardly arrived in Hong Kong, after the receipt of the Imperial rescript on the 15th September and the payment of the first instalment of the twenty-one millions on the 28th, before his fears were realized.

---

[1] Pottinger to Aberdeen, 29 Aug. 1842 (F.O. 17/57).
[2] Peel to Stanley, 23 Nov. 1842 (Add. MSS. 40467, f. 303).
[3] Auckland to Ellenborough, 20 Dec. 1841 (Add. MSS. 37717, f. 21).
[4] Pottinger to Ellenborough, 12 Sept. 1842 (Add. MSS. 43198, f. 237).

European females were exposing themselves in a manner that was an offence to Chinese conceptions of decency, and several people were openly talking of selecting sites for country houses. Three factories had been burnt in Canton and the lives and property of many British and other foreigners had been put in jeopardy as the result of a fray between Chinese of the lower class and Lascar sailors of whom there were some two hundred in the suburbs without proper discipline. He was not at all certain that it was his duty, when the provocation had come from the foreigners, to call upon the Provincial Government to repay the consequent losses, and the British Government concurred with their representative's view. They would refuse to protect or indemnify persons who by their misconduct or culpable negligence, 'render themselves obnoxious to the Chinese Government or People'[1]. He asked the foreign merchants, British and others at Canton, whether they could 'assert, that you have studied the complexion of the times, that you have in any single iota or circumstance striven to aid me in my arrangements, by endeavouring to dissipate and to soothe the very excitement and irritation of which you so loudly complain?'[2] Hong Kong being a British colony could and did become the centre of government, both of the inhabitants of the island, and of the British community throughout the treaty ports. Its possession therefore was to be not only of great commercial importance, but of high political value, in that its legislature and court by exercising discipline over some at least of the wilder elements of the British community were enabled to remove some of the readiest sources of friction and explosion.

At the same time Pottinger suggested to Elepoo and Keying, at Nanking, the advisability of an Imperial edict against the 'low and scurrilous language hitherto at times published officially regarding Foreigners , which was calculated to excite feelings of animosity and was totally unworthy of a Great Empire pretending to a high degree of refinement and civilization.

The Chinese interpretation given to the treaty, which had just been signed but not yet ratified, was in several respects different from that of the British. On the 1st September the High Commissioner, Keying, suggested that the British with their families should be allowed to live on shore at the treaty

[1] Draft No. 46 to Pottinger, 1 Apr. 1843 (F.O. 17/64).
[2] Pottinger to Aberdeen, 20 Dec. 1842 (F.O. 17/59).

ports only during the trade season. To this Pottinger replied that he expected a quarter to be set aside where his countrymen might reside as long as they wished; he would do his best to restrict the British merchants to the five ports; but for this the British navy must needs be used and therefore have access to the treaty ports. He readily agreed that the Chinese should reconstruct such fortresses as they pleased and dispose their troops where they would. But he could not agree wholly with Keying's view of jurisdiction. The Chinese minister had stated:

'It will be right forthwith to settle distinctly regulations whereby in any future cases of English merchant people being involved in legal proceedings with the people of the country, the English merchants shall be given over to English jurisdiction, while natives shall receive punishment from their own country, thus avoiding all cause of blood-shedding disputes.'

Permanent Chinese residents in Hong Kong, Pottinger maintained, should be placed under English law as they were, for example, in the Straits Settlements. Keying rejoined that though the Island of Hong Kong 'has been graciously given by the Great Empire to the English merchants as a place of residence, nevertheless the people dwelling in Hong Kong ought, as of old, to be subject to the rule of the Central Kingdom', for owing to its proximity to the mainland Hong Kong could not be regarded in the same light as Singapore. Pottinger agreed that Chinese who were guilty in Hong Kong of serious offences such as murder or arson should be handed over to the native authorities for punishment at Kowloon, but insisted on retaining police jurisdiction. Keying who was aware that Keshen had been degraded by the Peking Government for agreeing to submit Chinese to British jurisdiction, evidently attached as much importance to this point as did Pottinger.[1] The sequel, however, will show that Macao, where a system prevailed which Keying openly said he preferred, was not to become the model for the government of Hong Kong and its inhabitants, foreign and Chinese. On another point the British and Chinese differed. Keying suggested that what was done at Nanking must not be regarded as a precedent for other foreigners. England should explain to them that 'this extension is due to the Emperor's surpassing and heavenly favour, and that they might continue to have their commercial intercourse at Canton'.

[1] Pottinger to Aberdeen, 18 Oct. 1842 (F.O. 17/58).

In pointing out that other foreigners were subjects of independent countries, and that Britain could not dictate their policy or make demands upon them, Pottinger frankly stated that 'The government of England has asked for no privileges and advantages with regard to trade and future intercourse that she will not be glad to see granted to other Nations provided it shall so please the Emperor.'

Apart from settling the affairs of the infant colony of Hong Kong for which, after ratifications of the Treaty of Nanking were exchanged on the 26th June 1843, he became responsible to the Colonial Office, the most important work of the Plenipotentiary was the negotiation of a supplementary commercial treaty. A committee of the British merchants, whom he asked to consider what alterations they desired in tariffs and other matters of trade regulation, refused to co-operate. Some of them regarded 'with regret and dissatisfaction the Peace that has been concluded and the prospect of things being placed on a permanent footing'[1]: others were quite honestly incapable of telling what they had paid for the entry of their goods into Canton.

'The fact is, every individual has been used to make the best bargain he could for himself and his employers, through the Hong Merchants, linguists, and other such persons, all open to corruption and ready to evade payment of the just dues of the Chinese Government by the most barefaced and wholesale smuggling which was moreover winked at, and its unlawful gains shared in, by the whole of the local authorities, from highest to lowest.'[2]

However, he did receive a good deal of valuable information from some merchants,[3] and at least could not be blamed for refusing to give them an opportunity for stating their point of view. There was some delay in the transaction owing to the death on the 4th March of the High Commissioner Elepoo, already a sick man during the Nanking negotiations, at a great feast given him by the Hong merchants. An old man of seventy-three years, he expired, according to Pottinger, of 'apoplexy brought on by repletion'[4]. Elepoo had been obliged to draw up a schedule of trade regulations to please the Hoppo, but he had said that there would be little likelihood of any objection

---

[1] Pottinger to Aberdeen, 19 Jan. 1843 (F.O. 17/66).
[2] Pottinger to Aberdeen, 6 Feb. 1843 (ibid.).
[3] Pottinger to Aberdeen, 21 Feb. 1843 (ibid.).
[4] Pottinger to Aberdeen, 10 Mar. 1843 (ibid.).

to a British draft, for the Chinese officers placed 'the utmost reliance in your moderation and reasonableness'. Pottinger was making it his 'earnest study to prove to the Chinese officers by the terms I shall submit to them for the approval of the Board of Revenue at Peking that their confidence in my fair dealing is not misplaced'[1]. Two subordinate Chinese officers discussed Pottinger's proposals, to which by the end of June Keying (who much to the British Plenipotentary's relief was appointed in April as Imperial Commissioner) gave his general approval. The rates of duty were very moderate; arrangements were made for pilots, clearances of vessels, and the like. The new system was brought into operation on 27th July 1843. After that date both the Chinese authorities and the British merchants knew exactly where they stood. Illegal exactions were at an end and not only was the Imperial revenue considerably increased, but the trade was placed on a more certain basis. The local officers of course were the losers as they were precluded from recompensing themselves for the purchase at high prices of their offices. So was effected, after force had played its part, the first change in the direction of the rule of law under the impetus of the Western Powers, with Great Britain as the foremost champion of a conception of public life new to the Chinese.

These trade regulations and the new tariff comprised the first two articles of a supplementary treaty which was agreed between Keying and Pottinger in November 1843 and duly sanctioned by the Chinese Board of Revenue. Others stipulated that the Chinese authorities could confiscate British ships and cargo trading elsewhere than at the five ports, that British subjects at the ports should not go into the surrounding country beyond a certain short distance to be arranged by the local authorities in concert with the British consul, while the ships' crews should be allowed to land only in accordance with rules to be similarly fixed. In article VII it was agreed that ground and houses should be set apart, on the same principle, for the use of the British community. Article VIII gave the British any future advantage the Emperor might grant to other foreigners. Mutual extradition of criminals, the stationing of one warship by Great Britain at each port and the handing over of all buildings intact at the evacuation of Chusan and Koolangsoo, and the free entry into Hong Kong of Chinese were other points

[1] Pottinger to Aberdeen, 20 Mar. 1843 (F.O. 17/66).

arranged. British consuls were obliged to give what information they possessed of smuggling, and smuggled goods could be confiscated by the Chinese. British schooners and lorchas plying between Canton and Hong Kong were to carry a register in both languages under the Chief Superintendent's sign and seal and were to pay a small fixed fee.

The most noteworthy feature of the whole settlement is the complete absence of any clause dealing with the opium traffic. It has been said that the war was fought by Great Britain in order to compel the Chinese to smoke opium. The British had indeed suggested that the legalization of the trade would be an advantage alike to China and the foreigner by preventing the necessity of smuggling and the consequent disputes and violence. The London Government was glad of the Chinese declared intention of confining their anti-opium measures to their own people in the statement made to Pottinger that 'whether the merchant ships of the various countries bring opium or not China will not need to enquire or to take any proceedings with regard thereto'[1]. But even if the Chinese authorities were to legalize the sale of opium 'it will be right that Her Majesty's servants in China should hold themselves aloof from all connection with so discreditable a traffic. The British opium smuggler must receive no protection or support in the prosecution of his illegal speculations and he must be made aware that he will take the consequences of his own conduct.' As soon as Hong Kong was formally ceded to the Crown on the exchange of ratifications, the British Government contemplated preventing opium trade there or in its waters, though they were sensible that such action would do little to mitigate the existing evils. If the Chinese would legalize the trade for one port, the British would help them to carry this limitation into effect by withholding clearance certificates from ships which disregarded the rule. 'But so long as the prohibition against the introduction of opium into China is absolute, Her Majesty's government can do no more for China in that respect than prevent the Island of Hong Kong from being a resort and market for British smugglers.' With this end in view an Order in Council was passed empowering the British Plenipotentiary to forbid the opium traffic in Hong Kong. It was for reasons connected mainly with this traffic that Peel had decided that Hong Kong must be a dependency of the

[1] Aberdeen to Pottinger, 4 Jan. 1843 (F.O. 17/64).

British Crown, rather than like Aden of the East India Company.

'India and the East India Company', he wrote to the Colonial Secretary, 'have too strong a pecuniary interest in the profits of the opium trade to be enabled to exercise a perfectly unbiased judgement in respect to the commercial intercourse with China. At least however honest their judgement may be it will always labour under a disadvantage of suspicion.

'I believe that a regulated trade in opium would be the wisest policy for the Chinese. The Home Government is more likely to speak with authority upon this point—I mean the authority of reason and not of force—than a party immediately interested on the double ground of commercial profits and of Reason.'[1]

If the Government in London was not at all clear what exact line of policy to adopt in regard to the opium trade, the Governor-General of India was insistent that the British Government should do 'nothing to place in peril our opium Revenue. As for preventing the manufacture of opium and the sale of it in China, that is far beyond your Power.'[2] Peel wished for Pottinger's advice on 'all points connected with the conduct of this Trade for the future, in a manner less discreditable to us than that in which it has hitherto been conducted'. He thought Pottinger 'should have as wide discretionary authority to deal with opium questions that may arise before definite instructions can be sent from home as we can give him'[3]. Pottinger was of opinion that the steps which he had already taken to discourage the traffic in Hong Kong 'would lead very shortly to most of the vessels belonging to British subjects, employed in the opium trade in the waters of China, appearing under foreign Flags. Such a contingency might be met perhaps by Her Majesty's government proposing to all foreign governments in alliance with England, to prohibit the use of their Flags for such a purpose, but I doubt if even that step would be effectual.' But it was not really necessary. 'For whatever the terms in which the trade in opium is spoken of in this and other (official) communications, I have the strongest causes for doubting whether even one in 100 of the officers of the Chinese government is at all disposed to check the Trade.'[4] Indeed, Pottinger

---

[1] Peel to Stanley, 15 Dec. 1842 (Add. MSS. 40467, f. 331).
[2] Ellenborough to Aberdeen, 17 Nov. 1842 (Add. MSS. 43198, f. 28).
[3] Peel to Aberdeen, 22 Dec. 1842 (Add. MSS. 40453, f. 291). Aberdeen to Pottinger, 6 Jan. 1843 (Add. MSS. 43198, f. 247).
[4] Pottinger to Aberdeen, 3 Nov. 1843 (F.O. 17/70).

knew of the case of a Mandarin commanding one of the re-constructed Bogue Forts who had openly bought sixty chests in the office of a mercantile firm in Canton, while several vessels flying foreign colours were selling the drug in the Canton River above the Boca Tigris. The report of the British Consul in Canton in the spring of 1844 should have satisfied his Government that there was no need from the point of view of the maintenance of good relations with China to take the question too seriously. 'For many months past the sale and the use of opium have had a universal toleration throughout the Empire of China. The High Authorities see that any measures against it are not only futile, but while they increase the evil itself tend to others of a far more serious character.' If its introduction by sea and from the West could effectively be stopped, the result would be the rapid extension of cultivation in Yunnan Province, with a consequent shortage of grain, accompanied by famine, tumults, and pillage.

'The difficulty in admitting opium rests only in a thought that it would be a violation of decorum for His Imperial Majesty to legalize a thing which has been so strongly condemned. To help this difficulty it has been suggested that the barbarous names now employed should be exchanged for one implying that it is the juice of the Poppy, a preparation which finds a place in the native pharma-copeias. The suggestion cannot be made the subject of a memorial to the Throne, but it will reach the Imperial ear through the medium of conversation, where it is likely to be received, as His Majesty is known to be sincerely desirous to witness a change so calculated to enrich the Treasury and to benefit the country.'[1]

Consul Lay had a clear and explicit understanding with the Cantonese authorities. They declared their inability to deal with the question, and he his lack of authority and inclination to initiate any proceedings against the traffic so long as it was carried on beyond the precincts of the legal trade. And the attitude of Lay was shared by the consuls at other ports and by the Chief Superintendent. It need therefore cause no surprise that Aberdeen minuted on a dispatch from Pottinger: 'I think that Sir H. P. may be permitted to suspend the exclusion of opium from the waters and harbours of Hong Kong for the present, if he should continue to think it expedient to do so.' Pottinger's successor, Davis, urged upon the British Government the

---

[1] Lay to Pottinger, 1 Apr. 1844 (F.O. 17/81).

difference between connivance in the opium trade at Hong Kong and the more positive act of recognition by taxation. Between exclusion and countenancing 'there is doubtless the middle term of "laisser faire" most agreeable to English notions of freedom, and which as the subject of Chinese complaint might certainly be met with this answer: "Look to your own custom houses and coast guards." '[1]

These successful negotiations which began the opening of China to influences political, religious, and economic of the West had been carried out with great civility on both sides. Indeed, one of the least difficult of the tasks of the British representatives was to obtain a recognition of their claim to equality of status. Keying even went beyond a bare formal correctness in his relations with his British colleague. The interchange of social visits began at Nanking where 'old Yellow Girdle', or 'Royalty' as Keying was known in the Army, 'especially seemed pleased with the wine, cherry brandy, and other cordials'[2], and it was continued in the south. At the beginning of 1843 Pottinger went up to Whampoa and was met by the High Commissioner and the Governor of Kwantung Province. It was noteworthy that the Prefect of Canton was regarded as a Mandarin of rank too inferior to be introduced to the Plenipotentiary, whereas a few years before Elliot had been compelled to correspond through him with the Viceroy. A visit of two assistant commissioners to Hong Kong showed, perhaps to the surprise of some of the hosts, that they were able 'to enjoy society with all that easy politeness and total absence of constrained feeling that could be expected from well educated and refined gentlemen of any foreign nation'[3]. Pottinger laid stress on the value of social intercourse as the 'surest way of gradually removing all arrogant or exclusive feelings on the part of the High Officers of China', while the sight of their Mandarins coming to reside amongst, and on such cordial terms with, the British officers, could not fail to impress the ordinary people of the country.

Keying's visit to Government House in Hong Kong was the climax of these entertainments. Two steamers were sent to Whampoa to bring him and his suite to the colony. After

[1] Davis to Aberdeen, 26 Dec. 1843 (Add. MSS. 43198, f. 307).
[2] *The Last Year in China*, by a Field Officer, letter xxviii, 4 Sept. 1842.
[3] Pottinger to Aberdeen, 14 May 1843 (F.O. 17/67).

official calls Keying dined with Sir Henry Pottinger *en famille*. Before dinner he asked for a miniature of the Plenipotentiary's son, which was given him, and at dinner for one of Lady Pottinger—a request to which, after some hesitation, the husband acceded. Keying treated the picture with great reverence, putting it on his head, drinking a glass of wine while holding it in front of him, and ordering his attendant to send it home in his State chair. After dinner Pottinger presented his colleague with a handsome sword and belt and in return received a gold bracelet and Keying's upper robe of silk given by Kienlung to his father who had been that Emperor's Prime Minister. At the State banquet on the following day the Chinese Commissioner asked to be excused if he became so tipsy as to need a bed in Government House. He and other Chinese entertained the Englishmen by singing Tartar songs. Such were the scenes of rejoicing and friendship which set the personal seal to the exchange of the ratifications of the Treaty of Nanking. The Procureur Libois was forcibly impressed by the great change which such an entertainment signified. 'The English overwhelm this good Commissioner with honours', he wrote. 'How low the poor Chinese have sunk! Where is their old pride? Only eight years ago even the Mayor of Canton would not have liked to speak to a European envoy. To-day one of the chief dignitaries of the Empire pays a humble visit to a "Fan-kwei"[1] in an island which he has been forced to cede.'[2] Keying had asked Pottinger to keep up a private correspondence with him under the style of my 'familiar friend'. So long as he remained charged with the Empire's relations with the foreigners, considerable harmony between the races was maintained. When Pottinger was relieved he introduced his successor to the Imperial Commissioner at Hoomun-chai on the occasion of the signature of the Supplementary Treaty. The meeting was very cordial and Pottinger reported with some vanity that he had been asked to get a life-sized portrait of himself painted for presentation to the Emperor.

But in spite of this 'wonderful change', giving promise of 'permanent stability and cordiality of the Alliance' as Pottinger imagined in the early days of 1843, it remained true 'that in our intercourse with China and her subjects we are dealing

[1] 'Fan-kwei', or 'foreign devil', a term of abuse.
[2] Libois to Gauthier, 24 June 1843 (M.E., vol. 324, f. 439).

with an Empire and People who have no notion, however small, of international law and rights'.[1] This was made quite clear when the terms of an Imperial edict which had been issued on the subject of the Canton riot in December 1842 became known. 'These foreigners having but newly been brought back to peace, a border quarrel must not be suffered again to break out.'[2] In spite of the formal equality insisted upon in the ratification of the treaty by an Imperial seal and the place of equal honour in the texts accorded to the Queen and the Emperor, the British were still to the Peking court barbarians on the sea-border not much different except in warlike ability from Annamites or Thibetans. Pottinger therefore thought that it was 'equally insufficient and useless to desire that China shall be simply treated like all other civilized nations'[3]. Yet it was incumbent upon the British authorities naval as well as civil to pay due respect to rights, institutions, and usages of the Chinese, although all three might be at variance with Western ideas. And it grieved him to think that, in a variety of instances during the year and a half following on the treaty, the Chinese, who had refrained from protesting, partly from habitual apathy, partly from a dread of bringing forward any stormy question, had good cause for remonstrance. True to this conception of his duty Pottinger reprimanded the captain of H.M.S. *Plover* who, with Keying's approval, had been conducting a survey of the coasts, for attacking alleged pirates close to the shore. For the officers at Amoy in the autumn of 1842 had declined Pottinger's suggested help of the British navy in suppressing piracy, apparently even within the three-mile limit. The treaty did not allow such action, and the good faith of Pottinger was compromised if this ship engaged in any other than its 'humanitarian work'[4].

But if the Imperial court were blind to the new phenomenon of the demand for national equality which implied the possibility of international law, and if its officers, particularly Keying, were personally on good terms with the British representative and determined at any cost to keep the peace, the people of Canton were very aggrieved. They had not felt the war within their

[1] Pottinger to Aberdeen, 20 Mar. 1843 (F.O. 17/66).
[2] Pottinger to Aberdeen, 19 April 1843 (F.O. 17/67).
[3] Pottinger to Aberdeen, 1 Mar. 1844 (F.O. 17/80).
[4] Pottinger to Aberdeen, 16 Mar. 1844 (F.O. 17/80).

walls, as had the citizens of Amoy, Ningpo, or Shanghai, their trade had continued, and now they had lost their monopoly and feared ruin. Nothing indeed makes a greater contrast in the early days after the inauguration of the new system than the attitude of the local inhabitants in Canton and Shanghai. Before his death Elepoo had received a petition praying 'for leave to vindicate the dignity of the Empire by exterminating the hateful Barbarians'. It would appear that the Cantonese are a much quicker-tempered folk than the Chinese in the more northerly provinces, and they were as irritated as those disgruntled foreigners[1] who saw in the new trade regulations order and law take the place of easy bribery and profitable corruption. But whereas in time the authorities in Hong Kong were able to exercise control over the British merchants, it was of the essence of Chinese society that the officers of the Government were dependent in the last resort upon the good pleasure of the people—and by the people in fact was meant the mob which could be inflamed and set in action by interested parties.

One of the chief causes of delay in starting the trade under the new system was removed at the beginning of September 1843 by the death of Howqua. A man over seventy-five years old, he had been head of the Hong for nearly forty years. He had been violently opposed to the change and from his local influence and vast wealth—he died worth twenty million dollars—he necessarily carried great weight.[2] During the winter trade formed an effective though temporary antidote to exasperated feelings.[3] Over 174,000 packages of tea were exported from Canton in the last two months of 1843. The customs arrangements were working smoothly, and in February 1844 prices were said to be so excellent that 'one might almost think that there was a plan to get us to deal exclusively in Canton, and so virtually give up the other ports'[4].

Having by the Treaty of Nanking brought the war to a successful termination and secured the ratifications of the commercial treaty, Pottinger was now recalled. The successful fighter and negotiator arrived back in October 1844 and was

[1] Pottinger to Aberdeen, 21 Sept. 1843 (F.O. 17/69).
[2] Pottinger to Aberdeen, 21 Feb. 1843 (F.O. 17/66).
[3] Pottinger to Aberdeen, 14 Dec. 1843 (F.O. 17/71).
[4] Pottinger to Aberdeen, 12 Feb. 1844 (F.O. 17/79).

received by the Foreign Secretary. He told his former chief that so long as Keying remained in power, and his influence had increased recently, there was little likelihood of serious difficulties in China. He thought there was no doubt that the Chinese would legalize the opium traffic. 'But he spoke with strong censure of our merchants and their practices in China, each of whom, he said with a genuine Irish accent, was a bigger rogue than the other.' He thought that British trade, which was flourishing, was capable of indefinite expansion and that neither France nor the Americans were likely to hurt it.[1] Lord Aberdeen went with him to Windsor on the 22nd October, where he was received very civilly by the Queen,[2] 'who seems to take a peculiar interest about China'[3]. Aberdeen regarded him as a man of very friendly manner and of scrupulous character. 'He is evidently a remarkable man, and is perhaps the more striking from his comparative ignorance of Europe and European affairs.'[1]

[1] Aberdeen to Peel, 17 Oct. 1844 (Add. MSS. 40454, f. 278).
[2] Aberdeen to Peel, 22 Oct. 1844 (Add. MSS. 40454, f. 292).
[3] Aberdeen to Peel, 27 Dec. 1842 (Add. MSS. 40453, f. 305).

III

THE NANKING TREATY PERIOD, 1844–52

A. THE ADMINISTRATION OF SIR JOHN DAVIS, 1844–8

JOHN FRANCIS DAVIS, 'whose conduct after the death of Lord Napier was marked by great good sense and judgement'[1], took over the duties of Sir Henry Pottinger as Superintendent of Trade and as Governor of Hong Kong in May 1844. In his former capacity he received his instructions from the Foreign Office, while the Secretary of State for War and Colonies was his chief for colonial matters. Davis had long been connected with China. As a servant of the East India Company he had learnt Chinese and had been attached to Lord Amherst's fruitless Embassy in 1816. The British Government, advised by Sir George Staunton, thought that a former president of the Company's Select Committee was best fitted to promote that expansion of trade which might be expected to result from the Treaty of Nanking.[2] One of his earliest tasks was a tour of the newly opened treaty ports where consuls had already been established, consuls who were from the beginning on a footing different from those in European cities. They could not be purely commercial officers, but from the first were brought into direct touch with the local Chinese officers, and though subordinated to the Superintendent they had, owing to the difficulty of communication, to be allowed considerable latitude. A word may, therefore, be said about the development of these ports—Amoy, Foochow, Ningpo, and Shanghai, as it presented itself to Davis on his first tour.

1. *The New Ports*

At Amoy the situation left by the war had still to be liquidated. The island of Koolangsoo, opposite the city of Amoy, itself on an island, was in the occupation of British forces. Davis's instructions allowed him to arrange for its rendition on the 1st January 1845, if the indemnity instalments were duly paid.[3] The communication of this intelligence to Keying at his first interview made a good impression on the Chinese plenipotentiary, who desired to have the statement in writing, so that he

[1] Aberdeen to Pottinger, private, 6 Jan. 1844 (Add. MSS. 43198, f. 296).
[2] *Memoirs of Sir George Staunton*, p. 93; Peel to Stanley, 2 Dec. 1843 (Add. MSS. 40468, f. 85).   [3] Draft No. 7 to Davis, 28 Feb. 1844 (F.O. 17/85).

could acquire credit for the move at the court in Peking.[1] The offer, however, made the Chinese authorities suspect that in return for the earlier rendition of Koolangsoo the British Government might delay the evacuation of Chusan, to which they attached great importance.[2] There was considerable difficulty connected with the evacuation of the island, as the Consul and all Europeans had taken up their residence in Koolangsoo owing to 'the filthy and close nature of the Chinese town making residence there all but impossible'[3]. Keying had interpreted evacuation to mean that the merchants as well as the armed forces of the British Crown would leave Koolangsoo, while Davis regarded it as applying only to the removal of the military forces.[4] Business at Amoy was flourishing; the value of British trade exceeding £72,000, a figure more than three times as great as all other foreign trade combined. During the following year there was a further increase, but although its harbour afforded splendid access, the poverty of the inhabitants suggested that Amoy was not likely to become a trade centre of first-class importance.[5] There were twenty-six resident British merchants, and a good deal of the trade consisted in supplying coolies on a system of contract labour for working in the plantations of Cuba and other West Indian islands. Davis was much worried by this, which he characterized as 'virtual slave trading'[6]. There also developed a considerable British carrying trade between Amoy and the Straits, which threatened the interests of the native junkmen.[7] Both of these economic activities we shall meet again as they were to grow in magnitude and endanger pacific relations between Chinese and British.[8]

The early years of the trade with Foochow were very disappointing: by the middle of 1844 not a single ship had entered the port.[9] On his tour of inspection Davis was unable to sail to the city in his frigate owing to the 'very dangerous and impracticable character of the river for commercial navigation'

---

[1] Davis to Aberdeen, 13 June 1844 (F.O. 17/87).
[2] Davis to Aberdeen, 12 Aug. 1844 (F.O. 17/88).
[3] Davis to Aberdeen, 21 Oct. 1844 (F.O. 17/89).
[4] Davis to Aberdeen, 20 Dec. 1844 (F.O. 17/90).
[5] Davis to Palmerston, 29 Jan. 1847 (F.O. 17/123).
[6] Davis to Palmerston, 10 Mar. 1847 (F.O. 17/124).
[7] Davis to Palmerston, 1 Sept. 1847 (F.O. 17/130).
[8] See pp. 168 sqq.   [9] Davis to Aberdeen, 15 July 1844 (F.O. 17/88).

for rocks and shoals abounded and there was an 18-foot tide.
A small American schooner of two hundred tons was at the
city—the largest ship that could penetrate so far. The native
trade was primarily in timber.[1] The Governor of Fukien
Province, whose capital city Foochow was, belonged to the
anti-intercourse, illiberal faction of the Chinese Government
and seemed to encourage the natives in acts of hostility towards
foreigners. The British Consul was miserably housed and some
Englishmen had suffered acts of gross personal violence and
had been spat upon. The Commissioner Keying, however,
used his influence to modify this attitude,[2] so that before the
end of 1845 the situation had improved, and Davis was hoping
that Foochow might yet show itself to be a good mart.[3]

The statistics for 1845 were encouraging: British trade was
worth upwards of £140,000, American somewhat over £12,000.
The local authorities acted with firmness in suppressing in the
summer of 1846 a riot[4] due to the presence of Cantonese who
proved themselves the source of trouble again in the following
year.[5] Trade, however, made such little progress, that Davis's
successor early proposed its abandonment as a port, and
suggested keeping a vice-consul there, under the direction of
the consul in Amoy, primarily as a means of communication
with the provincial governor.[6] Just as Foochow suffered partly
from its proximity to Amoy where the black tea trade could
more easily be tapped, so Ningpo was too near to Shanghai.[7]
There was no mercantile progress there in 1846[8] and its total
British trade in the following year amounted to but £12,000.
It became more of a missionary than a trading centre.

Davis found an altogether different situation when he visited
Shanghai in September 1844. It had been opened for foreign
trade in the previous November. Robert Fortune the botanist,
who visited the city shortly after it had been opened, had
appreciated its possibilities.

'Shanghae is by far the most important station for foreign trade

[1] Davis to Aberdeen, 21 Oct. 1844 (F.O. 17/89).
[2] Davis to Aberdeen, 23 Aug. 1845 (F.O. 17/100).
[3] Davis to Aberdeen, 13 Oct. 1845 (F.O. 17/101).
[4] Davis to Aberdeen, 23 Apr. and 22 June 1846 (F.O. 17/111 & 112).
[5] Davis to Palmerston, 1 July 1847 (F.O. 17/128).
[6] Bonham to Palmerston, 26 Dec. 1848 (F.O. 17/146).
[7] Davis to Aberdeen, 21 Oct. 1844 (F.O. 17/89).
[8] Davis to Palmerston, 29 Jan. 1847 (F.O. 17/123).

on the coast of China, and is consequently attracting a large share of public attention. No other town with which I am acquainted possesses such advantages; it is the great gate—the principal entrance in fact—to the Chinese Empire. . . . The port of Shanghae swarms with boats of all sizes . . . which bring down large quantities of tea and silk to supply the wants of our merchants who have established themselves here, and return loaded with the manufactures of Europe and America. . . . There can be no doubt that in a few years it will not only rival Canton, but become a place of far greater importance.'[1]

Davis agreed with this opinion. 'The vicinity of Shanghai to the Grand Canal gives it advantages which will make it the first of the 4 new Ports.' A great quantity of raw silk was being exported, one-quarter of the Indian opium production imported, while the demand for English cotton was not yet satisfied. British trade which in 1844 had been worth just under one million sterling had risen to over $2\frac{1}{4}$ millions during the following year, being ten times greater than that of the United States, the next largest trading community.[2]

Captain Balfour, the Consul, was on excellent terms with the Taoutai[3] who agreed to the English making here, as at Amoy and Foochow, day excursions into the country.[4] In November 1845 Balfour and the Taoutai Kung Moo-Kew signed an agreement whereby a piece of agricultural land of 138 acres outside the city with a frontage on the Whangpoo River was reserved as a place where British subjects could purchase plots of land for residences and warehouses from the Chinese owners, and obtain from the Taoutai, through the Consul, titles of perpetual lease, for a small annual rent reserved for the Emperor. But from the first the British authorities did not restrict this privilege to British subjects; other foreigners could secure through their own consuls plots inside the reserved settlement area.

The good relations between the Consul and the Chinese officers continued, and in 1847 the British residents arranged for the construction of roads in their area, built a church and endowed a chaplaincy,[5] and later they appointed and paid for

---

[1] R. Fortune, *Three years Wanderings*, 1847, ch. vii.
[2] Davis to Aberdeen, 23 Apr. 1846 (F.O. 17/111).
[3] The chief Chinese Officer in Shanghai: translated sometimes 'Intendant'.
[4] Davis to Aberdeen, 21 Oct. 1844 (F.O. 17/89).
[5] Davis to Palmerston, 5 May 1847 (F.O. 17/126).

a constable.[1] The climate appeared suitable for Europeans, and substantial buildings were being erected. But the want of a series of beacons was a serious impediment to shipping in the river, and Davis was urging the necessity for regular steam communication between Shanghai and Hong Kong.[2] There were difficulties at times, however, even in the comparatively placid life of Shanghai. Early in 1848, 13,000 men had been thrown out of work as, owing to the silting of the inland waterways, the canal junks could no longer convey grain to the court at Peking, which had to be diverted to the sea route. Some of these idle persons attacked two missionaries at a place some thirty miles distant from Shanghai. The local people and officers had kindly done what they could to assist those British subjects, but Consul Alcock pressed the Shanghai authorities for the punishment of the guilty. Unanimously supported in this attitude by the Consuls of France, the United States, and Belgium, he stopped the grain junks and sent a warship to Nanking, the seat of the provincial governor. This pressure procured the execution of two of the malefactors.[3] In spite of this incident trade in Shanghai six years after the Nanking Treaty was in a very flourishing condition. British imports and exports in seventy-six vessels totalled close upon 40,000 tons, which was sixteen-twentieths of the total, the Americans were second with three, and all other foreign trade amounted to but one-twentieth. But the British were at a disadvantage. For the other foreigners, who had been given their opportunity to trade as a direct result of the British war, were not under 'any salutary control to prevent the abuse of those privileges'.

'As a necessary consequence the trade under the American, Spanish and other Flags has been carried out with such regard to Treaty obligations, Tariffs and Trade or Port Regulations as suited the taste and convenience of those interested—this is to say they have been continually infringed, disregarded and set aside, to the obvious prejudice of their British competitors in the same market.'

So long as the great predominance of British trade lasted this was of minor importance, but the proportions might alter to the advantage of the American 'who meets us with his cotton

[1] Davis to Palmerston, 3 July 1847 (F.O. 17/128).
[2] Davis to Palmerston, 18 Mar. 1848 (F.O. 17/141).
[3] Bonham to Palmerston, 25 Mar. 1848 (F.O. 17/141); 12 Apr. 1848 (F.O. 17/142).

fabrics in these markets'. Moreover, the activity of the British Consul had the unfortunate effect of giving to his measures in the eyes of his compatriots an 'unpopular, irritating and oppressive character'. If foreign Powers were unwilling to make their subjects and citizens 'amenable to the authority of duly accredited agents resident at the Ports' it might be necessary for the British Government to consider giving their subjects 'American freedom'.[1]

2. Canton

However tolerable in spite of minor difficulties was the position of foreigners in the newly opened ports, the same cannot be said with regard to Canton. There had been a nasty episode in May 1844, when the vane on the American flagstaff was supposed to have caused sickness among the Chinese population. The superstitions of the crowd were possibly turned into riotous activity by the authorities who resented the presence of the President's commissioner, Caleb Cushing, on board the U.S.S. *Brandywine*, as that 'gentleman had publicly avowed himself as American Envoy to the Court of Peking from the first'. The crowd on this occasion was dispersed by American marines.[2]

The hostility of the scholars and people of the city, which found vent not only in riot but in a manifesto ending with the words 'Ye men of America may truly dread local extermination'[3], tended to modify the views which Cushing had earlier expressed in the House of Representatives in a debate on the 16th March 1840 on the attitude of the United States towards the Anglo-Chinese war. He had thought that the moment when the Chinese Government were grateful for the upright deportment of American citizens in showing a proper respect for the laws and public rights of the Chinese Empire was a favourable opportunity to endeavour to put American trade on a just and stable footing.

'But God forbid', he said in his deep suspicion of British motives, 'I should co-operate with the British Government in the purpose—if purpose it have—of upholding the base cupidity and violence which have characterized the operations of the British individually and

[1] Bonham to Palmerston, 14 Apr. 1848 (F.O. 17/142).
[2] Davis to Aberdeen, 17 May 1844 (F.O. 17/87).
[3] Cushing to Sec. of State, 24 July 1844 (Sen. Ex. Doc. 67, 2 Sess. 28 Cong., at p. 21).

collectively in the seas of China. . . . I trust the idea will no longer be entertained in England, if she chooses to persevere in the attempt to coerce the Chinese by force of arms to submit to be poisoned with opium by whole provinces that she is to receive aid or countenance from the United States in that nefarious enterprise.'[1]

Even the hostile reception which he received in Canton was, he supposed, the result of the late war which had made the court of Peking more averse than ever to admit embassies from Western States.[2] He was personally piqued because 'some of the English newspapers have commented rather boastfully upon the fact that the English arms had opened the ports of China to other nations, and at the same time have, with flippant ignorance, ridiculed the idea of a mission from the United States. . . .'[3] 'The opening of the Five Ports to other nations was in fact, as it certainly was in form, the spontaneous act of the Chinese government.'[4] Though it was no doubt the desire of the British Government, as the Queen said to Parliament, that equal favour should be shown to the industry and commercial enterprise of all nations, yet 'it was the part of necessity —certainly it was the part of the only true view of her own interest for England not to seek (what she could not have held) any "exclusive (commercial) advantages" '[5]. At the same time Cushing ascribed 'all possible honour to the ability displayed by Sir Henry Pottinger in China' and recognized 'the debt of gratitude which the United States and all other nations owe to England for what she has accomplished in China'[3]. Hong Kong was open freely to the ships of all nations, and the American Minister had 'ample cause to be satisfied with the honorable manifestations of good will with which my own mission was received by the British functionaries in the East'[5].

The American Treaty of Wanghia differed but little from the British Treaty of Nanking. The most obvious contrast was furnished by a clause in the American Treaty prohibiting trade in opium. The sequel was to show that American participation in the trade was to be no less in the future than it had been in the past, and that the British officials were to give no more countenance to it than had Elliot in 1839. It is difficult to suppose

[1] Congressional Globe, 16 Mar. 1840.
[2] Cushing to Sec. of State, 15 July 1844 (Sen. Ex. Doc. 67, 2 Sess. 28 Cong., at p. 58).
[3] Cushing to Sec. of State, 5 July 1844 (Sen. Ex. Doc. ibid., at p. 77).
[4] Cushing to Sec. of State, 16 Aug. 1844 (Sen. Ex. Doc. ibid., at p. 88).
[5] Cushing to Sec. of State, 26 Aug. 1844 (Sen. Ex. Doc. ibid., at p. 100).

that Caleb, cousin of J. P. Cushing, head of the firm of Perkins, whose finances were dependent on the Calcutta market,[1] would have been easy at the disappearance of the opium trade. As it was J. P. Cushing died in 1851 leaving a fortune estimated to amount to two million American dollars.

The demonstrations at Canton which had in part influenced Cushing to remain in the south had disturbed Davis. A 'rabble which is the most vicious in the whole world and which, before the new order of things, was systematically tutored by the government to hate and ill-use foreigners', was now almost beyond the control of their own Government, and their ruffianly outbreaks threatened to drive away all trade from the place.[2] Shortly after he had expressed these views Davis felt it his duty to instruct the Consul at Canton, if he felt endangered, to strike his flag, hoping that the fear of the loss of duties and disorders among English traders, which might result from such a step, would induce the Cantonese authorities to keep their people in better control.[3] For a time there was some improvement,[4] but placards abusive of foreigners were appearing in the autumn. Perhaps the Cantonese mob would have been better behaved had they not believed that the humane action of General Gough during the late war in sending a Mandarin to persuade the crowd to disperse instead of firing upon it, was a proof of their own superiority.[5] Still in spite of all the troubles British commerce at Canton, especially cotton imports, was of very great importance. The trade for the first half of 1844 was worth close upon three millions sterling.[6] The new system was working well, and as the duties were moderate there was no temptation to smuggle, and, in spite of the brisk trade elsewhere, the Canton trade was throughout the year increasing. The value of British woollens was nearly three and of cotton nearly five million dollars. The opium imports, which of course did not enter by the customs, were valued at twenty million dollars, in 40,000 chests. British trade was worth close upon four times the American, while that of other foreign countries was of practical insignificance.[7]

[1] See p. 8.   [2] Davis to Aberdeen, private, 8 June 1844 (F.O. 17/87).
[3] Davis to Aberdeen, 19 June 1844 (F.O. 17/87).
[4] Davis to Aberdeen, 30 July 1844 (F.O. 17/88).
[5] Davis to Aberdeen, 24 Oct. 1844 (F.O. 17/89).
[6] Davis to Aberdeen, 16 Oct. 1844 (F.O. 17/89).
[7] Davis to Aberdeen, 7 Feb. 1845 (F.O. 17/97); 1 Mar. 1845 (F.O. 17/98).

Yet the mob could still be indisciplined. To the interior of
the city the foreigners had no access, and this exclusion, degrading as it was universally regarded, was one of the factors
provoking the insolence of the people,[1] who on one occasion
attacked the Vice-Consul and two other British subjects as they
were walking in the suburbs. Though the natives who insulted
the party were punished, no improvement was probable so
long as the foreigners were derisively defied entrance to the city
as they passed its gates. Davis pledged himself, if supported
by the sanction of his Government, to carry that point. The
twelfth article of the treaty had made the retrocession of Chusan
dependent upon the completion of arrangements at the ports.[2]
Though the Cantonese authorities had given ample building
sites for the needs of the merchants and had issued a proclamation which granted them the right, as at other ports, of making
expeditions of a day's journey,[2] Davis proposed to refuse the
acceptance of the last instalment of the indemnity and to hold
on to Chusan until the Canton city question was settled.[3] The
Commissioner Keying argued that no right to enter the city
had been granted and urged Sir John Davis,[4] who felt very
strongly that there was a decided wish to keep up the old system of degradation at Canton, not to be in a hurry in regard
to that claim.[5] Keying maintained that the people were disin-
clined to allow the foreigners to enter. But Davis thought that
this attitude had been produced 'by the government by whom
not a single proclamation had been issued since the war (altho'
so often promised) calculated to urge or enforce that right
which foreigners enjoy at every other Port of Trade—a right
which was also denied last year at Foochow on precisely the
same plea of the "people's wishes" '[6]. 'Keying, however, while
deploring the fact that 'the spirit of the Canton people differs
from that of all other ports', agreed to issue a proclamation as
a kite to test the strength of public opinion. When the proclamation was issued, Davis enjoined on British subjects a
prudent demeanour, and claimed from Keying protection from
the authorities, as he had no intention, except on their express

[1] Davis to Aberdeen, 4 Apr. 1845 (F.O. 17/99).
[2] Davis to Aberdeen, 24 Apr. 1845 (F.O. 17/99).
[3] Davis to Aberdeen, 27 June 1845 (F.O. 17/100).
[4] Created Baronet in July 1845.
[5] Davis to Aberdeen, 26 Nov., 10 and 22 Dec. 1845 (F.O. 17/102).
[6] Davis to Aberdeen, 8 Jan. 1846 (F.O. 17/109).

application, of attempting himself the control of the populace. Although the Cantonese were immediately excited by the appearance of fresh placards,[1] through the Chinese New Year celebrations the city remained tranquil until the Prefect punished, by burning down his house, a native who had obstructed his way.[2] Keying interpreted the ensuing disturbance as a protest against the entrance of foreigners into the city.[3] He himself might, thought Davis, be sincere, but there was little doubt that the other Cantonese officials were really unwilling to make any change in the old practice of exclusion existing previous to the peace.[4]

The situation was indeed extraordinary, for whereas respectable British subjects at Whampoa and Canton were unable to move about unmolested, 'there was perfect freedom and immunity enjoyed by the opium smugglers at Namoa, and Kumsingmoon, places interdicted by treaty. Here houses are built, roads are made with the connivance of the government authorities.'[5] Davis had already contemplated the possibility that the unrestrained exercise of the right to enter the city of Canton might be postponed for the present. In a difficult question of this kind a mutual accommodation of the difference might prove the best mode of terminating it.[6] The Emperor gave Keying authority 'to manage the affair'. As Gützlaff, a German missionary and Chinese scholar on the Staff of the Government at Hong Kong, advised Davis 'that to carry the entrance into Canton City at present British bayonets would be wanted', he finally agreed to postpone the exercise of a right which the Emperor was not unwilling to admit in principle. The first article of the convention dealing with the cession of Chusan read: 'His Imperial Majesty having stated that after a lapse of time when tranquillity is insured it will be safe and right to admit foreigners into the City, and the Chinese Government being unable at present to coerce the people of Canton, the Plenipotentiaries agree it be postponed, though the claim is not yielded by Her Britannic Majesty.' The second article gave British subjects full liberty to walk in the neighbourhood

[1] Davis to Aberdeen, 20 Jan. 1846 (F.O. 17/109).
[2] Davis to Aberdeen, 27 Jan. 1846 (ibid.).
[3] Davis to Aberdeen, 10 Feb. 1846 (ibid.).
[4] Davis to Aberdeen, 16 Feb. 1846 (ibid.).
[5] Davis to Aberdeen, 24 Feb. 1846 (ibid.).
[6] Davis to Aberdeen, 27 Jan. 1846 (ibid.); 22 Mar. 1846 (F.O. 17/110).

of, but outside, the city on both sides of the river in certain specified localities.[1]

There had been some suggestion that on the evacuation of Chusan by the British forces the French might step in. Aberdeen attached no weight to these rumours and thought that they were invented for the purpose of giving the Government a pretext to remain in occupation. 'On the other hand,' wrote the Foreign Secretary to the Prime Minister, 'the bare possibility of such an event is sufficient to justify a reasonable watchfulness. Anything would be better than ridicule so overwhelming.' Accordingly, Davis was instructed to obtain a declaration from the Chinese Government in the convention by which Britain agreed to restore the island, to the effect that China would never alienate Chusan to another Power. In return for this Great Britain bound herself to China to defend for China the island of Chusan if menaced by another Power. The Foreign Secretary indeed informed the French Ambassador in London that Davis was authorized, without waiting for orders from England,[2] to attack any power which might occupy Chusan. Peel thought that the case of Chusan was very difficult, and that though the carrying out of the instructions might impose great responsibility, they were the best that could be given.[3]

In the summer of 1846 a serious riot broke out in Canton. An Englishman, assaulted by a Chinese, knocked his assailant down, secured him and brought him into the factories. A mob thereupon gathered which the Chinese military, who did not appear for three hours, were unable to restrain. The British Consul agreed to repel the Chinese if the foreigners refrained from firing. The crowd was pushed back, but in another quarter some of the foreigners, of whom several were injured, fired causing the death of three Chinese.[4] Foreigners remained on watch during the following night, but they and the Chinese military were successful in preventing further trouble. Business was soon resumed, the Governor issued a quietening proclamation, though there were ominous meetings of the gentry and literati in the city, the tenour of whose discussions was unknown to the British authorities. By the end of August Davis

---

[1] Davis to Aberdeen, 11 Mar. 1846 (F.O. 17/110).
[2] Aberdeen to Peel, 21 Oct. 1845 (Add. MSS. 40455, f. 230).
[3] Peel to Aberdeen, 20 Oct. 1845 (Add. MSS. 40455, f. 228).
[4] Davis to Aberdeen, 9 July 1846 (F.O. 17/113).

was reporting that the city remained quiet, and that 'though the death of three Chinese is to be lamented in the abstract, I cannot help thinking (from the experience of the previous American incident in 1844) that the example will tend to deter thieves and vagabonds' of which the Cantonese mobs were composed.[1] Keying was converting the late Consoo House into barracks and intended to keep an adequate number of Chinese soldiers there under an officer of respectable rank. When this change had been effected Davis considered that it would be his duty 'by every means to check armed associations of British subjects'[2]. He was glad that Keying was removing from the neighbourhood of the factories the hucksters whose presence had been a source of annoyance to the foreigners and a centre of disturbance.[3] But at the close of the year Kwantung was in a very disturbed state owing to the subversive activities of the Triad Society, which defeated the Government troops but twenty-five miles from the capital, and threatened Canton itself.[4]

Meanwhile the Conservative Government of Peel had fallen, and with it Lord Aberdeen. Davis regretted the departure of his chief.

'I may still turn to account those lessons of moderation and justice which were conveyed in your dispatches—principles which during your too short administration have maintained a universal peace more glorious than any war. . . . I am persuaded that the Chinese think better of us than ever, and if I may judge from the unbounded and reiterated terms of acknowledgement in which Keying expresses himself, their astonishment at the strict observance of all the terms of the treaty in the restoration [of Chusan] is equal to their expressed admiration of our mild and just rule of the island (infinitely superior to their own) during its occupation. Our troops were hardly removed before the Chinese soldiers began their usual trade of squeezing the inhabitants.'[5]

Palmerston was back in the Foreign Office in July 1846. On hearing of the riots the new Foreign Secretary instructed Davis to inform the Chinese Government of the regret of Her Majesty's Government that the people of Canton should by violence have

[1] Davis to Aberdeen, 27 Aug. 1846 (F.O. 17/113).
[2] Davis to Aberdeen, 28 Oct. 1846 (F.O. 17/114).
[3] Davis to Aberdeen, 31 Oct. 1846 (F.O. 17/114).
[4] Davis to Palmerston, 23 Dec. 1846 (F.O. 17/115).
[5] Davis to Aberdeen, 28 Sept. 1846 (Add. MSS. 43198, f. 403).

compelled the British residents to fire upon and kill several Chinese. It would be a kindness if the Cantonese authorities would tell their people that 'British residents are not to be attacked or insulted with impunity, and you will request the Chinese authorities to bear in mind that if they shall be unwilling or unable to keep order, the British subjects will defend themselves, and the greater the violence of the mob, the greater will be the loss of life which will be inflicted upon them.' It was to be hoped that in future the Chinese would keep an adequate police force to ensure the tranquillity of the city, and that they would make examples of the instigators of the July riots. Davis was to send a British ship-of-war up river to be stationed off the factories.[1] With this warning to the Chinese went characteristically a warning to the British community. If upon an inquiry Davis found it justifiable he was to issue a public notice cautioning British subjects, should their proceedings end in the commission of acts of violence by the Chinese, not to expect their Government to insist upon the Chinese making reparations for losses or injuries received.[2] Davis combated the view that the presence of a British warship at the factories would be of value, as only a small ship could go up stream. Palmerston, who was thinking not so much of the defence of the factories against the Chinese Government, as of the moral effect upon the mob, finally agreed that the naval officer in charge should use his discretion in the matter.[3] But he disagreed with Davis's view of the undesirability of an armed association of the British merchants. If they could defend themselves they were not so likely to be attacked. 'Depend upon it, that the best way of keeping any men quiet is to let them see that you are able and determined to repel force by force; and the Chinese are not in the least different in this respect from the rest of mankind.' He was fully convinced that 'we shall lose all the vantage ground which we have gained by our victories in China, if we take the low tone which seems to have been adopted of late by us at Canton'. On the other hand, the English in Canton ought 'to abstain from giving the Chinese any ground of complaint and much more from anything like provocation and affront'[4].

[1] Palmerston to Davis, 3 Oct. 1846 (F.O. 17/120).
[2] Palmerston to Davis, 17 Oct. 1846 (F.O. 17/120).
[3] Addington to Sec. to Admiralty, 12 Apr. 1847 (F.O. 17/120).
[4] Palmerston to Davis, 9 Jan. 1847 (F.O. 17/121).

It appeared to Davis that one Compton had been the person responsible for the beginning of the late riot. He had kicked down the stall of a Chinese trader, and for this act the Consul fined him $200.[1] Compton had been guilty of repeated acts of violence, yet his punishment caused a ferment among the English merchants. 'I am not the first', wrote Davis, 'who has been compelled to remark that it is more difficult to deal with our own countrymen at Canton, than with the Chinese government'[2]. It had been far harder to get the fine paid by Compton, who admitted the whole of the repeated acts of violence and agreed 'that these circumstances led to the riot is very probable', than to secure the compensation of $46,000 damages suffered, partly through the fault of some of their number, by the British merchants. Unfortunately for Davis, Hulme, the Chief Justice of Hong Kong, to whom Compton appealed, not only quashed the sentence on a point of form, but in his judgement made remarks which were likely to encourage violence on the part of the British. Davis intended to pass an ordinance giving the Superintendent powers of deportation of English offenders on the just complaint and requisition of the Chinese Government.[3] The law officers of the Crown to whom Palmerston referred the case of Compton agreed with the decision of the Chief Justice.[4] Had the Chief Justice confined himself in his judgement to the legal aspect of the case, Davis would have had no serious grounds for complaint. But he referred to matter which was not in the evidence, and virtually attacked the policy of the Superintendent.[5] Personal motives lay behind his attitude. Davis had felt obliged to remonstrate with him for taking a six-months' holiday in the hot season, leaving witnesses waiting for the resumption of the court, and prisoners in jail.[6] 'It will never answer', complained Davis, 'to have two Plenipotentiaries in China, one doing justice to our ally, and the other immediately undoing it'. It was highly dangerous to the Hong Kong executive that the British judicial officer should be so completely independent of the Governor. He laid an accusation against the Chief Justice of being an habitual drunkard.

[1] Davis to Palmerston, 26 Sept. 1846 (F.O. 17/114).
[2] Davis to Palmerston, 12 Nov. 1846 (F.O. 17/115).
[3] Davis to Palmerston, 25 Nov. 1846 (F.O. 17/115).
[4] Palmerston to Davis, 11 March 1847 (F.O. 17/120).
[5] Davis to Palmerston, 15 Dec. 1847 (F.O. 17/115).
[6] Davis to Palmerston, private, 30 Oct. 1846 (F.O. 17/114).

'The sooner Silenus gives up officiating in the temple of Themis the better, and a sober judge on £2000 per annum (an ample salary) will be better than Silenus on £3000.'[1] Though there was some truth in the charge of drunkenness, Hulme was, after an inquiry, exonerated and reinstated much to the joy of the British community.[2] Palmerston let Compton know that he strongly disapproved of him and that the law officers of the Crown had ruled that a charge of murder might be brought against a person whose actions gave rise to a riot which ended fatally.[3] To the China merchants in London he complained angrily of the younger residents who 'amuse themselves by kicking over fruit-stalls and by making foot-balls of the Chinese'[4].

Yet difficulties followed on the riot in the summer. In October 1846 two sailors who had entered the city were mal-treated. Palmerston immediately ordered Davis to demand the punishment of the assailants, and to inform Keying that if the Chinese authorities would not prevent such outrages, the British Government would be obliged to take matters into their own hands. It would be the fault of the local authorities, if in consequence the innocent suffered with the guilty.[5] The day before this instruction reached Davis in March 1847, the British Plenipotentiary had asked Keying to punish those guilty of an aggression on another party, consisting of six Englishmen (includ-ing a lieutenant-colonel in plain clothes), which had taken place at the village of Fatshan fifteen miles above Canton. A Chinese Mandarin who was present had tried in vain to protect the party, and his attendants had been severely injured by the mob.

In face of the demands of the Foreign Office in regard to the October incident, and of the dispatch from Palmerston com-plaining of the 'low tone' which had been adopted by the British authorities recently, Davis decided to back up his demands by a show of force. He explained that his recent inaction was due to instructions from home: 'The records of the F.O. will convince Your Lordship that during the last three years, I have been rigidly tied down by my instructions to the most forbearing policy.' The major-general in command of the Hong Kong garrison agreed to give military support, and

[1] Davis to Palmerston, 28 Nov. 1846 (F.O. 17/115).
[2] Forth-Rouen to Min. des Aff. Étr., 21 June 1848 (Chine 5).
[3] Palmerston to Davis, 11 March 1847 (F.O. 17/120).
[4] Memorandum, 28 June 1847 (F.O. 17/135).
[5] Palmerston to Davis, 12 Jan. 1847 (F.O. 17/121).

the admiral, who was in the Straits, was urgently pressed to come to Hong Kong.[1] Keying's reply to the demands of the British Government was held by Davis to be unsatisfactory. 'It mixes up the subjects of three of my separate notes, and takes no notice whatever of the principal point, Your Lordship's direct demand for redress on account of the two seamen.' Major-General d'Aguilar agreed to go to Canton provided that he was not called upon to occupy the factories unless he had the Boca Tigris forts in his hands. He decided to embark at night time in order to effect a *coup de main*. As a result of his operations the whole river from Hong Kong to Canton within thirty-six hours was in British hands, all the guns had been spiked or captured, and the forts disabled, without the loss of a single man. Arrived in Canton, the general informed Davis that he was in a position to seize two of the city gates and from them and the adjoining rampart to dominate the city in half an hour. But if this action was necessary it would have to be completed, owing to the paucity of his troops, within the following twenty-four hours. Hence Davis was obliged to present an ultimatum to Keying, after expressing in strong terms his disgust and disappointment of the manner in which the treaty engagements had been trifled with at Canton. Having failed to obtain an extension of the period during which the city should continue to be closed to foreigners from two years to four or five, Keying agreed to all Davis's demands. British subjects were to be free from molestation, the aggressors of October and March were to be punished, and various local improvements at Canton designed to minimize the danger to the factories from the lower classes of the city were promised. The foreign community expressed its great satisfaction at this action and its outcome. The French Consul thanked Davis for promoting the cause of *la civilisation Européenne*, while the American Consul called upon the British representative in order to voice his concurrence in the necessity and policy of the measures.[2] The demonstration resulted, according to the American Consul, in a marked improvement in the tone of all the Chinese 'from the Imperial Commissioner down to the lowest of the rabble'[3]. So much had been gained by a force of 900 men, three steamers,

---

[1] Davis to Palmerston, 27 Mar. 1847 (F.O. 17/124).
[2] Davis to Palmerston, 5 Apr. 1847 (F.O. 17/125).
[3] Davis to Palmerston, 30 Apr. 1847 (F.O. 17/125).

and a brig at a cost of £700.[1] Keying prohibited anonymous anti-foreign placards. His conduct in this regard was perhaps due, thought Davis, 'to instructions from Peking, cautioning him against the chance of a serious rupture with the British, at his peril'[2]. Every day impressed Davis with the fact that there would be no more need of using force at Canton.[3] The small British guard left at the factories was withdrawn early in July,[4] while in the three months following the *coup de main* the export of tea increased by one million pounds over the corresponding period of the previous year,[5] a state of affairs very different from that imagined by Compton's 'Chamber of Commerce' which asserted that the expedition had done 'incalculable injury to trade'[6].

Lord Palmerston fully approved of the step which Davis had taken, and the promptitude and judgement with which the arrangements for it had been made.[7] After hearing criticisms of Davis's conduct by the China merchants,[8] the Foreign Secretary confirmed this approval, but indicated that he had

'indeed no wish unnecessarily to have recourse to force in order to compel the Chinese authorities to listen to their just demands. But H.M.G. cannot doubt that the lesson which those authorities have now learnt, that forbearance has its limits and that Her Majesty's servants in China relying upon the support of their government are prepared, if necessary, promptly to assert the rights which British subjects in China are by Treaty entitled to enjoy, will have a salutary effect on the future conduct of Chinese affairs.'

On the other hand, the recent action ought not to encourage ill-disposed individuals to provoke collisions; every tendency to such conduct ought to be suppressed by Her Majesty's servants to the full extent of their legal powers.[9]

The confidence of the British authorities was, however, misplaced, for in December another attack was made upon a party of six young Englishmen who had gone on an excursion to a village three miles up river from Canton. They got into an

[1] Davis to Palmerston, 12 Apr. 1847 (F.O. 17/125).
[2] Davis to Palmerston, 8 May 1847 (F.O. 17/126).
[3] Davis to Palmerston, 23 June 1847 (F.O. 17/127).
[4] Davis to Palmerston, 10 July 1847 (F.O. 17/128).
[5] Davis to Palmerston, 13 Aug. 1847 (F.O. 17/128).
[6] Davis to Palmerston, 19 Aug. 1847 (F.O. 17/128).
[7] Palmerston to Davis, 24 June 1847 (F.O. 17/121).
[8] Memorandum, 28 June 1847 (F.O. 17/135).
[9] Palmerston to Davis, 5 July 1847 (F.O. 17/122).

affray with a party of Chinese, of whom they killed one, and
wounded two. The British party were subsequently over-
powered, killed, and horribly mutilated. Keying did his best
to apprehend the guilty Chinese, but as he was slow in making
his captures, Davis threatened to remove the British community from Canton.[1] Though Davis denied Keying's
contention that the British were the aggressors he was willing
to admit to his chief that affairs of that kind were very likely
to arise from a reckless use of firearms.[2] Nine Chinese were
apprehended and Keying promised, according to Chinese
custom of a life for a life, after taking into account the losses
sustained by the Chinese in the fray, to execute four of his
prisoners. Davis, who at first counter-demanded that every one
guilty should be executed—and executed in the offending
villages,[3]—agreed to be satisfied with the immediate execution
of four and the remission of the remaining to the Board of
Punishments at Peking. But their punishment and the exhorta-
tions of the officers would not, thought Keying, influence the
villagers to change their minds, and the Canton Consul concurred in this judgement. He thought there would be great
difficulty in making a satisfactory arrangement for the personal
safety of British subjects, so long as the local militia existed in
the rural districts maintained by the gentry and landowners,
who were avowedly opposed to foreign influence, and over
whom the officers of the Government did not seem to be able
to exercise the least control.[4] Davis was prepared to use force
again and requisitioned an extra regiment from India.[5] Keying
thereupon suggested keeping a body of twenty Chinese police
who should attend any party desirous of making excursions.
Davis thought the plan might be of some use if these police
were in British pay, as they would at least be able to identify
aggressors. The establishment of this system coupled with a
pacificatory address which Keying prevailed upon the gentry
to issue to the people gave Davis some encouragement, and he
considered himself bound to give it a fair trial.[6] The British
Superintendent notified the merchants of the existence of the

[1] Davis to Palmerston, 13 Dec. 1847 (F.O. 17/132).
[2] Davis to Palmerston, 29 Feb. 1848 (F.O. 17/140).
[3] Davis to Palmerston, 18 Dec. 1847 (F.O. 17/132).
[4] Davis to Palmerston, 8 Jan. 1848 (F.O. 17/140).
[5] Davis to Palmerston, 10 Jan. 1848 (F.O. 17/140).
[6] Davis to Palmerston, 17 Jan. 1848 (F.O. 17/140).

new police protection, and while informing them that the use
of these Chinese was not compulsory, stated that 'those who
take them will be entitled to a more favourable construction
of their intentions and conduct than those who do not'[1]. There
seemed, however, to be a 'combination to oppose what the
consul has done for the peace and security of persons wishing
to make excursions to a distance'[2]. The Foreign Secretary was
unable to understand that the mere circumstance of its being
more agreeable to go without an escort than with it could be a
sufficient reason for not adopting a precaution which, though it
might not absolutely ensure their safety, would tend to make
any danger far less likely.[3] Davis could congratulate himself
that another incident had passed without the necessity on that
occasion of using coercive measures, as he had received during
the negotiations instructions from Her Majesty's Government
peremptorily forbidding any further offensive operations to be
undertaken without their previous sanction.[4] He seemed to
think that the permanent feeling of hostility of the Cantonese
had 'commenced with the violence suffered by their women
from the Sepoy troops in 1841' and that killing several hundreds
of them would hardly reconcile the survivors to the British.[5]
Soon after the appeasement of this affair Keying departed to
Peking, leaving his second-in-command Hwang in office, and
Davis himself was relieved by Bonham fourteen days later.[6]
Looking on the events of recent months a French observer
wrote:

'With all their guns the English cannot get their treaties executed
and are worse off at Canton to-day than before the War. . . .'[7]
'They have threatened it is true but I do not think that they are
anxious to come to blows; they are not at present in a position to
do so honourably. . . . Canton deserves a sharp lesson, but it is
being spared because of the enormous trade here, which would of
necessity suffer from a major disturbance. In spite of this, when the
English . . . have all the necessary means of attack, Canton will
certainly get its lesson.'[8]

[1] Davis to Palmerston, 25 Jan. 1848 (F.O. 17/140).
[2] Davis to Palmerston, 29 Feb. 1848 (F.O. 17/140).
[3] Palmerston to Bonham, 29 May 1848 (F.O. 17/138).
[4] Davis to Palmerston, 28 Jan. 1848 (F.O. 17/140).
[5] Davis to Palmerston, 8 Feb. 1848 (F.O. 17/140).
[6] Davis to Palmerston, 8 Mar. 1848 (F.O. 17/141).
[7] Libois to Directeurs, 27 Feb. 1848 (M.E., vol. 314, f. 158).
[8] Libois to Directeurs, 24 June 1848 (M.E., vol. 325, f. 247).

Another Frenchman, the new Minister, Forth-Rouen, thought that a policy of goodwill on the part of the British Government, as exemplified in Palmerston's strictures on the conduct of some of the trading community,[1] was all very well in itself, but it unfortunately diminished the respect with which the British had been regarded.[2]

B. THE ADMINISTRATIONS OF SIR (SAMUEL) GEORGE BONHAM AND SIR JOHN BOWRING FROM 1848 TO 1852

1. *The Triumph of Seu*

Before his appointment to China Bonham had had considerable experience of Eastern affairs. The son of a father drowned while in the maritime service of the East India Company, after employment under the Indian Government he became in 1837, at the age of thirty-four, Governor of Singapore and Malacca. Ten years later he was made Governor of Hong Kong and British Plenipotentiary in China. Bonham appears to have been a cautious administrator, inclined, with as little trouble to himself as to others, rather to watch over than actively to promote the interests entrusted to his charge. Towards the end of his period of office especially he dreaded the opening of thorny questions which might interfere with his plans for enjoying in retirement the fruits of his quiescent policy and a not inconsiderable fortune. In that same year, 1847, there set out for the East, through the friendship of Lord Palmerston, John Bowring, who was destined to succeed Bonham in 1854 at the age of sixty-two as the representative of the British Crown in Hong Kong and China. Very different from his younger contemporary and chief in China, Bowring was a man of precipitation, of definite ideas, and of a reforming zeal with a high conception of his duty and his position. He was too a man of piety, the author, among others, of the well-known hymn, 'In the Cross of Christ I glory'. Until his assumption of the office of Consul in Canton he had had no personal knowledge of oriental affairs, but was already a much-travelled man of wide experience, particularly in the fields of economics and commerce. He came of a west country woollen family, was a great linguist, and a radical in tradition, a friend of Jeremy Bentham and of

[1] Forth-Rouen to Min. Aff. Étr., 21 June 1848 (Chine 5).
[2] Forth-Rouen to Min. Aff. Étr., 21 July 1848 (Chine 5).

Cobden. He had been elected member for Bolton, as a repealer,
in 1841, but the depression of 1847 threatened his fortune,
wholly invested in ironworks in South Wales, and on obtaining
his consulate, he resigned his seat and resided in the East for
the next twelve years.

Keying had left Canton for the capital on the 16th March,[1]
and six days later Bonham was sworn in as Governor of Hong
Kong and took over the duties of Her Majesty's Plenipotentiary.[2] On the 29th April the new British chief, accompanied
by the major-general and other civil and military officers, and
escorted by a guard of honour, had an interview at Hoomun-
chai with Seu, the acting, soon to be the substantive, Imperial
Commissioner. Seu declared that he was determined to abide
by the provisions of the treaties and to make 'no distinction
between the central and outside people, so long as the foreigners
were properly restrained'. He struck Bonham as a determined
man; he had already executed 500 people owing to the disturbances in Kwantung. Yet he had to tread warily with the
unruly Cantonese, knowing full well the limitations of his
power over them.[3] He had, for instance, given it out that his
journey to Hoomun-chai was a tour of inspection of the Bogue
Forts, as he feared a riot if the Cantonese suspected that his
real purpose was a ceremonial visit to his British colleague.[1]
The new Imperial Commissioner, a man of fifty, was, reported
Bonham, a voluptuary without business ability, whose wealth
at once obviated the necessity of indulgence in corrupt practices, and furnished the means for the acquisition of popularity.[4]
He was too a man learned in the literature of the Chinese
classics and 'haunted by all the narrow-minded prejudices with
which this inspires its students'. He was led both by his education and his feeling for popularity to be a 'staunch champion
of Chinese rights and an advocate of antiquated principles'[5].
Bonham was to find that Seu was a friend of Commissioner Lin,
and as anti-foreign as his friend.[6] Such were the actors.

The British Plenipotentiary's earliest impressions of the new
Chinese authorities did not lead him to expect the continuance

[1] Bonham to Palmerston, 4 May 1848 (F.O. 17/143).
[2] Bonham to Palmerston, 21 Mar. 1848 (F.O. 17/141).
[3] Bonham to Hammond, private, 30 Nov. 1848 (F.O. 17/145).
[4] Bonham to Palmerston, 22 Aug. 1848 (F.O. 17/144).
[5] Bonham to Palmerston, 20 Jan. 1849 (F.O. 17/153).
[6] Bonham to Palmerston, 19 May 1849 (F.O. 17/155).

of that close and friendly co-operation which had marked the relations of Keying with Bonham's two predecessors. The restrictions imposed by the Treaty of Nanking were, he thought, bad from a moral and political point of view, as they had the effect of keeping alive the arrogant spirit and ministering to the vanity and prejudices of a semi-barbarous people. The pretensions of the Chinese so fostered were the greatest obstacle to a more enlarged and beneficial intercourse. These anti-pathetic feelings were sedulously nourished by the authorities who wrote and spoke of the foreigners officially and privately in terms of the greatest opprobrium, even when they had been compelled to use decorous terms in their communications to British officers. Past history and the then unsatisfactory position after a war and treaties dictated by the British afforded the strongest arguments, apart from the advantage which would ensue to the trading interests of the country, for the total abolition of trading and travelling limitations. 'Improved social and political position must be the cause rather than the effect of a more extended and beneficial commercial intercourse.'[1]

The first step in this direction which might be taken without the necessity of a revision of treaties was the fulfilment of the agreement relative to the entry of British subjects into the city of Canton. In the summer of 1848 Bonham suggested that subordinates of his own and of the Imperial Commissioner should meet to discuss arrangements for the opening of the city which was due to take place the following April. But he met with a refusal.[2] It was clear that Seu would not execute the agreement, without which Bonham would continue to be debarred from direct access to the Viceroy. The authorities had not enough power to compel the people to behave in a proper manner, and Bonham was precluded by his instructions from moving troops from Hong Kong.[3] The state of trade at home and in India could not alone account for the commercial stagnation of the summer of 1848. There was a general feeling of insecurity consequent upon the possibility of the British authorities having recourse to arms for a final settlement of the city question. A naval force of some strength would be

[1] Bonham to Palmerston, 14 Apr. 1848 (F.O. 17/142).
[2] Bonham to Palmerston, 21 June 1848 (F.O. 17/143).
[3] Bonham to Palmerston, 20 July 1848 (F.O. 17/144).

necessary to effect this purpose, and the whole or part of the
city would probably have to be held for a considerable time.
Yet to forgo the right would create a dangerous precedent.
It might be advantageous to effect a compromise on the basis
of the cession of Danes Island in the river near the city and the
limitation of the right of entry to the Superintendent of Trade
and the Consul at Canton.[1] It certainly appeared that the
city itself would be quite unsafe for the British community
generally, for the Canton people were as insolent as ever and
aggression against foreigners had only been avoided by their
confining themselves to the immediate vicinity of the factories.
Bonham was of opinion that the precedent condition of foreign
security was an entire change in the minds of the people which
would never be effected until the city and its inhabitants had
felt British power. The populace and 'braves'[2] of the adjacent
country, as things were, would resist heartily and a respectable
force would be necessary. A temporary stoppage of trade
would inevitably follow and a long time would ensue before
confidence could be again fully restored. Bonham suggested
that he should go to the city gate on the day agreed upon for
the entry and request access to Seu, who would probably reply:
'You have a right, but I cannot guarantee your safety.' Then
Bonham would inform him that he intended to go to Peking.
If that threat was not effective, he would go to the Peiho with
as formidable a naval force as the admiral might have at his
command. In the capital Keying and Hwang, who understood
the British position, would probably attempt to procrastinate
in order to get the expedition away, but in that event pressure
could be applied by the blockade of Tientsin and Chin-kiang.
In itself entry into the city was a matter of comparative unimportance and the question might have been waived if so
much negotiation had not taken place on the subject.[3] It was
significant of the changed attitude of the Canton authorities
that Seu showed inexplicable rudeness in refusing at the same
time to receive John W. Davis, the United States representative.
He seemed to be departing from the traditions of Keying, who
had well understood the existence of Anglo-American rivalry
in China, and had given his special confidence to the American

[1] Bonham to Palmerston, private, 24 July 1848 (F.O. 17/144).
[2] As the popular militia was termed.
[3] Bonham to Palmerston, 23 Oct. 1848 (F.O. 17/145).

K

Consul in order to secure his goodwill in case of difficulties with the British. When Davis was prevented by adverse winds from keeping an appointment eventually fixed by Seu, the Imperial Commissioner refused to accept his excuse and went so far as to indulge in menacing language; but upon the appearance of an American ship before Canton, Seu quickly agreed to meet Davis in Howqua's[1] counting-house.[2]

The British Government were anxious to know whether there was any practical advantage to be gained by entering Canton.[3] By the end of 1848 they had definitely come to the conclusion that Bonham was not to be allowed to use force against the city, nor to go on a mission to Peking. Even if, as was possible, the Chinese were led by the seeming weakness of Great Britain on the question of the Canton entry to violate other agreements, it was quite certain that for such an object alone Great Britain ought not to risk the issues of peace and war. It would be just as easy to use force for more important objects. Bonham was, therefore, instructed by Palmerston to inform Seu that Her Majesty's Government, in order to preserve harmony, did not intend that British subjects should avail themselves of the right at once, but that they hoped the two authorities would draw up regulations on the subject and that for this purpose Bonham was to express a wish to visit the High Commissioner under a suitable escort.[4]

In February 1849 Bonham had an interview with Seu in H.M.S. *Hastings* in Anson's Bay. While affirming that it was not in his power to carry out the agreement made between Keying and Sir John Davis, and that those two officers knew at the time that it was incapable of fulfilment, the Chinese officer promised to write to the Emperor on the subject.[5] As the date approached there were unmistakable signs of popular agitation among the Cantonese. The people enlisted a large body of militia, taxing themselves on an assumed capacity to pay, and agreeing to inflict penalties upon those who refused to conform. Numerous placards of an inflammatory nature appeared. The woollen traders declared their determination

[1] Son of the former senior Hong merchant who inherited the trade name Howqua, by which father and son were known to the foreign community.
[2] Forth-Rouen to Min. Aff. Étr., 26, 27 Sept. and 18 Oct. 1848 (Chine 5).
[3] Palmerston to Bonham, 7 Oct. 1848 (F.O. 17/139).
[4] Palmerston to Bonham, 30 Dec. 1848 (F.O. 17/139).
[5] Bonham to Palmerston, 21 Feb. 1849 (F.O. 17/153).

to forgo and prevent trade with, or brokerage on behalf of, the Barbarians either directly or through other guilds, to refrain from all connexion with any merchant or broker who might sell goods on British account, to fine heavily those who violated or connived at the violation of these rules, and refuse employment to all who failed to give information in their possession against such guilty parties. The cotton and cotton yarn guilds passed similar resolutions. Bonham wrote to Seu pointing out the futility of these attempts by the guilds to compel Her Majesty's Government to forgo a right. But to Seu, who, thought the Consul, was the impulse behind these manifestations, the question was: 'As the people are the essential part of a State, how can they be stopped by legal enactments?' 'In transacting affairs it is absolutely necessary to yield to public feeling. It is quite impossible for me to force the merchants to comply with my own desires.'[1] Seu's views on the nature of government were identical with those of his august master, who, in reply to his Commissioner's dispatch, also refused to comply with the wishes of the foreigners in opposition to his own people. The High Commissioner declined to see the newly arrived Consul Bowring and the Plenipotentiary in the city, though he was prepared do so in Howqua's gardens. Bonham objected to meet him in these circumstances, and Seu would not himself receive a person of merely consular rank. In face of the rigid attitude of the Chinese authorities and of the unwillingness of the British Government to take forceful measures, Bonham could not but regard the discussions on the entry question as closed.[2]

The distaste of the local Cantonese inhabitants for the foreigners was apparently quite genuine. At the same time this natural hostility 'received no slight impulse from the machinations of all interested in the continuance of the old and restricted state of things'. These men, justly apprehensive that improvements in the condition of the foreigners would lessen their own influence as the agents in everything to do with Western trade, sought to push the people in an anti-foreign direction. At the same time these powerful vested interests by means of corruption were able to work upon the avarice of the local Mandarins and induce them to encourage the popular clamour against the concession of the treaty rights to the British.

[1] Bonham to Palmerston, 5 Mar. 1849 (F.O. 17/153).
[2] Bonham to Palmerston, 18 Apr. 1849 (F.O. 17/154).

The lower classes, thought Bonham, needed to be taught a lesson which had perhaps been too long delayed. But, to the British authorities, the means, the possible destruction of the city of Canton, were disproportionate to the desired end, the entry of officials to the city. Yet so long as the entry was delayed, so long would the future discussion of all other matters be inevitably embarrassed.[1] For as the French Minister, Forth-Rouen, wrote to the Quai d'Orsay: 'La plume à la main les Chinois sont très forts pour éterniser les questions, mais mis en présence des Européens un peu au fait de leurs ruses, les habitants du Céleste Empire perdent tous les avantages.'[2]

The French Minister had foreseen that if Great Britain was forced to abandon her rights she would sink and lose all her influence. This would be an event much to be regretted by other Europeans, for 'we have all a joint interest in China and I do not share the view of those who hold that we can profit by England's loss. If the Chinese regain their former pride we should, I think, soon feel the serious consequences of it.'[3] This, however, he acknowledged was not the view of the Americans in general, who imagined that the only result of the strained relations between the British and the Chinese would be their own commercial advantage.[4]

Forth-Rouen thought war between Britain and China was inevitable. 'Sooner or later she will have to take up the task she left unfinished at Nanking . . . and the English will be represented in Peking: that is the goal of all their desires.'[5] He had been talking to Consul Bowring who he understood had come to China with the mission of forming a close under-standing with the representatives of France. It is probable that, from conversations with Bowring, Forth-Rouen got the view that the English 'do not mean Russia to have the monopoly of representation in Peking'.

'They believe that that Power is at work through its agents against the consolidation of English influence in China and they mean to fight it in the very place where it is hatching its plots . . . indeed China will not really be open to foreigners until they can reside in the capital of China.'

[1] Bonham to Palmerston, 23 Apr. 1849 (F.O. 17/154).
[2] Forth-Rouen to Min. Aff. Étr., 18 Oct. 1848 (Chine 5).
[3] Forth-Rouen to Min. Aff. Étr., 5 Nov., 29 Dec. 1848 (Chine 5).
[4] Forth-Rouen to Min. Aff. Étr., 28 Mar. 1849 (Chine 5).
[5] Forth-Rouen to Min. Aff. Étr., 26 Apr. 1849 (Chine 5).

In spite, however, of Bowring's desire to bring about an understanding with France on Chinese affairs, the French minister had to confess that the relations of Frenchmen and Englishmen in China were very cold, while with the Americans his countrymen were on such a friendly footing as to be at times embarrassing.[1]

Indeed, it was not long before it became apparent that owing to the forbearance of the London Government, the British suffered a considerable loss of prestige. The gentry and literati proposed to erect a tablet to commemorate the services of Seu the Viceroy and Yeh the Governor of Kwantung in excluding the British from Canton, while the Emperor joined with the people in honouring Seu for his ability in disposing peacefully of the question.[2] In return Seu recommended to Imperial favour certain officers, literary graduates, and others of the gentry, for 'the precautionary measures' they had taken for the defence of the city. Both the authorities and the people considered that they had gained no small triumph by keeping the city closed to the British.[3] Yet there was some compensation, for the Chinese traders and others with whom the Europeans were in the habit of coming into contact were more than ordinarily civil.[4]

2. *Protest to Peking*

Palmerston declined either to waive the right or to enforce it at the moment. The British Government preferred waiting to deal with future violations of the treaty according to the circumstances of the case. Bonham was instructed to forward a note to the Imperial Commissioner, expressing his surprise and displeasure and inquiring whether the Emperor were unwilling or unable to carry out his Treaty promise, and he was to request that Seu should forward this communication to the capital.[5] Bonham was later ordered to protest against the proposal to erect a tablet of honour to Seu and Yeh, a proposal which had been circulated certainly with the knowledge and probably with the approval of the Canton officers. 'If that document', wrote Palmerston, 'is to be considered as expressing in any

[1] Forth-Rouen to Min. Aff. Étr., 22 Apr. 1849 (Chine 5).
[2] Bonham to Palmerston, 18 May 1849 (F.O. 17/155).
[3] Bonham to Palmerston, 22 June 1849 (F.O. 17/156).
[4] Bonham to Palmerston, 23 June 1849 (F.O. 17/156).
[5] Palmerston to Bonham, 25 June 1849 (F.O. 17/152).

degree the sentiments of the Chinese Government or of the great officers at Canton, Her Majesty's Government would despair of being able to continue to maintain relations of peace between Great Britain and China'[1]. In 1839 the Chinese had thought Great Britain too far away to be an effective danger, but as they had been conquered then, they could be defeated again. The British Government abstained from forceful measures only from a knowledge of its strength, trusting that the mistakes of Lin would not be repeated, and in the hope that the high officers would endeavour to cultivate decent relations with the foreigners and set an example to the people over whom they were placed. This second protest Bonham was likewise instructed to forward to Peking by Seu, and in addition through Alcock by the Taoutai of Shanghai.[2] If both these notes failed to reach their destination by either of those two channels, Palmerston instructed his representative to send them by one of H.M. ships to the mouth of the Peiho.[3]

In September Seu finally agreed to forward the substance of Palmerston's first protest to the Central Government.[4] Bonham could not send the second protest to the Minister for Foreign Affairs as there was no such officer in Peking, but he determined to forward it addressed to Muchangah and Keying—the two principal ministers. It was clear too that the Taoutai would never be able to send Palmerston's note to Peking, for at best he might send it to his Provincial Governor of Chekiang, who would forward it to the Viceroy at Nanking. The latter officer would almost certainly send it to Seu, and therefore the Shanghai *démarche* would end in the same channel as Bonham's direct request. In the event the Taoutai refused to receive Palmerston's letter.[5] Bonham asked permission to go himself to the north—not to Peking, but to the Peiho—if the Canton channel should prove to be blocked by Seu's intransigence. He hoped that a conference in the north

'with the High Officers would have the effect of showing the Commissioner and his successors that we have it always within our power to appeal to his superiors, and tend to affect materially our

---

[1] Palmerston to Bonham, 18 Aug. 1849 (F.O. 17/152).
[2] Palmerston to Bonham, 18 Aug. 1849 (F.O. 17/152).
[3] Palmerston to Bonham, 9 Oct. 1849 (F.O. 17/152).
[4] Bonham to Palmerston, 17 Sept. 1849 (F.O. 17/157).
[5] Bonham to Palmerston, 30 Jan. 1850 (F.O. 17/165).

position at Canton, where the arrogance of the people towards us is confirmed by their conviction that without force we have no resource against their insolence or passive opposition'[1].

Palmerston gave Bonham leave to hold conversations with the Chinese ministers in Peking if his letters were not forwarded by other means, though he was to be careful not to regard the visit as a mission to the court, involving him in questions of etiquette, and exposing him to the refusal of reception.[2] When the season arrived for a journey north, it was impossible for Bonham to set out as he had intended, owing to the death in February 1850 of the Emperor Taoukwang. In May, however, he went to Shanghai. As the Taoutai now promised to forward Palmerston's letter to his Viceroy, Bonham agreed to wait twenty days to learn whether the Viceroy would forward it to the capital.[3] Tired of waiting, he eventually dispatched H.M.S. *Reynard* to the Peiho, whereupon the Viceroy replied favourably.[4] He was informed that Muchangah and Keying had duly received Palmerston's first protest of August 1849, but had given a verbal answer that by the laws of China they had no powers to deal with foreign affairs, which were in the hands of the Viceroy in Canton.[5] The commander of the *Reynard* was likewise rebuffed. He waited for fourteen days off the Peiho, and attempted in vain to persuade the officers there to receive the Foreign Secretary's communication.[6] By the end of the year Bonham was convinced that it was futile to attempt to establish communication with the court either by a personal visit to the Peiho or through the medium of the Nanking Viceroy.[7]

Besides the refusal of the entry of the British into Canton another invasion of treaty rights called for protest. The Commissioner was believed to have contemplated a measure tending to establish a close monopoly in the tea trade, by which, it was thought, he hoped to secure the old debt of the ex-Hongists to the Chinese Government. By this new system the ex-Hong merchants were to be granted the sole authority to

[1] Bonham to Palmerston, 28 Oct. 1849 (F.O. 17/158).
[2] Bonham to Palmerston, 2 Jan. 1850 (F.O. 17/164).
[3] Bonham to Palmerston, 13 May 1850 (F.O. 17/167).
[4] Bonham to Palmerston, 4 June 1850 (F.O. 17/168).
[5] Bonham to Palmerston, 11 June 1850 (F.O. 17/168).
[6] Bonham to Palmerston, 22 July 1850 (F.O. 17/168).
[7] Bonham to Palmerston, 23 Dec. 1850 (F.O. 17/170).

'secure' the tea warehouses.[1] In the summer new changes had been effected whereby half a farthing in the pound would be added to the price of tea. Though the charge was so trifling, Bonham objected strongly to what was, in effect, the revival of the Hong system by forcing new warehouse-men, or rather through them, foreign traders in general, to liquidate the debt due to the Provincial Government by the former Hongists. He toyed with the idea of stopping an equivalent amount from the duties payable by the Chinese. But such a course would be too dangerous, for the Chinese would be likely to retaliate by putting an embargo on British trade, especially as the influential Howqua, one of the chief of the ex-Hongists, was a partner in an American firm.[2] As soon as the Foreign Office heard that certain bonded ware-houses for tea had been licensed on the payment of a fee for the benefit of the Chinese Government, Palmerston stigmatized such action as an illegal imposition, inconsistent with the treaty, and instructed Bonham to demand its immediate cancellation.[3] Seu, however, refused to alter the new regulations. He con-tended that the extra charge was merely a deduction from that which had been charged throughout for storage of teas in bonded warehouses—a sum earmarked not for rent, but for securing the loan lent by the Chinese Government to Chinese of the ex-Hong to enable them to meet their obligations to British merchants. This charge was not a tax in excess of the tariff and could not raise prices. On Bonham's dispatch cover-ing this rejoinder there is in Palmerston's hand the following note:

'Prepare reply to Ch. Comiss[r] stating concisely the ground upon wh. we think ourselves intitled by Treaty to demand the abrogation of this arrangt. and instruct Sir S. Bonham[4] to send a note to Comm[r] to this effect and to say to him that H.M. Govt. require him to transmit this Representation to the Govt. of Pekin not doubting but that the Imperial Govt. will see the justice of this Demand and will give orders that it shall be complied with. Sir S. B. shd. say that H.M.'s Govt. have desired him to send this Representation to Pekin Govt. through the Comm[r] because H.M. Govt. think it will be more

[1] Bonham to Palmerston, 30 Jan. 1850 (F.O. 17/165).
[2] Bonham to Palmerston, 22 May 1850 (F.O. 17/169).
[3] Palmerston to Bonham, 18 Oct. 1850 (F.O. 17/164).
[4] Created K.C.B. in 1851.

agreeable to Pekin Govt. so to receive it than that it should be transmitted to them by British officers sent to Pekin by the Peiho River.'[1]

The Chinese Commissioner, however, refused to memorialize
the throne on the question of the extra tea duty. Were he ever to
do so, Bonham was of opinion that the British authorities would
never hear anything of it. This intelligence inclined Palmerston
to advocate strong measures. He asked his Under-Secretary for
a memorandum

'stating our various grievances against the Chinese Govt. and its
officers, and of the endeavours we have made by Remonstrances
and Representations to obtain Redress, and let me know which is
the Season of the year at which an interception of the supplies to
Pekin by stopping the passage of vessels across the Yangtze Kiang
in their way up the Canal to Pekin, would be the most effectual'.

In reply he was informed that there were only two grievances
outstanding—the question of the right of entry into Canton,
and this attempt to interfere with the freedom of the tea trade
at Canton, with which the Chinese Commissioner refused to
deal. Fear of a rumour getting abroad of an intended attack
on China and its dangerous effect on trade precluded consultation with either Morrison (son of the missionary and lexico-
grapher) of the Consular Service, then on leave in England, or
the Admiralty on the question of the best season of the year
to interfere with the grain junks. Bonham was, therefore, instructed in October 1851 to advise the Government on the
suitability of seasons.[2]

Bonham appears to have been somewhat alarmed at the
energetic attitude of the Foreign Secretary. As an excuse for
Seu's attitude on the tea question, he suggested the smuggling carried on by foreigners which was 'truly detestable',
while the British Government, he argued, in order to protect
the revenue, pursued itself a restrictive policy in regard to the
tea trade, by allowing its importation only at certain British
ports. Seu's plan might be contrary to treaty, but it was difficult to see how the evil of smuggling could be prevented by
any other plan; and in any event the imposition was a 'mere
trifle'. Above all Bonham argued that he would be sorry to see
coercive measures resorted to at that juncture, 'inasmuch as

[1] Bonham to Palmerston, 21 Jan. 1851 (F.O. 17/175).
[2] Bonham to Palmerston, 18 July 1851 (F.O. 17/178).

such a measure might throw the whole of the two Kwangs into a confusion from which it might be very difficult to extract them; and it is clear that such a state of things could not be conducive to our interests'[1].

Palmerston had been ready to contemplate the possibility of recourse to force in the case of a violation of a right conceded by the Chinese by treaty, even though the violation was in itself as trivial as a charge of half a farthing on a pound of tea. That he did not in fact take forceful measures was due to the consideration that consequences disproportionately dangerous might follow. But it should be noted that he resolutely opposed the suggestion of using force as a means of gaining new rights, for force should be the handmaid of justice and not the instrument of policy. He seems, in the international sphere, as any English statesman was bound by tradition and experience to be in that of municipal law, deeply conscious of the Rule of Law. It is true that in his handling of Chinese affairs, as of other international affairs, he perforce had to constitute the British Government at once the judge and the policeman—the interpreter and the enforcer of what he regarded as the lawful rights of his Sovereign. It is noteworthy that he remitted many cases to the law officers of the Crown for legal opinion, and how he sharply rebuked his subordinates for any breach of the law of nations. Thus he denied the right of the master of the *Mayflower* to compensation for the loss of his cutter as, on his own showing, he had on board sixteen chests of contraband goods—opium. But at the same time, the persons who had been guilty of a murderous assault on the crew without legal process or authority should be punished, whether in the employment of the Chinese Government or not.[2]

---

[1] Extract of letter from Bonham, Hong Kong, 29 Dec. 1851 (F.O. 17/181). The disturbed condition of Kwantung had, for some time, caused Bonham anxiety. In April 1849 he had reported that the insurgents in that province were more menacing than the Government at Peking thought.* In the summer of 1850 the central authorities in alarm demoted Seu four places,† owing to his failure to check the rebel robbers of his province, though by October Bonham thought there was no insurrection in progress, and that the bandit menace had subsided.‡

[2] Palmerston to Bonham, 2 Jan. 1850 (F.O. 17/164).

---

* Bonham to Palmerston, 23 Apr. 1849 (F.O. 17/154).
† Bonham to Palmerston, 23 Aug. 1850 (F.O. 17/169).
‡ Bonham to Palmerston, 29 Oct. 1850 (F.O. 17/170).

Again, no matter what inconvenience it might cause,
Bonham was not allowed to withhold from the Chinese courts
any Chinese subject who was wanted as a defendant or a
witness, even if such subject was in the employ of a consul.[1]
Nor, again, could the Governor of Hong Kong demand from
the Chinese Commissioner a Chinese who was wanted for trial
for an offence committed in the colony and had fled to the
country of his allegiance. 'According to International law,
unless it be otherwise stipulated by Treaty, the Government
of one Country is not bound to give up any of its subjects.'
So that Bonham's request 'could rest only upon grounds of
general comity, and could not be founded upon any ground of
right'[2]. A British naval officer had by force released a British
subject from jail in Macao. Palmerston at once disavowed this
action and instructed Bonham to consider with the Portuguese
authorities what compensation was due.[3] The British Government objected emphatically to the smuggling practised by the
foreign merchants. 'It is an evasion of Treaty engagements,
a fraud upon and a loss to the Chinese government, an injury
to the honest trader and a discredit to European commerce,
and Her Majesty's Government consider that it would be very
desirable to put a stop to it.' Bonham ought to address a
representation to the Government of Peking, giving facts to
prove that the Chinese local authorities connived at such
illicit practices. British consuls were bound by treaty to see
that the duties legally chargeable were duly paid by British
subjects, but they would be powerless to fulfil that obligation
'if the local Authorities of the Chinese government encourage
the foreign traders to evade payment of the full amount'.[4]
When Consul Alcock at Shanghai fined a British smuggler,
Palmerston agreed that he had acted rightly. The permanent
officials in the Foreign Office thought that in view of the fact
that other Western Governments had no such treaty obligations
and were doing nothing—unlike Alcock in this case of the *Lady
Mary Wood*—to coerce their subjects or citizens into paying
their lawful duties, British merchants were being placed at a
disadvantage. They were prepared to use the laxity of the

[1] Palmerston to Bonham, 18 Jan. 1850 (F.O. 17/164).
[2] Palmerston to Bonham, 24 Jan. 1850 (F.O. 17/164).
[3] Palmerston to Bonham, 1 Aug. 1850 (F.O. 17/164).
[4] Palmerston to Bonham, 11 Sept. 1850 (F.O. 17/164).

Chinese officials as an adequate reason for absolving the British consuls from this unpopular duty. Palmerston, however, intent on observing the law, turned down a draft dispatch which instructed the consuls in future to take no part in securing the payment of duties, and merely stated that 'Her Majesty's Government will *have to consider whether they will not* be obliged to cease to take any part in regard to these matters in so far as the agency of H.M. consuls is concerned'[1]. By May of the following year Palmerston, while still maintaining that the British Government would prefer a properly regulated system of customs duties, observed that neither the American nor the French Treaties stipulated for any consular control with a view to securing the Chinese Government their customs duties. On the principle, admitted in the Supplementary Treaty, of the British Government acquiring any rights conceded to other Powers, he thought he could justify a suspension of such consular activities by Treaty stipulation, and added, 'we can fairly claim it on the ground of gross negligence of the Chinese authorities'. A system proposed by the British Government, and accepted by the Chinese, which had sought to interpose the consuls between the merchants and the Chinese authorities as a means of avoiding disputes, thus lapsed. It is abundantly clear that the British Government and Lord Palmerston would have preferred the proper enforcement of this system. It was not their fault that it was not maintained; on grounds of law and of equity the Foreign Secretary thought himself justified in consenting to its abrogation in order to remove an unfair discrimination which put honest traders at a disadvantage, and to relieve British merchants of a disability under which their American rivals had never laboured.[2] Characteristically enough the Commissioner Seu, in reply to a communication from Bonham stating the grounds on which the British Government had decided to withhold for the future all interference by British Consuls for the protection of the Chinese revenue, treated the whole matter very lightly.[3]

If Palmerston was insistent with the Chinese that 'Her Majesty's Government cannot permit the Treaty to be broken'[4],

---

[1] Palmerston to Bonham, 27 Nov. 1850 (F.O. 17/164).
[2] Palmerston to Bonham, 24 May 1851 (F.O. 17/174).
[3] Bonham to Palmerston, 22 July 1851 (F.O. 17/178).
[4] Palmerston to Bonham, 25 Mar. 1850 (F.O. 17/164).

he was at least consistent. There was nothing dearer to the hearts of the mercantile community than the acquisition of further ports where trade might lawfully be carried on. The ports of Ningpo and Foochow had proved, at least by 1849, of very little use for trading purposes.[1] The British Government thought that it might be advisable to exchange them for others better situated, and Bonham agreed that it would be of material benefit to trade to have consular stations established at Hangchow and Soochow, 'the great centres of consumption'. 'What we now require is a footing inland, either on the Banks of the Yangtze Kiang or upon the Grand Canal, or, if practicable, upon both.' Chin-kiang, at the crossing of the Yangtse and the Canal, was moreover a place of the greatest political importance. If the British Government could not get access to Peking, an establishment at Nanking or Chin-kiang would prevent an 'entire dependence on the whims and caprices of an Imperial Commissioner stationed at Canton'. But Bonham thought that 'to gain the ends in view all attempts at negotiation with the Imperial Commissioner at Canton would be a pure waste of time', for it would require at least a naval demonstration before Chin-kiang to induce the Chinese to listen, much less to agree, to such proposals. The revision of the Treaty of Nanking, due in 1854, would provide the opportunity for such amendments, or possibly the accession to the Dragon Throne of the new Emperor, who could not be more hostile than his predecessor, might prove a suitable occasion for seeking a more extensive intercourse.[2] Palmerston agreed with Bonham that British trade and influence would be advanced if consular ports were established at Soochow, Hangchow, and Chin-kiang,

'but it appears to Her Majesty's Government that any proposal to this effect should be made diplomatically and should not be accompanied by a naval demonstration. Such a demonstration might be proper for the purpose of supporting a demand for redress for a breach of Treaty, but would not be proper in support of an application for that which Her Majesty's Government do not demand as a right, and which the Chinese Government is at liberty to withhold without giving thereby to this country any just cause of war.'[3]

All the indications, however, suggested to Palmerston that 'the Time is fast coming when we shall be obliged to strike another

[1] Bonham to Palmerston, 24 Dec. 1849 (F.O. 17/159).
[2] Bonham to Palmerston, 15 Apr. 1850 (F.O. 17/166).
[3] Palmerston to Bonham, 3 Sept. 1850 (F.O. 17/164).

Blow in China. . . . These half-civilized Governments such as those of China Portugal Spanish America all require a Dressing every eight or Ten years to keep them in order. Their Minds are too shallow to receive an Impression that will last longer than some such Period and warning is of little use. They care little for words and they must not only see the Stick but actually feel it on their Shoulders before they yield to that only argument which to them brings conviction the argumentum Baculinum.'[1]

But the question of the exchange of ports was not one which could be properly solved by such an argument. Bonham was therefore instructed to apply to the Government of Peking and not to the Commissioner in Canton for the exchange, and to offer to go up to the capital for detailed discussion if the Emperor should desire. The grounds of the application would be that the Treaty of Nanking had envisaged Ningpo and Foochow as centres of considerable trade and 'that this expectation has been disappointed and that, therefore, the intention with which the two Governments concluded the Treaty of Nanking has been defeated, that intention having been to increase the commercial intercourse between England and China'. Bonham was further to propose that British subjects should be allowed to travel in the interior for business or health, provided they were in possession of passports issued by the Consul and countersigned by Chinese authority. Generally speaking the aim should be to encourage a freer ingress for British goods, but, however grievous the imposition of internal duties might be, 'we cannot claim for British goods treatment not given to Chinese goods'. Thirdly, Bonham was instructed to point out that the arrangement for the settlement of British subjects at the ports had been systematically violated at Canton.[2] The Manchester Chamber of Commerce had been urging the British Government to secure for their members liberty of trade in the interior, and the establishment of a mission in Peking,[3] while the Canton Chamber of Commerce hoped for Tientsin in exchange for Ningpo.[4] In April 1851 Bonham, realizing that a direct appeal to Peking would be useless, as the new Emperor had degraded Muhchangah and Keying for alleged adherence to anti-Chinese principles and favourable leanings to foreigners,[5]

[1] Palmerston, autograph note, 29 Sept. 1850 (F.O. 17/173).
[2] Palmerston to Bonham, 3 Sept. 1850 (F.O. 17/164).
[3] Palmerston to Bonham, 5 July 1850 (F.O. 17/164).
[4] Palmerston to Bonham, 16 July 1850 (F.O. 17/164).
[5] Bonham to Palmerston, 23 Jan. 1851 (F.O. 17/175).

requested the Commissioner to address a memorial to the Throne on the subject of the exchange of Foochow and Ningpo.[1] Seu, however, refused to consider such an exchange, and declared 'we ought on both sides to maintain the established boundaries'[2].

Meanwhile, Seu was facing more troublesome antagonists than the Western foreigners. After a few months' quiescence banditry had again become very active. By January 1851 Kwangsi was devastated with the scourge and the Provincial Governor had been dismissed. In February Bonham thought the movement of no political significance;[3] in May, however, it was believed that the 'Prime Minister' was travelling south to suppress the Kwang rebels.[4] Next month Seu himself was deprived of three grades on account of local disturbances, and the gravity of the situation began to be more clearly seen.[5] Yeh, the Governor of Kwantung, was left as Trade Commissioner, while his chief was attempting to bridle the disaffected. By the autumn things were no more settled, and the rebellion was being, for the first time, attributed to the propagation of 'strange doctrines'[6]. Seu was away from Canton all winter.[7] Bowring characterized the disturbance in Kwantung as 'rather predatory than political movements' and informed the Foreign Office that 'the character, habits and institutions of the Chinese people have so little analogy with what exists elsewhere that the most erroneous notions generally prevail as to the causes and consequences of social agitations in these vast Dominions'[8]. But whatever the character of the trouble, it was on a considerable scale, and cost the Imperial Treasury one and a half millions Taels a month.[9]

Such was the state of affairs when at the beginning of the new year Palmerston's dispatch of October 1851 arrived in Hong Kong. Both Alcock and Bonham concurred in the view that the most effective time to blockade the junction of the Grand

[1] Bonham to Palmerston, 22 Apr. 1851 (F.O. 17/177); 21 May 1851 (F.O. 17/177).
[2] Bonham to Palmerston, 27 Jan. 1851 (F.O. 17/175).
[3] Bonham to Palmerston, 27 Feb. 1851 (F.O. 17/175).
[4] Bonham to Palmerston, 23 May 1851 (F.O. 17/177).
[5] Bonham to Palmerston, 21 June 1851 (F.O. 17/178).
[6] Bonham to Palmerston, 29 Sept. 1851 (F.O. 17/180).
[7] Bonham to Palmerston, 29 Mar. 1852 (F.O. 17/188).
[8] Bowring to Granville, 23 Apr. 1852 (F.O. 17/188).
[9] Bowring to Malmesbury, 22 June 1852 (F.O. 17/190).

Canal and the Yangtse would be March or April at the latest. But Bonham thought that other points would have to be blockaded as well, and it was to be remembered that in the grain depots of Peking and Tung-chow near the capital a three years' supply was kept in reserve. Bonham too was of opinion that success at court in obtaining an order to the Commissioner for the opening of the city of Canton to foreigners would be ineffective, for Seu's prolonged absence from the city on his campaign against the bandits had greatly reduced his power and influence over the Cantonese.[1] Though Alcock thought that the rebellion in Kwangsi was a strong reason for acting at once, Bonham was unwilling 'to see any attempt at coercion commence with a less naval force than is now at the disposal of the Naval Commander-in-chief in China and India con-jointly'[2]. In fact, as he told the new French Minister, de Bourboulon, with great frankness at the end of 1851, his was a pacific policy. Though there might be some substance in the complaints against China, British commerce there was bringing in a revenue of three million pounds to India and six to Great Britain, and he had no intention of disturbing such a valuable asset. 'If the Chinese do not love us,' Bonham said, 'it must be confessed that they have hardly reason to do so, and if they often oppose us by duplicity and bad faith, is not that the natural defence of the weak?'[3] To this rational appreciation of the situation his personal predilections came perhaps as an unconscious support. To the Procureur of Hong Kong Bonham appeared 'un bon vivant qui fait tranquillement ses affaires sans trop faire parler de lui'[4].

3. *Bowring's Début*

At the end of March 1852 Bonham sailed from Hong Kong on home leave. His temporary successor, Bowring, the Canton Consul, was, as we have seen, a very different man. For long enough Bonham had found Bowring's *'activité dévorante' 'un peu fatigante'* and he had in consequence been in very cold relations with his subordinate.[5] Early in their association Bowring had

---

[1] Bonham to Palmerston, 26 Jan. 1852 (F.O. 17/187).
[2] Bonham to Palmerston, 20 Feb. 1852 (F.O. 17/187).
[3] De Bourboulon to Min. Aff. Étr., 28 Dec. 1852 (Chine 11).
[4] Libois to Legrenée, 19 Mar. 1850 (M.E., vol. 325, f. 297).
[5] Forth-Rouen to Min. Aff. Étr., 20 July 1849 (Chine 7).

shown himself capable of rapid and decisive action. The Chinese had seized and imprisoned an Englishman for a debt owing to a native. Upon failing to receive a reply to his demand for the instant release of his compatriot, the Consul had ordered marines on shore and duly rescued the Englishman. On another occasion Chinese officers had burst into an Englishman's house in search of contraband which was in fact American property. Though Bowring received no answer to his complaint of the violation of the house, he refused to hand over to the Chinese the comprador who was implicated in the affair. To Forth-Rouen his conduct on this occasion seemed very reasonable, but 'il paraît que M. Bonham n'en a pas jugé ainsi'[1].

Bowring, who had been a leading member of the Peace Society when in the House of Commons, had hoped that his residence in Canton might have brought about a complete change in Anglo-Chinese relations. He had flattered himself that he could turn the hostility of the Chinese into an abiding friendship. But the early refusal of Seu to receive him caused him to regret having left London. 'Cependant son cœur répugne à une guerre contre la Chine', reported Forth-Rouen in cipher to his Government in the early summer of 1849. 'He would like, before having recourse to this extremity, to try a *démarche* in common with the foreign representatives in China to invite the Imperial Commissioner to act in accordance with the treaty. He expects a very great result would be produced by such a demonstration, the idea of which he has certainly suggested to his Government. I do not, however, think', added the French Minister, 'that it will be possible to establish a perfect understanding between them. Without a shadow of doubt the Americans will refuse to come in, and if they were to, it would only be with very bad grace.'[2]

To the replies of Bonham and Alcock to Palmerston's inquiry regarding the best methods which should be employed in order to bring pressure to bear upon the Chinese Government, Bowring added his views in a private letter to his patron, which Palmerston communicated to the Foreign Office from which, after having arranged for Bowring to relieve Bonham temporarily while Sir George came home on leave, he had been recently dismissed by Lord John Russell. It was written from

[1] Forth-Rouen to Min. Aff. Étr., 26 Aug. 1849 (Chine 7).
[2] Forth-Rouen to Min. Aff. Étr., 18 May 1849 (Chine 6).

Ceylon, where the Canton Consul was on holiday. He had had a long discussion with Sir Henry Pottinger in Madras. Bowring was

'pleased to find that in the opinions I had formed on China questions and which I have so often intruded on your lordship, he completely concurred. He thinks that every encroachment on the Treaties, every attempt to evade or delay an engagement, should be promptly and peremptorily resisted; he believes that such resistance would not lead to a rupture, but that a system of concession and forbearance will certainly bring about the very disasters it seeks to prevent, and that war not peace will be the result of seeming indifference and real inaction.'[1]

The easy-going Bonham had served under Palmerston: now the more active Bowring was to receive instructions from Granville which caused him considerable anxiety. To begin with, his powers were to be curtailed: his legislative authority over British subjects was held in suspense, and he was not allowed to sign any treaty without previous reference to the Foreign Office. He read 'with the utmost anxiety and attention' that paragraph of his Lordship's dispatch which laid down the course of policy which he was to pursue in China.

'While I am called upon "to watch over and to insist upon a performance by the Chinese authorities of the engagements which exist between the two countries", I am at the same time "to avoid all irritating discussions",—to push no "arguments or doubtful points so as to fetter the free action of Her Majesty's Government", to resort to no measures of force without reference home, except in the extreme case of such measures being necessary to repel aggression or to protect the lives and properties of British subjects.'[2]

Such instructions must have been galling to one who had just written to Palmerston from Ceylon that 'the sense of being in a position where I can do so little, and where so much might be done, oppresses me like a nightmare' and who had hoped to have been allowed home 'to tell my tale'[1]. Two years before, Forth-Rouen had noted that the former parliamentary defender of China 'aurait déjà modifié sa manière de voir, et écrivait que son gouvernement doit prononcer sur le *casus belli* qui est

---

[1] Bowring to Palmerston, Ceylon, 15 Jan. 1852 (F.O. 17/187).
[2] Granville to Bowring, 19 Jan. 1852 (F.O. 17/186); Bowring to Granville, 19 Apr. 1852 (F.O. 17/188).

arrivé'[1]. It was but to be expected that Bowring would submit to the British Government

'a few observations on the policy of the Chinese Government and respectfully suggest a course of action by which . . . the honour and influence of my country may be best maintained—the security and extension of commerce best provided for—and the permanent interests of peace best promoted'.

Though the Pottinger treaties had inflicted a deep wound upon the pride, they had by no means altered the policy of the Chinese Government. The British had sought in them the establishment and gradual expansion of friendly commercial relations, and offered in return honourable and lucrative commerce to the Chinese. But this object had never met with the concurrence of the Chinese authorities. 'Their purpose is now, as it ever was—not to invite but to impede and resist the access of foreigners. This policy is impressed upon all the High Officers of the Empire, associated however with the most stringent commands to avoid collisions.' Seu's popularity at court and in the country was in Bowring's judgement attributable to the success he had won in repelling the advances of foreigners while at the same time preserving the peace. The truth was that the objects of the British and Chinese Governments were diametrically opposed, except that both Governments earnestly desired to avoid all hostile acts. 'Our hesitation—our delay—our caution—are misunderstood and often render the settlement of questions and the redress of grievances difficult.' Bowring was firmly convinced that exclusion from Canton rendered it impossible to protect, let alone increase, British commercial interests. For the British Plenipotentiary to be able to communicate personally with the eight Mandarins in Canton who could correspond directly with the Emperor, would materially help 'to remove that ignorance as to the purposes of Foreigners which is the mainspring of the national policy'. As it was, the aims of British policy could always be kept back from the Emperor at the sole desire and discretion of the Imperial Commissioner. Entrance into Canton would have been gained before without the use of force 'had it not unfortunately happened that Howqua (whose informant was probably the American consul) was enabled to assure the Imperial Commissioner that he might safely resist'. The result had been the

[1] Forth-Rouen to Min. Aff. Étr., 21 Apr. 1849 (Chine 6).

erection of six triumphal granite arches to record the fact that the wisdom and the patriotism of the Imperial Commissioner had compelled us to surrender our claims—the assertion of which had been characterized by Yeh as 'a seditious endeavour'.

Bowring thought that the time had now come to press the British claims to enter the city. Popular passions had died down, placards and public meetings had ceased to appear; hatred and distrust of foreigners had given place to more friendly and habitual intercourse. He thought too that he was specially qualified for the task. During his three years' residence in the factories he had become well acquainted with the people. His administration of justice had inspired such confidence that he had been asked to decide cases arising among Chinese. He had walked twenty or thirty miles in the environs of the city without any feeling of anxiety or meeting with incivility, had attended military parades, open-air theatres, and religious, civil, and social ceremonies. He accordingly notified the Imperial Commissioner of his appointment as Bonham's deputy and asked for a reception, which, however, he was determined to decline unless it were to take place in the official Yamen.[1]

Ten days later he formally asked the Home Government permission to insist on an entry into the city. He wanted authority to tell Seu that he wished to go as a friend and a guest, but to point out that 'I am quite prepared if he aver his inability to protect me to surround myself with such military force as is needful for my safety'. If he could hold such language he was convinced that the Chinese authorities would show their 'anxiety to calm the popular passions'[2]. It was doubtless true, as Bowring suggested, that scarcely any Chinese of rank or position considered the English 'as other than powerful sea marauders, too strong to be resisted but to be dealt with as marauders, should the opportunity ever present itself of so dealing with us in safety. The Chinese believe as they have been taught, as all their literature teaches them—and they act accordingly.' He was persuaded that 'nothing but intercourse —habitual intercourse—social relations gradually enlightening —intellectual, moral, and scientific superiority perpetually pressing upon the Chinese mind—will shake the prejudices

---

[1] Granville to Bowring, 19 Jan. 1852 (F.O. 17/186); Bowring to Granville, 19 Apr. 1852 (F.O. 17/188).
[2] Bowring to Granville, 29 Apr. 1852 (F.O. 17/188).

which the Chinese have been accumulating from generation to generation'. This was the fundamental reason why Bowring despaired of the existing diplomatic machinery. It was abundantly clear to him, of whom Pottinger had said,[1] 'no official in China had ever so well succeeded' as had Bowring 'in winning the good opinions and confidence of the Chinese', that 'China must be influenced from China'. The British representative stationed at Hong Kong could hardly be placed diplomatically in a more disadvantageous position, for that Colony 'represented separation—isolation—non-intercourse, and nothing more'[2].

To his request for an interview with Seu Bowring received a reply that it was impossible to arrange one at that time as the High Commissioner was out of the city, engaged in dealing with the rebels in south-west Kwantung.[3] At the beginning of June 1852 it was officially announced that Pih-Kwei had been appointed Commissioner for Foreign Affairs. Bowring, still waiting for an answer from London to his earlier dispatches, hoped to be allowed to call upon him with authority to enforce his request if necessary. This had, however, been expressly forbidden him,[4] and it was the intention of the new Derby Administration that Bowring should adhere strictly to the instructions given him by Granville. He was to abstain from mooting the question of the right of British subjects to enter the city, and was himself not to be received in any other way than had been his predecessors.[5] In fact, it were better that he should not enter into further correspondence with the Chinese authorities relative to his reception, for Sir George Bonham would take up again the duties of Plenipotentiary on his expected return at the end of the year, and the British Government remained of the opinion that there was no solid advantage to be gained by the user of the right to enter the city comparable to the disadvantages and dangers which would attend a possible collision.[6] Bowring could but give it as his opinion and that of Alcock, who feared that relations at Shanghai might become as distant as those at Canton, that it was safer and wiser to resist promptly

[1] Bowring to Palmerston, Ceylon, 15 Jan. 1852 (F.O. 17/187).
[2] Bowring to Granville, 3 May 1852 (F.O. 17/188).
[3] Bowring to Granville, 29 Apr. 1852 (F.O. 17/188).
[4] Bowring to Malmesbury, 7 June 1852 (F.O. 17/190).
[5] Malmesbury to Bowring, 21 June 1852 (F.O. 17/186).
[6] Malmesbury to Bowring, 21 July 1852 (F.O. 17/186).

every infraction of the treaties than to temporize or in any way seem to give a triumph to the unfriendly and repulsive policy of the Mandarins. With deference he ventured to think that a change of policy was most desirable 'in order to prevent future disasters—to secure our present position and to give our Merchants those fair chances for the extension of their commercial relations in these vast unexplored and undeveloped Regions'[1]. Nor was he alone in advocating a more active policy. From 1848 the French, represented by a Minister resident in Macao, had obtained from the Mandarins on occasion concessions and redress for their Catholic missionaries. But since the English had several times drawn back before Chinese threats, the French agents had been treated in a manner *assez insultante*. The Procureur, a friend of Bowring, was of opinion that 'pour remonter l'influence européenne il faudrait maintenant en venir aux faits et donner une leçon au Céleste Empire. Mais à tort ou à raison on ne le fera probablement pas. Nos Français n'y pensent pas et les Anglais ne le veulent pas non plus.'[2] The Procureur had correctly gauged the situation. The French Foreign Office, in commenting upon the difficulties of their agents in China had ascribed them to 'the inevitable consequence of the weak, evasive attitude of the English', and indicated the line of conduct to be followed by the representatives of France.

'Only if the English forsook their present policy and returned to the hostile attitude of the days of the Hong Kong expedition, could the French try means of intimidation. So long as they remain unmoved in face of the outrages which the Chinese make them swallow, threats on our part not effectively followed up, or a demonstration with insufficient force, will only make our bad position worse and increase the insolence of the Chinese.'[3]

If Bowring's hands were to be tied for the moment, four years later as Governor and Plenipotentiary he was to put into effect, with the approval of his Government, his forward policy; a policy which was to lead Lord Elgin to the capital of China.

[1] Bowring to Malmesbury, 26 Aug. 1852 (F.O. 17/192).
[2] Libois to Directeurs, 28 Sept. 1851 (M.E., vol. 314, f. 844).
[3] Instructions, 1851 (Chine 11).

IV

THE PERIOD OF STRAIN, 1852–6

A. THE REBELLIONS AND THEIR CONSEQUENCES, 1852–6

THE interest of the four years from the summer of 1852 lies in the development of the internal difficulties of China which caused great embarrassment to the Powers, and the gradual drawing together of the Governments of London, Paris, and Washington, which prepared the way for the second great series of treaties negotiated in 1858 and finally ratified in 1860. In this movement Great Britain was no longer alone in arms, as she had been from 1839 to 1842, for the France of the Second Empire, associated with her in the Crimean War, was to join her military forces with those of the British, while the United States and Russia added their diplomatic influence.

1. *First Impressions*

The Chinese, we have seen, were a rebellious people. Secret societies with political aims had persisted since the collapse of the Ming dynasty, but had not proved serious until after the abdication of the great Emperor Kienlung at the end of the eighteenth century. From that time disturbances had been endemic in every part of the country, and particularly in the mountainous district on the borders of Kwangsi, Kwantung, and Hunan Provinces. Though the disquiet had given the local officials a great deal of anxiety, and had cost no little effort to quell, no leader arose to discipline and weld together the discontented elements before the appearance of Hung Siu-tsuee. 'A soured and disappointed member of the learned proletariat', rejected in the examinations, this man, though never baptized, had been in touch with Christian teachings through an American Protestant missionary in Canton. Having formed an enthusiastic and formidable band of followers, in 1850 he proclaimed himself the Third Person of the Trinity, the 'Taiping Wang', or Heavenly Younger Brother. With these claims to divinity he directly challenged the position of the Son of Heaven, and bid for the Imperial Throne of Peking.

Having consolidated their position on the borders of Kwangsi and Kwantung in the winter of 1851–2, the Taipings spread north to Changsha in the autumn of the latter year, straddled the Yangtse at Hankow by mid-winter, and controlled the river from that point eastwards to the former imperial capital of Nanking, which fell to the rebels in March 1853. From thence a thrust was made northwards which reached the environs of Tientsin during the winter of 1853–4. It was this rebellion which forced Seu to hand over the offices of Viceroy and Imperial Commissioner to Yeh in September 1852,[1] and caused the downfall of the chief minister Sae Shangah.[2] By January 1853 the Chinese authorities were reported as having spent six million sterling and to be in straits for money.[3] In February the appointment of Keshen as chief minister was announced at the same time as the news of Seu's degradation was confirmed.[4] On his belated return to China in February 1853 just as the situation was beginning to affect foreign interests, Bonham had to consider what attitude to adopt if the Chinese Government asked for the help of British warships in the defence of Nanking. He realized that his first duty in that region would be the defence of his own countrymen at Shanghai,[5] but if he could thereby gain advantages for British commerce such a proposal might be entertained.[6] When Bonham arrived in the northern port he came to the conclusion that foreign aid to the Imperialist forces might only prolong the struggle. He was deeply impressed by the material and psychological results of the fall of Nanking and of Chin-kiang which soon followed, for the Grand Canal could now be blocked by the rebels and the fall of the southern capital was a great blow to the prestige of the Manchu dynasty.[7] While it was the prevailing opinion amongst the Chinese and foreigners of Shanghai, in which Bonham concurred, that the insurgents would eventually succeed, foreign interests seemed adequately protected by the presence of three British warships and one each from the French and American navies.

It was of importance to British interests for Bonham to form some judgement on the attitude of the Taipings of Nanking towards

[1] Bowring to Malmesbury, 27 Sept. 1852 (F.O. 17/192).
[2] Bowring to Malmesbury, 27 Dec. 1852 (F.O. 17/194).
[3] Bowring to Malmesbury, 27 Jan. 1853 (F.O. 17/199).
[4] Bowring to Malmesbury, 5 Feb. 1853 (F.O. 17/199).
[5] Bonham to Malmesbury, 10 Mar. 1853 (F.O. 17/200).
[6] Bonham to Malmesbury, 11 Mar. 1853 (F.O. 17/200).
[7] Bonham to Russell, 28 Mar. 1853 (F.O. 17/200).

foreigners. The interpreter Meadows, sent beyond Soochow to gather information, brought back news of the supposedly high moral standard of the insurgents. He learnt that they were 'puritanical and even fanatic. The whole army pray regularly before meals. They punish rape, adultery and opium-smoking with death—Tobacco smoking with the Bamboo.' Bonham himself determined to go to Nanking in H.M.S. *Hermes* to find out for himself the rebels' attitude towards foreigners.[1] Bonham managed to inform the leaders that there were great British interests at Shanghai, interference with which he would resent, but that he meant to preserve neutrality. As the weeks went on it seemed that the Taipings were unlikely to make the once threatened advance to Hangchow, taking Soochow and Shanghai on their way.[2] The attitude of the other two Treaty Powers towards the insurgents was distinctly less favourable than was Bonham's during the summer of 1853. It was his opinion that 'more political and commercial advantages were likely to be obtained from the insurrectionists than we shall ever obtain from the Imperialists'. On the other hand, Marshall, the American envoy, was visiting Eleang, the Viceroy of the Two Kiangs, and de Bourboulon 'did not disguise from me that he considered the views of the French government were, to a certain extent, favourable to the cause of the Imperialists', and though he thought, with Bonham, that the struggle would be a long one, added that he also thought that the British Government would be obliged on account of the commercial paralysis existing at Shanghai to intervene on the side of the authorities.[3] To Bonham the time was not yet ripe for active interference on either side. His personal position probably influenced his natural inclination to let things take their course; for, possessing a considerable fortune and having been made a baronet while recently on leave after more than thirty years' service in India and China, he had hoped to have been dispensed from returning to the Far East. He was due to retire from the service in the following spring, and the last thing he wanted was the outbreak of any disturbance which might cause a postponement of his retirement.[4]

---

[1] Bonham to Clarendon, 22 Apr. 1853 (F.O. 17/200).
[2] Bonham to Clarendon, 7 May 1853 (F.O. 17/201); 6 July 1853 (F.O. 17/203).
[3] Bonham to Clarendon, 4 Aug. 1853 (F.O. 17/204).
[4] de Bourboulon to Min. Aff. Étr., 5 Aug. 1853 (Chine 14).

2. *Shanghai Customs*

In September 1853 the walled city of Shanghai was seized by another force of rebels, the 'Small Swords Society'. War of a sort now raged between the Imperialist forces and the rebels in the city, and brought trouble close to the foreign settlements. The situation gave rise to one repercussion of enduring importance.[1] The Imperial authorities evacuated the custom-house, but by November the Taoutai established, close to the anchorage of the foreign vessels, another temporary office on a war junk which was moored down stream from the rebels. Though indeed the import trade was at a standstill in November, tea and silk exports were lively.[2] The British Consul took bonds for the duties payable from the merchants of his nation, and the disposal of this question caused much anxiety to the Foreign Office. Bowring, who relieved Bonham in April 1854, suggested sending the bonds home in compensation for the extra tea duty levied illegally at Canton.[3] The British Government agreed with the merchants that as the Chinese Government had *de facto* broken down no duties could properly be levied on a trade which was wholly unprotected.[4] Payment was therefore for the moment to be suspended. This meant that some at least of the British community who had charged the duties to their constituents would escape payment of them.[5] The Americans made an arrangement with the Taoutai to pay a proportion of the value of the bonds, but the Foreign Secretary strongly disapproved of Bowring's promise that Her Majesty's Government would make good bonds which were themselves legally invalid.[6] Similarly, he instructed Bowring to withdraw a promise that the British Government would set off the amount claimed by the Shanghai customs against the extra duty of $\frac{1}{2}$ a farthing a pound levied on tea at Canton. The law officers of the Crown had ruled that no duties were payable to the Chinese Government at Shanghai in respect of the period from the

---

[1] For exhaustive treatment of the Customs problems in the early days of Foreign Inspectorate see J. K. Fairbank, *Nankai Social and Economic Quarterly*, vol. ix, no. 1, and *Chinese Social and Political Science Review*, vol. xviii, no. 4, and vol. xix, nos. 1 and 4.

[2] Bonham to Clarendon, 10 Nov. 1853 (F.O. 17/205).

[3] Bowring to Clarendon, 15 Apr. 1854 (F.O. 17/213).

[4] Clarendon to Bonham, 4 Oct. 1853 (F.O. 17/198).

[5] Bowring to Hammond, 18 May 1854 (F.O. 17/213).

[6] Clarendon to Bowring, 9 Nov. 1854 (F.O. 17/211).

7th September 1853 to the 9th February 1854.[1] If the Chinese authorities who regarded the non-payment of the duties as typical of the 'fraudulent conduct of Western Barbarian nations' threatened to stop the trade at Shanghai until these back duties were paid, Bowring was to give the reasons of the law officers' opinion—that the custom-house was closed, and any protection of foreign trade had ceased *de facto*,[2]—and to urge that to put an embargo on the trade of the port would be a foolish action owing to the great efficiency of the customs service as it existed in Shanghai already by 1855.

This greater efficiency was the permanent result of the civil war and disturbance at the great northern port. On the 29th June 1854 an agreement was drawn up between the Taoutai, then in the British settlement, and the consuls of the three Treaty Powers whereby each of these nations furnished an officer to assist the Chinese superintendent of customs. Wade, whose resignation of the office of Vice-Consul was accepted by Clarendon,[3] was chosen as the British member, and as he alone had any knowledge of the Chinese language the actual control of the new machinery fell into his hands. Consul Alcock was able to report in the new year of 1855 on the smooth working of the new custom-house scheme, whereby the ruinous competition of unscrupulous with honourable merchants no longer existed and one million taels had been collected from exports alone during the first six months of its existence.[4] Wade was succeeded in January 1855 by Lay.[5] The British Government was pleased with the success of the new system, but though anxious that the Chinese Government should receive its proper dues, it was afraid that if the new rigorous system prevailed at Shanghai alone the trade of that port might be destroyed.[6] Bowring was able to assure the Foreign Secretary that trade was not leaving Shanghai and that the respectable merchants were thoroughly satisfied with the admirable conduct of the new administration.[7] Indeed, the teas exported thence in the 1854/5 season exceeded in amount those of the previous year by more than 20 million

[1] Clarendon to Bowring, 24 Jan. 1855 (F.O. 17/224).
[2] Clarendon to Bowring, 9 Apr. 1855 (F.O. 17/224).
[3] Clarendon to Bowring, 14 Oct. 1854 (F.O. 17/211).
[4] Bowring to Clarendon, 29 Jan. 1855 (F.O. 17/227).
[5] Bowring to Clarendon, 31 Jan. 1855 (F.O. 17/227).
[6] Clarendon to Bowring, 29 Jan. 1855 (F.O. 17/224)..
[7] Bowring to Clarendon, 15 May 1855 (F.O. 17/230).

pounds.[1] Clarendon had another reason for hoping that the same system would be extended with similar advantages to all other ports in China, for in this way the Chinese Government was likely to become more reconciled to foreign trade while foreigners could have no just grounds of complaint.

'Still it is very essential both as regards the Chinese government and the foreign trader that the collection of the Chinese Revenues and the nomination of the officers appointed to collect it, should be exempt from any avowed interference on the part of foreign nations; and that the Foreign Inspectors should be to all intents and purposes Chinese officers, and not nominees and delegates of foreign countries.'

The independence of this service was thus early recognized by the British Government: the officers were to be, as in fact they became, servants of the Chinese authorities, they had no right to return to the service of the British Crown, and the British Government refused to recognize any responsibility for their actions or omissions.[2]

In spite of the fact that the Inspectorate system at Shanghai had the great advantage of improving navigation through the provision of buoys,[3] the British Government became more and more doubtful of its value when it was not extended to other ports. Clarendon asked whether it had received Imperial sanction: if it had not, then its continuance would seem to depend upon local caprice; if it had, how was it that local officers elsewhere objected to its establishment in their ports? Bowring was instructed to inform the High Commissioner that it was desirable to set up the system everywhere, but that his Government could not continue to recognize an 'unequal system'. There was, moreover, a danger to British and Indian interests if the foreign inspectors enforced the prohibition of the opium trade. 'It would seem impossible to deny their authority altogether to put a stop to the Trade in opium', and if such were to be the result, the efforts of Her Majesty's Government to obtain the consent of the Chinese to the legalization of the opium trade would be rendered superfluous.[4]

Throughout 1856 Bowring was reporting favourably on the

[1] Bowring to Clarendon, 6 July 1855 (F.O. 17/231).
[2] Clarendon to Bowring 'seen by Ld Palmn', 8 Sept. 1855 (F.O. 17/225).
[3] Bowring to Clarendon, 12 Nov. 1855 (F.O. 17/234).
[4] Clarendon to Bowring, 2 Jan. 1856 (F.O. 17/242).

economic position of Shanghai in spite of forebodings that the stricter enforcement of duties would drive trade from the port.[1] In 1855 British exports increased by 75 per cent. and imports by 200 per cent., compared with the previous year,[2] while clearances had increased from 46½ to 77 thousand tons.[3] Through the influence of the inspectors reductions were made in the duties on silk piece goods, coarse silk, dyed cotton hand-kerchiefs,[4] and on cotton chintzes.[5] The most substantial mer-cantile houses, with the exception of Dent & Co., thought the new order a great advantage,[6] though there might be some temporary disadvantage to the small men. Bowring hoped that at Foochow the new system might come into operation,[7] for the Mandarins there had been instructed to prevent customs frauds, which could only be stamped out with foreign co-operation. Even if it were not universally established, and at Canton at least it seemed that the only course would be connivance at 'licensed fraudulent competition', he regarded the possibility of its abolition at Shanghai as 'one of the greatest disasters with which our real and permanent interests in China could be visited'[8]. Great was his disappointment, therefore, when in the new year of 1857 he learnt that the Board of Trade and the British Government had reached the conclusion that the time had come to abolish the Foreign Inspectorate at Shanghai unless it was immediately extended to the other ports.[9] Had the troubles and preoccupations of the *Arrow* affair not prevented action on these instructions, China might not now possess the fine service which is a tribute to the capacity of men loyally to serve States other than their own. As it was, de Bourboulon, the French Minister, agreed with Bowring that at a time of such crisis the system established at Shanghai could not be abolished.[10] It remained, as we shall see, for Lord Elgin to arrange for the Foreign Inspectorate to be set up in all Treaty Ports.

[1] Bowring to Clarendon, 7 Feb. 1856 (F.O. 17/245).
[2] Bowring to Clarendon, 12 Apr. 1856 (F.O. 17/246).
[3] Bowring to Clarendon, 6 May 1856 (F.O. 17/247).
[4] Bowring to Clarendon, 13 Mar. 1856 (F.O. 17/246).
[5] Bowring to Clarendon, 17 Apr. 1856 (F.O. 17/246).
[6] Bowring to Clarendon, 4 Dec. 1855 (F.O. 17/235); 6 May 1856 (F.O. 17/247).
[7] Bowring to Clarendon, 9 May 1856 (F.O. 17/247).
[8] Bowring to Clarendon, 26 May 1856 (F.O. 17/247).
[9] Clarendon to Bowring, 9 Dec. 1856 (F.O. 17/243).
[10] Bowring to Clarendon, 27 Feb. 1857 (F.O. 17/264).

3. *Shanghai Municipality*

The disturbed conditions which gave rise to the establishment in Shanghai of the Foreign Inspectorate system affected that city and the rest of the open ports in other and various ways. In Shanghai the foreign representatives were compelled to take up the question of their attitude towards the contestants and to watch carefully the interests committed to their charge. Bowring had no sympathy for the 'low vagabonds who have got the city'—the Shanghai rebels were quite distinct from the Taipings,[1]—nor for the less thoughtful members of the British community who 'have no more notion of government than half-a-dozen Newgate birds would have'[2] and were in declared sympathy with the rebels.[3] Though Alcock punished his nationals for infractions of neutrality, he felt obliged to call upon Her Majesty's forces to attack and destroy an Imperial encampment near the settlement owing to a series of unprovoked attacks by Imperial soldiery upon British subjects.[4] In this operation, vulgarly called the 'Battle of Muddy Flat', American forces joined the British.[5] A large number of Chinese took refuge in the limits of the settlement, and the Consul actively engaged with his French and American colleagues in taking measures to bring these persons 'under some sort of temporary jurisdiction, for their own well-being, not less than our own'[6]. Both Bowring and Clarendon urged caution in such an assumption of jurisdiction over Chinese subjects, wholly unwarranted by Treaty or international law.[7] Alcock recognized that in order to keep the peace, it would be necessary 'to afford protection and exercise jurisdiction over Chinese subjects, which will practically be an assumption of government and lead to an absolute appropriation of territory'[8]. With the approval of the British and American ministers 'the foundation of a further municipal government for this settlement' was laid with singular unanimity, and on the 11th July 1854 a Municipal Council was

[1] Bowring to Clarendon, 20 Apr. 1854 (F.O. 17/213).
[2] Bowring to Clarendon, 18 May 1854 (F.O. 17/213).
[3] Bowring to Clarendon, 15 Apr. 1854 (F.O. 17/213).
[4] Bonham to Clarendon, 13 Apr. 1854 (F.O. 17/212).
[5] Bowring to Clarendon, 18 Apr. 1854 (F.O. 17/213).
[6] Bowring to Clarendon, 29 Apr. 1854 (F.O. 17/213).
[7] Clarendon to Bowring, 6 July 1854 (F.O. 17/211).
[8] Bowring to Clarendon, 14 June 1854 (F.O. 17/214).

created.[1] Clarendon offered no objection to the formation by the residents of an association for purposes of self-defence, and observed that 'the comfort and safety of European residents may also require internal police and sanitary arrangements'. But at the same time, the Consul was directed 'to avoid pledging Her Majesty's Government to the continuance of the regulations, by becoming parties to them in the name of Her Majesty's Government'[2]. This voluntary association was, moreover, to have no power to call upon the British navy 'in the event of a danger to the settlement from the intrusion of armed men'[3].

The French were in a peculiarly difficult position in Shanghai as their concession abutted on the walled Chinese city, which early in 1855 they decided to attack. In view of this decision the American and British naval commanders were prepared to prevent armed Chinese entering into the settlement in which their nationals lived, whether Imperialists or rebels.[4] Though the French attack on the 6th February was a failure and created a bad moral effect, famine played a decisive role.[5] Twelve days later, the recovery of the city by the Imperialists,[6] and the freeing of the immediate neighbourhood from insurgents,[7] rendered the life of the foreigners in the settlements more normal, and trading prospects rapidly improved.[8]

Bowring took care to prevent the life and soul of the Shanghai rebel movement, Chin-a-lin, a former stable-boy to British residents, from stirring up trouble afresh. Upon the fall of the city this man had been harboured by a British subject Scarth, the Belgian Vice-consul, who had brought him as a servant to Hong Kong. Thence he had gone on to Singapore. Bowring requested the Governor of that colony to warn Chin-a-lin that he was not to use it or Hong Kong as a base from which to trouble the peace of China under pain of the high displeasure of the British authorities. It was feared that he would be provided with funds by the secret societies so prevalent in Hong Kong and Singapore.[9] Throughout the rest of 1855 and the

---

[1] Bowring to Clarendon, 22 July 1854 (F.O. 17/215).
[2] Clarendon to Bowring, 25 Oct. 1854 (F.O. 17/211).
[3] Clarendon to Bowring, 24 Nov. 1854 (F.O. 17/211).
[4] Bowring to Clarendon, 22 Jan. 1855 (F.O. 17/226).
[5] de Bourboulon to Min. Aff. Étr., 12 Feb. 1855 (Chine 16).
[6] Bowring to Clarendon, 14 Mar. 1855 (F.O. 17/228).
[7] Bowring to Clarendon, 13 Apr. 1855 (F.O. 17/229).
[8] Bowring to Clarendon, 17 May 1855 (F.O. 17/230).
[9] Bowring to Clarendon, 1 June 1855 (F.O. 17/231).

following year there were no anxieties arising in connexion with the northern port.

4. *The Coolie Trade*

During these four troublous years in Shanghai the degeneration of Imperial authority was manifesting itself also in the other ports. In the waters adjacent to Ningpo, an open port of considerable missionary importance, but of little commercial value, there was continued activity of piratical bands. As the pirates, taught by many a lesson, paid no small respect to ships bearing foreign flags, a flourishing British coastal trade had grown up,[1] and a convoy system, in which British vessels had by 1854 almost superseded Portuguese lorchas, had come into being for the protection of Chinese junks. Foochow seemed to be prospering by the difficulties experienced by Shanghai. There an exceptionally brisk tea trade was developing.[2] Exports for the last six months of 1853 amounted to $57\frac{1}{2}$ million pounds, an increase of 10 millions over the corresponding period of the previous year.[3] It was found in practice that when sufficient inducement was offered, the navigation of the Min was not so serious a handicap as had been supposed.[4] But there were difficulties here too. Not only had Consul Medhurst to exert himself to the utmost to maintain for the Church Missionary Society the position which it had obtained in the city,[5] but he had to protest to the Prefect against the levy of excessive transit duties on teas. Anxiety was increased during the summer of 1856 by the presence in Fukien of rebel hordes.[6] Fortunately, though smuggling and customs defalcations were rife, the trade continued to flourish, as indeed it might have done from the opening of the port in 1842 had not a secret Imperial ordinance for more than ten years prohibited the export of tea from Foochow.[7]

If the convoy trade at Ningpo and the increase of trade in Foochow were the consequences of the general disturbances, the chief problem at Amoy was the traffic in human labour

---

[1] Bowring to Clarendon, 22 Nov. 1854 (F.O. 17/217); 26 May 1855 (F.O. 17/228).
[2] Bonham to Clarendon, 4 Aug. 1853 (F.O. 17/204).
[3] Bonham to Clarendon, 7 Feb. 1854 (F.O. 17/212).
[4] Bonham to Clarendon, 15 Oct. 1853 (F.O. 17/205).
[5] Bowring to Clarendon, 10 Oct. 1855 (F.O. 17/234).
[6] Bowring to Clarendon, 5 May 1856 (F.O. 17/247).
[7] Bowring to Clarendon, 21 July 1856 (F.O. 17/249).

carried on at that port.[1] Though the laws of China prohibited the expatriation and emigration of its subjects to foreign lands, the Chinese authorities were powerless or unwilling to interfere in an illegal trade carried on under their very eyes: the great barracoons where the coolies were collected at Amoy almost touched the custom-house. Bowring rightly suspected that 'the most false and fraudulent misrepresentations were made by the Chinese crimps and brokers who collected the coolie population together for shipment'. In many cases, at least at the beginning, the emigration was voluntary. For ages past Chinese had migrated for a season to the East Indies and Malaya. Foreign shipping now enabled the teeming population to go farther afield where, consequent upon the abolition of the slave trade, cheap labour was much in demand. The mortality, however, on board ship was exceedingly high, and from some places such as the Peruvian guano islands shocking accounts of the conditions of life and labour were received. Frequently the unwilling cargo revolted—as did the coolies in the American ship *Robert Bowne*, which sailed from Amoy in 1852. On the plea of cleanliness the master of this vessel had cut off the pig-tails of a very large number of Chinese and had caused their bodies to be scrubbed with a broom.[2]

The British Government, disturbed at the great mortality on board the British coolie ships *Lady Montague* and *Susannah*, desired the consuls to adopt all legal means to check abuses and decided to seek additional statutory powers.[3] Scandalous cases of this kind would make it difficult to complete the contracts arranged in July 1852 for the shipment of eight to fifteen thousand men to Havana.[4] Bowring regretted that instead of a 'quiet, steady and progressing system of well-digested emigration', we have a sudden irruption of a fleet of ships which might well mean that 'we may see the jails of China emptied to supply "labour" to British Colonies'. He had himself seen disgraceful arrangements for the shipment of coolies at Amoy.

'Hundreds of them gathered together in barracoons, stripped naked, and stamped or painted with the letter C (California), P (Peru), or S (Sandwich Islands) on their breasts, according to the

[1] See p. 116.
[2] Bowring to Malmesbury, 17 May 1852 (P.P. 1852–3, lxviii, p. 348).
[3] Malmesbury to Bowring, 21 July 1852 (ibid., p. 349).
[4] Bowring to Malmesbury, 16 July 1852 (ibid., p. 349).

destination for which they were intended. A trifle advanced to give their hungriness food, a suit of clothes to cover their nudity, a dollar or two for their families, and candidates in abundance are found for transportation to any land.'[1]

The great obstacle to the success of any energetic action by the British Government was the impossibility of expecting co-operation from the Chinese authorities, and the existence of abundant places of shipment other than the legal ports where alone British consuls could exert their authority. Strong legis-lative enactments might exercise some deterrent effect on British shippers, but there was the obvious danger that if British subjects were effectively controlled, the coolie trade might not be diminished, but merely fall into the hands of other foreigners.[2]

From Amoy merely the refuse of the population had hitherto enrolled themselves, or as the Chinese saying was 'sold himself to an English merchant'. Assistant Consul Winchester hoped to see established a strict system of regulation, an officer appointed to determine the number of men each vessel could carry, to inspect provisions and water supply and lime juice, to con-trol ventilation and berth fittings, to witness and explain con-tracts to the emigrants and to decide summarily any disputes between them and the brokers. He should be a health officer with powers to prevent embarkation in cases of small-pox. It was essential to regulate an emigration technically forbidden by the laws of a quasi-friendly country, for Britain ought either to forbid and prevent the engagement of her vessels or to enforce principles of humanity: the character of the English nation could not be allowed to suffer at the moment at which its duty to the Chinese emigrants began—at the time of embarkation. He recommended the extension to the Superintendent of Trade of the powers allowed to colonial governors by the Passengers Act, by which statutory means the master of the vessel would be amenable at the start of his voyage to the British consuls in Chinese ports, on landing in a foreign country to the British Consul, or in a British colony to the usual colonial courts for infringement of the law.[3]

The British Government accordingly sent out in August an

---

[1] Bowring to Malmesbury, 3 Aug. 1852 (P.P. 1852, lxviii, p. 349).
[2] Bowring to Malmesbury, 25 Sept. 1852 (ibid., p. 352).
[3] Bowring to Malmesbury, 25 Sept. 1852 (ibid., p. 385).

officer, White, as an emigration agent to arrange for the proper supervision of coolies destined for British colonies. He was to see they were fairly treated both in the matter of the contract and of ship-room. If the Chinese Government objected to his appointment on the ground that emigration was against their law, White would have to establish himself in Hong Kong. If Chinese labourers wished by flocking to the British colony to run the risk of such penalties as their own Government might inflict that was their own affair.[1] Bowring hoped that White's presence would do something to prevent much of the crime and misery which had lately seriously compromised public tranquillity at Amoy. For while the local Chinese authorities might gain both financially by their connivance and politically by ridding the district of a miserable surplus population, nothing could be more fatal to British trade generally than serious disturbances which would inevitably wreck the growing disposition to friendly intercourse.[2]

'The abuses, many in number and great in amount, connected with the irregular and fraudulent shipment of coolies, abuses which even now are not far from placing the coolie emigration in the category of another Slave Trade' might easily jeopardize 'the immense interests, both British and Anglo-Indian, involved in the opium trade, giving at the present moment more than three millions sterling of revenue to India, and furnishing the means of payment for a large portion of the exports from China to Great Britain, her colonies and the United States.'[3]

Indeed, the coolie traffic caused a serious riot to break out in Amoy on the 21st November 1852. Two British subjects were violently assaulted, warehouses were threatened and in particular that of Messrs. Syme, Muir & Co. British sailors were eventually compelled to open fire, killing four and wounding five people: an action of which the local authorities fortunately fully approved. A British subject Syme and his assistant Cornabé had gone to a police station and rescued a cooliebroker of their employ from the hands of the Mandarins. They were both fined at a Consular Court.[4] Clarendon added his approval of the condemnation of 'those persons who have brought disgrace on the British name and have endangered

[1] Malmesbury to Bowring, 20 Oct. 1852 (F.O. 17/186).
[2] Bowring to Malmesbury, 20 Dec. 1852 (F.O. 17/194).
[3] Bowring to Malmesbury, 24 Dec. 1852 (F.O. 17/194).
[4] Bowring to Malmesbury, 27 Dec. 1852 (F.O. 17/194).

British interests in China'. By January of 1853 Amoy had resumed its former peaceful aspect. Except ships already loaded
with coolies, no emigrant vessels had left since the disturbances
of November. There would be no lack of a stream of labourers
willing to depart for the Straits Settlements—indeed 100 such
left of their own accord for Singapore. The Mandarins had
taken means to deter the brokers whose villainies had brought
about such an unpleasant clash. But instead of to Amoy, two
Spanish and one English ship were going to Namoa, long an
irregular opium station in the vicinity,[1] whither also Tait, the
principal shipper and also consul at Amoy for Spain, Holland,
and Portugal, had removed his receiving ship.[2] The other great
centre of the coolie trade was at Kumsingmoon near Macao,
the station which supplied Canton and its district with opium.
In these places there was no consular control: and the question
naturally arose whether the British Government would extend
to the traffic in coolies the principle of non-interference which
it already practised in regard to opium. Certainly some of the
chief opium houses were getting alarmed at the possible consequences of the intrusion of the coolie trade into their stations.
To Bowring's observation that the British Government had
ample and plenary power to stop this trade if they chose to exercise it, the Foreign Office commented 'Is it not the business and
the duty of the Chinese Government to prevent these abuses
and enforce their own laws?' If Great Britain, argued Bowring,
prevented her nationals from all trade at the illegal places, she
would have a strong claim on the Chinese to prevent other
foreigners from doing so also. To this suggestion of Bowring's
a marginal query was made in the Foreign Office: 'whether it
might not be a question whether the Chinese Government, in
consideration of its own weakness, is not entitled to expect us to
assist them in maintaining their authority, in the assertion of the
principle that no other nation shall be allowed to enjoy privileges in China which are denied to us?' The greatest scandal
was in connexion with the emigration undertaken by foreign
non-British agents in ships not flying the British flag to foreign
colonies and countries.

'There is every reason to fear that iniquities scarcely exceeded by
those practised on the African coast and on the African middle

---

[1] Bowring to Malmesbury, 18 Jan. 1853 (F.O. 17/199).
[2] Bowring to Malmesbury, 7 Feb. 1853 (F.O. 17/199.)

passage, have not been wanting. The statements which have reached China of the condition of the coolies in the Guano Islands —the reported sale of coolies in the public market-places of Peru— the deceits practised in order to obtain labourers for the railways of the Isthmus of Darien, are rather subjects of general conversation than of official cognizance.'[1]

The West Indian interest was concerned to maintain a supply of good coolies on a decent footing. A regular stream of emigrants was necessary as Chinese females never left the country and the males went abroad for a limited period. Opportunity was taken of the presence in England of Bowring and Winchester, the assistant in the Amoy consulate, and of the emigration agent White and Sir Henry Barkly, ex-governor of British Guiana, to discuss the situation in the summer of 1853. There was general agreement that nothing could be done by British officers to control the collecting of emigrants, but that steps ought to be taken to ensure their good treatment on board and when in service. It was thought that heavy penalties should be imposed on British ships taking coolies from other than the legal ports; and that the Passengers Acts, modified to allow of 12 instead of 15 superficial feet for each adult, should extend to the trade. The head-quarters of the official emigration should be at present confined to Hong Kong.[2] These recommendations were adopted by the Government,[3] and the necessary legislation was passed by Parliament.[4] But White on his return to Hong Kong, unable to get any shipping at the price he was authorized to pay, had resort to Messrs. Tait & Co. of Amoy, who guaranteed to procure the shipping provided they could take up the emigrants from Namoa. To this course White agreed. He also agreed to give to a few of the better emigrants $40 on condition they purchased a respectable girl each. Clarendon was surprised to see such deliberate disregard shown for treaty engagements—White's expression of regret for his action in dealing at Namoa was quite inadequate—and he pointed out to Bowring that White, though in the British Government's employment, was as amenable to the jurisdiction of English law as any other British subject. Clarendon was alarmed at the plan White formed for procuring female

[1] Bowring to Malmesbury, 5 Jan. 1853 (F.O. 17/199).
[2] Merivale to Addington, 15 Sept. 1852 (P.P. 1854–5, xxxix, p. 161).
[3] Clarendon to Bonham, 19 Sept. 1853 (F.O. 17/198).
[4] 16, 17 Victoria, c. 84.

emigrants which he stigmatized as 'a trade little different from the Slave Trade'[1].

There was a renewed attempt in 1855 by Syme & Co., who could no longer obtain men at Namoa, to engage in the coolie trade at Amoy. Though Syme promised that operations should be carried on twenty miles off, and that he would exert every possible supervision over his brokers, the acting vice-consul was prepared to apprise the Mandarins that he was willing to afford them every necessary support if they wished to check this emigration. It was apparently proposed to obtain women to accompany the emigrants, and Bowring pointed out that this could only be done by direct sale or covert kidnapping of females. He hoped the British Government would see fit to call upon the Governments of Spain and Peru to direct their representatives to co-operate in order to avoid a succession of abuses disgraceful to humanity.[2] He refused to allow a British subject who was a member of a coolie firm to accept appointment as Peruvian Consul on the ground that his private interests and public duties might be irreconcilable, for to the consuls alone the coolies could look for protection and justice.[3] The British Government, acting on Bowring's suggestion, intervened with success at Lima and the conditions in the Guano Islands were greatly improved. But the disgraceful nature of the trade was glaringly revealed by an incident at Ningpo in 1855. A British vessel, the *Inglewood*, shipped at that port kidnapped or purchased girls, the eldest of whom was only eight years old. When the ship arrived at Amoy the sailors reported the fact because they were nauseated by the stench, misery, and disease of these unprotected children. The Consul was put in some difficulty as the principal parties were Spanish and Portuguese subjects, and the ship was consigned to the house of a British subject who was Spanish Vice-consul and the principal emigration agent.[4] However, the captain was fined £100,[5] and the children were sent back to their place of origin. The British Admiral, when apprised of this incident, agreed in future to put into force the Anti-Slavery Acts if such a scandal came to the knowledge of the British navy. The Foreign Office fully concurred in the punish-

---

[1] Clarendon to Bowring, 5 Apr. 1854 (F.O. 17/210).
[2] Bowring to Clarendon, 8 Feb. 1855 (F.O. 17/227).
[3] Bowring to Clarendon, 5 Mar. 1855 (F.O. 17/228).
[4] Bowring to Clarendon, 5 Mar. 1855 (F.O. 17/228).
[5] Bowring to Clarendon, 16 May 1855 (F.O. 17/230).

ment of the miscreants who had so dishonoured their flag.[1]
After the rupture in the autumn of 1856 there was a further
scandal due to the heavy mortality on board two British ships,
the *John Calvin* and the *Duke of Portland*, bound from Hong
Kong to Havana. In the former 135 out of 298, in the latter
128 out of 332, died on the voyage. The British Government
took a very lively interest in the investigation of these cases, but
were obliged to come to the conclusion that there was no lack
of humanity and that the sickness was not due to overcrowding.
A bona-fide mistake had been made by the emigration officer
in his calculations in the case of the *John Calvin*. This ship was
licensed for 301 passengers, all but 81 declined to sail, and yet
she sailed with over 200 more persons. The law officers were
called upon to examine whether there had not been such an
infraction of the letter, as there certainly had been in the judgement of the Foreign Office of the spirit, of the Chinese Passengers
Act of 1855,[2] as would justify a prosecution. If they agreed that
a conviction could be obtained, the Superintendent of Trade
was instructed to put the bond in suit against the master and his
sureties. This was in fact successfully done, though ultimately
only a mitigated penalty of £50 was inflicted.[3]

The whole story of the coolie trade shows that the British
Government were desirous to use their authority over their own
nationals to ensure decent conditions on board British ships,
and to prevent unwilling embarkations that amounted to slave-
trade enterprises, and at the same time to exert that influence
which they had used incessantly since 1815 over friendly
Powers to the same effect. But their beneficent activities were
to an extent paralysed by the difficulty of co-operation with
Chinese authorities. It was impossible to stop adult males
emigrating at least for a season, and yet the mere fact of the
unlawfulness of such emigration meant that it could only be
conducted in a clandestine way, with the interested connivance
of the Mandarins. The prohibition of the emigration of females
was an additional difficulty from the point of view of the colonial governments of the West Indies. Bowring maintained, no
doubt quite rightly, that it was impossible to expect women of
good character to cross the seas. But even if it were only pos-

[1] Clarendon to Bowring, 17 Aug. 1855 (F.O. 17/225).
[2] 18, 19 Victoria, c. 104.
[3] Full correspondence on these cases in P.P. 1857-8, xliii, and 1857, x.

sible to secure women of loose morals, Malmesbury argued that no obstacle should be placed to their emigration, as people going to a new country had a chance of reform. 'Almost any women in such places are better than the crimes which result from a great disproportion of the sexes.'[1] Though the consuls were to be made emigration agents to assist the labour market of Trinidad and British Guiana, they were to be careful to observe strictly the Chinese Passengers Act. It was with great concern that in 1858 he heard of a mortality rate of 14¾ per cent. on two British emigrant ships which had arrived at Havana. The Act would be strengthened[2] and must be rigorously enforced.[3] It is not surprising, therefore, that one of the aims of the British Government was to secure legalization through treaty of a traffic[4] which could not be effectively stopped, but which might well be decently controlled and supervised by the loyal and legal co-operation of Chinese and British officers. In this way the dictates of humanity and the economic necessities of the West Indian planters could be reconciled.

5. *The Colonial Register*

The southern group of rebels were already pressing towards Canton in the summer of 1852.[5] Though Seu and Yeh returned to the city in September proclaiming that they had wiped the rebels off the face of the earth, in fact they had merely temporarily bought them off,[6] and Seu was soon ordered into action in Hunan Province,[7] where Yeh joined him before the winter.[8] Disaffection in the city was so widespread that terrorist methods were used by the authorities in an attempt to crush it. On ten days between the 13th September and the 28th October no less than 237 persons were executed, while over 2,000 were put to death in the city during the year.[9]

The Government troops were defeated at a distance of only thirty miles from Canton on the 13th November. The situation was no better during the following year. There were daily in-

---

[1] Malmesbury to Bowring, 6 Apr. 1858 (F.O. 17/292).
[2] Malmesbury to Bowring, 17 Apr. 1858 (F.O. 17/292).
[3] Malmesbury to Bowring, 31 May 1858 (F.O. 17/292).
[4] Malmesbury to Bruce, 14 Dec. 1859 (F.O. 17/311).
[5] Bowring to Malmesbury, 23 July 1852 (F.O. 17/191).
[6] Bowring to Malmesbury, 7 Sept. 1852 (F.O. 17/192).
[7] Bowring to Malmesbury, 27 Sept. 1852 (F.O. 17/192).
[8] Bowring to Malmesbury, 27 Oct. 1852 (F.O. 17/193).
[9] Bowring to Malmesbury, 11 Nov. 1852 (F.O. 17/193).

creasing popular disturbances near Canton,[1] leading to frequent
collisions between the people and the authorities.[2] Yet in spite
of these untoward events tea exports from Canton remained
normal, though prices ruled high.[3] Even in October 1853 there
was still fighting between the rebels and the military.[4] In the
spring of 1854 there were violent clan feuds in the neighbourhood of the city with which the authorities deemed it expedient
not to interfere. Great inconvenience and danger to foreign
property and persons were caused by the presence of rebels in the
river; communications between Whampoa and Hong Kong were
frequently interrupted,[5] and the colony itself was threatened with
unrest by the presence of rebels in Kowloon.[6] Before the end
of the year these rebel pirates had rendered the Hong Kong
and Canton waterway impassable for Chinese vessels: foreign
boats were attacked and trade was at a standstill.[7] This appal-
ling state of affairs caused a daily improvement in the sentiments
towards foreigners of the wealthier Chinese who were willing to
offer money for protection on the waters round Canton and
Hong Kong. Even the Imperial Commissioner himself readily
agreed that Her Majesty's ships should act as a supporting
squadron to Chinese vessels of war—the first manifestation
of any desire to co-operate with British naval forces.[8] Yeh
was led to ask for foreign help against the rebels generally.
'Great must be the alarm and extreme the perplexities and
perils which have induced this proud Mandarin to supplicate
the aid of outer nations', observed Bowring. Indeed, the rebel
forces from Blenheim Reach with 200 sail moved against the
Government's fifty war junks to a distance of only three miles
from the city. Bowring however, in perfect accord with the
American commissioner, refused to be a party to the domestic disputes of the Chinese Empire, and was only willing to interfere
when British subjects were in danger.[9] Though trade had vanished
completely there was no fear for the foreign settlements.[10]

[1] Bowring to Malmesbury, 27 Nov. 1852 (F.O. 17/193).
[2] Bonham to Clarendon, 22 July 1853 (F.O. 17/203).
[3] Bonham to Clarendon, 4 Aug. 1853 (F.O. 17/204).
[4] Bonham to Clarendon, 26 Oct. 1853 (F.O. 17/205).
[5] Bowring to Clarendon, 21 Aug. 1854 (F.O. 17/215).
[6] Bowring to Clarendon, 26 Aug. 1854 (F.O. 17/215).
[7] Bowring to Clarendon, 28 Oct. 1854 (F.O. 17/216).
[8] Robertson to Hammond, 10 Nov. 1854 (F.O. 17/217).
[9] Bowring to Clarendon, 11 Dec. 1854 (F.O. 17/218).
[10] Bowring to Clarendon, 25 Dec. 1854 (F.O. 17/218).

At the beginning of 1855 rebel and Imperial forces were in action again near the foreign shipping at Whampoa,[1] but the situation on the river was eased by a great victory gained by the Government over their opponents in March.[2] During the struggle pillaging had been continually in progress, and the success of the Imperialists had been due in part to a notification by the British Plenipotentiary that the rebels' blockade would not be recognized and that he would not tolerate warlike acts in the neighbourhood of peaceful foreign shipping.[3] At midsummer the province of Kwantung was reasonably quiet, though the Government had need to resort to violent measures of repression. Capital punishment was being inflicted in the city of Canton at the rate of two hundred heads a day[4]—ten times the rate of 1852—and during the past year three thousand persons had been executed: yet the secret societies were still in being.[5]

To prevent the severance of communication between Hong Kong and Canton, the British and American authorities (the latter represented since January by Dr. Parker as chargé d'affaires on McLane's leaving China) agreed that it was a matter of necessity, in order that the legitimate trade might not be absolutely cut off, to grant 'English and United States flags with a passport to Chinese lighters for a single trip to and from Canton and Whampoa to be immediately returned and filed at the consulates by which they were issued'[6]. In consequence of this agreement the Colonial Government of Hong Kong passed two ordinances in 1855 and 1856 giving to residents in Hong Kong under certain conditions the right to carry the British flag. In November 1855 lorchas bearing the British flag were seized by the Chinese authorities on a charge of smuggling salt. When they were not handed over to British authority on the requisition of the Consul, Her Majesty's sloop *Rattler* took possession of them. Bowring directed the Attorney-General to proceed against the parties concerned in the alleged smuggling for a breach of the colonial ordinance under which the registers

---

[1] Bowring to Clarendon, 4 Jan. 1855 (F.O. 17/226).
[2] Bowring to Clarendon, 9 Mar. 1855 (F.O. 17/228).
[3] Bowring to Clarendon, 28 Feb. 1855 (F.O. 17/228).
[4] Bowring to Clarendon, 6 July 1855 (F.O. 17/231).
[5] Bowring to Clarendon, 13 Oct. 1855 (F.O. 17/234).
[6] Parker to Marcy, 13 Mar. 1855 (Sen. Ex. Doc. 22, 2 Sess. 35 Cong., at p. 569).

were granted. At the same time he stated categorically: 'I cannot allow the Chinese authorities to encroach upon my jurisdiction, however little sympathy I may feel for those who disregard the conditions on which the protection and privilege of the British flag have been accorded to them.'

He had pointed out to Yeh that, according to the twelfth article of the Supplementary Treaty, it was within the province of the Chinese Government to seize smuggled cargo found in a British ship, but that the ship herself, though she might be prohibited from further trading, could not legally be held. As Hong Kong was British territory it was competent to the Queen's Government to authorize all residents in the island to fly the British flag. He informed Yeh that a bond of $1,000 was required as a sanction for compliance with the laws binding on British subjects. He had no sympathy either with smugglers or with persons who might seek to make Hong Kong a base for seditious practices against the Chinese Emperor.[1] Yet Bowring acknowledged to the Foreign Office that before the regulations were tightened in the early part of 1856 Chinese lorchas having colonial registers had 'been participating in nefarious deeds'[2]. The law officers of the Crown were in agreement with Bowring that he was within his rights in calling upon the naval authorities to rescue the vessels detained by the Chinese.[3] But by the end of the summer of 1856 questions were constantly arising concerning the conditions in which foreign vessels were allowed to hoist the national flag: for instance a large Chinese junk left Macao in April 1856 illegally under American colours, whilst an American house in Shanghai was offered $100 for the privilege of using its name to procure American registry for a Chinese ship. There were vessels assuming the flags of foreign Powers without authority, and vessels flying flags granted by trading consuls of other European States having no authority to give registers. The Chinese officials were 'utterly unable to distinguish between the claims of the subjects of non-Treaty powers, as the recognition of the consular authorities of such powers was of the most loose and irregular character'[4]. There was clearly in this chaos of rebellion and anarchy and in the

[1] Bowring to Clarendon, 22 Nov. 1855 (F.O. 17/235).
[2] Bowring to Clarendon, 4 Mar. 1856 (F.O. 17/245).
[3] Clarendon to Bowring, 22 Mar. 1856 (F.O. 17/242).
[4] Bowring to Clarendon, 17 Sept. 1856 (F.O. 17/250).

attempts of the British and other foreigners to safeguard their trading interests, ample opportunity, if there was a will on either side, to find material for conflict and war.

B. GROWING CO-OPERATION OF THE TREATY POWERS, 1852–6

1. *Marshall and McLane*

The second significant feature of the period from 1852 to 1856 is the change in the relations between the Treaty Powers from a sullen suspicion to a growing co-operation; a change due partly to personal factors and partly to the outbreak of the Crimean War and the emergence of Russia in the waters of the Yellow Sea.

In January 1853 Colonel Marshall arrived as the representative of the United States in China, with a letter from the President to the Emperor. A man of between forty-five and fifty years of age, educated at West Point, he had served several years in the army, rising during the Mexican war to the rank of colonel. He was now a lawyer-politician and had been a member of the House of Representatives.[1] From the first it was apparent that so long as he remained charged with the safeguard of American interests it was not likely that cordiality would mark Anglo-American relations in China. Marshall was placed in too great an advantage, in Bowring's eyes, owing to the fact that Forbes, the United States Consul, enjoyed, as a consequence of his business connexion with Howqua, a virtual monopoly of intercourse with the Chinese authorities. The British Plenipotentiary was afraid that his American rival would be received inside the city of Canton if he was determined upon such reception; and in that event the United States would be 'at the summit of foreign influence in the Chinese mind'[2]. Fortunately, however, for Bowring's fears, Forbes had a keen sense of his economic interests, and did his best to persuade Marshall to agree to a reception without the walls. Much delay in making any arrangement was occasioned by the absence of Yeh from the city on an expedition against the rebels, and when he did finally return Marshall was given an evasive answer. Thereupon Mar-

[1] De Bourboulon to Min. Aff. Étr., 1 Feb. 1853 (Chine 13).
[2] Bowring to Malmesbury, 24 Jan. 1853 (F.O. 17/199).

shall decided to leave Macao and the south for the northern ports.[1] He was in fact quite disgusted.

'It is a mockery to keep the representatives of Great Britain, France and the United States dancing attendance at Canton, in order to transact business with an Imperial Commissioner when years are permitted to elapse during which time no such public functionary visits Canton to confer with them on public affairs.'[2]

It was not long afterwards that Bonham, back from leave in England, also went north to Shanghai. Before he arrived, Marshall in U.S.S. *Susquehannah* had left for Nanking, but the vessel returned to Shanghai in three days after having been aground for twenty-four hours within ten miles of Woosung.

'What his object was', wrote Bonham of Marshall's visit to Eleang,[3] 'I know not—but I believe he says his intention was to deliver his credentials. . . . I much regret this move on the part of the Americans as I fear it will induce a belief in the rebel mind that foreigners intend to side with the Imperialists. The Commissioner, Marshall, is a very coarse headstrong man—has never been out of Kentucky before he came here and I fear will give us annoyance and embarrass our proceedings—he already wants to have a squabble with me, but I will not afford him the opportunity if I can possibly avoid it. His proceedings and measures since he has been here have been generally disapproved of by his countrymen.'[4]

Bonham, however, successfully went to Nanking, as we have seen.[3] Marshall commented to his Government that 'the version given by H.E. of the visit leaves me so mystified by the insignificance of what he has attained that I shall wait for further revelations'[5]. It was not long before he suspected the worst—that Bonham's intercourse 'with the rebels' camp and their princes had served to awaken in his person the warmest sympathy in their cause'. He thought that Great Britain might be aiming at 'a protectorate of the young power', 'at least so far as to mould its first steps to suit the policy of that government'. He feared that Great Britain might obtain from the new Empire at Nanking the opening of a west China inland port and 'the right to navigate the Yangtse Kiang closed from foreign commerce beyond the existing port of entry. I do not doubt that

[1] Bowring to Malmesbury, 9 Feb. 1853 (F.O. 17/199).
[2] Marshall to Sec. of State, 19 Mar. 1853 (H. Doc. 123, 1 Sess. 33 Cong., at p. 87).
[3] See p. 161.
[4] Bonham to Hammond, 13 Apr. 1853 (F.O. 17/200).
[5] Marshall to Sec. of State, 6 May 1853 (H. Doc. 123, 1 Sess. 33 Cong., at p. 112).

with that view her war with Burmah has been waged and her
Indian Empire extended. The portage from the Ihrawaddy to
the Yangtsze Kiang is very short.'[1] It is hardly necessary to
state that there is no trace of such a suggestion in the records
of the Foreign Office, nor was it likely that a trade route comparable in value to the Pacific could be dreamt of between
Burmah and the Yangtse. Only a backwoodsman, suspicious
and jealous, could have expressed such thoughts when it had
been Great Britain's repeatedly declared policy, upon which she
had invariably acted, never to seek any exclusive commercial
advantages for herself in China. Yet in spite of this distrust of
Great Britain, and indeed of Russia, either of which States in
his judgement might be tempted to make such prizes that the
fate of Asia would be sealed, the American representative gave
it as his opinion that it would be very important to the United
States, indeed to the world, could the Western Powers unite
in sending their diplomats to Peking or Nanking and 'so by a
timely interference put an end to the internal strife'. 'An interference of the United States to quiet and tranquillize China
would be a mission of humanity and charity. It would be
essentially a work of peace, unlike the ruthless conquest of India,
made upon the sordid calculations of a cruel avarice.' But, on
the other hand, Marshall would not suggest that such disinterested interference should be undertaken until the Emperor
had granted to citizens of the Powers the right to travel in the
Empire, had opened the Yangtse for foreign trade, granted an
amnesty to his present opponents and religious equality, set up
a department of Foreign Affairs, nor finally until 'he shall
become a subscriber to the laws of nations'[2]. It was an advantage to Anglo-American relations in the Far East that Marshall
did not long represent Washington in China, for he seems to
have thought co-operation between the two Anglo-Saxon countries quite impossible. The President had left the propriety of
co-operation with the British authorities to his judgement, and
it can well be imagined that co-operation was not likely to be
realized by one who could write: 'China has not been inattentive
to the policy of Great Britain in India, and actually trembles

---

[1] Marshall to Sec. of State, 30 May 1853 (H. Doc. 123, 1 Sess. 33 Cong., at
p. 168).
[2] Marshall to Sec. of State, 21 June 1853, 10 July 1853 (ibid., at pp. 182 and
203).

for her own safety—I think not without good cause—for Great Britain has exhibited in her eastern conquests neither fear of Heaven nor love of justice among men.' Indeed, to him reciprocal confidence in Great Britain was 'an event I am not simple enough to anticipate from my past experience or observation'[1]. It is not without interest to observe that less than a year after the United States representative had contemplated the possibility of a conquest of China by Great Britain, Bowring was comparing the origins of the British Indian Empire with the conditions in China during the summer of 1854.

'The history of British India is full of instruction', he wrote. 'When our merchants settled in India and made their earliest appeals to military or naval authority for their defence, how small was the British interest involved compared with that which now exists in China! . . . India did not supply, and never has supplied, like China, ⅛ of the gross revenues of Great Britain, while to the resources of India itself, China has become an equally valuable market, and perhaps the most valuable, contributor. The races of China are no more able to resist the pressure of British superiority in arts and arms than were those of India, and it is no unusual characteristic of the Anglo-Saxon race, when settling in foreign regions, that they begin by trading and end in governing. . . . I do not hesitate to state to Your Lordship that I have often my misgivings lest the future should re-tell the tale of British India, over a vaster field, on a grander scale, and with larger interests involved.'[2]

No stronger evidence of the complete misunderstanding of the British attitude by the American Commissioner could be given than Bowring's openly expressed dread of the possibility of great new British responsibilities in the larger Chinese field.

Marshall was succeeded by McLane who arrived at Hong Kong in March 1854. He noticed a great change in the tone of the British authorities, who were now expressing undisguised hostility to the rebels; this difference he thought due to the changed personal opinion of Sir George Bonham. Bonham had indeed deplored Marshall's action in seeking an interview with the Viceroy Eleang and his strong pro-Imperialist sympathies. He had thought that there never was a more unpropitious time to enter upon a new treaty than the autumn of 1853. With whom could it be made? If with the Emperor, did that imply

[1] Marshall to Sec. of State, 21 Sept. 1853 (ibid., at p. 268).
[2] Bowring to Clarendon, 5 June 1854 (F.O. 17/214).

that the Treaty Powers were to aid him against the rebels? His authority anyhow was practically nil. It were better to wait at least to see whether the Taipings, who in the winter 1853–4 were at the gates of Tientsin, became masters of Peking. If they succeeded in capturing the capital, the Powers ought to consider whether they would not be likely to obtain greater political and commercial advantages from them than from their Imperialist rivals.[1] Since then, however, the repulse of the rebels from the north had saved the prestige of the dynasty. The approach of the period at which the British Government thought itself entitled to demand a revision of the treaty, as well as the outbreak of the war with Russia, influenced the Foreign Secretary to instruct Bowring to work in harmony for the general interests of the western powers with his American and French colleagues.[2]

The right of treaty revision was claimed by the British Government under the most-favoured-nation clause. Though there was no such specific right in the Treaty of Nanking, the American Treaty contained a clause which envisaged the possibility of modifications. This ran: 'Experience may show that inconsiderable modifications are requisite in those parts which relate to commerce and navigation.' The French treaty, however, gave a better ground for real and substantial modifications. The clause in it which affected the issue was worded: 'Si par la suite le grand Empereur des Français jugeait convenable d'apporter des modifications aux articles du présent Traité, il pourra entamer de nouvelles négociations avec la Chine après que douze ans se seront écoulés, à partir du jour de l'échange des ratifications de ce Traité.' The Chinese version of this clause, on the other hand, instead of talking of the *articles du présent Traité* referred to 'these regulations and provisions'. Keying had already laid stress, when discussing the question of treaty alteration, on the phrase 'inconsiderable modifications', and had denied that it was to be understood that 'after twelve years, the Treaty should be disregarded and ministers appointed to determine upon other provision': in his view all that was contemplated was that 'the minutiae of the commercial points may possibly after a term of twelve years stand in need of slight alteration'. There was not much therefore in any admission of

[1] Bonham to Clarendon, 4 Aug. 1853 (F.O. 17/204).
[2] Clarendon to Bowring, 5 July 1854 (F.O. 17/211).

Keying to Davis to justify the British and other Governments in asking for a complete overhaul of the three treaties,[1] and Clarendon agreed that there was nothing to be gained in calling the attention of the High Commissioner to that correspondence.[2]

The Foreign Secretary admitted that, although Great Britain had not obtained all the advantages expected from the Treaty of Nanking, still her commerce had made great strides and was capable of further expansion.

'It was not to be expected', he remarked, 'that the notions of superiority over other governments, which the isolated position in which the government of China had so long entrenched itself had served to foster, should at once give way to a conviction that its claims in that respect were unfounded or that the arrogance of the authorities and the prejudices of the people should be altogether exchanged for feelings of cordiality and goodwill towards those who by force of arms had acquired a right to be treated with consideration and respect.'

It was, he thought, a disregard of these considerations which had brought a certain amount of disappointment. If the Chinese authorities pleaded that the state of civil war prevented them from engaging in negotiations for treaty revision, Bowring was instructed at least to obtain an acknowledgement of the right of Great Britain to a revision on the twelfth anniversary of the Nanking Treaty—29 August 1854. A postponement of the actual negotiations might be advantageous to Great Britain by giving her an opportunity of obtaining a better idea of the possible outcome of the rebellion, and of bringing about conjoint action with the United States and France. But whether the representatives of these states co-operated or not it was still, as it had been in the days of the Melbourne and Peel ministries, the desire of Her Majesty's Government 'that all the nations of the civilized world should share equally with them in whatever benefits, commercial or political, circumstances may enable them to secure for the British nation'. To this end copies of Bowring's instructions were forwarded for the information of the Governments of Washington and Paris.

But the British Government had no intention of pressing its requests for revision by force of arms. Bowring was bidden to avoid using an authoritative tone which might compel his

---

[1] Bowring to Clarendon, 25 Apr. 1854 (F.O. 17/213).
[2] Clarendon to Bowring, 5 July 1854 (F.O. 17/211).

Government to choose between loss of consideration and dignity by retracting and the risk of an interruption of commerce or even of war in support of their demands. Great caution should be exercised, especially in urging the rights which the Government regarded as already conceded by treaty but not enjoyed in practice, such as free intercourse with the Chinese authorities and admission to the city of Canton. What they wished was the opportunity for making proposals and of 'receding from them without dishonour, if found unpalatable to the Chinese government'[1]. This unwillingness to contemplate the use of force was particularly necessary 'at a moment when the aid of the British naval force in China Seas might not be available for that purpose'[2].

Bowring was fully alive to the significance of the weakened naval forces in the China Seas as a result of the outbreak of the Crimean War. He was even afraid that Russian warships, or vessels with letters of marque, might attempt to interfere with British shipping.[3] Indeed, until its termination in the spring of 1856 the Crimean War made an active policy in the Far East impossible. Bowring himself understood 'at a moment when the cares of the great European contest must necessarily be peremptory and paramount, that questions so remote and in many respects so intricate, as those which present themselves in China cannot obtain the attention which an altered and more active policy would demand'[4]. Not only was there no possibility of a sufficient material force for the time being, but it seemed that the British Government and the Foreign Office had not adequate time to devote to a study of the problems of the Far East. Yet both would be needed. 'These stubborn mandarins, though stiff, are as subtle as otters. Before we end I am quite afraid we shall have to employ something harder than brainbullets.'[5]

2. *Negotiations at Shanghai and the Peiho*

Bowring, as we have already seen, was perhaps the first Englishman in a position of responsibility to advocate close cooperation with the Governments of the Treaty Powers. The instructions which he received so to act must, therefore, have

[1] Clarendon to Bowring, 13 Feb. 1854 (F.O. 17/210).
[2] Clarendon to Bowring, 5 July 1854 (F.O. 17/211).
[3] Bowring to Clarendon, 20 Apr. 1854 (F.O. 17/213).
[4] Bowring to Clarendon, 14 May 1855 (F.O. 17/230).
[5] Bowring to Hammond, 18 May 1854 (F.O. 17/213).

been very welcome, and owing to the change in the personnel of the American legation, it would seem that they might afford some opportunity of making such a demonstration of unity as to cause a change in the attitude of the Imperial Commissioner and Government. As soon as he assumed office he got into touch with de Bourboulon and McLane. The French Minister formed the opinion from his conversations with Bowring that the new British Plenipotentiary was 'very anxious to mark his arrival in China by an important move, and also impatient— perhaps a little more than custom and circumstances warranted —to tackle all at once the various questions connected with a most complicated mission'[1].

Bowring admitted to McLane that the Russian war and his consequent naval weakness made it impossible for him to insist upon a reception by the Imperial Commissioner in his Yamen in the City,[2] yet he wished to give Yeh an opportunity of meeting him and discussing the situation.[3] He announced his assumption of office in a dispatch to the Imperial Commissioner dated 17 April 1854. Receiving no reply, he wrote again eight days later. On the same day Yeh replied postponing an interview to a 'fortunate' day.[4] Twelve days later Yeh agreed to meet Bowring outside the city in Howqua's packhouse on the 22nd May. The British Plenipotentiary refused to meet the High Commissioner otherwise than at a public office inside the city.[5] The newly arrived United States representative could not prevail upon Yeh to meet him anywhere and decided to make the 'discourtesy and repulsiveness' of the Imperial Commissioner a prominent reason to justify his going to the Peiho, whither he was bent on sailing with a fleet which contained —unlike the British squadron—ships suitable for river service.[3] Bowring arranged to meet the American representative at Shanghai and hoped on his way there to prevail upon the Viceroy at Foochow to forward a remonstrance on the behaviour of his Canton colleague to Peking. He contemplated a joint Anglo-American move to the capital. This would be a grave step to take and perhaps it would prove futile, for the

[1] De Bourboulon to Min. Aff. Étr., 19 May 1854 (Chine 15).
[2] McLane to Sec. of State, 20 April 1854 (Sen. Ex. Doc. 22, 2 Sess. 35 Cong., at p. 23).
[3] Bowring to Clarendon, 25 Apr. 1854 (F.O. 17/213).
[4] Bowring to Clarendon, 3 May 1854 (F.O. 17/213).
[5] Bowring to Clarendon, 15 May 1854 (F.O. 17/213).

Jesuits had suggested that the Emperor, by the simple process of travelling into Manchuria, would avoid all negotiations if he and his French and American colleagues went to the capital. Perhaps, commented Bowring, the best answer the Governments of the three Powers could make to Yeh's intransigent behaviour would be a declaration firstly that, on the broad ground of violation of the Treaty by the Chinese, the subjects of the three Powers were emancipated from the restrictions placed upon them by the Treaty, and could trade where they wished, and secondly, that so long as the foreigners behaved peacefully, their persons and their property would be protected by their respective Governments.[1]

Arrived in Shanghai, Bowring had two discussions on the 27th June and the 3rd July with the local Chinese authorities, mainly concerning the position of the Imperialists and insurgents, between whom the British had attempted in vain to mediate. He was able at the latter of these interviews to complain to Keih the Provincial Governor of Kiangsu of the attitude adopted by Yeh. 'Yeh was an old man', replied the Governor, 'and unable to force the people: in Chinese politics, the two influences attended to were above, Heaven, and below, the people.'[2] On the 25th July, after a conference between Bowring, his American colleague, and Admiral Sir James Stirling on the one side, and Keih and Woo, the Taoutai of Shanghai, on the other, the Governor agreed to report to Peking his meeting with the foreign authorities and his discussion with them concerning the local situation. But he declined to forward a representation of theirs to Peking as he feared the consequences of a charge of meddling in matters foreign to his jurisdiction. He agreed, however, to convey the substance of their representation to the Emperor, and to inform him of their desire to place British and American commerce on a more extended basis and to settle the question of the extra duty levied upon tea. If he were disgraced as a result of such action, an inquiry into Yeh's proceedings would probably be held and result in that officer's removal. McLane impressed upon Keih how anxious Her Majesty's Plenipotentiary had always been to persuade the Chinese authorities to give effect to treaty stipulations, how unsuccessful his applications at Canton had been,

[1] Bowring to Clarendon, 18 May 1854 (F.O. 17/213).
[2] Bowring to Clarendon, 6 July 1854 (F.O. 17/214).

'that he had decided in consequence never again to go back to the Commissioner at Canton and that with that determination he, the United States Commissioner, entirely concurred; that there was no alternative left to them but to go in person to Peking and state their case to the Emperor himself'. They were, however, aware how distasteful such action would be to the Court and therefore accepted Keih's suggestion that he would be their mouthpiece.

In accordance with the Governor's request the memorandum which the two Plenipotentiaries presented to him showed 'a desire to advantage China as well as Great Britain and America'. It recalled the fact that Bowring, finding on his arrival in June, the 'subjects of Great Britain endeavouring to evade the Treaties, and the Imperial authorities scarcely able to enforce them', had made the merchants pay their duties regularly and had promised payment of back duties.[1] It was agreed that in forty days the British and American representatives should meet again in Shanghai to hear the result of Keih's move,[2] though if this were unsatisfactory Bowring and McLane were prepared themselves to go to the Peiho in September. Clarendon entirely approved of the proposed expedition and learnt with great satisfaction that if it took place the Americans would be there, and he hoped the French also.[3]

But any hopes there might have been of Keih's intervention proving effective were soon dashed. As McLane was on the point of leaving for Canton, Keih asked for another conference, at which the Chinese officer explained that an Imperial edict had been issued commanding the two foreigners to go to Canton and settle affairs with Yeh, while the Taoutai who had adopted a conciliatory attitude was to be impeached on a charge of embezzlement. Bowring felt 'no surprise at our having reached this crisis, and I have never accommodated my policy to a confidence in the value of any promises made by any Mandarins in the Chinese Empire'. McLane, he thought, had assuredly exhausted every means of friendly action at Canton, at Foochow where he had attempted to pay a personal visit to the Viceroy, and at Shanghai. He was now completely converted

---

[1] This was of course before the law officers had advised the British Government that the back duties were not legally recoverable. See p. 162.

[2] Bowring to Clarendon, 27 July 1854 (F.O. 17/215).

[3] Bowring to Clarendon (and Clarendon's minute thereon), 28 July 1854 (F.O. 17/215).

to Bowring's opinions. Keih who would have to defer forwarding the substance of the memorandum until the Taoutai's examination was complete and his successor appointed, begged McLane to make another attempt with Yeh, who had been instructed to receive all foreign envoys for the future. McLane replied, and his rejoinder was immediately confirmed by Bowring, that he was going down to Canton to look into the disturbed condition of that neighbourhood, that he would not seek an interview with Yeh, and that if he did see him he would be most unwilling to discuss general questions with him, but would tell him plainly his opinion of his conduct—that he considered him unfit to negotiate national questions with foreign envoys and totally unworthy of his confidence.[1]

On his way to Hong Kong Bowring called in at Foochow and Amoy. After some preliminary difficulties, which included an attempt to persuade Bowring to enter by a door of insufficient honour and the use of the term 'Barbarian', Wong, the Viceroy of Fukien, who had been in the habit of publicly expressing contempt and hatred of foreigners, agreed to receive a visit in due form from the British Plenipotentiary. Their conversation turned solely on local questions.[2] At Amoy Bowring found the merchants too much disposed to emancipate themselves from consular control, but hoped that, through the joint influence of a newly appointed Taoutai and Consul Parkes, the trade of Amoy would flourish, especially as the Canton region was so disturbed.[3]

When the three Western representatives met in Hong Kong on the 28th August they had all been instructed by their respective Governments to act in loyal co-operation. McLane and Bowring had indeed anticipated these instructions,[4] and now the French representative joined them. After some discussion they agreed to refuse an interview with Yeh, to sail for the Peiho, and obtain a conference with an Imperial Commissioner authorized to discuss the conditions of new Treaties.[5] On the 30th September the three were back in Shanghai and there they again met the Governor and Taoutai. The French

---

[1] Bowring to Clarendon, 3 Aug. 1854 (F.O. 17/215).
[2] Bowring to Clarendon, 14 Aug. 1854 (F.O. 17/215).
[3] Bowring to Clarendon, 19 Aug. 1854 (F.O. 17/215).
[4] Bowring to Clarendon, 5 Sept. 1854 (F.O. 17/215); McLane to Marcy, 20 Aug. 1854 (Sen. Ex. Doc. 22, 2 Sess. 35 Cong. at p. 169).
[5] Bowring to Clarendon, 11 Sept. 1854, 29 Sept. 1854 (F.O. 17/215).

and American ministers informed the Chinese that they were instructed to act with the British representative. McLane told Keih that while in the south he had again been in communication with Yeh who could not discuss other than minor modifications to the existing treaties, whereas the aim of the three ministers was the establishment of international relations on an improved and proper basis. The French Minister added that he especially desired to protect Catholic converts who had recently been suffering much persecution. Bowring remarked that the forbearance of his Government had not been properly appreciated. Keih agreed that Yeh's letter in regard to treaty revision was a 'vague and unsatisfactory document, unworthy of a man charged with the Commissioner's responsibilities', but he impressed upon the foreign ministers the difficulty of their enterprise: they might find a state of rebellion at the mouth of the Peiho; anyhow there would only be minor officials present. He suggested that he could now charge himself with their communication. In July he had just heard the Emperor's edict. 'Now however the case was different. His advice to return to Canton had been taken, an effort had been made to induce Yeh to do his duty and it had failed.'[1] But Bowring admitted that 'the strength of my desire to adopt a particular course of action is generally measured by the amount of resistance to it which I experience from the Imperial Authorities'. The three ministers decided to postpone their departure for the Peiho a few days in order to give the Governor time to notify Peking of their impending arrival.[2]

On the 10th October Bowring and McLane left Shanghai accompanied by the attaché of the French Minister, who was later censured by his Government for refusing to travel with his colleagues on the ground that he had no French man-of-war in which to make the journey.[3] Five days later they anchored 8½ miles off the forts which guarded the entrance to the Peiho. On the 16th October the secretaries of the American and British ministers having passed some way up the river, the bar of which

[1] Bowring to Clarendon, 2 Oct. 1854 (F.O. 17/216).
[2] Bowring to Clarendon, 4 Oct. 1854 (F.O. 17/216).
[3] The difficulty about the warship was indeed a pretext. The Procureur expressed frankly his opinion of the abstention of de Bourboulon: 'Je doute qu'il soit très aisé de traiter de concert avec les Anglais. Je sais du moins que cela ne plaît pas à son entourage tandis que Mr. Bowring au contraire le désire ardemment.' Libois to Directeurs, 10 Nov. 1854 (M.E. vol. 314, f. 1470).

was wide and dangerous, were asked to return to the forts, where with marked civility they were welcomed by a high military functionary who 'happened' to be in the forts. They had been instructed to press for permission for the ministers to journey to Peking but not to close the door to any proposals that might be made. As the secretaries were of opinion that they were being trifled with they returned to their ships. To the suggestion made on the 26th by the local authorities that they should return to one of the Five Open Ports, the ministers answered that they would allow their secretaries to wait three days in the hope that an Imperial answer to their request to enter the capital might reach the Peiho on the 28th. Eventually on the 3rd November an Imperial Commissioner duly arrived and received the foreign envoys with distinction in tents especially erected on the river bank near the forts—the American Minister escorted by 150 marines and Bowring by a retinue of 50 persons.

There Bowring presented eighteen heads of a new treaty. One group concerned the relations of the two Governments and their agents. It was desired to maintain a resident minister in Peking, or at least for the British Minister to pay occasional visits to the capital and enjoy direct communication with the Cabinet, while to deal with local matters Bowring asked that the Plenipotentiary should have access to the official Yamens of the Viceroys, including that of Canton, whenever desired, and the consuls on needful occasions. An Imperial decree should grant to British subjects the right of entry into Canton, promised in April 1847. There were clauses dealing with the extension of trade through the whole interior of China or at least up the Yangtse as far as Poyang Lake, in the coastal harbours, and at Tientsin, for which Ningpo would be surrendered. It was sought to modify the tariff and to legalize the opium trade, to sanction the practice of the carrying trade in foreign bottoms, to arrange for co-operation in the suppression of piracy and in a regulated system of emigration. To assist the flow of goods transit duties on articles of export and import should be abolished, coins should be received at their intrinsic value and bonded warehouses established. To avoid the considerable difficulties that had been experienced at Whampoa and Shanghai Imperial instructions should be issued to enable British subjects to acquire quiet possession of purchased land, and to recover debts. The new and illegal tax on tea should be abolished, and greater protection should be given to foreign life and property. The new treaty, the English version of which should prevail, was to be reconsidered after the expiration of twelve years. The American proposals differed in some points. McLane thought it useless to take measures against piracy, and wished to prevent the coolie trade. In regard to the opium trade though his instructions precluded him from advocating any step towards its legalization, he desired to end the existing system of chaotic connivance. To all points except those dealing with measures of debt recovery and the additional tea duty, which should be dealt with at Canton, the Commissioners returned either an absolute negative or, as for example to the proposal for bonded warehouses, a bland answer 'you must adhere to old engagements'. Seeing that he could not even countenance these requests, how, asked the High Commissioner, could he presume to present them to the Throne? Bowring and his colleagues felt that they had at least done all they could to find a channel for amicable negotiation. They had been heard, though in vain, by an exalted person specially appointed by the Emperor. Their arguments to the effect that the Peking Government, in view of the rebellion, would be well advised to cultivate the best relations with the foreign Powers proved unavailing, because the rebellions were considered by the Chinese officers but as extensive outbreaks of robber confederacies. The capital itself seemed safe and as long as it was so 'large portions of the Empire may be disrupted without producing such alarm as to induce the Emperor to submit to the humiliation of seeking the aid or alliance of "outer nations" '.

Bowring, clearly convinced that peace could not be maintained without a demonstration of war, hoped to receive instructions from Her Majesty's Government that 'may be such as will enable Her representative to accommodate his action to the varying uncertain and unforeseen destinies through which it will probably be the fate of China to pass'[1]. McLane in reporting the failure of the Peiho negotiations asked for further instructions. Was he to go on as the United States had been doing—protecting American lives and property and generally waiting on events, or was a more active policy desired? If the latter course were adopted, the President might forward to the Peiho a letter to the Emperor, a refusal to accept which should

[1] Bowring to Clarendon, 10 Nov. 1854 (F.O. 17/217).

be followed by a blockade of the Peiho, Yangtse, Min, and Whampoa by the three Treaty Powers, whose recent harmony he hoped to see continued. There was also a possibility that in return for aid against the rebels the Chinese might be willing to grant extended facilities for trade.[1] He hoped himself that the President would adopt 'a new and perhaps aggressive policy, as the only means of preserving the commercial privileges now possessed by the western nations in China'[2].

But the British Government were not prepared, any more than the American, to adopt a policy which might lead to forceful measures. It was clear to Lord Clarendon that nothing had been gained by the visit except 'further evidence of the impracticable nature of the Government with which we have to deal in China and of the little hope of any advantage arising from conciliatory representations or attempts to bring on closer intercourse between Her Majesty's Servants and the Imperial Authorities'. Yet warlike demonstrations would be 'doubtful as a matter of right and very questionable as a matter of policy'. Though it was true there were just complaints, they did not in themselves justify war; and war might endanger the existing commerce. But even if the British Government had legality and commercial expediency on its side,

'the circumstances of the present time would make any such demonstration singularly inopportune. For the war in which we are engaged with Russia necessarily calls for all the naval and military force of the Empire which can be devoted to its prosecution. . . . It is therefore the positive injunction of Her Majesty's Government that you abstain from raising unnecessarily questions with the Chinese Government calculated to render a recourse to force incumbent on this country. . . . Your duty is to remain a quiet observer of the events which may be passing around you, . . . holding yourself aloof from all participation in the intestine troubles of the country.'[3]

The prosecution of any plan for more extensive and intimate relations with China was thus dropped for the moment. The next attempt was to be made at the suggestion of a former American medical missionary who took over the United States Legation as chargé d'affaires on McLane's retirement from the Far East.

[1] McLane to Sec. of State, 19 Nov. 1854 (Sen. Ex. Doc. 22, 2 Sess. 35 Cong., at p. 285).
[2] McLane to Sec. of State, 25 Nov. 1854 (ibid., at p. 349).
[3] Clarendon to Bowring, 24 Jan. 1855 (F.O. 17/224).

3. Parker's Forward Policy

During the summer of 1855 Dr. Parker proceeded to Washington. He acknowledged to the Secretary of State that the 34th article of the Treaty of Wanghia gave the United States a right to demand 'inconsiderable modifications', but that 'the experience of the last 12 years has evinced that not only inconsiderable modifications but radical changes are indispensable in order to attain the highest interests of the respective governments'. To effect this, 'high ground must be taken'[1]. He won the approval of the American Government for a policy of diplomatic activity, backed by a demonstration of force, to be pursued in co-operation with the other two Treaty Powers. Arrived in London on his return journey to the Far East he had an interview with Lord Clarendon in October 1855 which both regarded as highly satisfactory.[2] To Parker's observation that were he a Chinese and the greatest patriot of the Empire he could desire nothing better than what was contemplated by their Governments, the British Foreign Secretary replied: 'Yes, not only do our consciences approve, but the whole world must commend our policy.' Clarendon was delighted to hear that the Chinese people would welcome an extension of trade and agreed to Parker's suggestion that the Anglo-French force stationed in the China Seas might just as well, during the forthcoming negotiations with Russia, anchor for a fortnight in the Gulf of Pechili as in the harbour of Hong Kong.[3] The object of this force would be purely to give prestige to the negotiations. Parker having found an equally favourable atmosphere in Paris,[4] went on by Marseilles and Alexandria to Hong Kong where he arrived on the last day of 1855.

Meanwhile Bowring had become impressed by the desirability of establishing British influence in Peking, in order to strengthen the Chinese Government in a policy of resistance to the steady advance of Russia in the North.[5] Only a joint advance on Peking could prevent the Russians, with the Amour River as a base, from establishing settlements on territories inhabited by Tartars, Japanese, or Coreans which they might wish to conquer

[1] Parker to Marcy, 20 Sept. 1855 (Sen. Ex. Doc. 22, 2 Sess. 35 Cong., at p. 612).
[2] Clarendon to Bowring, 8 Nov. 1855 (F.O. 17/225).
[3] Parker to Marcy, 26 Oct. 1855 (Sen. Ex. Doc. 22, 2 Sess. 35 Cong., at p. 618).
[4] Parker to Marcy, 8 Nov. 1855 (ibid., at p. 621).
[5] Bowring to Clarendon, 10 Dec. 1855 (F.O. 17/235).

or to claim.[1] There was too a possibility that the Chinese authorities might make use of Russia to drive the Western Powers out of the five ports.[2] And the check which Russian activities in the Near East received as a result of the Treaty of Paris might give a fresh impulse to invasions and usurpations in the remoter regions of eastern Asia. Bowring warned the Foreign Office that 'a few years of Russian activity and of European neglect in localities so shattered and disorganized as China offers in her vast dominions may lead to a state of things far more menacing to our substantial interests both in China and India, than the possession of the Bosphorus or the freedom of the Sound would give Russia in the field of European activity'. The prospect of Russian irruption into Tartary, as the herald of projects upon Corea and Japan and ultimately upon China herself, would place in jeopardy the £40 millions of British capital and £10 millions of British and Indian revenue dependent upon the China trade. The problem was no longer one merely of securing trade concessions and an extension of commercial posts from the Chinese Government. By getting a footing in Peking 'the door may be opened to the discussion of other topics which cannot but be considered as intimately connected with our trading relations with China'[3].

In the course of a private correspondence with de Bourboulon's temporary successor, the Comte de Courcy, Bowring had asked: 'Is not this the moment for the Plenipotentiaries of the two Allied Powers to go to Peking, to fight there against an influence so contrary to our interests, and to seize, if necessary, such advantages as might give us an honourable and useful compensation?' De Courcy was alarmed at these ideas: he thought that France should not embark on such an enterprise, in which the Americans would certainly not participate. This scheme of Bowring's, he thought, 'sied bien à son esprit aventureux qui a eu déjà l'occasion de se signaler plusieurs fois depuis son retour en Chine'[4].

The Foreign Office, as much impressed as was its representative in China by the danger of Russian activities, was anxious to consider the possibility of an 'undertaking for the protection of

---

[1] Bowring to Clarendon, 27 Nov. 1855 (F.O. 17/235).
[2] Bowring to Clarendon, 13 Mar. 1856 (F.O. 17/246).
[3] Bowring to Clarendon, 1 May 1856 (F.O. 17/246).
[4] De Courcy to Min. Aff. Étr., 8 Feb. 1856 (Chine 17).

the Chinese Empire against Russian aggression'. Bowring's opinion was sought 'not only as to the manner in which such a Protectorate[1] could be established and made effectual, but also as to the measures which would be necessary for obtaining the assent of the Chinese authorities to it'[2].

Though Bowring thought that the United States would probably rather invite than repel Russian influence in China,[3] he naturally welcomed the intention of Parker to attempt to win the Chinese Government's approval not only to the opening of further ports to foreign trade, but also to the establishment of foreign ministers in Peking. Great changes would inevitably follow if American policy were as vigorous in action as it appeared to be decided in intention.[4] The close harmony between the representatives of the Anglo-Saxon States was evident from the presence in Government House at Hong Kong of Dr. Parker as Bowring's guest. The British host was in full agreement with his guest in desiring an extension of trade, though he would not go so far as Parker in wishing to secure an unlimited trade, for in his opinion it would be safer to confine it to specified ports on the Yangtse and on the coast. Nor did he think it practical to insist, as Parker desired, on the universal grant of freedom of opinion. The establishment of the legations at Peking would be a blessing to China, for the machinery of government might be employed to advance the greatest reforms —educational, social, and political, but such 'results must grow out of influence only slowly to be acquired, and most prudently to be exercised'. Bowring thought that Parker's proposal of an agreement for a reform of the tribunals 'can form no part of diplomatic action or Treaty discussions',[5] and that it was far more important and practical to attempt to settle the immediate and specific questions relating to piracy, emigration, currency, and tariff reform. The vague and benevolent suggestions of Parker, in which the French Government concurred, were, he confessed, tasks beyond his capacity. 'The moral influence of the Western nations may in the progress

[1] Though the words 'Protectorate could be established' on the draft dispatch were underlined and a query inserted opposite to them in the margin, the initial of the Foreign Secretary was appended at its foot.
[2] Clarendon to Bowring, 7 Mar. 1856 (F.O. 17/242).
[3] Bowring to Clarendon, 1 May 1856 (F.O. 17/246).
[4] Bowring to Clarendon, 5 Jan. 1856 (F.O. 17/244).
[5] Bowring to Clarendon, 6 Feb. 1856 (F.O. 17/245).

of centuries of intercourse, change the opinions, ameliorate the codes, and reform the tribunals of 3 or 400 millions of men.'[1]

After Parker's visit to Lord Clarendon, Bowring was informed that the British Government intended to co-operate with those of America and France.[2] On the receipt of further instructions sent in March Bowring held a conference with Admiral Seymour. The British naval commander, who had been active off Kamchatka during the previous summer,[3] could promise no help to the civil authority until 'the great European question has reached some solution'[4]. Although news of the termination of the Crimean War reached Bowring officially by the 26th May,[5] Seymour was intending in July to sail back to India on the break of the monsoon.[6] Bowring had already given it as his opinion in the previous September that the success of any attempt to reform the existing treaties would depend upon the disposal of an adequate naval force in China,[7] and he now urged upon Parker the uselessness of moving to the Gulf of Pechili with only two ships of war. McLane and he had exhausted the possibilities of amicable representations in 1854, and a weak demonstration would but confirm the Peking Government in their obstinacy.[8] The American representative, however, persisted in his desire to effect something: he was full of high hope and appeared not to doubt for a moment of success. Common negotiations and the mere presence of naval forces off the Peiho would, he thought, be enough. 'I know', he told de Courcy, 'that there are in Peking statesmen of integrity, intelligence, and devotion to their master'. For long they had misunderstood the evil which was undermining the throne, and ruining the reputation of China, and therefore they naturally knew not the remedy to be applied. Yet if he and his colleagues appeared in the north 'these men would eagerly grasp the hands we hold out to save them'. De Courcy had no illusions concerning the alleged intelligent docility of the Emperor's advisers— 'cela serait trop contraire aux précédents historiques'. Indeed,

[1] Bowring to Clarendon, 21 Aug. 1856 (F.O. 17/249).
[2] Clarendon to Bowring, 8 Dec. 1855 (F.O. 17/225).
[3] Bowring to Clarendon, 1 Aug. 1855 (F.O. 17/232).
[4] Bowring to Clarendon, 16 May 1856 (F.O. 17/247).
[5] Bowring to Clarendon, 26 May 1856 (F.O. 17/247).
[6] Bowring to Clarendon, 1 July 1856 (F.O. 17/248).
[7] Bowring to Clarendon, 13 Sept. 1855 (F.O. 17/233).
[8] Bowring to Clarendon, 1 July 1856 (F.O. 17/248).

were the Emperor to act as Parker hoped, he would be completely discredited and deemed to have humbled himself before the Barbarian.[1] De Courcy's advice to his Government was very different from the American's conception: 'Before beginning we should above all be certain of our capacity to carry on and bring the affair to a successful conclusion.'[2] But as he was not yet in receipt of instructions from the Quai d'Orsay, de Courcy felt himself unable to do more than announce to Yeh that his Emperor was counting upon a revision of the French Treaty.

On his way to Shanghai, which was as far north as ever he got, Parker had persuaded the Viceroy of Fukien to transmit to Peking a letter of which he was the bearer from the President to the Emperor.[3] The Imperial Privy Council opened and returned it with a caution to the Fukien Viceroy that foreign affairs were in the sole charge of his colleague at Canton, 'the most popular and powerful minister in the Empire'. To treat the President's letter in this fashion was in Parker's judgement 'a fresh indignity to the sovereignty of the United States, and one more argument, would that it were the final one, that the past and present policy of the Manchus towards the Americans as well as all foreign nations can and shall be endured no longer'[4]. It was not his fault, he wrote to Washington in September, that he was not already in Peking. Co-operation between the powers was a necessity and Bowring with the best will in the world was unable to proceed north. The British representative had, however, fully endorsed his policy of entering upon negotiations at Shanghai with accredited plenipotentiaries provided that they agreed at the outset to the residence of foreign ministers in Peking.[5]

Throughout the summer of 1856 indeed co-operation was perforce limited to the diplomatic sphere. Bowring agreed in the middle of May to give formal notice to Yeh, the Imperial Commissioner, of the existence of British co-operation in an attempt to redress existing grievances and for placing future relations upon a more satisfactory footing.[6] At the beginning of July Yeh had answered neither that communication nor an

---

[1] De Courcy to Min. Aff. Étr., 8 Feb. 1856 (Chine 17).
[2] De Courcy to Min. Aff. Étr., 22 May 1856 (Chine 18).
[3] Parker to Sec. of State, 24 July 1856 (Sen. Ex. Doc. 22, 2 Sess. 35 Cong., at p. 857).   [4] Parker to Sec. of State, 5 Sept. 1856 (ibid., at p. 940).
[5] Parker to Sec. of State, 30 June 1856, 3 Sept. 1856, 20 Oct. 1856 (ibid., at pp. 846, 920, 981).   [6] Bowring to Clarendon, 16 May 1856 (F.O. 17/247).

earlier dispatch of the 15th April on the subject of the Customs Inspectorate system. Bowring might well characterize this sullen attitude as 'this neglectful and insulting silence' which 'is in itself a grievance of an intolerable character'[1], and his judgement was fully endorsed by Parker:

'His Excellency Yee, in some respects', he wrote to Washington, 'stands alone and pre-eminent in his insane and insufferable conduct towards foreigners. . . . The same demeanour on the part of an officer of his rank of any other nation would be deemed an outrage justifying summary redress; but hitherto foreign governments have treated that of China as ignorant and barbarous, and have not applied those principles of international law and etiquette which obtain in the intercourse of civilized nations.'[2]

The succession of honours showered upon Yeh since his success against the rebels had made him 'wild with pride and vanity', so that Bowring harked back to his old panacea and advised the Foreign Office 'that the simplest and safest policy would be to humble that pride by insisting on an official reception at Canton'. It was quite probable, he thought, that 'were he informed that it would be *enforced* by us, if it should be denied by him', the right of official entry and reception in the city would not be denied.[3] A rumour which got abroad that Bowring was about to enter Canton by force was thought by the British Plenipotentiary to be the reason which prompted Yeh finally to reply to his dispatch. Of the reply, which was a refusal to help in the inauguration of the Inspectorate system elsewhere than at Shanghai, and a denial of the right of the British to claim under the Treaty of Wanghia a revision of their own treaties, Bowring wrote 'nothing can be more contemptuous'. Quite clearly 'no becoming attention would be paid by the Chinese authorities to any representations which are not associated with a display of physical force'[4]. Incendiary placards had already begun to appear, the Imperial authorities were again stirring up the people as in 1849, and only the nearness of serious personal danger would lead the Chinese Government to extend friendly relations with foreigners.[5] The present enforced policy of non-action was fraught with increasing perils

---

[1] Bowring to Clarendon, 1 July 1856 (F.O. 17/248).
[2] Parker to Sec. of State, 7 May 1856 (Sen. Ex. Doc. 22, 2 Sess. 35 Cong., at p. 760).   [3] Bowring to Clarendon, 1 July 1856 (F.O. 17/248).
[4] Bowring to Clarendon, 3 July 1856 (F.O. 17/248).

which exposed British interests to certain danger. On the other hand, the presence of a respectable force of the three Powers, with a number of light draught ships able to make their way to Tientsin, anchored in the Gulf of Pechili the following May or June, might well lead to the withdrawal of the whole court into Manchuria. But even that would be better than inactivity.[1]

Clarendon approved of Bowring's decision to refrain from going to the north in view of Admiral Seymour's inability to accompany him. But now that the Crimean War was over he requested the Admiralty to furnish their officer with sufficient force and to instruct him to be at liberty to take Bowring to the northern ports in company with the ministers and naval forces of the United States and France. Joint action by the three Treaty Powers at the moment, thought Clarendon, was of great importance.[2] These instructions arrived in China at the beginning of October. The season was too late to allow of an immediate move to the Gulf of Pechili, the Admiral still wished to visit India, the French and Americans were not ready, steamers of shallow draught were a technical necessity and appear not to have been at hand. Bowring contemplated being in a position to move the following spring.[3]

The situation then in the autumn of 1856 was one of expectancy. The British Admiral, now that the overpowering necessity of watching Russian activities in the Far East had been removed, had received his instructions from the Admiralty to co-operate with Sir John Bowring in a move towards Peking in order adequately to reinforce demands for a radical alteration in the existing state of affairs. The British Government had agreed that a policy of enforced inaction must come to an end and that a real attempt must be made not only to extend trading facilities but to break through the icy wall of Yeh's coldness by means of a direct advance to the capital. Bowring had again quite recently suggested that the best place to attempt to melt the Chinese obduracy was Canton, and that the threat of force was the only chance of success without bloodshed. The time was favourable in that the American Government was prepared to co-operate loyally towards ends in effect similar to those

[1] Bowring to Clarendon, 21 Aug. 1856 (F.O. 17/249).
[2] Bowring to Clarendon, 16 May 1856 (minute of Clarendon thereon dated 17 July) (F.O. 17/247) and Clarendon to Bowring, 30 July 1856 (F.O. 17/243).
[3] Bowring to Clarendon, 3 Oct. 1856 (F.O. 17/251).

of the British Cabinet, and the common work of the Second Empire and Great Britain in withstanding Russia in the Near East augured well for the continuance of an intimacy in the more remote regions of the Far East, where the murder of a Catholic missionary, Chapdelaine, in February[1] 1856 was to provoke Napoleon III to a determination to exact ample reparation.[2]

This murder was a culminating incident in a long story of imprisonment, persecution, and death. In 1850 a French Catholic missionary had been imprisoned for baptizing the daughter of a Mandarin and her son. Eventually released after removal to Canton through the efforts of the French Consul and Forth-Rouen, he complained of the continued maltreatment to which the native Christians were exposed by the evil will of the authorities of China, 'who only act when compelled and when they cannot do otherwise'. 'Our poor Christians . . . whom we teach to look upon France as their support and liberator, are groaning in oppression.'[3]

The fathers of 'Les Missions Étrangères' were thus creating an important French interest, and like the British merchants were critical of the alleged supineness of the national representatives in the Far East. One of them, Guillemin, soon to be consecrated Bishop by the Pope himself, exclaimed that the French diplomats 'ne semblent venir ici que pour se moquer de nous sous la voile d'une bienveillance apparente'[4]. 'Mon Dieu! pourquoi n'avons-nous pas un homme capable de comprendre ces choses, et de conduire les affaires de manière à les faire tourner à la gloire de Dieu et la conversion de ce pauvre peuple chinois.'[5] From April to November the missionary Jacquemin was held in prison in the interior. Twice de Bourboulon wrote to Yeh, but without apparent effect: 'all this proves', wrote the future Bishop, 'more and more that we need a man here, who knows his duty and who has the strength and the will to do it'[6]. Yet though he complained thus bitterly to the Directors of the Mission, he did not advocate a recourse to war. 'I am not one of those men who wants the guns fired at all costs; they may very often do us more harm than good; but for goodness' sake let

[1] Bowring to Clarendon, 19 July 1856 (F.O. 17/249).
[2] Clarendon to Bowring, 29 Sept. 1856 (F.O. 17/243).
[3] Le Turdu to Directeurs, 17 Nov. 1850 (M.E., vol. 550, f. 145).
[4] Guillemin to Albrano, 22 July 1853 (ibid., f. 323).
[5] Guillemin to Legrégeois, 16 Jan. 1854 (ibid., f. 359).
[6] Guillemin to Legrégeois, 10 July 1855 (ibid., f. 543).

us stick to our treaties—which are not much to boast of anyhow.'[1] The Procureur Libois, though admitting that de Bourboulon might have been more active, thought that his conduct
had been too severely criticized, especially in the columns of the
Univers which were written by the pen of his own assistant. The
Viceroy had indeed treated the Minister in a cavalier fashion,
but he had nevertheless communicated with the Magistrate of
Kia-yn, who after great delay, attributable in part to the disturbed condition of the country, had dispatched Jacquemin in
accordance with the treaty stipulations under escort to Canton.[2]
For it should be remembered that no foreigners were under
treaty allowed beyond the treaty ports. When therefore missionaries transgressed the rule they were apt to complain of the
treaties as being *mesquins*. Though it was obviously illegal to
imprison or put to death a foreigner, they could have no valid
reason to object to removal to the nearest treaty port. The
Catholic missionaries who lived *à la chinoise* had penetrated in
great numbers and even into the far interior, but though they
were criticized by the Protestants for justifying the means by the
end, their critics were at one with them in disregarding the
treaty limitations. J. S. Burdon, looking back on the 'system of
itineration' followed by the missionaries of the Church Missionary Society before 1858, justified a practice which he agreed to be
'a direct violation of the Treaty of Nanking' by the thought that
'no one who acknowledges the supremacy of the Saviour over all
earthly things will condemn the missionary who *judiciously*
seeks to obey that Saviour's last command'[3].

Libois took the troubled position of the Catholic missionaries
very calmly. When in the summer of 1856 he heard of the death
in the previous February at Sin-lin in the Province of Kwangsi
of Chapdelaine he uttered a pious expression of hope in his
report of the fatality to the Directors that the murdered man's
blood might so water the ground as to cause it to bring forth
fruit abundantly.[4] To some of his colleagues Libois had indeed
to bear a heavy responsibility, for according to one of them:

'L'envoi de ce cher confrère au Kouangsi était contraire à
toutes les lois de la prudence, on l'a fait observer au p. Libois de

[1] Guillemin to Directeurs, 10 July 1855 (ibid. f., 547).
[2] Libois to Directeurs, 14 Nov. 1855 (ibid., vol. 314, f. 1719).
[3] Burdon to Secretary, C.M.S., 22 Nov. 1858 (C.M.S., China 14).
[4] Libois to Directeurs, 7 July 1856 (M.E., vol. 314, f. 1843).

plusieurs côtés; mais son parti était pris, et il a fallu marcher. Pour moi, j'étais persuadé que tôt ou tard il lui arriverait malheur. Mr. Guillemin ne l'était pas moins que moi et Mr. Perny l'avait annoncé au p. Libois.'[1]

De Courcy was acting as chargé d'affaires when the cruel torture and death of Chapdelaine became known. To his request that Yeh should himself propose adequate terms of reparation the Imperial Commissioner returned a procrastinating refusal. De Courcy thereupon demanded the punishment by degradation and exile of the offending magistrate and, as a warning to others and as some security for the future, the publication of the sentence in the *Peking Gazette*. As Yeh would neither himself propose any satisfaction nor accept the terms demanded by the French chargé, de Courcy refused further discussion and referred the matter to Paris.[2] Although previous régimes had not been unmindful of the important French interest represented by these fathers, it was certain that Napoleon III would be especially sensitive to the call of an active policy which could be pursued at once side by side with Great Britain and in the interests of the Catholic Faith. In the murder of Chapdelaine he was presented in the summer of 1856 with an adequate reason for making common cause with the British in an attempt to establish closer relations with the Imperial Government in Peking, if need be by force of arms.

On the Chinese side it is clear that the Cantonese Imperial Commissioners had effectively done their best to bring to an end the friendly and harmonious relations of the days of Pottinger and Keying. Yeh had triumphed—for the moment —over the indigenous rebels with the support of popular opinion, again recently manifested in the city. Could there be any doubt that he would continue to retain the confidence of his countrymen and the favour of the Son of Heaven? A crisis was approaching, but would not have arrived until the spring of 1857, had not an incident happened on the 8th October which brought about a state of hostilities locally in Canton which was not to be closed until four years later the Treaty of Tientsin was duly ratified in the capital of the Celestial Empire. It is clear that it is entirely misleading to regard the affair of the lorcha *Arrow* as the main cause of a formal breach in

---

[1] Le Turdu to Legrégeois, 4 July 1856 (M.E., vol. 550, f. 719).
[2] Cordier, *L'Expéd.* i, ch. II.

relations between Great Britain and the Chinese Government. In a real sense there had hardly been any relations between the Western Powers and the Imperial Commissioners for some years, and the fundamental cause of the ensuing war was the desire of the Western Powers to perfect the work inaugurated as they imagined in the treaties of the forties.

By a rigid insistence upon the narrowest interpretation of the treaty contracts, the Chinese had so far successfully resisted the advances of the British and other foreign Powers in the direction of a closer and more extensive intimacy. But the patience of the Western governments was now exhausted. They were determined, if necessary by force, to humble what they could only regard as the arrogant pride of the Emperor and his Ministers, and to compel China, which they persisted in treating as a Sovereign State, to take her proper place in the family of nations.

V

THE LORCHA *ARROW*, 1856–7

A. THE INCIDENT AND ITS CONSEQUENCES IN CHINA

ON the morning of the 8th October 1856 near the Dutch Folly, an island in the river opposite the British factories at Canton, the lorcha *Arrow*, commanded by a British subject, Thomas Kennedy, was boarded by a large party of Chinese police consisting of four officers and forty soldiers,[1] and twelve of her Chinese crew of fourteen were carried off to a Chinese war junk. The *Arrow* had received a colonial register, according to the local Hong Kong ordinances, in the name of her owner Fong-Ah-ming, a Chinese Crown leaseholder who had been settled in the colony for the previous ten years. The register was in fact a few days out of date, as it had been issued for one year on the 27th September 1855. Kennedy, a Belfast man aged twenty-one, described as 'very respectable of his class', had been engaged as her nominal master by Block, the Danish Consul at Hong Kong who, with one Douglas Lapraik, in accordance with the colonial ordinance, had gone security to the Hong Kong Government for the vessel under a penalty of $3,000. The *Arrow* had been sold to Fong-Ah-ming by pirates who had captured her from her lawful owners, with whom Fong, however, had subsequently compounded for $1,000. That the vessel, engaged lawfully in the importation of rice, had committed an offence against the regulations of the Colonial Government there is no doubt, but the offence was at most technical. For Kennedy had left Hong Kong on the 1st September with a valid register and would no doubt have renewed it on the 9th October, by which date, had the vessel not been held up at Canton, he would again have arrived at the colony. Since the 1st September he had been to Macao and Canton. The *Arrow*'s papers were on that morning of the 8th October lawfully deposited at the British Consulate, and Parkes, the Consul, seems to have been ignorant that the period of their validity had just elapsed. It is clear, moreover, that this irregularity was unknown to the Chinese who authorized the boarding of the lorcha and the arrest of the twelve members of the crew.

[1] De Courcy to Min. Aff. Étr. 10 Nov. 1856 (Chine 19).

It is hard to believe that they were unaware that she claimed at least to be entitled to British protection. Though there was subsequently a denial by the Chinese that the British flag was flying at the time, that it had been hoisted and was torn down by the boarding party was averred on oath by Kennedy, who was 150 yards away at the time on board the *Dart* lorcha with that vessel's master, Leach, who gave concurrent testimony. The two Chinese who were left in the *Arrow* also agreed that the British flag was flying and had been torn down. The evidence in the possession of the Imperial Commissioner Yeh on the question of ownership was provided by a member of the crew 'lying bound with thongs before his interested inquisitors at the time he made his statement'. Moreover, though Kennedy was absent when the ship was boarded, he quickly arrived, and it was at his request that two of the fourteen crew were allowed by the boarding party to remain on board. He knew Chinese well enough to make such request, and the officer in charge of the boarding party must therefore have known before the men were actually taken to the war junk that a British subject was master of the vessel. The *Arrow* had been engaged for five days in unloading her cargo, and it seems that the Hoppo must have been apprized of her status by the Consul who held her papers. That she was flying the British flag was in itself probable, as she appears to have had flying also the 'Blue Peter'—the signal that she was shortly departing. For when in port it was not the custom to fly the national flag. There can be little doubt, as Lord Clarendon observed, that 'the national character of the lorcha was well-known to the authorities'.

Assuming that the *Arrow* was, in accordance with the Supplementary Treaty of the Bogue or in any other way, an English[1] ship, there is no doubt that the Chinese authorities had committed a breach of the 9th article of the Supplementary Treaty. That article required that a Chinese malfaisant in a British ship should only be dealt with by the Imperial authorities after he had been handed over by the British Consul on requisition from, and subsequent to an examination by, the Consul in the presence of Chinese officers. The treaty, that is to say, made an exception in favour of English ships and their crews to the normal international rule, that in the territorial waters of any

[1] The words 'English' and 'British' are used in the Supplementary Treaty indiscriminately.

State, the officers of that State have sovereign jurisdiction over all ships and persons of whatever nationality. It was a specially favourable position enjoyed by the Treaty Powers in China—one of limited extra-territoriality for Chinese in treaty vessels analogous to the complete extra-territoriality enjoyed by persons who were subjects or citizens of the three Treaty Powers. And this specially favoured position demanded and conceded in the forties, as it had been already in the case of Turkey and Persia, was necessary if foreign persons and foreign commerce were to be allowed in the Chinese Empire.

The British Consul in Canton, Harry Parkes, had come out to China fifteen years before at the age of thirteen. He had acquired a fluent knowledge of Chinese and was a young man of 'nervous eagerness and quick apprehension' according to Alcock under whom at Amoy, Foochow, and Shanghai he had served his apprenticeship. He was to show himself fearless and clear-headed, of untiring energy and of extraordinary tenacity of purpose. On being informed of the event of the morning of the 8th October Consul Parkes repaired immediately to the war junk to demand the return of the twelve in as public a manner as had been their capture. He was prepared to examine them in accordance with the Treaty at the Consulate and to hand them over to Chinese officers if his examination of the case showed that there was adequate ground for their trial by the Chinese authorities. The officers of the junk, however, protested that they would resist Parkes by force if he attempted to rescue the men. They had received orders to arrest the father of a notorious pirate, who was stated to have been among the crew. Failing to get satisfaction from the immediate captors, Parkes preferred a complaint to Yeh, and requested him to deal with the matter, as he was himself prepared to do, in accordance with the Treaty. Two days later, after a second remonstrance from the Consul, Yeh in reply changed the ground for the arrest, alleging that three of the captured seamen had a month ago perpetrated a piracy at St. John's Island. He had accordingly directed an Assistant Magistrate to return nine of the men. He denied that the vessel was a foreign lorcha and declared that it was therefore useless to enter into any discussion respecting her. Parkes refused to receive these nine men as they were not delivered by the captain of the war junk to the *Arrow* in the Consul's presence.

The action of Yeh was tantamount to a declaration that he would respect neither the British flag nor a British register, whenever any Chinese stated to him that a vessel so provided was not British owned. The main question was, in Parkes's words:

'Are British ships to be subject, whenever information happens to be laid against any of the men on board, to be boarded by the Chinese military without communication being made to the consul; to have their national flag hauled down, and their crews carried away as prisoners, and is the Imperial Commissioner to be at liberty to declare a vessel to be Chinese owned, in the face of an assurance given by the British Consul of her British nationality and of his own admission of her being in possession of foreign papers?'

Sir John Bowring, appealed to by the Consul, instructed Parkes to inform Yeh that he required an apology and an undertaking for the future that the British flag should be respected. At the same time Parkes was to give an assurance that proceedings would be taken against British ships or subjects engaged in acts of piracy, and that there was no desire to harbour Chinese offenders on British ships. If the apology was not forthcoming within forty-eight hours the Senior Naval Officer at Canton was instructed to seize one naval junk until redress should be made.[1]

Although Yeh refused an apology for the past on the ground that the *Arrow* was not British, he gave a qualified promise that Chinese officers would not seize people belonging to foreign lorchas—qualified by the words 'without reason', of which the Chinese would apparently be the judges, and accompanied by an admonition that foreigners should not sell registers to Chinese owners of lorchas.[2] In consequence of the unsatisfactory nature of this reply, Commodore Elliot proceeded to fulfil his instructions. Fortunately the junk he seized offered no resistance; but as the vessel taken was in fact a merchantman and not a war junk, the menace produced no effect upon the Imperial Commissioner. Bowring warned Yeh of 'the grave consequences which may follow any further hesitation on your part to fulfil the Treaty engagements'[3]. On the 20th Parkes advocated that reprisals should be extended to the capture of the forts between Whampoa and Canton and ultimately to

---

[1] Bowring to Clarendon, 13 Oct. 1856 (recd. 1 Dec.) (F.O. 17/251).
[2] Bowring to Clarendon, 15 Oct. 1856 (F.O. 17/251).
[3] Bowring to Clarendon, 16 Oct. 1856 (F.O. 17/251).

those of Canton if within another twenty-four hours a fresh appeal to Yeh brought no satisfaction, for otherwise there would be no security for the small vessels of the colony whose crews were almost wholly or invariably Chinese. This plan was agreed to by Bowring and the naval commander-in-chief. Both the United States and French consular officers concurred in the justice of Parkes's demands. On the morning of the 22nd October the Imperial Commissioner handed over ten, and shortly before noon the remaining two of the captured Chinese seamen. But as no officer of rank nor letter of apology accompanied them, Parkes refused to receive them. So although Yeh gave 'a sort of assurance that the Consul should be applied to in future in cases of Chinese offenders being found on board foreign lorchas', his action fell short of the British demands. The forts were, therefore, duly captured on the 23rd and Bowring thought that Yeh would then 'feel the absolute necessity of complying to the demands that had been made', and indeed 'the *vexata questio* of our entrance into the city' might also be settled. But though the operations were successfully extended to the capture on the 24th of the forts in the immediate vicinity of the city, nothing further came from Yeh beyond a menace of popular anger. Indeed, a number of armed men threatened the factories, but they were dispersed with some loss to themselves by British armed guards. On the 27th October, after notice had been given to the Consuls of France and the United States, fire was opened upon the residence of the Imperial Commissioner. To confine the damage the fire was at ten-minute intervals from one gun. Thereupon Yeh issued a proclamation offering $30 for an English head and considering himself in a state of war with Great Britain. On the 29th a representative of Yeh, accompanied by Howqua, called upon Parkes. The Consul informed them of Bowring's opinion that 'the want of proper communications between the British and Chinese authorities' was one of the main causes of the present difficulty, and that operations would be continued until the Imperial Commissioner was prepared to allow to all foreign representatives for the future free personal access to all the authorities at Canton. The naval fire having effected a breach in the walls on the 29th, a storming party of marines placed the British flag over the Tsing-Hai gate, the approaches to the Yamen were cleared, and the Admiral and Consul entered the

official residence of the Imperial Commissioner. Unfortunately
the entrance into Yeh's Yamen was accompanied by scandalous
scenes of vandalism. Following the British forces an idle and
curious throng began to pillage the residence and to obtain
whatever spoils lay to hand. Nor was the damage done by the
British alone. De Courcy reported to the Quai d'Orsay:

'Mr. Kinnan, United States Consul at Hong-Kong, formerly a
militia general, did still better than the others. While his countrymen, under his administration perhaps, ransacked with great haste
the Viceroy's rooms and harem, he tried partially to rob the English
of the honour of the victory by resolutely planting the flag of the
United States on the breach. He forgot that his colleague, Mr.
Perry, who himself was taking part in the looting, had proclaimed,
at the beginning of hostilities, the neutrality of that flag. But, as the
American merchants say, you must not be too angry with General
Kinnan seeing that he was drunk.'[1]

Though the British forces thus dominated the city they were
not numerically strong enough to occupy it. Such scenes of
brutality as had been enacted would do much not only to confirm Yeh and his fellow citizens in their opinion that it was
advisable to maintain the exclusion of foreigners from their
midst, but also, when the knowledge of these events reached
Peking, to strengthen the belief of the Son of Heaven that the
dwellers in the Celestial Empire were alone truly civilized and
that the Barbarian should at all costs be kept beyond the geo-
graphical as he was beyond the spiritual pale of that Empire.

On the 3rd November the bombardment was extended to
the official residences of the General and the Provincial Governor, and on the 4th the Kwang-yin hill at the end of the city
farthest from the river, imagined by the Chinese to be too
remote to be reached, was effectively shelled. Howqua as the
leader of the gentry pleaded for consideration, while Yeh
affirmed that the Kwantung people were as unwilling in 1856
to see foreigners in their provincial city as they had been in
1849. As 'in the administration of all matters in China, the
rule adhered to is that which Heaven shows', and as 'Heaven
sees as my people see: Heaven hears as my people hear', it was
impossible for him to concede the claim for official entry into
the city. Equally impossible was it in Bowring's judgement
that 'a small and turbulent fraction of the population of China'

<hr />

[1] De Courcy to Walewski, 10 Nov. 1856 (Chine 19, No. 31).

should 'be allowed to supersede the engagements of their Emperor to the Sovereign of Great Britain'.

In spite, therefore, of the bombardment of the official residences, the breaching of the city walls, and the destruction on the 6th November of a fleet of war junks which put up a lively resistance, no serious modification had been made in Yeh's original position regarding the *Arrow*, nor had any concession on the newly raised entry question been granted. The only action open to the British was the maintenance of the positions already acquired. Bowring was convinced 'that whatever may have been the importance of the question which necessitated the first appeal to hostilities, it has now assumed a character seriously involving all our present and future relations with China'. Some little hope of a solution was entertained by Parkes as a result of a conversation on the 8th November with certain leading members of the gentry who disapproved of Yeh's attitude to what they described as the reasonable demands of the British. They thought, however, that it would be very difficult for the Imperial Commissioner to yield on the city question, different as the demand might now be from the right of general entry claimed in 1849, in that it was restricted to the entry to officials. They discounted the hostile attitude of the people, and hoped to address the Imperial Commissioner whose principal officers, however, regarded him as immovable in his opposition.[1]

On the 14th November the last military pressure was used— the capture with the loss of one boy killed and four men wounded of the Bogue Forts which put the whole river effectively in British hands. Bowring himself went up to Canton on the 16th November, and further appealed in vain to Yeh to receive a visit from him by assuring him that he could arrange for his own protection from a hostile populace on his way to the Yamen. Meanwhile, as there were at the factories no French subjects to protect, the French consular flag was struck and the Americans expressed 'most cordial sympathy' with British proceedings, and thought the demand to hold official communication with the Chinese authorities a most reasonable one, though they had no instructions from their own Government to insist upon the general right to enter the city.[2] Parker, who arrived

---

[1] Bowring to Clarendon, 23 Oct.–15 Nov. 1856 (F.O. 17/252).
[2] Bowring to Clarendon, 18 Nov. 1856 (F.O. 17/252).

in Hong Kong after his fruitless negotiations in Shanghai on the 11th November, agreed that 'the spirit manifested by the imperial commissioner as usual was not courteous or satisfactory'[1]. The barrier forts had been reoccupied by the Chinese, and from them the American flag had been fired upon. After the American Plenipotentiary had attempted in vain to obtain redress for this insult, as a becoming punishment upon the Chinese the batteries were silenced by the fire of United States men-of-war. This was 'the first blow that has ever been struck by our navy in China', commented Parker, and it was necessitated by the 'quite inscrutable obstinacy' of the Imperial Commissioner. 'Either he has become desperate and determined to adhere to his insane policy to the death, or he is ambitious of attaining to an illustrious apotheosis as model-hater of foreigners.' Though he felt full sympathy with the British, he was unwilling and unable to make common cause with them as 'the ostensible question in the present dispute—satisfaction for the violation of the Treaty in the case of a British ship and the entrance to the city of Canton'—was a controversy solely initiated by her Britannic Majesty's Government, and specifically British in its origin, and the two points raised were 'trifles compared with the questions at the foundation of all our grievances—viz. are the Treaty Powers, the equals of China, to say the least, to be acknowledged and treated as such by the Manchu Government?' Yet though he must remain neutral in the particular quarrel, he asked Bowring 'to rest assured of the deep interest I feel in the success of the measures adopted to bring to a speedy and satisfactory conclusion the present contest, and the attainment of an end so replete with interest, social, and commercial and political to China, and ultimately to all the Treaty Powers'[2]. But in spite of the action of the U.S. ships, relations between Parker and Yeh were not re-established until the 13th December, when the American Minister expressed himself satisfied with the correspondence on the question of the insult done to the American flag.

The British forces captured 'French Folly' Fort on the 4th December to prevent the Chinese from annoying foreign shipping in that branch of the Canton river. But trade was at a

[1] Parker to Sec. of State, 13 Nov. 1856 (Sen. Ex. Doc. 22, 2 Sess. 35 Cong., at p. 984).
[2] Parker to Sec. of State, 22 Nov. 1852 (ibid., at p. 1019).

standstill. By mid-December (when there were only one American firm and twenty British subjects left at Canton[1]) the whole of the foreign factories, with the exception of one leased by the British Government, were burnt to the ground in the middle of the night.[2] Bowring thought that the Imperial Government should be held responsible, but that compensation for the very heavy material losses should be made to fall upon the Cantonese, and a considerable additional space for factories should be secured. 'An absolute triumph at Canton will be the very best initiative to successful negotiations elsewhere, and it appears to me that these negotiations must be carried on elsewhere, for the viceroy of Canton is of all men the least fitted for negotiation and the locality of Canton would be of all places in the Empire the least desirable.'[3] Thus a position of stalemate had been reached, for though singularly few British casualties had been incurred in the course of assuring the domination of the fleet on the river, the naval forces, harassed by fire rafts, were quite inadequate to attempt the capture of the city. There Yeh had concentrated the armed forces of the provinces, thus letting loose brigandage and pillage in the countryside, and in addition some 20,000 'braves', ill-disciplined men, half of whose wages found their way into the pockets of the gentry, who were often not men of property but hangers-on of the Government, financially interested in the mobilization of these forces.[4]

The Chinese did not resist according to the rules of war known in Europe. The Government of Canton set a price on the heads of Englishmen, recalled servants from Hong Kong (many of whom were obliged under threats of reprisals on their families resident on the mainland, to leave their service), and inflicted penalties on Chinese who supplied the foreign markets.[5] The most flagrant violation of Western international conceptions of hostilities was the attempt made in the middle of January 1857 to poison with arsenic the bread baked in Hong Kong. Fortunately for the foreign community so much poison was put in that it was easily detected. Protests were made by the American Minister, the French chargé d'affaires, and the Portuguese Governor of Macao, as it seemed that some Chinese

[1] Bowring to Clarendon, 25 Nov.—14 Dec. 1856 (F.O. 17/252).
[2] Bowring to Clarendon, 16 and 17 Dec. 1856 (F.O. 17/253).
[3] Bowring to Clarendon, 22 Dec. 1856 (F.O. 17/253).
[4] Bowring to Clarendon, 27 Dec. 1856 (F.O. 17/253).
[5] Bowring to Clarendon, 10 Jan. 1857 (F.O. 17/263).

officials were implicated in the design thus to rid themselves of all foreigners in the colony.[1] Yeh denied any complicity in the poisoning attempt and asserted that he would punish any one guilty of such an offence, but he begged the French representative to remember that the people's hatred of the English made them blind.[2] Papers seized in April from a fleet of Mandarin junks and lorchas 'implicated the Mandarins in the plots of assassination, poisoning and incendiarism'. And they showed also that Yeh himself was connected with troubles that broke out at Kowloon.[3] The Chinese apparently thought then, as in days gone by, that the British had

'no purpose to serve, no care or concern but in direct and immediate subordination to questions of commercial profit and loss, and that in addressing themselves to motives which they suppose influence all our purposes and policy they may direct the course of Her Majesty's government whose functions they believe principally to consist in keeping barbarian merchants in order and securing for them the all important benefits of a Trade with China'[4].

The Imperial Commissioner desired, thought Bowring, to 'conciliate the Americans in the hope of using them hereafter as intermediaries', and he thought too that that was a position which Parker would be willing to accept.[5] Yeh had apparently given the Peking Government to understand that the Americans and French thought Great Britain in the wrong. Parker, however, disabused him by declaring 'the foundation of all difficulties between China and foreign nations is the unwillingness of China to acknowledge England, France, America, and the other great nations of the West as her equals . . . so far as respects this grave matter the American government is sensible that the English are in the right'[6]. Bowring was interested not only in the fundamental causes of the quarrel, but also in the specific points at issue, in regard to which he believed it to be impossible to modify his conditions by reference to any foreign authority— American or Chinese.[7]

Though Parker clearly could not engage in any enterprise

[1] Bowring to Clarendon, 19 Jan. 1857 (F.O. 17/263).
[2] Bowring to Clarendon, 18 Feb. 1857 (F.O. 17/264).
[3] Bowring to Clarendon, 11 Apr. 1857 (F.O. 17/267).
[4] Bowring to Clarendon, 31 Jan. 1857 (F.O. 17/263).
[5] Bowring to Clarendon, 14 Feb. 1857 (F.O. 17/264).
[6] Bowring to Clarendon, 10 Mar. 1857 (F.O. 17/265).
[7] Bowring to Clarendon, 10 Mar. 1857 (F.O. 17/265).

against Canton without instructions from Washington,[1] by the beginning of April the French minister de Bourboulon had been ordered by the Government of Napoleon III to press for a settlement of the fatal outrage upon the Catholic missionary M. Chapdelaine. Urged by Bowring he altered a draft dispatch to Yeh with a view to an early answer, while the British Plenipotentiary on his side agreed to support his demand for adequate reparation. The Imperial Commissioner was to request the Emperor to banish the offending Mandarin, and to insert the decree of banishment in the official *Peking Gazette* with a declaration that exemplary punishment should follow any repetition of the offence. There was thus a specific French grievance which gave ground for a joint Anglo-French operation against Canton, if, as was generally believed, Yeh were to refuse the request of M. de Bourboulon.[2] Whatever might be done ultimately, there was apparently agreement among the representatives of all three Treaty Powers that the first thing was to settle matters outstanding with Yeh in Canton.[3] Parker stated that 'the settlement of the Canton question must be admitted by all acquainted with the subject, as an indispensable preliminary to a solution of all others now pending'[4]. The American representative informed his Government that France, and especially Great Britain, desired the co-operation of the United States. There was always a danger of 'England under force of circumstances possessing herself of exclusive jurisdiction or privileges at Canton'. It was a vital necessity to the United States that the position of foreigners in Canton should be improved, one 'worthy of their decided efforts to aid in obtaining, rather than ingloriously to rely on others to secure these advantages for her'. He was satisfied of the entire good faith of both the English and French Governments

'in their sincere desire for the cordial co-operation and concurrent action of the three Treaty powers *only*, for the attainment of advantages of common interest to those powers, and which will be of incalculable benefit to the Chinese Empire if obtained. . . . Should the United States decline to pursue with these governments a concurrent policy for the revision of treaties and the establishment of occidental-

[1] Bowring to Clarendon, 30 Mar. 1857 (F.O. 17/266).
[2] Bowring to Clarendon, 4 Apr. 1857 (F.O. 17/267).
[3] Bowring to Clarendon, 7 Apr. 1857 (F.O. 17/267).
[4] Parker to Sec. of State, 13 Mar. 1857 (Sen. Ex. Doc. 22, 2 Sess. 35 Cong., at p. 1242).

oriental relations upon a new, wise and just foundation, I can't resist the honest conviction that it will prove, one day, a calamity rather than an advantage.'

Parker suggested that if the quarrel was regarded as local and war was not declared, the American constitutional difficulty arising from the concurrent congressional and presidential right to declare war would be met and at the same time an important political consideration would be attained by avoiding the calamity of war with China.[1] For he was fully convinced that

'nothing short of an imposing physical force, or the exhibition of it, will enable any minister to succeed under existing circumstances. . . . Great Britain, France and the United States are very similarly situated in respect to China. It is a settled point that the former two governments will apply themselves to the task with vigour; and every sentiment of national respect and interest demand that the United States should do the same. The character of the future of China for a long time to come depends,' under Providence, upon the action of the western governments at the present time; and it is devoutly to be hoped the United States will stand in their true position in the campaign already initiated.'[2]

B. REACTIONS IN ENGLAND

The British Government, having consulted the Queen's Advocate, were in entire agreement with Bowring and Parker in their protest against the seizure of the crew of the *Arrow*, in demanding the return of all twelve men and a formal request for the extradition in due form of any alleged criminals. In the circumstances they were not opposed to the seizure of a war junk. Lord Clarendon also approved of the subsequent operations in the river and at Canton.[3] He had been on the point of sending Bowring instructions for opening negotiations with China for the revision of the existing treaties, in conjunction with the French Plenipotentiary and also with the Plenipotentiary of the United States if the latter were empowered to act in concert, when the intelligence of the Canton outbreak

[1] Parker to Sec. of State, 10 Apr. 1857 and 5 May 1857 (ibid., at pp. 1276 and 1319).
[2] Parker to President Buchanan, 13 Feb. 1857 (ibid., at p. 1205).
[3] Clarendon to Bowring, 10 Jan. 1857 (F.O. 17/261).

reached Great Britain. It was vitally necessary to provide against the continuance at Canton of the old exclusive system, and it appeared to the London Government that the recent troubles entitled them to a revision of the existing treaties. They desired to acquire the right of residence for a British Minister in Peking, and an extension of commercial intercourse, especially in the large towns in the neighbourhood of Shanghai and Ningpo, free access to the great rivers and the right to have consuls and trade establishments in the towns on their banks. For the rest Bowring was given a free hand as the British Government realized that he knew far better than themselves the situation in the Far East. Clarendon agreed in principle with the American desire for the establishment of freedom of opinion and of judicial reform, but thought the idea impracticable, nor did he see the utility of the French proposal of the residence of Chinese agents in European capitals. Whatever was gained by Great Britain, Bowring was to remember that it was the settled policy of the Government not to receive exclusive advantages.[1] By the middle of March, however, the Government had determined to send out a new Plenipotentiary to arrange the Canton affair and to put British relations on a more permanent footing. Bowring was to remain as the accredited Minister, but he was not to exercise his functions in questions related to the recent troubles, to military and naval operations, and to the securing of peace and a revision of treaties.[2] Already correspondence beginning in September 1856 had passed between the Governments of London and Paris on the subject of treaty revision. The French had insisted on a *réparation éclatante* for the murder of Chapdelaine, and the British Government, prepared to make common cause with them on this question, agreed not to complete the revision of the treaties until the French had received adequate amends for this incident. It was agreed first to try negotiations at the Peiho and, if they failed, to exert pressure on the Yangtse. The British Government regarded the opening of that river to commerce as of vital importance, to be secured either by negotiation or by force and negotiation.[1] On the 25th March Clarendon notified Bowring of the selection of Lord Elgin as head of the special embassy. In Singapore 2,500 men were to be

---

[1] Clarendon to Bowring, 9 Feb. 1857 (F.O. 17/261).
[2] Clarendon to Bowring, 10 Mar. 1857 (F.O. 17/261).

mobilized and to await Elgin's arrival unless the Commander-in-Chief and the Chief Superintendent were of opinion that their immediate dispatch was indispensable.[1]

The approval of the British Government of their agents' actions did not, however, carry with it the approval of the British House of Commons. A great debate started by resolutions moved by Cobden and supported by Lord John Russell, Gladstone, and Disraeli, began on the 26th February 1857, was continued on four evenings and resulted in the policy of the Government being defeated by a majority of 16 in a House of 510 members. The attack of the majority was directed in three main directions. From the evidence supplied by a voluminous publication of dispatches, the honesty of Bowring was doubted, the legality of his proceedings was denied, and his political wisdom was questioned, and for all three the Government was held responsible by its endorsement of its agents. The majority was made up of Conservative opponents of the Palmerstonian Government together with the radical and Peelite dissidents, and although the speakers generally disclaimed that they were influenced by party considerations, the resolutions were regarded by the Government as tantamount to a vote of no confidence.

Cobden characterized Bowring's conduct as utterly flagitious. He argued that on the 11th October Bowring had written to Parkes that as the register of the *Arrow* was out of date she was not entitled to British protection, while on the 14th November he averred to Yeh that the *Arrow* 'lawfully bore the British flag under a register granted by me'. He had further stated to Parkes that the fact that she was not entitled to British protection made no difference to the right of the Consul to demand from Yeh recognition of her British quality, on the ground that Yeh was ignorant of the fact of the expiry of the register. This proposition of Bowring's Bulwer Lytton thought a 'miserable argument; falsehood embraced a wilful suppression of the truth, and falsehood and prevarication have nothing to do with the honour of the English nation'. In his defence of Bowring on this score Palmerston made play with Cobden's statement that Bowring had been his friend for twenty years. 'The whole question is, what did the Chinese know and believe this vessel to be? Did they or did they not consider her to be a British

[1] Clarendon to Bowring, 25 Mar. 1857 (F.O. 17/261).

vessel?' The Prime Minister was convinced that they really thought she was British. Therefore

'when it was said that it was a falsehood on the part of Sir John Bowring when he said that the Chinese Government did not know that the licence had expired, I say, on the contrary, that that is a correct statement of the real principle at issue between the British and Chinese authorities. Instead of being a flagitious attempt at imposition, it was a statement of the principle upon which the question between the British and Chinese authorities was to be adjusted. The animus of an insult, the animus of violation of the treaty was in the Chinese, and you have a right to demand not only an apology for the wrong that was done, but an assurance that it should not be repeated.'

The contrast that Lord Derby in the Upper House as well as Cobden and Gladstone in the Commons drew between the courtesy and forbearance they noticed in Yeh's communications and the tone of arrogance and presumption they alleged in the dispatches of Parkes and Bowring was a tribute rather to the skill of the Chinese in literary composition and evidence of the opposition's desire to champion the cause of other nations than their own rather than an indication of the true relative positions of the Canton contestants in the field of actual relations. Courtesy had not marked the way Yeh had treated the representatives of foreign Powers, as not only Bowring but his American colleague would be prepared to state. If there is truth in Palmerston's criticism of Cobden 'everything that was English was wrong, and everything that was hostile to England was right', there is some truth in the view that to Palmerston 'everything that was hostile to England was wrong'. Cruel and clever as Yeh undoubtedly was, Palmerston's summary of him as 'one of the most savage barbarians that ever disgraced a nation' was a manifest exaggeration, for Yeh was most certainly not a barbarian. Bowring's conduct must have come to Cobden and his friends as a bitter disappointment. For while a member of the House of Commons Sir John had been Secretary of the Peace Society. Palmerston had said that there were no men so pugnacious as the members of the Peace Society, and he had been proved right.

Bulwer Lytton was not far wrong when he said that Bowring was 'a man of enthusiastic temperament, and like all men of genius, is very desirous of carrying out his own wishes'. Sir

James Graham from his own knowledge of the man told the House that he was apt to form strong opinions, to adopt them with precipitation, invariably pushing those opinions to the utmost extreme, and on the whole, more remarkable for his self-confidence than for the soundness of his judgement. There is no doubt much truth in Derby's criticism that he evinced a 'monomania about getting into Canton'. His experience first as Consul at Canton and then as Governor of Hong Kong and Plenipotentiary had planted this *idée fixe* firmly in his mind. Like his predecessors he had been warned against pushing the right, never renounced but temporarily waived, to the extent of hostilities. The necessity of caution while the Crimean War was in progress he fully understood. But now the war was over, the American and French Governments were in general agreement with the British on the urgent necessity of placing the relations of Western States with China on a more satisfactory basis, and a larger British naval force than had ever been in China Seas in peace time was based on Hong Kong. The *Arrow* affair had given rise to reprisals which had developed into local hostilities. At that juncture he came forward with his demand, not indeed for a fulfilment of the suspended Treaty, but for the lesser point of official Entry to the city. By so doing he made it more difficult to end the state of hostilities. Of that there is no doubt. But on the evidence it would be impossible to hold that Bowring deliberately sanctioned reprisals with a view to creating a situation favourable for an advancement of his purpose of official entrance. He thought that the strong measures of Seymour in clearing the river, bombarding the official residences, and penetrating to Yeh's Yamen by force, would so overwhelm the Imperial Commissioner as to compel him at once to give ample apology for the past and security for the future in the matter of the shipping, and to grant to the Treaty Powers the right of official audiences within the walls. A conversation which Bowring had had with de Courcy two months before the incident of the lorcha *Arrow* throws a significant light upon the future conduct of the British representative. Bowring had declared that

'It would be of advantage in several respects if our squadron brought us to Canton and opened its gates for us before sailing for the Peiho. Such a victory won at the start of the negotiations over the ill will of the high functionary to whom the Chinese Government has given its entire confidence and to whom it has entrusted the task of keeping the insolent Barbarians in check, would produce in Peking the most favourable impression. At one blow it would repair many mistakes and rebuffs and would avenge many a humiliation.'[1]

But Bowring's self-confidence was far too great. Yeh who had been so obstinate in the paper war was to prove himself as obstinate under the rain of bullets and shells. He, like Bowring, had his *idée fixe*, and nothing, not even eventual capture and confinement at Calcutta, where he ended his days, could shake his imperturbable, unapproachable isolation.

That Bowring had made things more difficult was certain. But perhaps things had to get worse before they could get better. Lord John Russell said with some truth that no attempt should have been made to settle the Canton question, which had been so long in abeyance, without the full, solemn, and deliberate determination of the British Government. Had Bowring been content with the qualified promise in regard to shipping for the future, and instructed Parkes to receive back the twelve captives when Yeh offered to return them, while at the same time reserving all rights for the determination of the London Government to take further steps, one fresh claim for treaty revision would have been given to the British Government. As it was, his action tended to put a false complexion on the relations between Britain and China. Hostilities at least appeared to have come about for what Lord John could say was 'after all but a paltry affair'. To any one cognizant of the past Sidney Herbert's view that time should have been given to Yeh to communicate with Peking on the question of the Entry before the expiration of the ultimatum was the sheerest absurdity. But to make some kind of immediate settlement with reservation of the final right of the British Government would have been a counsel of prudence humanly impossible of acceptance to the British authorities on the spot, exasperated as they were by a whole series of slights and annoyances stifled through the Crimean years, but ready to flare up into activity now that they knew the French and English Governments were on the point of taking a strong line. After all, was Lord John's view that the affair was trifling quite true? Palmerston was more correct

---

[1] De Courcy to Min. Aff. Étr., 28 Aug. 1856 (Chine 18).

than his former colleague in his assertion: 'This violation of our treaty in regard to the lorcha is not the first or only one that occurred, but a part of a deliberate system to strip us step by step of our treaty rights'. Cobden said at the opening of his speech that he would begin at the beginning—the 8th October 1856. Starting from that date the affair was a trifle, but then it was a false start.

On the question of legality there were three main points to consider. It was argued by the opponents of the Government that as the colonial ordinance was at variance with Imperial Statute—the Merchant Shipping Act—it was void; that even if the colonial ordinance was valid, the *Arrow*'s register, being irregular by reason of the expiry of the period, was therefore invalid; and thirdly, if both ordinance and the register were valid, it was unlawful to clothe a Chinese with the right to possess such a vessel, or, if it were Chinese property, to exempt it from the jurisdiction of the Emperor of China.

It was pointed out by Labouchere, the Colonial Secretary, that there could be two classes of ships entitled to British protection, one possessed of an Imperial register governed by the maritime Statute Law, the other granted a colonial or local register. For more than two hundred years there had been in existence a 'Mediterranean pass' entitling a person having for a period of fifteen years a fixed abode in Gibraltar (and after 1815 in Malta), not necessarily a British subject, to have a local register for a vessel neither British built nor British manned. The right sprang not from Statute but from the prerogative of the Crown exercised in conquered and ceded territory. A ship possessing such a right had always enjoyed the protection of the British Crown, and the Mediterranean pass had been in the mind of the Colonial Office when they had sanctioned, on behalf of the Crown, the ordinances passed by the legislature of Hong Kong regulating the colonial register. The Attorney-General argued that the phrase 'British Ship' was one of artificial, not of natural, meaning. In the old navigation law it did not mean a ship belonging to a British subject, but a vessel entitled to the privileges conferred by the Act. For this purpose a ship owned by a British subject, if built abroad or manned by foreigners, was not a British ship. But the words of the Supplementary Treaty spoke of a vessel 'owned by a British subject'—not necessarily, he contended, a British-born subject; but a person resident in British territory and living under British rule. Article 17 concerned 'small vessels belonging to the English nation' which could be built anywhere, and manned anyhow, but they had to belong to a British subject and to possess a sailing register. The Imperial Statute was therefore of no import as the treaty gave birth to a special class of vessel. An Imperial register and a colonial register did not give rise to two conflicting rights: they were supplementary and parallel, as they were concerned with two different categories of vessels, essentially on two different planes. As therefore there were under the old Navigation Law and the Supplementary Treaty two distinct classes of vessels entitled to British protection, the modification made by the Merchant Shipping Act of 1854, whereby a British ship was defined as one owned by a British subject, natural born, or one who had become so by cession of territory, naturalization, or denization, had no effect on the local Hong Kong category which might embrace a wider category in one way and a narrower in another. It was narrower in that it was confined to the coasts of China, as the Gibraltar or Malta passes were confined to the Mediterranean, and it had been, at least before the Act of 1854, wider in its embrace of ships which had not to be either British built or British manned. Hence, after the passage of the Act of 1854, it was lawful for the Crown, whose legislative powers in Hong Kong were restrained by Statute from passing ordinances inconsistent with English law, to sanction ordinances regulating the rights enjoyed by persons under its protection in a matter which was essentially different from the matter regulated by the Statute of 1854. This the Crown had done by allowing the two ordinances of the Hong Kong legislature No. 4 of 1855 and No. 9 of 1856.

Not only therefore were the ordinances not inconsistent with Statute Law but separated from it and parallel to it; but it also followed that the effect of the ordinance was simply to define duties owed to the Crown by the persons protected by it. The ordinances were no part of the Supplementary Treaty, but a regulation and definition as between the British Crown and the owners of the class of vessel privileged in that treaty. Therefore the question of the expiry of the *Arrow*'s licence was an irrelevant consideration in the dispute between the British Government and the Chinese authorities. It would have given a right to the

Hong Kong Government to institute proceedings against the owner of the *Arrow*, but in itself it did not deprive the *Arrow* of its status under the Treaty nor debar the British authorities from protecting her. It was, moreover, questionable whether the fact that the licence had not been renewed five days before the 8th October, when the *Arrow* was boarded by the Chinese, even constituted in the circumstances an offence under the ordinances which gave grace to a vessel 'when at sea'. It was true that the *Arrow* was not at sea but in the river; it was also true that she could have run into Hong Kong from Macao before going up river to Canton. It would certainly have been more prudent to have done so, but it would have necessitated a very literal interpretation of the ordinances by a court before a conviction could have been sustained.

The international question had therefore nothing to do with the validity or invalidity in municipal law of the Hong Kong Ordinances, or of the register of the *Arrow* under those ordinances. The question at issue was solely one of international law. Now the international law as between Great Britain and China in this matter must be looked for in the Supplementary Treaty which made a serious inroad, in favour of the British Crown, in the generally accepted international law governing the rights of a sovereign over foreign vessels in the ports of his territories. It was fatuous to argue, as some of the opposition did, that the British Government would resent a similar claim by French authorities to exclude British police from a French ship and French crews in Liverpool, for there was no treaty between the sovereigns of France and Great Britain similar to that existing between the sovereigns of China and Great Britain. The 17th Article of the Supplementary Treaty stated that 'every British schooner, cutter, lorcha, etc. shall have a sailing letter or register in Chinese and English under the seal and signature of the Chief Superintendent of Trade, describing her appearance, burden etc.' That, argued the Attorney-General, defined as between the Chinese and British a British vessel and was equivalent to saying that 'every lorcha receiving that sailing letter was, by the very terms of the Treaty, converted into a British lorcha'. Hence every lorcha producing a sailing letter was entitled to the privileges and character of a British vessel. If then the lorcha *Arrow* was a British vessel, the Chinese subjects on board her were entitled to the immunity from arrest by a Chinese officer expressly allowed in Article IX of the Supplementary Treaty which provided that

'if lawless natives of China, having committed crimes or offences against their own government shall flee to English merchant ships for refuge, and if . . . it shall be ascertained or suspected by the officers of the Government of China whither such criminals or offenders have fled, a communication shall be made to the proper English officer in order that the said criminal or offender may be rigidly searched for, seized, and on proof or admission of their guilt delivered up . . .'

Although the owner of the lorcha was a Chinese subject resident in Hong Kong, one not born in British allegiance, nevertheless his ship would be entitled to the privileges of a British-owned vessel. For that doctrine there was authority in the case of *Marryat* v. *Wilson*, in which Lord Kenyon had held that though a British subject by birth cannot throw off his allegiance to the sovereign of his native land, yet he may be adopted and become a citizen of another country for the purpose of commerce, and the circumstance of his being a natural-born British subject cannot deprive him of the advantage of being a citizen of the country of his adoption, so as to disable him from engaging in a trade forbidden to the subjects of his native country. That is to say, that although it is impossible for a man to throw off his allegiance to his natural sovereign, he may nevertheless become by residence or adoption so far a subject of another country as to be admitted to all the privileges and entitled to all the rights enjoyed by the subjects of that country. And it was to be observed that if the contention that only a natural-born subject can give British character to his ship was relied on, then the Merchant Shipping Act enshrined a principle contrary to international law, for a person having letters of denization or having been naturalized and having taken the oath of allegiance would, under that Act, confer British character upon his ship.

Serjeant Shee stated that in the case of the *Indiana* it had been held that she was British, although owned by a foreigner, on the ground that the foreigner was resident in England. He was convinced that the true interpretation of the Treaty of 1843 was 'that a ship, Chinese built, Chinese manned, the property of a Chinese resident in Hong Kong and registered by him at the British registry of Hong Kong, was to all intents and purposes, within that Treaty, "an English merchant ship" '. Indeed, unless that were a true proposition, no article of the Treaty would stand, and the whole trade stipulated for between Hong Kong and China was entirely unprotected and at the mercy of the Chinese. Articles 13, 14, and 16 of the Supplementary Treaty could be construed to mean that ships of Chinese residents in Hong Kong registered at the British registry were not to be regarded as Chinese ships. The phrase 'English merchant ship' was a much wider category than 'British ship'. It was true that at the time of the Treaty British ships were defined by the Act of 4 William IV, c. 34, not as ships owned by British subjects, but as ships sailing under a British master, three-quarters of whose crew were British, British built, registered in a special way, and carrying a certificate of registry. That definition could not be applied to the phrase 'English merchant ship' of the Supplementary Treaty without making that treaty meaningless, and if it could not be applied as being in the mind of the contracting parties still less could the new definition adopted in the Act of 1854.

When to these arguments is added the opinion of the Queen's Advocate, a non-party officer of the Crown, appointed by Lord Derby's Government, contained in Lord Clarendon's dispatch of the 10th December 1856 approving of the attitude of Sir John Bowring, it is difficult to come to any other conclusion than that as a matter of international law right was on the side of the British Government and their officer. The right that they claimed was essentially a right of extra-territoriality, a right claimed and recognized by the Chinese in the Supplementary Treaty because without it navigation would be rendered impossible.

There still remained the question of policy. Cobden declared that 'Civis Romanus sum' is not a very attractive motto to put over the doors of our counting-houses abroad. But it is germane to remember that the foreign community in Canton were in general agreement with Bowring's policy. Gregson, the Chairman of the East India and China Association, from his place in the House supported the Government. There was no need to adopt such a motto in Shanghai or in the other ports, but it is difficult to understand what measures, short of insistence on treaty rights acquired and granted in the interests of trade, could have enabled the counting-houses to flourish, given the attitude which Yeh had all along adopted. After all, such extension of commercial activity as had followed the opening of the four new ports after 1842 had been the result of resolute resentment at the humiliating conditions of the closed mono-polistic system of the old Hong days. And the future was to show, after the troublous period of Yeh was over and the Treaty of Tientsin had come into force, a further commercial develop-ment on a magnificent scale. The criticisms of Disraeli were more profound and more prophetic than those of his radical leader in this China debate. He reminded the House that fifty years ago Lord Hastings had offered to conquer China with 20,000 men. But there were no longer the Clives and Hastings of the past, and besides the position of affairs in the East had greatly changed.

'We have the Russian Empire and the American Republic there, and a system of political compromise has developed itself like the balance of power in Europe; and if you are not cautious and careful in your conduct now in dealing with China, you will find you are not likely to extend commerce, but to excite the jealousy of powerful states, and to involve yourselves in hostilities with nations not in-ferior to yourselves.'

British hostilities in Persia might well, when peace was made, end in the establishment of Russian ascendancy in the middle east, 'while in China, where also you may soon have peace, you will very probably have established the ascendancy of the United States'. There had been too great precipitancy. It was not possible to expect to be able to extend in a moment to coun-tries like China the same diplomatic intercourse which was adopted with other nations. The twenty-five centuries of civilization and isolation had resulted in deeply engrained habits and customs expressing themselves in a profound cere-mony and formal etiquette, and such a country was bound to be startled by the frank and occasionally brutal freedom of European manners. But with a policy of combination with other powerful European States in attempting to influence the conduct of China by negotiations and treaties, Disraeli thought that ultimately, slowly and surely, the end might be attained. He deplored the existing state of affairs because it would make such cautious advance in co-operation with other Powers more difficult, if not impossible.

The Fabian tactics advocated by the Conservative leader of

the Lower House were rejected by the Government of Palmerston which was supported by a majority in the new House after the dissolution provoked by the China Debate. Elgin was sent with an armed force and in co-operation with the French Government embarked upon a policy of resolute activity. He was not only to solve the local difficulties in Canton, but to extend lawful foreign trade to further seaports and to the great river cities, and above all to gain diplomatic representation at the court of the Son of Heaven.

The Foreign Secretary himself does not seem to have been convinced that Bowring's actions were beyond criticism, though no doubt he agreed there was no alternative in the circumstances but to support him. Bowring's son Edgar championing his father's cause pointed out to Lord Clarendon that although opposition speakers in both Houses had spoken of Sir John as a liar no member of the Government had explicitly vindicated his honour.[1] In reply Clarendon promised to consider the possibility of bringing the question before the Lords, but he thought it would be better to await a full explanation of Sir John's conduct than to base a defence upon a certain degree of supposition.[2] In a letter to his friend Lord Canning, the Governor-General of India, with whom he had been allowed to correspond on matters under discussion in the Cabinet, the Foreign Secretary stated:

'You will probably think the opposition right in their estimate of the proceedings at Canton, but you will also judge that they have acted most foolishly and have contrived to help Palmerston over a very difficult session. . . . The whole country, i.e. England and Scotland is Palmerstonian.'[3]

His correspondent congratulated the Foreign Secretary on his speech, but commented:

'I should not have liked to have had to make it. The subject w^d not have been sympatico. I think we (England) were wrong about the lorcha and right about the entrance to Canton, but that Bowring's presumption in swelling the small case into the great one was indefensible. I quite think that there was nothing to be done but to uphold him—or rather the War:—and that makes the awkwardness of the question.'[4]

---

[1] Edgar Bowring to Clarendon, 11 Mar. 1857 (G.D. 29/23).
[2] Clarendon to Edgar Bowring, 11 Mar. 1857 (G.D. 29/23).
[3] Clarendon to Canning, 10 Mar. 1857 (G.D. 29/21).
[4] Canning to Clarendon, 4 May 1857 (G.D. 29/21).

To de Courcy, a not unfriendly observer of the Lorcha *Arrow* affair, there seemed no doubt that the development of the quarrel was above all Bowring's responsibility. 'Sir John', he wrote to the French Foreign Minister, 'is more exacting and bellicose than the commander of the English naval forces; he it is who advises the admiral to take the Bogue forts and suggests the idea of an interview in the city . . . in a word it is he who takes the initiative in important decisions and vigorous measures'[1]. By the end of the year, however, it was apparent to every one that Bowring would not be able to achieve his aim of securing entrance, even for Government representatives, into the city of Canton. De Courcy's main criticism of his colleague's action was its rashness. 'It must be acknowledged that the task undertaken by the British authorities was, when they attempted it, beyond their power. The English plenipotentiary and Admiral did as a matter of fact act imprudently, without the authority of their government when there was no danger in waiting.'[2]

On the other hand, an unsolicited testimonial to Bowring's conduct from Dr. Parker reached Clarendon through a Liverpool merchant who had entertained the American Minister on that officer's return via England to the United States at the close of the year 1857. Parker considered

'that every step taken by Sir John Bowring and Admiral Seymour was right. He strongly approves of everything they did, and says if England and France and the United States would unitedly make a demonstration against the present Chinese policy, they would carry their point. . . . The disinterested evidence of such a man as Doctor Parker the Minister of another State is about the strongest we could have that our Chinese affairs have not suffered in Sir John Bowring's hands.'[3]

---

[1] De Courcy to Walewski, 6 Dec. 1856 (Chine 19, No. 35).
[2] De Courcy to Walewski, 27 Dec. 1856 (ibid., No. 36).
[3] William Brown to Clarendon, 14 Dec. 1857 (G.D. 29/23).

VI

LORD ELGIN'S FIRST MISSION, 1857–9

A. THE CAPTURE OF CANTON

LORD ELGIN was commissioned as Her Majesty's High Commissioner and Plenipotentiary on the 20th April 1857. He was entrusted with an immediate force of 1,500 men sent from Great Britain together with 750 European and 350 native Indian troops already in Hong Kong; while preparations were being made for the dispatch of further troops and additions to the existing naval forces in the East. Elgin was instructed on his arrival in China to proceed to the Peiho, and obtain reparation for injuries inflicted, complete execution in Canton and elsewhere of existing treaties, and compensation for destruction of property. If these points were granted he was still to endeavour to procure, but by diplomatic means alone, two further points—the residence of a British Minister at, or at least an occasional visit to, the Court of Peking with the right of direct communication with the Chinese Government through messengers of British selection, and the revision of the existing treaty in order to obtain access for British commerce to the great rivers and the city of Chefoo. If, however, the Chinese Government were to refuse to enter into any negotiation, or should they not agree to the first three demands, Elgin would be justified in having immediate recourse to coercive measures, and in that case he was instructed to insist upon the last two requests, and to demand in addition payment of the necessary expenses. If operations were decided upon the British Government contemplated actions such as the blockade of the Peiho, the Grand Canal, Chefoo, and other ports, the occupation of Chusan, the seizure of the heights above Canton by a land force and the retention of that city.[1] In a secret and confidential dispatch Elgin was informed that as it was the opinion of the law officers that a claim by the British Government based on the 8th Article of the Treaty of Hoomun-chai to a revision of the Nanking Treaty could not be sustained, he was to rest his claim for treaty revision on recent events, which had themselves

---

[1] Clarendon to Elgin, 20 Apr. 1857 (P.P. 1859, Sess. 2, xxxiii, no. 1).

shown the need of placing relations between the British and Chinese Governments on a more satisfactory footing.[1]

Elgin left London on the 21st April and after a four-day visit to Paris, where he was enabled to consult with Napoleon III's Government on Chinese affairs, he arrived in Ceylon on the 20th May. There he heard the first rumours of the Indian Mutiny which led him to the opinion that he must press matters in China to a quick conclusion.[2]

However, in Singapore on the 3rd June he received urgent letters from the Governor-General requesting immediate reinforcements. Elgin at once agreed to respond to this call to the utmost of his ability.[3] When, therefore, after a considerable delay in the Straits waiting the arrival of the *Shannon* steam frigate, he arrived in Hong Kong on the 2nd July he was not in a position to dictate any terms to the Chinese authorities. The British Government, who fully approved of the diversion of the troops originally intended for the China service, promised to replace them by 1,500 marines, but Elgin could not expect them until December.[4] He desired, however, to carry out at least the first part of his programme, the attempt at negotiations at the Peiho. In this he was opposed to Sir Michael Seymour, Sir John Bowring, and the local community, who held that the Canton trouble being essentially of a local character should be dealt with locally—and that meant the reduction of Canton. But such an operation would necessitate the employment of 4,000 or 5,000 troops, and the General had but 1,240 fit men. To Elgin it appeared as though the choice was one between a diplomatic visit to the Peiho and inactivity in the south, and after all the court of Peking was, in his eyes, chiefly to blame, for it was its obstinate refusal to place itself on a footing of equality with other powers which was the root of the whole difficulty. The Emperor had honoured Yeh and broken those who were faithful to the treaties; his was to Elgin the major responsibility. Moreover, if Yeh were overthrown, the Emperor might well affirm that he had viewed all along with supreme indifference and contempt this miserable squabble between a provincial official and a handful of outward Barbarians. So

---

[1] Clarendon to Elgin, 20 Apr. 1857 (no. 7) (F.O. 17/274).
[2] Elgin to Clarendon, 23 Apr. to 26 May 1857 (F.O. 17/275).
[3] Elgin to Clarendon, 4 June 1857 (F.O. 17/275).
[4] Clarendon to Elgin, 20 and 27 July 1857 (P.P. 1859, Sess. 2, xxxiii, nos. 7 and 8).

that the advocates of strong measures at Canton independently of reference to Peking might be, unconsciously no doubt but still very powerfully, abetting the haughty and anti-commercial policy of the court. Elgin had no sympathy with those who contended that the frank and unreserved concession by the Emperor of all the claims which the British Government were entitled to urge, would, if unaccompanied by an act of signal vengeance upon the people of Canton, be an evil rather than a benefit. But he was quite convinced that the concessions to be granted must be so ample in substance, and so uncompromising in form, as to put it out of the power of even that 'ingenious and sophistical people' to attribute to weakness or pusillanimity a moderation prompted by humanity alone. If such an unequivocal settlement by diplomatic means were not reached in the north he agreed that hostilities should properly begin at Canton.[1]

There was, however, one insuperable difficulty which presented itself—the necessity in which Elgin would be of proceeding alone. Parker had received no instructions from the State Department, over which the Secretary of a new Administration presided. Though the new French Plenipotentiary, Baron Gros, had not yet arrived, de Bourboulon had been virtually superseded by his Government, as had Sir John Bowring by the British.[2] Elgin pressed the French Admiral on his arrival on the 13th July to persuade de Bourboulon at least to join with the British representative in preliminary negotiations at the Peiho, for he feared that Baron Gros would not arrive in the East until too late in the year for communication to be had with the north. But the French Admiral could not act himself without Gros's presence, and agreed with de Bourboulon that it was impossible for him to assume such a responsibility in view of his recent instructions. The French Admiral was willing to fix a rendezvous at Shanghai at the end of September and to expedite the arrival of Baron Gros, who unlike Elgin had been sent by the long route via the Cape. In this way October could still be used for an attempt at a pacific settlement, and the whole year would not then be wasted. Impressed by the greatly increased risks to a pacific solution that an isolated appearance at the Peiho would entail, convinced that a rebuff there would necessitate, for the sake of prestige, the immediate employment

---

[1] Elgin to Clarendon, 9 July 1857 (ibid., no. 16; F.O. 17/275).
[2] Elgin to Clarendon, 9 July 1857 (P.P. 1859, Sess. 2, xxxiii, no. 14).

of a force of which he was not in command, and alarmed by the receipt on the 14th July of still graver news from India, Elgin decided to abandon his idea of an immediate appeal to the court of Peking. The time might indeed be well spent in a journey to Calcutta, where he would be in a better position to find out the time when the Viceroy or the British Government could release troops for the China Expedition. He would then know what means he could rely upon before meeting Baron Gros at the end of September. Accordingly, he instructed Bowring in the event of Yeh making any overture to reply to the Chinese Commissioner that Her Majesty's Plenipotentiary would soon be returning with the force he had gone to organize.[1] He left Hong Kong on the 16th July in the *Shannon* for Calcutta,[2] where he learnt that Canning could send one or two battalions of sepoys to Hong Kong, but dared not release Elgin's European troops.[3]

Elgin was back again in Hong Kong on the 24th September, but had to wait until the 15th October for Baron Gros, while on the 14th November Mr. Reed, the new American Plenipotentiary, announced his appearance and assumption of office, and Count Poutiatine, the head of the Russian Mission, called upon the British Commissioner. Elgin had thought to send his brother and secretary, Bruce, to the Peiho with a letter intimating his assumption of office. Such a notification would be a compromise between his instructions to open negotiations at the Peiho, and the necessity in which he was placed, in the absence of a force adequate to avenge an insult, of avoiding any serious prejudice to his prestige, already lowered by Yeh's knowledge of the Indian situation. He awaited the arrival of Baron Gros before he adopted such a plan, and was therefore in possession of the latest views of the British Government, modified as a result of the Mutiny in India. In a dispatch of 26th August which Elgin received on the 14th October Clarendon authorized him, if he should not have gone to the Peiho, and if the military and naval commanders were satisfied that they were in a position to do so, to use force at Canton to bring the local Government to terms.[4] During Elgin's absence the British Admiral

---

[1] Elgin to Clarendon (confidential), 29 July 1857 (F.O. 17/275).
[2] Elgin to Clarendon, 29 July 1857 (P.P. 1859, Sess. 2, xxxiii, no. 20).
[3] Elgin to Clarendon (confidential), 2 Sept. 1857 (F.O. 17/276).
[4] Clarendon to Elgin, 26 Aug. 1857 (P.P. 1859, Sess. 2, xxxiii, no. 13).

had instituted a blockade of the city and river of Canton, which, while not completely depriving the inhabitants of food caused them much distress. Palmerston minuted on the 7th November on Bowring's dispatch: 'It seems to me that if Yeh could be brought to terms by a rigid naval Blockade of Canton that would be just as good an ending as the capture of the Town.'[1] The British Government would seem to have reduced their aims to the settlement of the immediate and local questions of Canton, and under the stress of the Indian situation to have abandoned the more ambitious project of increased commercial openings and direct political access to the Imperial Throne.

By the time Gros had arrived[2] Elgin had become deeply convinced that it was essential before the winter closed that either the British demands should be granted or Canton occupied.[3] Gros reported that

'Lord Elgin is under the influence of the merchants driven out of Canton who mean to be revenged for the treatment they have undergone, and he is carried away too by the unanimity which reigns at Hong Kong and Macao alike. He is as convinced as are Admiral Seymour and Sir John Bowring that Canton must be blockaded, attacked, taken and held as a security not to be given up until all demands on China have been met.'[4]

The fear which many people in Hong Kong entertained was that Elgin's policy was to *tâcher d'arranger tout pacifiquement*. It appears to have been unfounded: doubtless he had been greatly impressed by the opinion of the Colony, which was described by a Catholic missionary thus: 'A Hong Kong il n'y a qu'une voix: *delenda est Carthago*, lisez Canton-Canton-Canton.'[5]

In order to be assured of adequate means of pressure Elgin urged the immediate dispatch of troops from India, and discussed with Baron Gros the steps to be taken. Gros was in a difficult position as he had not yet received any modifications to his instructions, similar to Elgin's, authorizing an immediate attack on Canton. Though finally convinced of the futility of a preliminary pacific approach to the Gulf of Pechili, he nevertheless insisted on addressing a communication to Peking through Yeh who was still, as he argued, after all not only

[1] Bowring to Clarendon, 11 and 14 Aug. 1857 (F.O. 17/271).
[2] Gros to Walewski, various (Chine 21).
[3] Elgin to Clarendon, 15 Oct. 1857 (P.P. 1859, Sess. 2, xxxiii, no. 44).
[4] Gros to Walewski, 26 Oct. 1857 (Chine 21).
[5] Rouseille to Libois, 23 Sept. 1857 (M.E. vol. 316, f. 901).

Viceroy of the Two Kwangs but also Imperial Commissioner. Elgin agreed to conform to that procedure provided that it was made plain that Great Britain would not suspend hostilities at Canton, even momentarily, until such time as the reparations demanded by England had been obtained *de droit et de fait*.[1] If Elgin were thus being pressed to a strong line of action by the opinion of the British merchants, Gros had to consider the views of the French missionaries. These men were far from desiring armed French intervention at Canton. 'De l'intervention française à Canton, point! Elle serait peu honorable pour la France et funeste à notre mission. . . . Ce n'est qu'à Canton qu'on doit faire des hostilités, mais c'est à la Chine qu'on doit imposer les conditions de la civilisation européenne.'[2]

Gros embodied the result of his discussions with Elgin in a memorandum written on the 16th November. The naval and military authorities were to be called upon to state whether they were in a position to seize, hold, and police the city until a treaty had been negotiated with the Emperor. If they were able to act, the two Plenipotentiaries would address notes to the Viceroy, or in his absence from the city, to the senior Chinese officer therein, by way of a last overture with a time limit attached. Failing an answer, or on the receipt of an unsatisfactory answer, the military and naval authorities were to capture the city, taking care to avoid all acts of violence and pillage. With this memorandum Elgin was in entire agreement.[3] Before the end of November Admiral Seymour announced that in order to establish a base for future operations at Canton, he thought it necessary to occupy a portion of Honan Island. Elgin, who had no objection to any plan of the Admiral's for strengthening the blockade, insisted that no step should be taken towards operations directed against Canton until the Plenipotentiaries had been advised that the naval and military commanders were in possession of adequate force to capture and hold the city, and that a final communication had been addressed by them to Yeh.[4] Elgin was compelled to impress on Seymour the necessity of preserving the good understanding with the French and his dislike of placing the forces

[1] Gros to Walewski, 26 Oct. 1857 (Chine 21).
[2] De Fontaine to Legrégeois, 9 June 1857 (M.E., vol. 550, f. 911).
[3] Elgin to Clarendon, 24 Nov. 1857 (P.P. 1859, Sess. 2, xxxiii, no. 51).
[4] Elgin to Clarendon, 28 Nov. 1857 (ibid., no. 53).

within pistol shot of Canton before the reinforcements which were on their way from India had arrived.[1]

The plan of the British Admiral was for the British to land men at the south-west angle of the city wall, the French below the south-east, for both parties to scale and to proceed along the walls until they met on the heights near the centre of the north front. As the advance would necessarily be made in single file, or at most three abreast, the men would have to destroy by fire the buildings of the city adjacent to the walls to preserve their safety. Hence would result a great loss of property especially as the Chinese 'pack so close'. The Admiral thought that the hardihood of the plan would prevent the Chinese from opposing the Allied advance. Elgin pointed out that past events had proved that the Allies might well underestimate the power of resistance possessed by the Chinese. It was vitally important that the operation should be successful, but subject to that paramount consideration Elgin hoped that a plan would be adopted which was likely to be attended with the smallest sacrifice of life and property.[2] On his part Gros was equally critical of Seymour's scheme. He criticized him for lack of foresight: no steps had been taken in the long months that had passed to organize any kind of espionage service whereby reliable information might have been obtained of the military state of the city, such for example as the condition of the roads, whether they had been barricaded or mined.[3]

Therefore before committing themselves to the irrevocable decision of sending an ultimatum to Yeh, Elgin asked for the joint opinion of Major-General Van Straubenzee and Rear-Admiral Sir Michael Seymour, and Gros for the advice of the French Admiral. When they were assured by the naval and military commanders that they were ready to undertake the capture and occupation of the city, Elgin and Gros sent ultimata to Yeh on the 12th December requiring the complete execution at Canton of all treaty engagements, including the right of entry, not only of British and French officers, but of their nationals generally to the city; together with compensation for losses suffered during the recent disturbances by British and French subjects and protected persons. If these demands and

[1] Elgin to Clarendon, 28 Nov. 1857 (F.O. 17/277).
[2] Elgin to Clarendon (confidential), 10 Dec. 1857 (F.O. 17/277).
[3] Gros to Walewski, 9 Dec. 1857 (Chine 21).

those of the French were conceded, the British, in conjunction with their allies, would immediately raise the blockade, but would retain the island of Honan and the river forts until a definitive treaty had been made with the Imperial Government and duly ratified by both parties. Elgin, making little of the *Arrow* incident, contented himself by stating that 'finally an insult to the British flag, followed by the refusal of the Imperial Commissioner to grant adequate reparation or even to meet in the city the Representatives of Her Britannic Majesty, has forced the officers who are charged with the protection of British interests to have recourse to measures of coercion against Canton'. In his covering dispatch to the Foreign Secretary Elgin commented on his note to Yeh: 'I have given to the *Arrow* case as much prominence as it deserves, when I represent it as the drop which has caused the cup to overflow.'[1] For Baron Gros, as Elgin wrote to his wife, 'has a much better case of quarrel than we; at least one that lends itself much better to rhetoric'—whereas 'that wretched question of the *Arrow* is a scandal to us, and is so considered, I have reason to know, by all except the few who are personally compromised'. He was most anxious to do what he thought had not been done by Bowring, 'to use calm and dignified language, and to be moderate in our demands and resolute in enforcing them'[2].

The ultimata being duly delivered, the British and French forces proceeded to take possession without opposition of Honan Point. Yeh's reply dated the 14th December was received two days later by Elgin in Hong Kong. It repeated the old arguments that there was no right of entry into Canton by the Treaty of 1842, that for raising the question in 1847 Sir John Davis had been recalled at the instance of the foreign community, while for relinquishing the claim Sir George Bonham had been decorated. It was in vain that Bonham and Bowring had gone to the Peiho in 1850 and 1854, and it would be impossible for the Emperor to do otherwise than refuse any further concessions. Compensation was out of the question, and after all Parkes's foolish action had resulted in greater loss to the Chinese than to British subjects. Yeh wished Elgin to understand that an occupation of Honan would be distasteful to the inhabitants, and he refused therefore any responsibility for consequences

---

[1] Elgin to Clarendon, 12 Dec. 1857 (P.P. 1859, Sess. 2, xxxiii, no. 59).
[2] T. Walrond, *Letters and Journal of Lord Elgin*, 9 Dec. 1857, p. 209.

which might ensue from such a measure.[1] The reply to Gros was equally evasive. To the main French demand for adequate reparation by China for the murder of Chapdelaine, Yeh replied that the person executed was one Ma tzu Nung whereas the Catholic missionary was known as Ma chen Fu.[2] At a conference of the Plenipotentiaries and military commanders held on the 21st December on board the French ship *Audacieuse* it was agreed that Elgin and Gros should notify Yeh that, as his reply was unsatisfactory, the Plenipotentiaries had handed the matter over to the naval and military commanders who would summon the authorities at Canton to remove their troops and surrender the city.[3] In sending, on Christmas Eve, this notification Elgin and Gros warned Yeh that they reserved the right of making such additional demands as the Imperial Commissioner's refusal to agree to the two original points might seem to them to justify.[4]

By the 27th December operation orders were issued. Bombardment was to begin at daylight on the 28th to continue slowly day and night and to be accompanied by a landing of the forces at Kuper Passage. On the following day the walls were to be captured and an advance made northwards to the two northern gates with Magazine Hill and Five-storied Pagoda.[5] These operations were entirely successful, but the authorities headed by Yeh still refused to communicate with the victorious allies. They were discovered on the 5th January, captured, and while every courtesy was shown them Yeh was placed on board ship and the Provincial Governor Pih-Kwei and the Tartar General were kept in confinement. The allied officers assumed the government of the city. The troops effecting the seizure of the treasury and other public offices were strictly forbidden, in order to prove the supremacy and the civilized character of the invading nations, to loot or commit any acts of wanton destruction.[6]

It soon became apparent that the British and French forces had no machinery for controlling such a vast population as the citizens of Canton. After considerable hesitation it was finally decided to reinstate Pih-Kwei as Governor in his Yamen to

---

[1] Elgin to Clarendon, 22 Dec. 1857 (P.P. 1859, Sess. 2, xxxiii, no. 68).
[2] Elgin to Clarendon, 22 Dec. 1857 (F.O. 17/277).
[3] Elgin to Clarendon, 22 Dec. 1857 (P.P. 1859, Sess. 2, xxxiii, no. 69).
[4] Elgin to Clarendon, 24 Dec. 1857 (ibid., no. 70).
[5] Elgin to Clarendon, 27 Dec. 1857 (ibid., no. 72).
[6] Elgin to Clarendon, 5 Jan. 1858 (ibid., no. 77).

control the Chinese, while in the same building a tribunal of officers, selected by the commanders, was to sit to try cases in which any foreigner was concerned, and to give their approval to any draft proclamation of the Governor before it was issued. The maintenance of a guard in his residence and of this foreign tribunal gave adequate safeguards against any danger of treachery. To show that they were in fact the masters of the city and the situation the two ambassadors staged a little ceremony at Pih-Kwei's Yamen which made it apparent that he was acting by their leave and under their authority.[1] At first there was naturally some confusion, and complaints of serious outrages committed by the Allied forces were brought before the Commissioners. Three disorderly French sailors were arrested and placed in confinement on the 16th January. An English marine was found guilty by the Commissioners of robbery and a sentence of four dozen lashes was inflicted in the courtyard of the Governor's Yamen.[2] Stringent measures were taken to prevent Chinese from selling alcoholic liquor to the soldiers and marines.[3] However, after a considerable effort by the Commissioners, a police corps was organized consisting of 100 English and 30 French distributed in six zones from which patrols could constantly supervise the streets. The efficiency of this force was greatly increased by the association with them in the discharge of their duties of an equal number of Chinese police. The plan was well received both by the Chinese authorities and people.

By the end of January people were coming back to their homes in the city[4] and the Chinese New Year passed off without trouble.[5] Two measures helped this gradual restoration of tranquillity—the lifting of the blockade on the 10th February and the removal of Yeh to Calcutta. The one measure promised to give employment to the inhabitants, and the other ease of mind to many of the minor functionaries who so long as a possibility of the restoration of the former Imperial Commissioner remained, were perplexed as to the course which it would best suit their interests to pursue.[6]

[1] Elgin to Clarendon, 26 Jan. 1858 (P.P. 1859, Sess. 2, xxxiii, no. 80).
[2] Elgin to Clarendon, 13 Jan. 1858 (ibid., no. 83).
[3] Elgin to Clarendon, 24 Jan. 1858 (ibid., no. 88).
[4] Elgin to Clarendon, 27 Jan. 1858 (ibid., no. 93).
[5] Elgin to Clarendon, 27 Feb. 1858 (ibid., no. 115).
[6] Elgin to Clarendon, 6 Feb. 1858 (ibid., no. 100).

Trade seemed at first to be hesitant, but Parkes was able to report to Elgin on the 25th February that four pack houses had been engaged, the reaches above Honan were covered, nearly as thickly as in former times, with craft of all descriptions, while the goldsmith's guild was considering bringing back to Canton the valuable stock in trade which had been removed to Fat-shan.[1] The newly revived trade necessitated the functioning of the consulate. For the time this was situated, with the concurrence and approval of Pih-Kwei, at Whampoa[2] in order not to introduce an element of complication to the military commanders in the city which continued, and was likely for some considerable time to continue, under a state of martial law.[3]

Thus the first step towards a solution of Anglo-Chinese relations had been successfully accomplished. The Anglo-French forces were in complete and peaceable control of the exclusive city of Canton, and the chief representative of the exclusive system left the waters of China on the 20th February to live in comfort and inscrutable silence in Calcutta.[4] The distinctive Anglo-French operations being concluded, there yet remained the more important and delicate task of a joint diplomatic effort which might now well embrace the representatives of Russia and the United States, to obtain enlarged commercial and political intercourse.

B. THE MOVE TO TIENTSIN

The new American Government, in which Cass was Secretary of State, influenced by internal political considerations, supplanted Parker, 'the excellent Parker whose activities have the approval of the Government'. In his stead was appointed a lawyer Reed, a man of some fifty-odd years, 'of a rather remarkable distinction and elegant simplicity' who impressed Gros as sympathetic towards France, though he exhibited some coolness towards Britain and her Plenipotentiary,[5] and soon showed himself as lacking in tact. Reed was bidden to co-operate with the French and British, whose objects were recognized by the new President as just and reasonable. But his co-operation was

---

[1] Elgin to Clarendon, 27 Feb. 1858 (ibid., no. 119).
[2] Elgin to Clarendon, 27 Feb. 1858 (ibid., no. 112).
[3] Elgin to Clarendon, 12 Feb. 1858 (ibid., no. 105).
[4] Elgin to Clarendon, 27 Feb. 1858 (ibid., no. 113).
[5] Gros to Walewski, 26 Nov. 1857 (Chine 21).

to be entirely diplomatic; only firm representations and an appeal to justice and policy were permitted. At the same time an increase was contemplated in the United States forces in the Far East, the commanders of which were to be instructed to act at the suggestion of the new Minister.[1] On his arrival in the Far East Reed was disposed to criticize his predecessor. He imagined that Parker had led Bowring to believe in the possibility of armed co-operation by the United States on the one hand and then had repelled suggestions for friendly concert on points of common interest.[2] His first impression was that the British were determined to chastise Canton at any cost.

'There is a great irritability among them all. They are fretful, not only at their dependence on the French, without whom they could not take a step in advance, but by their inability to involve the United States in their unworthy quarrel, for such, as it now stands, I confess, it seems to me. On the other hand, the Chinese every hour are putting themselves in the wrong.'[3]

Yet while he was writing thus to the Washington Government, he was saying to Elgin that he regarded the British and French hostile movement as inevitable and that no friendly intervention would do the least good. Elgin welcomed Reed's cordial communication even if 'the Government of the United States has declined, for reasons, chiefly of a constitutional character, the force of which it would of course be impertinent in a foreigner to presume to judge, to join the governments of England and France in proceedings which Your Excellency justly describes as inevitable'[4].

Reed had written to Yeh on the 16th November announcing his arrival and asking for a meeting at which he could deliver a letter from the President to the Emperor. He concluded by remarking that relations of a very satisfactory character subsisted between the United States and China. In a subsequent letter regretting the non-receipt of an answer by Yeh, Reed had asked the Chinese Commissioner whether he confounded the United States with the hostile powers. Elgin, not unnaturally in light of Reed's former communication, regretted that his American colleague should in so marked a manner have

[1] Cass to Reed, 30 May 1857 (Sen. Ex. Doc., 47, 1 Sess. 35 Cong., at p. 6).
[2] Reed to Cass, 10 Nov. 1857 (Sen. Ex. Doc., 30, 1 Sess. 36 Cong., at p. 16).
[3] Reed to Cass, 25 Nov. 1857 (ibid., at p. 19).
[4] Elgin to Clarendon (confidential), 12 Dec. 1857 (F.O. 17/277).

directed attention to the difference in the attitude assumed at
the time by the United States and by the other Treaty Powers
in respect of Canton affairs. Though Reed assured Elgin that
his words had no such intention as that which the British
Plenipotentiary had ascribed to them, and thought that they
would not be so understood by the Imperial Commissioner,[1]
yet it seems clear that Reed hoped that Yeh might have been
induced to use the good offices of the American Government.
For after the fall of Canton he criticized the Imperial Commissioner's refusal 'to receive a visit from a friendly power such
as he admits the United States to be, at a time when some good
offices of mediation might have been rendered'[2]. This cold
neglect prevented Reed from taking any advantage from the
status of a non-belligerent in which his Government had placed
him.

Before the operations against the city began Reed agreed to
attempt to reconcile his Government and fellow citizens to what
he regarded as the anomalous state of affairs in the river, where,
though there was no declared war, a blockade was imposed.
Elgin, naturally anxious that the United States, who were the
only power in a position to impede the operations, should not
put obstacles in the way, laid stress on the fact that in enforcing
claims for redress and violation of treaty rights by measures of
coercion to which civilized nations were wont to resort, Great
Britain and France were adopting a course strictly in conformity with public law.[3] Fortunately for him Reed made no
further reference to the subject and, during the period in which
final arrangements for the attack were being made and the
newly won position in the city was being consolidated, there
was a stop put to the correspondence between the British and
American ministers.

When the operations in Canton had been successfully undertaken Elgin sought to regain contact with the American Minister, which was made all the easier by Reed's attitude. He asked
Elgin if he could be vouchsafed a glimpse of the future action
of the Allies, though he quite understood that this might not be
thought possible. He congratulated his British colleague on the
capture of the city, and 'the great success of a bloodless victory,

---

[1] Elgin to Clarendon (confidential), 12 Dec. 1857 (F.O. 17/277).
[2] Reed to Cass, 14 Jan. 1858, 13 Feb. 1858 (Sen. Ex. Doc. 30, 1 Sess. 36 Cong.,
at p. 86).   [3] Elgin to Clarendon, 15 Dec. 1857 (F.O. 17/277).

the merit of which I am sure is mainly due to your Lordship's gentle and discreet counsel'[1]. An opportunity offered itself of establishing communication, since the troops had found in Yeh's Yamen the originals of the American as well as of the British and French Treaties with the Chinese Emperor. In agreement with Baron Gros the American document was sent to Reed by Elgin through his brother Bruce, Secretary to the British Mission.[2] Reed fully agreed with Elgin's plans for the government of the city, including the establishment of the tribunal, and, in order to prevent undesirable foreigners from entering the city, of a pass control system—two steps which naturally gave to the Allies jurisdiction over American citizens in the city. He read to Bruce the dispatch which he had written to Washington on the capture of the city. Since his mind had cleared on the China question, he was more certain than ever of the necessity of the course the British and French Governments had pursued; his own dispatches had become more warlike during the last month, and his impression was much stronger of the duplicity and bad faith of the Chinese, who could only be worked on through their fears. He was convinced that the way in which the President's letter had been treated and the destruction of the docks at Whampoa gave the United States an adequate *casus belli*, and he had impressed on his Government that friendly representations were of no use.[1]

The great care which Elgin and Gros had taken to make the capture of the city as merciful an operation as possible was duly recognized by Reed. Elgin had indeed said: 'I never felt so ashamed of myself in my life—Here we were accumulating the means of destruction under the very eyes and within the reach of a population of about one million people, against whom these means of destruction were to be employed.' The attack, he observed, was to begin on the day of the Massacre of the Innocents. 'If we can take the city without much massacre, I shall think the job a good one.'[3] Reed was quite correct when he wrote to his Government that it was impossible to read the letters of the British and French Plenipotentiaries without being impressed not only by the moderation of their demand, but by their reluctance to resort to arms. 'I believe

[1] Elgin to Clarendon (private and confidential), 27 Jan. 1858 (F.O. 17/285).
[2] Elgin to Clarendon, 26 Jan. 1858 (P.P. 1859, Sess. 2, xxxiii, no. 91).
[3] Walrond, op. cit., p. 213.

everything was done to confine the inevitable suffering within the narrowest limits. The discipline of the assailants, though the town was taken by actual assault, was very strict.' Elgin's action was therefore not only morally right but politically sound. On the other hand, Yeh had created the worst impression on Reed's mind.

'I have no hesitation in saying', he wrote to the Secretary of State, 'now that this result has occurred, that it was a disgraceful surrender, for such it is, without the grace of being voluntary; an indifference to the sacrifice of human life; an obstinate and unreasoning faith in a superiority of race made more absurd by a cowardly dereliction of duty; the insolence of Yeh one day, and the neglect of all means of defence, though with abundance of resources, and running out of back doors the next, in view of all this, I do not hesitate to say that a new policy towards China ought to be, and I have no doubt by others will be, initiated, and that the powers of western civilization must insist on what they know to be their rights and give up the dream of dealing with China as a power to which any ordinary rules apply.'[1]

A captured Imperial decree, forwarded to Reed by the Allied Ministers, settled definitely

'the question as to any distinction being taken among the nations of the west to our advantage. Steadfast neutrality and consistent friendship make no impression on the isolated obduracy of this empire. I never thought there was, on the part of the officials, any such distinction. I am sure of it now.'

The decree also showed that the Imperial Government must have known precisely what was afoot, and therefore in Reed's judgement the real responsibility was with them. And as the Central Government showed extreme anxiety to prevent the access of foreigners to Peking, he concluded that 'decisive action is necessary with the officials who rule this people' and that 'actual approach to the neighbourhood of the capital with a decisive tone and available force, might produce a result, and that nothing short of this will'[2]. It was therefore clear that Elgin could count on the co-operation of the American representative, though Reed was precluded by his instructions from making a contribution to that material force which by February 1858 he was convinced would necessarily have to be employed.

---

[1] Reed to Cass, 14 Jan. 1858, 13 Feb. 1858 (Sen. Ex. Doc. 30, 1 Sess. 36 Cong., at p. 86). [2] Reed to Cass, 4 Feb. 1858 (ibid., at p. 118).

The United States were therefore to act in the closest friendship with the Russian representative who was likewise prevented by his Government from the use of force.

Admiral Count Poutiatine, the Governor of the lately appropriated provinces on the Amour River arrived in the steamer *America* at Shanghai in the summer of 1857.[1] 'Behind a very modest and simple exterior', wrote the Procureur of the Missions Étrangères of him, 'is concealed great ability. Our ambassadors look upon him as a very capable and active man—above all as a very shrewd politician.'[2] He had been sent on a mission to the Imperial Court, but it had been a failure.[3] He had gone to the mouth of the Peiho, but from information which Elgin received confidentially through French missionaries the Emperor of China was only willing to receive the Russian Envoy if the Count were the bearer of tribute,[4] and would perform the kotow. He had previously attempted at Kiakhta to gain admission to the capital through correspondence with what he believed to be the Foreign Office in Peking, but which Elgin knew in fact to be the tribunal which dealt with colonial or dependent states, though for the past 150 years it had been with this office that the Senate in Russia had been in relations. It was of course of the utmost importance that Elgin should divine the motive which underlay the desire of Russia for closer communication with the Chinese Government. Economic connexion there was, but slight, through the overland Siberian trade route; territorial connexion had recently been established by the advance of Russia down the Amour. Under the energetic leadership of Nicholas Muraviev, appointed in 1847 Governor-General of Eastern Siberia, a factory had been established at the mouth of that river, Saghalien annexed, and Mariinsk and Imperial Harbour founded. In 1854 Muraviev made the first of a series of expeditions from Lake Baikal to the river Shilka and thence past Aigun to the mouths of the Sungari and Ussuri to the sea. The activity of the Franco-British naval force in the Pacific during the Crimean War had converted the Russian Government, initially dubious of the value of Far Eastern expansion, to the view that the acquisition of the left

[1] Bowring to Clarendon, 8 Sept. 1857 (F.O. 17/272).
[2] Libois to Directeurs, 27 Sept. 1858 (M.E. vol. 314, f. 2561).
[3] Bowring to Clarendon, 13 Oct. 1857 (F.O. 17/272).
[4] Elgin to Clarendon, 16 Oct. 1857 (F.O. 17/276).

bank of the Amour was the only practical means of ensuring
the defence of Kamchatka. It had been to secure such a cession
that Poutiatine had recently attempted in vain to make a treaty
with the Chinese authorities.

It was not improbable that there might be ulterior aims in
this Russian diplomatic activity. Indeed, Lord Wodehouse, the
British Ambassador in St. Petersburg thought, after a discussion
with Gortchakoff, that Russia might be aiming at a political
connexion not unlike that with Turkey. Already such a dream
had occurred to Muraviev who had said in 1853: 'If Russia
became stronger in the East, she might even act as Protector
of China.'[1] Elgin therefore asked Poutiatine whether the
Chinese had affected to construe his application for admission
to Peking which he had addressed to them from Kiakhta into
a tender of Russian assistance to suppress the rebellion in
China. 'He seemed a little put out when I hasarded this remark
and proceeded to assure me that he had made no such offer
although he might no doubt have intimated that Russia as a
neighbour would be ready to give to the Chinese her best
advice in their difficulties both domestic and foreign.' 'We may,
I think', commented Elgin, 'infer something respecting the
attitude which Russia would not be unwilling to assume in this
quarter if the Chinese were more manageable'. Baron Gros
was told by his British colleague that Poutiatine did not deny
his suggestion and appeared 'fort troublé'[2].

Joint action would be less detrimental to British interests than
the isolated diplomacy of Russia. Elgin, therefore, assured
Poutiatine, that when the local quarrel which Great Britain
and France had with Canton was concluded, 'we should be
prepared to go northwards in force, and very glad to be accompanied by the flags of other nations interested with us in
extending commercial relations with China, and in inducing
that Court to abate its absurd pretensions of superiority'. The
conversation was, reported Elgin, 'on the whole of a very
amicable character'. The Russian envoy had allowed Elgin
to see confidentially the treaty, as yet unratified, which he had
just concluded at Nagasaki between his own and the Japanese
Governments.[3] While the Canton operations were in progress

[1] T. C. Lin, *Pacific Historical Review*, vol. iii, no. 1.
[2] Gros to Walewski, 26 Nov. 1857 (Chine 21).
[3] Elgin to Clarendon, 14 Nov. 1857 (F.O. 17/276).

Poutiatine remained in his little boat, 'au moins il se tait, n'élève aucune prétention et montre plus de tact que son collègue des États-Unis'[1], wrote the French Ambassador.

When, therefore, Elgin thought himself in a position to leave the neighbourhood of Canton, he drafted in consultation with Baron Gros a letter to the 'Prime Minister' of the Emperor of China, and invited the Ministers of the United States and Russia to adopt a similar course. It would appear that Elgin refused at first to abandon the hostile attitude which both he and Gros had naturally adopted while the British and French forces had been engaged at Canton, and to assume the more friendly character which the French Ambassador imagined to be more suitable, now that peaceful negotiations were to be undertaken in the north in conjunction with the neutral powers. Elgin had said to him: 'ce ne sont plus des négociations que nous aurons à entamer avec lui, nous n'aurons que des sommations à lui faire.' Such a policy would inevitably lead to a separation of France and Britain from Russia and America. Though Gros realized that in the last analysis he would have to agree to the course determined upon by Elgin owing to the relatively considerable forces at his colleague's disposal and the greater extent of the interests entrusted to his care, he successfully prevailed upon Elgin to send a justification of his course of proceeding by transmitting to Peking copies of the whole of his correspondence with Yeh and to address the Celestial Government, though in terms severer than Gros was prepared to use, yet with *paroles conciliantes*.[2]

To his own Government Elgin explained the difference in tone between his first draft and that of his French colleague, whose

'communication to the Court of Peking may be in phraseology and form somewhat more gracious than mine. If I suffer myself to be outdone by my distinguished colleague in that courtesy of language which it so well becomes the strong to employ when treating with the weak, I yield the palm to him only because I am convinced that in dealing with a race so stolid as the Chinese a stern and uncompromising tone not infrequently averts the necessity of resort to harsher measures.'[3]

[1] Gros to Walewski, 11 Dec. 1857 (Chine 21).
[2] Gros to Walewski, 3 and 27 Jan. 1858 (Chine 23).
[3] Elgin to Clarendon, 26 Jan. 1858 (F.O. 17/285).

Though in his final draft he agreed, at Gros's suggestion, to specify more fully the points on which he was instructed to negotiate with the Chinese Plenipotentiaries, Elgin drew attention to the fact that: 'I have not mitigated its tone which I consider to be not too imperative under the circumstances.'[1] This asperity and apparent brusqueness was to be a characteristic feature of Elgin's diplomatic dispatches and general dealing with the Chinese. He was convinced that harsh words which showed unmistakably that he meant what he said and was determined to achieve his ends, would give him the victory at a lesser cost in human suffering. His whole conduct at Canton is instinct with a deep humanitarian feeling. It was in this spirit that he warned the Chinese 'Prime Minister' that if no Plenipotentiary were to meet him in Shanghai by the end of March, fully accredited and empowered to accede to reasonable terms of accommodation, he would have recourse, without further announcement or declaration of hostilities, to such measures as he deemed advisable to adopt.[2] Elgin agreed with Gros's suggestion that they should both ask the Russian and American envoys if they would join in presenting similar notes to Peking. But he was afraid of lowering his prestige if he couched his invitation to them in terms too pressing especially in the case of Reed, who had shown in his notes to Yeh a clear divergence from the French and British standpoint. The two Plenipotentiaries agreed to compromise between Elgin's frigidity and Gros's warmth of expression.[3]

The Russian and American Ministers promised to support the method of communicating with the Peking Government through the Governor-General of the Two Kiangs and the Governor of Kiangsu upon which Elgin had determined. Poutiatine regarded as measures of general interest the establishment of regular diplomatic intercourse with Peking, the extension of foreign trade, and liberty of conscience to Christians. He added two points especially affecting Russia—settlement of frontier questions and compensation for the pillage of a Russian factory in western China.

In consequence of this understanding Oliphant with the British and American notes, in company with the bearer of

[1] Elgin to Clarendon (confidential), 12 Feb. 1858 (F.O. 17/286).
[2] Elgin to Clarendon, 12 Feb. 1858 (P.P. 1859, Sess. 2, xxxiii, no. 102).
[3] Gros to Walewski, 10 Feb. 1858 (Chine 23).

Baron Gros's note, went on in advance to Shanghai.[1] Arrived
in Shanghai on the 20th February, the French and British
officers found that the Taoutai was absent on a visit to his
superiors. They determined, acting on the advice of the Consuls, to go on to Soochow, the temporary head-quarters of the
Governor-General—a step calculated 'to invest the despatches
with a character of importance altogether exceptional, and to
engage for their delivery a publicity which would render it
impossible for the Governor to avoid using the utmost promptitude in their transmission'. In consequence of this decision the
French and British Secretaries, and the American Vice-Consul,
accompanied by Lay, the Inspector of Customs, started on the
24th February in seventeen boats for Soochow, which they
reached and entered two days later.[2] The reception of the notes
of the heads of the missions of the four Powers by Chaou
ensured their transmission to the 'Prime Minister' in Peking.[3]

Elgin first arranged that the Admiral should sail northwards
from Hong Kong on the 16th March, if nothing prevented him,
with as large a fleet as possible, especially of gunboats drawing
little water, and then at the beginning of March left in advance
for Shanghai.[4] He touched at Amoy and Swatow, where the
stories of the coolie trade appalled him,[5] Foochow, and Ningpo.[6]
He was thus brought into touch with conditions at the several
ports and in making this personal inspection acted like his
Russian colleague. 'It is amusing', he wrote to his wife, 'to see
how we play our parts. Poutiatine and I are always together,
visiting every port, looking into everything with our own eyes.
Our colleagues with their big ships, arrive sooner or later at
the great places of rendezvous.'[7] At Shanghai he received a
message from Yu, the Chief Secretary of State, through the
Governor-General of the Two Kiangs and the Governor of
Kiangsu that as the Emperor had appointed Hwang the new
Imperial Commissioner the British Plenipotentiary should repair to that officer's seat of government at Canton, where alone

[1] Elgin to Clarendon, 12 Feb. 1858 (P.P. 1859, Sess. 2, xxxiii, no. 103).
[2] Oliphant has written a graphic account of his journey and the reception
accorded to the foreign diplomats at the Governor's Yamen.
[3] L. Oliphant, *Narrative of Lord Elgin's Mission*, vol. i, chs. x and xi.
[4] Elgin to Clarendon, 2 Mar. 1858 (P.P. 1859, Sess. 2, xxxiii, nos. 120, 121).
[5] Elgin to Clarendon, 6 Mar. 1858 (ibid., no. 122).
[6] Elgin to Clarendon, 8, 19 Mar. 1858 (ibid., nos. 123 and 126).
[7] Walrond, op. cit., 11 Apr. 1858, p. 246.

foreign affairs could be transacted.[1] The other Plenipotentiaries were given similar messages. The answer to Reed, after making mention of America's faithfulness, ended with the admonition, 'the American Minister ought to be at Canton, waiting to perform his incumbent duties'[2]. Elgin, naturally dissatisfied with the content of the message, refused to receive a reply from the 'Prime Minister', which being thus indirectly communicated was also bad in form. Accordingly, he forwarded a second communication through the two local high officers to Yu, insisting upon the Treaty right of direct correspondence with the Chinese high officers both at the capital and in the provinces,[3] and returned the Viceroy's dispatch. Gros contented himself with the milder course of sending a note to Yu in which he stated that he regarded the Chinese answer as 'nul et non-avenue', Bruce had said to him:

'Ce n'est pas en mettant le couteau sur la gorge des Chinois qu'on obtiendra quelque chose d'eux, c'est en l'y enfonçant tout entier', though Gros believed that he was but expressing an idea which it was hoped would prevail, and that both he and his brother, Elgin, 'loin de pousser la main qui tiendrait l'arme, l'arrêteraient plutôt s'ils le pouvaient.'[4]

As March was now passed and Elgin had gathered from Poutiatine that the season for operations in the north would end by the beginning of June, he determined to push on at once to the Peiho. Such an immediate move would prevent the Chinese authorities from thinking that he was pursuing a vacillating policy and would also enable him to cut off the rice supplies bound for the capital.[5] As Yu refused to communicate directly and to send an accredited person to negotiate at Shanghai, Elgin had recovered his liberty.[6] Reed and the other Plenipotentiaries fully concurred in Elgin's judgement not to waste time by returning to Canton, but to move towards the capital, especially 'as every attempt to correspond on terms of equality elsewhere has for more than ten years failed'[7]. Therefore having arranged with the senior naval officer to dispatch

[1] Elgin to Clarendon, 30 Mar. 1858 (P.P. 1859, Sess. 2, xxxiii, no. 131).
[2] Elgin to Clarendon, 31 Mar. 1858 (F.O. 17/287).
[3] Elgin to Clarendon, 3 Apr. 1858 (P.P. 1859, Sess. 2, xxxiii, no. 136).
[4] Gros to Walewski, 10 Apr. 1858 (Chine 24).
[5] Elgin to Clarendon, 3 Apr. 1858 (P.P. 1859, Sess. 2, xxxiii, no. 137).
[6] Elgin to Clarendon, 1 Apr. 1858 (F.O. 17/287).
[7] Elgin to Clarendon, 3 Apr. 1858 (F.O. 17/287).

further ships, although the Admiral had not yet arrived at
Shanghai, the British Minister sailed north on the 10th April,[1]
accompanied by Lay, his brother Bruce, and Wade as Chief
Chinese Secretary. Though Gros understood Elgin's desire to
avoid the appearance of hesitation, he personally would have
waited until the whole force was ready to sail. No plan had
been clearly fixed in Elgin's mind, and the French Ambassador
complained of his colleague's *indécision habituelle*, which seemed to
have increased as his confidence of complete success diminished.
His frequent complaints to Gros of Seymour's conduct were
evidence that he was disturbed at the prospect of affairs.[2] He
arrived in the Gulf of Pechili on the 15th April, but it was not
until the 29th May that he was in a position to enter the river
and proceed to Tientsin. This delay of over a month was due
partly to the non-arrival of the gunboats, and partly to the
diplomatic activity of the Russian and American Ministers who
were precluded from the use of force. Elgin was certain that if
he had appeared with ten or twelve gunboats he could have
gone straight up river without opposition and announced to
the Chinese authorities that he and his colleagues were prepared
to meet accredited Plenipotentiaries of the Emperor in or near
Peking. In that way he would have shown that the mouth of
the Peiho was not, as the Chinese had thought, sealed to foreign
ships owing to the shallow water at the bar. He would have
had the additional advantage of being placed between the
Capital and the rice junks,[3] which 'were constantly passing
over the Bar with provisions for Peking'[4], 'at the rate of fifty
a day'. As it was he arrived in H.M.S. *Furious* with the gunboat
Slavey and the dispatch boat *Cormorant*, and had to anchor five
miles off the coast.[3] On the 24th April Seymour arrived on
board H.M.S. *Calcutta* accompanied by the *Sampson* towing the
gunboat *Coromandel* with the information that five gunboats
might be expected during May, but that the *Leven* was detained
at Amoy, and the *Opossum* and *Bustard*, which should have left
Hong Kong on the 10th April, were still in front of Canton two
days later. Many British gunboats were unserviceable owing
to the way they had been worked in the Canton River on duties

[1] Elgin to Clarendon, 9 Apr. 1858 (P.P. 1859, Sess. 2, xxxiii, no. 140).
[2] Gros to Walewski, 10 Apr. 1858 (Chine 24).
[3] Elgin to Clarendon, 23 Apr. 1858 (F.O. 17/288).
[4] Elgin to Clarendon, 22 Apr. 1858 (F.O. 17/288).

which, at least since the blockade had been raised, could have
been equally well performed by ordinary passenger or merchant
craft. Elgin complained that the Admiral had given him to
understand in the most uncompromising terms that he was
prepared to give the naval support for which he had been asked
and which he had never questioned. It was essential that those
who controlled 'the material force of Great Britain in this
quarter should lend to those who direct its diplomacy a vigorous
and intelligent support'. The net result of the delay would be
the arrival of the force at the worst season of the year for
European constitutions. When in early May the preliminary
negotiations had reached a point at which the British and
French Admirals were requested to move up the river by their
diplomatic chiefs, the commanders refused to move until the
forts were in their hands, and declared they would not be in
a position to attack until the gunboats had arrived.[1] It was not
until the 11th that all available reinforcements had arrived.
Even then Seymour and his French colleague again insisted
on their refusal to send them up the river until the forts were
in their hands.[2] Elgin seems to have disagreed with this view,
but was bound to bow to the professional opinion of the sailors.
He had hoped to have avoided the use of force, as the American
and Russian Ministers would be obliged to separate themselves
from the British and French at that point. He was fearful, too
fearful as the sequel showed, of the consequences.

'This decision, coupled with Admiral Seymour's omission to send up
the gunboats at the time originally agreed on between us, has deprived the Allied Powers of an opportunity for placing the relations
between the Western nations and China upon an improved footing
which may very probably never again present itself under conditions
equally promising.'[3]

The time between the 15th April and the assault on the forts
at the mouth of the Peiho on the 22nd May was spent in an
endeavour to reopen negotiations at Takoo. Elgin accepted
Gros's suggestion on the 22nd April that the four Powers should
again address the 'Prime Minister' and acquaint him with their
arrival in the gulf and their desire to negotiate either on board
ship or at some suitable place on land. Gros was as anxious for

[1] Elgin to Malmesbury, 9 May 1858 (F.O. 17/288).
[2] Elgin to Malmesbury, 20 May 1858 (F.O. 17/288).
[3] Elgin to Malmesbury, 15 May 1858 (F.O. 17/288).

a quick settlement as was his British colleague, recently instructed by the new Derby Government to do his utmost, even at the sacrifice of less important demands, to bring about a speedy solution of the difficulties.[1] 'Vous savez', he wrote to Elgin, 'mieux que moi qu'avec ces gens-ci, il faut agir avec promptitude, avec vigueur, et avec justice; ils ne comprennent les bons procédés que lorsque c'est une main de fer qui les leur montre'[2]. In consequence of this agreement Wade delivered to the Governor-General of Chih-li a letter from Elgin covering a request to the 'Prime Minister' for the dispatch of a Plenipotentiary to Takoo. A time limit of six days was given at the expiration of which he would regard himself free to adopt such further measures for enforcing the just claims of his Government on that of China as he might think expedient.[3]

In consequence of this *démarche* the Plenipotentiaries were notified on the 28th April by Tau of his appointment by the Emperor to conduct negotiations, but as the characters for the Queen and the Emperor were not placed on an equality the letter was returned. It came back amended two days later with the usual explanation that the error was due to the ignorance of a subordinate clerk. Elgin and Gros were anxious to find whether Tau had powers or instructions which would enable him to engage the Peking Government. The Russian Minister thought they were *assez restreints*. Tau avoided using the Chinese characters for full powers which had been used by Elgin's Chinese secretary and substituted others which signified 'power to treat so as to bring things to a settlement'.[4] Being unable to enter the river and make a display of force Elgin had to content himself with demanding on the 6th May from Tau the production within six days of powers similar to those granted to the Commissioners Keying and Elepoo before the discussions leading to the Treaty of Nanking had been undertaken.[5] Both Reed and Poutiatine held that the Chinese Government would not grant to any foreign Power whatsoever the most reasonable concession, even where such concession would be attended by the most manifest advantage to itself, except under the influence of fear. Yet, as the naval situation

---

[1] Walewski to Gros, 4 Apr. 1858 (Chine 24).
[2] Elgin to Clarendon, 22 Apr. 1858 (F.O. 17/288).
[3] Elgin to Clarendon, 25 Apr. 1858 (P.P. 1859, Sess. 2, xxxiii, no. 146).
[4] Elgin to Malmesbury, 9 May 1858 (ibid., no. 152).
[5] Elgin to Malmesbury, 9 May 1858 (ibid., no. 153).

prevented what Elgin had hoped might be possible—the advance of all four powers peaceably in gunboats to Tientsin—the two neutral ministers ardently desired success at Takoo and the avoidance of any rupture in diplomatic relations. They therefore almost constituted themselves mediators, and in doing so their influence tended naturally to exceed that of the French and British. Poutiatine was in a particularly strong position, for he was able to summon to his assistance two of his countrymen from Peking. One of them who kept a diary of his days in China had made himself useful, and had been admitted, to some of the highest courts of the Empire. He had had access to the plans of the Takoo fortifications. Arrived at the mouth of the Peiho on the 24th April he and his companion were well lodged and entertained to a sumptuous dinner, 'circumstances causing the Chinese to pay us extraordinary attention'. In conversation with the Chinese officers he was impressed by their complaints of the rudeness of the English 'who will not discuss affairs in the proper order and with due ceremony and who insult the dignitaries of China by their contemptuous bearing'. It was evident to the Russian that 'the Chinese were aware of their impotence, and were not averse to come to an accommodation with the European powers had the latter only moderated their feelings of repugnance and contempt'. The diarist and his friend visited Poutiatine in the *America* on the 25th. His view that the Chinese would yield in everything, provided that the prestige so dear to an Oriental Government was preserved, no doubt influenced the Russian Plenipotentiary's attitude. 'They were waiting for, and seeking, an opportunity of giving a plausible appearance to their concessions, but the opportunity was not afforded to them.' The anger of the Chinese against the English was accordingly extreme. One of their Mandarins, 'stretching out his hand and turning pale with rage, towards the East, as if he saw the English, cried out frantically, "Lai, Lai" (Come, Come here!)'[1].

On the 29th April Poutiatine had an interview with the Chinese on land, and it was his intervention that procured the alteration in the form of the original notification by Tau of his appointment. When Elgin criticized to the Russian Minister the powers given by the Emperor to Tau, Poutiatine replied that it was not to be expected that greater powers should be

[1] Erskine to Russell, 17 Sept. 1860 (F.O. 65/554).

given, nor was it necessary owing to the nearness of the capital. Similarly Reed announced on the 4th May that

'peace is too important to the relations subsisting between China and the United States to be imperilled by any adherence in a preliminary correspondence to the strict rules of Western diplomacy, and I was content to run the risk of ultimate or even preliminary failure on a point which according to circumstances might become either sub-stantial or merely technical'.

He was convinced that Tau's powers were limited by the requirement not that each clause but that an agreed Treaty should be referred as a whole to Peking. He was ready to negotiate at once if Tau, by producing copies of his letter to the 'Prime Minister' handed over at the Soochow interview the previous February, could demonstrate that he was charged to discuss the American demands, and if the Emperor agreed to receive the President's letter on a footing of equality. Elgin was convinced that a Government which would not communicate directly with foreign envoys and which sent a powerless Com-missioner was only trifling. He asked the American and Rus-sian ministers 'in all earnestness, is it possible that international relations can subsist under such a system?' However, he so far agreed with Reed that the only evidence of adequate power he would demand for starting to negotiate was the possession by Tau of a document similar to that issued to Keying in 1842. Poutiatine thought that what had once been given could be given again and urged Tau to produce the necessary document within the time limit stipulated by his British colleague.[1]

Elgin's analysis of the situation proved quite correct, for an interview which Reed had on the 10th May was far from satis-factory. Tau obviously would not be in a position to procure powers similar to Keying's, for he assured Reed that Keying must have forged the document in question, and that anyhow his policy had led to his degradation. Reed found the Chinese unwilling even to discuss the claim of occasional access to Peking or of the extension of commercial facilities up the great rivers to the internal marts. At most they might agree to grant foreign representatives the right of direct sealed correspondence with the Privy Council and the legalization of trade in those ports where irregular trade was being carried on. Moreover, the decree which had been issued on the subject of the recep-

[1] Elgin to Malmesbury, 9 May 1858 (F.O. 17/288).

tion of the President's letter was so unsatisfactory that Reed
refused to hand it to Tau. He was therefore bound to make it
clear to the Chinese 'that it is a necessity created by themselves
which reconciles me to what is about to occur'[1].

On the 11th May Elgin received an evasive refusal from the
court of Peking to give Tau powers similar to those entrusted
to Keying and Elepoo in 1842. Tau had in fact, thought Elgin,
been appointed a negotiator without powers in order to attempt
by persuasion or force to drive the foreigners away from the
neighbourhood of the capital.[2]

At one moment it appeared possible that an agreed solution
might be obtained through Russian intervention. For on the
night of the 13th/14th d'Osten-Sacken, Poutiatine's secretary,
reported that the Chinese Commissioner seemed prepared to
consider serious concessions: fresh ports would be opened to
foreign commerce, an indemnity would be paid for losses sustained by the subjects of the Treaty Powers at Canton, liberty
of conscience would be granted to Chinese Christians, while
missionaries might be allowed, under the protection of the local
authorities, to go anywhere in the Empire to preach the Gospel.
Though Tau refused to agree to the permanent residence of
political agents, he thought, subject to reference to Peking, that
there might be no objection to their entry into the capital to
discuss with the Emperor's ministers when grave questions
made such a course necessary. But Tau was adamant against
opening the Yangtse cities or the interior generally to foreigners
as well as to the payment of a war indemnity. Gros, whose
Government was concerned primarily to vindicate the rights
of the Catholic missionaries, would have accepted these terms,
though he doubted the sincerity of the offer. Elgin too initially
shared Gros's opinion and congratulated himself on the possibility of a door being opened in this way which would allow the
British and French to escape with honour from the impasse in
which they were then placed. But by the 15th Elgin's judgement had changed. He declared it absurd to accept a clause
by which Christian missionaries obtained freedom of access to
the interior while that privilege was withheld from foreign
traders, 'et il me disait', reported Gros to his minister, 'avec
énergie qu'on le brûlerait vif s'il avait le courage d'accepter de

[1] Elgin to Malmesbury, 11 May 1858 (F.O. 17/288).
[2] Elgin to Malmesbury, 20 May 1858 (P.P. 1859, Sess. 2, xxxiii, no. 155).

telles conditions'. He was, however, relieved of the necessity of considering seriously whether to accept these suggested terms by the news that the Emperor himself had given them his negative.[1] The possibilities of an amicable settlement were now exhausted.

On the 18th May, after the Admirals had made their reconnaissance, the British and French civil and naval authorities determined to take the forts and advance up river, and on the 20th Tau was notified of this decision. The result was the capture of the forts, whose garrison opened fire, with but slight British casualties, though the French had heavier losses owing to an accidental explosion. Tau had himself not ordered resistance, but protested at the impropriety of foreign boats entering the Peiho and advancing to Tientsin.[2]

C. NEGOTIATIONS AT TIENTSIN

After the passage had been secured, Elgin and his colleagues pushed on to Tientsin, which was reached on the morning of the 30th May, to find appointed as Commissioners two Tartars of long standing in the public service, and of more exalted rank than Tau: Kweiliang, the old and sickly Chief Secretary of State, who received his visitors resting on the shoulders of an attendant, and Hwa-shana, President of the Board of Civil Office, a vigorous man under fifty years of age with sharp severe features; the former was the second Manchu in the Empire, a brother of the Imperial Commissioner who had met Bowring when he visited the Gulf of Pechili in 1854.[3] Afraid that even at Tientsin his negotiations might prove abortive, Elgin made provisional arrangements for a large force to be dispatched north from Hong Kong. On their arrival in Tientsin the Chinese Commissioners sent the foreign envoys their cards on which they described themselves as 'Ministers with full authority to act as the occasion shall demand', and Elgin agreed to meet them to exchange full powers.[4] The first interview took place on the 4th June. Kweiliang at once stated that full powers in the Western sense were unknown to the Chinese Government, but to please the foreigners the Emperor had made use

[1] Elgin to Malmesbury, 22 May 1858 (P.P. 1859, Sess. 2, xxxiii, no. 157).
[2] Gros to Walewski, 19 May 1858 (Chine 24).
[3] Elgin to Malmesbury, 1 June 1858 (P.P. 1859, Sess. 2, xxxiii, no. 159).
[4] Elgin to Malmesbury, 4 June 1858 (ibid. no. 162).

of Elgin's words. The words used, however, in the decree of appointment were of an evasive character. They could be taken to be as full as Keying's or as restricted as in Tau's case. They were thus translated: 'In any conjuncture requiring that the action taken be suited to the emergency, unless the case (or article, or section) be in contravention of what is right or proper, their course is to deviate (from the beaten track) accordingly.' Elgin, who thought it advisable to take a high and stern line from the outset, insisted on taking time to consider whether he was even now justified in entering into discussion with the new Commissioners on the different questions at issue.[1] An additional difficulty was occasioned by the fact that Kwei-liang was not in possession of the appropriate seal of an Imperial Commissioner. The senior of the two had used the one attached to his Superintendency of the Board of Punishment. In the preliminaries to the Nanking negotiation Elepoo had stressed the fact that Keying was arriving possessed of the seal of an Imperial Commissioner. Kweiliang attempted to explain away the difference in the two cases on the ground that his master was unwilling to recognize the fact of a state of hostilities, and Keying's seal had been one issued only to Commissioners deal-ing with extraordinary military business.[2]

However, these points were to be met, and meanwhile, on the suggestion of the Imperial Commissioners, Lay was sent to their residence to discuss Elgin's letter to Yu of the 11th Febru-ary, as they found 'there are some points on which we are not perfectly clear'. In consequence Lay entered upon a discussion which began on the 6th and was continued every day until the 10th June. After a formal reception by the Commissioners, the real conversation began between their Secretary Pieu and the Shanghai Inspector of Customs. Pieu acknowledged that Yeh had been in the wrong at Canton and that Pih-Kwei's reports as to conditions actually prevailing in Canton differed materi-ally from Lay's. Such a state of affairs should not, however, happen again. Lay objected that there did not seem much chance of improvement when Yu refused to answer Elgin's February letter: 'After such conduct on the part of her chief Minister, could China wonder at a want of confidence in her professions?' But Pieu insisted that the remedy for such a

[1] Elgin to Malmesbury, 12 June 1858 (ibid., no. 164).
[2] Elgin to Malmesbury, 14 June 1858 (ibid., no. 166).

grievance could not be the right of access to Peking; indeed the Emperor would rather risk war than give up his policy of exclusion. Similarly, he feared that if the British demand for universal trade were granted, foreigners would monopolize all trade to the ruin of the native Chinese. Lay put the foreign point of view clearly when he observed

'China had been led by her past exclusiveness to regard herself as the "central nation", and her ignorance of the existence of powerful and wealthy countries had made her look upon all people not Chinese as "barbarians", beyond the pale of civilization. This was a grand mistake, which she would have now to unlearn; and she must, however much against her will, henceforth comply with the usages of western nations, intercourse with whom she was manifestly too weak, physically, to decline.'

After an hour's conversation in private with his chiefs, Pieu returned to ask Lay whether the British would be satisfied if her representative alone were admitted to Peking, and whether he and his suite, except on grand occasions, would wear Chinese costume so as to obviate the possibility of arousing popular excitement. Lay doubted whether Elgin would agree to the first suggestion, and at the second he almost laughed. On the following day the First Commissioner, having explained Yu's remissness in not answering Elgin's February note as due to his dotage and his ignorance of foreign nations, appealed to Lay (whom as a servant of the Chinese Government he regarded as 'one of ourselves') to prevail upon Elgin to withdraw the request for the residence of foreign ministers in Peking. All four Powers could not be admitted, though there was no objection to allowing that privilege to the minister of Great Britain. To grant all nations freedom of access to the capital would be fraught with evil to China. Lay could not help, from his knowledge of the country, acquiescing to a certain extent in this argument. Kweiliang made a personal appeal to Lay. He was seventy-four years of age and begged the British to spare him from the degradation and punishment which acceptance of the residence point would inevitably entail. He and his colleague, reported the Russian diarist who was in attendance on Poutiatine, 'were in a state of extreme humiliation and trembled at the approach of Lord Elgin's deputies. Kweiliang had entirely broken down and Hwashana had evidently sought solace in strong liquor.'[1]

[1] Erskine to Russell, 17 Sept. 1860 (F.O. 65/554).

On the following day Pieu submitted a memorandum to Lay in which all the propositions made by Elgin in February were more or less negatived. There was, in particular, to be no freedom of access either diplomatic to the capital or commercial to the Yangtse. Lay regarded this as sheer trifling and insisted upon immediate agreement to five propositions: the use of English in all official correspondence, toleration of Christianity, co-operation of the Chinese and British authorities in the suppression of piracy, a revision of the tariff and customs arrangements, and, lastly, access to the cities on the Yangtse and, under a system of passports, of all merchants to the cities of the interior. After an interview with Kweiliang and consultation among the Chinese officers, Lay was promised Chinese acceptance of these terms. Conversation then turned upon the question of a reception by the Emperor of Lord Elgin. Lay insisted that his chief should be received in audience according to Western forms: Elgin would kneel on one knee and while in Peking would select a building for the permanent accommodation of the British Minister. Though Kweiliang at first agreed to these propositions he afterwards urged, in deference to a protestation on the part of Pieu, that Elgin should kneel on both knees and objected to the idea of his going to the capital in the present conjuncture.

On the 9th June it was understood that the Chinese Commissioners would embody these terms in a letter addressed to Lord Elgin. Lay attended them, but finding the draft unsatisfactory dictated a fresh one. As their expected seal, however, had not arrived he would not take back the written answer. It was promised for 3 p.m. on the 10th, but five hours after that time, Lay was still waiting for the document.[1] The delay was due to the unexpected intervention of Keying, who, styling himself a Vice-President, had sent his card to Elgin on the 9th. The British Plenipotentiary had excused himself from a visit on the ground that his time was fully occupied with the negotiations with the accredited Commissioners. Wade and Lay, however, paid him a visit in the miserably furnished house in which he was established. He praised everything English, asked after every one with whom he had come into contact in the forties, enlarged upon his liberality to the English when at Canton, instancing among other proofs, that he had eaten with

[1] Elgin to Malmesbury, 14 June 1858 (P.P. 1859, Sess. 2, xxxiii, no. 167).

the British their 'ta-tsan'. Friendship for England had cost him
everything: he had been thrown into prison and charged with
taking a bribe of 40,000 taels from the English. He informed
the British secretaries that, as his name had been mentioned,
the Emperor had allowed him to try his hand at a settlement,
but that if he should fail he would lose his head. Wade and Lay
gathered that he was in little favour at court. They did not
hesitate to let Keying know that they were distrustful of his
good intentions in days gone by. When Lay, a young man of
twenty-seven, read one of Keying's Memorials, captured in
Yeh's office, in which he apologized to the Emperor for his
social intercourse as a mark of condescension and a means of
controlling the Barbarians, the enfeebled old Mandarin dis-
solved into tears.[1] His great solution was the withdrawal of the
foreign ships from the north: if that were effected he would
settle everything. It was clear to the British that the Imperial
intention was to employ a man, thought to be acceptable to
foreigners and experienced in 'cajoling' them. 'His conversation
was a perfect clatter of compliments and moral sentiments,
delivered with that mixed air of patronage and conciliation
which, it may be observed, was considered by the mandarins
earlier in contact with us as the true means of "soothing and
bridling the barbarian".' To the British secretaries it appeared
that the best way in which Elgin could help Keying from the
threatened anger of the Emperor was to decline to enter into
communications with him. On the 11th June, however, Keying
admitted himself as an Imperial Commissioner and Minister
Plenipotentiary having the requisite seal and empowered to
act 'as occasion demands'[2].

His intervention had been unavailing and, without sanction
from his Government he withdrew to the capital. On the way he
was arrested by Sang-ko-lin-sin, who commanded an army of
35,000 men barring the road to Peking, thrown into irons, and
condemned to death.[3]

On the 11th Elgin received the promised letter from the
Commissioners embodying the five points with two slight modifications. Until the Chinese officers were better acquainted
with English, they asked that a Chinese translation of English

[1] Gros to Walewski, 11 June 1858 (Chine 24).
[2] Elgin to Malmesbury, 14 June 1858 (P.P. 1859, Sess. 2, xxxiii, no. 165).
[3] Gros to Walewski, 21 June 1858 (Chine 24).

communications should accompany the originals, and that foreigners should not visit places held by the rebels, nor use the right of travel into the interior until the Emperor had had time to enjoin through his officers upon the Chinese population conformity with the new system. In addition it was agreed first that arrangements should be made at Canton for the payment of war expenses, and secondly, that in regard to diplomatic access to the capital, 'to the permanent residence of a Plenipotentiary of Her Britannic Majesty there is properly no objection', and that the Emperor would send a Commissioner to England. However, owing to the recent collision at Takoo, they urged that it would be better to postpone for the present the exercise of the right.[1] The following day it was agreed that Elgin should send officers on the afternoon of the 14th June to arrange with the High Commissioners, now in possession of the requisite seal, the drafting of a treaty in accordance with their reply.

Several days were taken up by Lay in reducing the agreed terms to treaty form, for the Chinese Commissioners were all the while negotiating separately with the other three foreign Powers. On the 21st the Chinese asked for postponement of the date, owing to the Taiping rebellion, of the opening of Chinkiang as a foreign trading port, and due time for the promulgation of a decree announcing the arrival of foreigners in the interior. They reiterated their fears of the destruction of the Chinese merchant by foreign competition, and finally suggested that Elgin should forgo a visit himself to the capital, though on a future occasion the British Government might send an officer to Peking. These four points which the Emperor by decree had commanded his envoys to consider with Elgin, the British Plenipotentiary refused to discuss. The treaty was ready by the 22nd, and two days later Elgin's brother and secretary considered its text. Some slight modifications were agreed upon. The words 'when coming with no hostile purpose or in pursuit of pirates' were added to the clause enabling British warships to enter Chinese harbours; words implying bad conduct in the past of the Chinese Government were struck out of the clause dealing with transit duties; a president of one of the boards could represent China in the future tariff conference in lieu of the original proposal to send the Chief Secretary of State. Bruce agreed to refer to Elgin the questions of the

[1] Elgin to Malmesbury, 14 June 1858 (P.P. 1859, Sess. 2, xxxiii, no. 168).

Canton indemnity and of the authority of the English over the Chinese text of the treaty, though at the same time he pointed out that the defectiveness of the Chinese version of the Nanking Treaty had given a handle to the Canton authorities to claim the legality of the exclusion of foreigners from their city. The Commissioners withdrew their desire to make special reference to contraband and prohibited articles in the clause allowing the Chinese authorities to confiscate articles shipped or landed at unauthorized ports, for since, as Bruce pointed out, all goods at such places were by the proposed treaty liable to confiscation, such an addition was otiose. The Chinese again protested against the establishment of a passport system enabling merchants to accompany their merchandise throughout the interior of the country, although the passport system had originated in a desire to avoid hurting Chinese prejudice. However, it was agreed to keep Chin-kiang closed for one year and to open Newchwang. Again an effort was made to exclude the possibility of the permanent residence of a foreign minister in Peking. Bruce categorically refused to consider a proposal, contrary to what every other nation was used to grant, that only when there was definite business to transact should a foreign minister come up to the capital, and then unaccompanied by foreign women.[1]

On the 26th Bruce and Lay again met the two Commissioners and explained Elgin's surprise at learning that the old objections had again been raised—this proceeding he could only consider evidence of the bad faith of the Commissioners. He was excessively indignant at an attempt which had been made by them to invoke the assistance of the other foreign representatives in matters which concerned Great Britain alone. The Imperial Commissioners rejoined that the alterations they sought were not introduced by them as ultimata, and when Bruce consented to change the words 'residence in perpetuity' in the clause dealing with the residence in Peking to 'constant residence' they agreed to sign the treaty as it stood.[2] And in consequence at 7 p.m. on that day, the 26th June, the Treaty of Tientsin between Great Britain and China was signed. Elgin, however, waited in that city until he learnt of the Imperial approval of the treaty. On the 30th June the Emperor announced:

---

[1] Elgin to Malmesbury, 1 July 1858 (P.P. 1859, Sess. 2, xxxiii, no. 174).
[2] Elgin to Malmesbury, 3 July 1858 (ibid., no. 175 and F.O. 17/289).

'We have perused your memorial and know all. Respect this.' This was not definite enough for Elgin, who refused to move until approval as definite as that given to the Treaty of Nanking was forthcoming.[1] On the 3rd July adequate approval was sent in the words: 'We hereby signify our assent to all the propositions in the English, French, Russian and American Treaties as submitted to us in their previous memorial by these ministers.'[2]

Elgin's anxiety and responsibility at Tientsin were not, however, exhausted by his transactions with the Imperial Commissioners. He had to bear in mind that his three colleagues had all somewhat different motives. The interests of Great Britain and France had been reconciled by the discussions between the London and Paris Governments preceding the appointment of Elgin and Gros. There was bound, however, to be a sharp difference of attitude between Gros and himself on the one hand and the American and Russian Plenipotentiaries on the other. The neutral ministers were obliged to take what they could themselves persuade the Chinese to grant without an appeal to the *ultima ratio*, while at the same time securing, by most favoured nation clauses, any additional concessions which the British and French could extort from the fears of the Imperial Government. The dominant position of Great Britain is abundantly clear, and yet it was not without its dangers. Doubtless the moral if not the material position of Elgin was strengthened by the presence of representatives of four Powers. But he had been unwilling to treat in common conference with them and the Chinese, for such a proceeding might unduly have tied his hands. The High Commissioners had originally desired such common conference, and though Elgin had declined, 'the Russian Minister had likewise stoutly objected to it'.

Poutiatine had a difficult task. For the most important point at issue between Russia and China was the question of the boundary between the Russian and the Celestial Empires. Owing to his previous failure to achieve a solution of the territorial problem he had been instructed to confine himself to obtaining the commercial and political objects upon which the alliance between Great Britain and France was based. Muraviev was

---

[1] Elgin to Malmesbury, 5 July 1858 (P.P. 1859, Sess. 2, xxxiii, no. 176).
[2] Elgin to Malmesbury, 5 July 1858 (ibid., no. 178).

given by the St. Petersburg Government exclusive power over the Amour question, and was actually negotiating at Aigun with the Chinese representative Ishan at the very time that Poutiatine was at Tientsin. Muraviev's hands were strengthened by reason of the fact that troops from the extra-mural provinces had been transferred to the capital as a defence against a possible advance of the Anglo-French forces from Tientsin. Though Ishan yielded to *force majeure*, the Emperor refused to ratify the agreements arrived at on the Amour beyond recognizing the right of Russia to occupy the left bank of that river from Aigun to the Sungari mouth.[1] Of these negotiations neither Elgin nor the British Government knew anything.

As we have already seen, the British Government had been suspicious of Russia's attitude; and when Lay heard from Pieu on the 7th June that Poutiatine had expressed the hope that the boundary question would be settled on the Amour and not even mentioned at Tientsin, he warned the Chinese Secretary that 'any act on the part of one power affecting the welfare of China would be, on the plea of protection of their common interests, fair ground for intervention on the part of the remaining powers'. Lay suggested that when the time came for the settlement of the Russian boundary, China would find it to her advantage if she invited the advice and assistance of Great Britain and France; and of this suggestion 'Pieu evidently approved'[2]. The day before Lay had emphasized that there was no design on the part of the powers to annex Chinese territory. He could well say so, as Poutiatine's demands which had been shown to Elgin had disclosed no territorial ambitions. Indeed, Lay thought that the four Powers would bind themselves by a formal engagement to abstain from the prosecution of any such design. 'If China were wise she would make Great Britain her friend, and in that case she would have nothing to fear from other powers. Great Britain was the most influential of the nations concerned.' The analogy of China and Turkey was present in the minds of the Chinese as well as of the British, for Pieu declared that his Government knew that the recent Russian war had been undertaken to prevent the Tsar from appropriating 'little Turkey'. Lay drove home the point—they might see that a foreign nation could not always commit what

---

[1] T. C. Lin, *Pacific Historical Review*, vol. iii, no. 1.
[2] Elgin to Malmesbury, 14 June 1858 (F.O. 17/289).

acts of aggression she pleased, for if one nation were unreasonable others could interpose to restrain her.[1]

This lesson the Chinese had possibly no need of learning, and they were not slow to demonstrate against Great Britain the principle inculcated in it. The Imperial Commissioners found fault with Lay's harsh manner in pressing them to communicate a draft agreement to Elgin before the seals had been received. Lay 'presently began to speak very improperly and boisterously. We were much grieved and displeased at such conduct', and as it was not 'suitable for us to inform the English Plenipotentiary of this rude conduct of his deputy, we therefore trouble their Excellencies the Russian and American Plenipotentiaries to express to him our views on this subject'. Poutiatine happened to be at the Chinese Commissioners' Yamen at the time and was tactful enough to call upon Gros and invoke the good offices of the French Ambassador to put an end to such proceedings, as the violence used was, he thought, unworthy of the high character with which the Plenipotentiaries were clothed. He added confidentially that it would be impossible for him to take part in any negotiations of a threatening nature, above all when the threats were used by an agent of such low rank towards the highest dignitaries of the Empire. Reed, on the other hand, whose want of tact had several times been commented upon by Gros and who was always anxious to play the part of mediator between the Chinese and the two Western Powers, sent an official note to Elgin who answered him *d'une manière assez dure*. Gros himself thought Lay's conduct regrettable and showed his sense of annoyance by observing an attitude of silence towards his British colleague.[2] Elgin informed Poutiatine and Reed that Lay, in acting as he had done, had exactly carried out his instructions, and sent Wade to the Imperial Commissioners to tell them that they must hold him, Elgin, responsible for the language in question. The Imperial Commissioners thereupon apologized for having complained of Lay's conduct, and the next day presented him with a horse, complete with saddle and bridle.[2]

But it was not only on a question of form that the Imperial Commissioners sought the intervention of the two non-belligerent Powers. To the Chinese the most unreasonable

---

[1] Elgin to Malmesbury, 14 June 1858 (P.P. 1859, Sess. 2, xxxiii, no. 167).
[2] Gros to Walewski (confidential), 11 June 1858 (Chine 24).

demand made at Tientsin was without doubt the claim of the British Government to a permanent legation in Peking.

'That Russia should not be particularly anxious to see Ministers representing the occidental nations established at Peking was intelligible,' wrote Elgin, 'and as owing to the part which I had taken in pressing these demands, the triumph of the objection raised would have been regarded as a blow to England, it was not difficult to discover a motive for the American plenipotentiary's advocacy of Chinese exclusiveness.'[1]

This outspoken criticism, withheld from publication to Parliament by the British Government, was provoked by the intervention of the other Powers with Elgin on the 25th June, when the terms of the treaty had been agreed upon and an hour on the day immediately following fixed for its signature. Gros called upon him with the news that he had been visited by Poutiatine and Reed,

'who came to him on behalf of the Chinese Imperial Commissioners to tell him that they had received a Decree from the Emperor apprising them that their lives would certainly be forfeited if they conceded two particular points which I claimed in my treaty, and which the French Plenipotentiary had seen fit to waive in his, namely: first, the right of Her Majesty's Government to establish a resident minister at Peking, and secondly, the right of British merchants to enter China with passports for trading purposes.'

This *démarche* placed Elgin in very considerable embarrassment, for he wanted neither to accept the responsibility for the deaths of the two Manchu negotiators nor on the other hand to deprive the treaty of its most valuable provisions, and in so doing 'to convey to the Chinese an impression in regard to Russian and American influence which would be highly injurious to British prestige in this quarter'. Fortunately Elgin was able to convince himself that it was doubtful whether such an edict had been issued and the minor modifications which Bruce allowed on the following morning did not depart from the terms of the letter dictated by Lay which the Imperial Commissioners had addressed to him on the 11th June.[1]

Elgin's reason for insisting upon a permanent legation at Peking was twofold. Though the local officers, with the exception of Seu and Yeh, had proved themselves amenable to

[1] Elgin to Malmesbury, 5 July 1858 (F.O. 17/289).

reason in their dealings with foreign consuls and ministers, grave difficulties had continually arisen from the omission or refusal to represent facts honestly to the Imperial court by its subordinates, who in their communications with Peking seemed to have been afraid to tell the truth. And secondly, the presence of the ministers of the Treaty Powers at the capital might be the means of stirring up the Imperial Government to do something towards controlling the lawless subjects of other foreign States, such as the Prussians and Swedes, who ran amok, paying no duties and obeying no law. Elgin looked forward to the possibility of invigorating the Imperial administration just as Great Britain was hoping to do in Turkey. 'The Imperial power is to be sustained and among the means of doing so is that which this treaty provides—a sort of diplomatic protectorate at the capital.' Reed was willing to confess that 'if out of these new concessions and new points of contact no political entanglements arise, Lord Elgin will certainly deserve great credit for the steadiness with which, from first to last, he has kept these ends in view'[1]. There had been indeed—perhaps inevitably when their different positions are borne in mind—a certain lack of intimacy between the British and the American Ministers. Reed had a great dread of 'western diplomatic involvements' which he thought so seriously refracted the truth, and was probably from the first somewhat suspicious that Great Britain had dark and ulterior aims. In this fear he would doubtless be confirmed by his co-operation with the Russian Minister closer as it inevitably was than with the envoys of the two western European Powers. On the other hand, he could complain, with some justice, of Elgin's criticism of the course pursued by the United States, 'when, either intentionally, or inconsiderately, information to which we were entitled in the friendly co-operation to which we suppose we were invited was withheld'. Had Elgin transmitted to him earlier than mid-October copies of the captured documents found in Yeh's Yamen, Reed's attitude might have been very different. 'I have no such confidence', he wrote to his Secretary of State, 'in my own equanimity and self-control as to determine what might have been my inclination before and after the fall of the Taku forts, had the contents of these papers been known to me.' For there was in them 'nothing to countenance the belief that the Chinese make any very clear

[1] Reed to Cass, 29 July 1858 (Sen. Ex. Doc. 30, 1 Sess. 36 Cong., at p. 382).

distinction between the United States and other nations', and the doubts he had 'expressed as to a permanent diplomatic residence at Pekin fade away in the very unpleasant light shed by these intercepted documents', which 'in a great measure justify the coercive policy pursued by the allies in the north. I do not think that Lord Elgin could have acted differently on the assumption which such disclosures as these seem almost to authorize, that the rules of public law applicable to nations civilized and christianized cannot be made to apply here.'[1] Yet it is somewhat surprising that Reed did not come to this conclusion when in Tientsin he received the Emperor's reply to the President's letter, which although making a distinction between tributary and friendly nations, began with the characteristic words: 'Having received with profound respect the commands of Heaven to sway with tender care the entire circuit of all lands, we regard the people everywhere, within and without the wide seas, with the same humane benevolence', and ended with the admonition to Reed that upon the conclusion of his treaty he should repair 'to Canton to attend to the commercial duties of his office as usual'[2]. Tau had asserted that the President, however great, was but an earthly potentate, while his Emperor had divine attributes, and was the Son of Heaven.[3] Whatever doubts Reed may have felt when he went to China, and during the course of events at Canton and Tientsin on the propriety of British policy, were finally set at rest before he left the country. In November 1858 he acknowledged: 'I am more and more impressed every hour by the identity or rather community of the commercial interests of the west, and that nothing is more likely to defeat the true ideas of American statesmanship here than a distempered jealousy of English or French progress.'[4]

There was another question which might have caused difficulty between the American and British ministers—the problem of the opium trade. Reed had mentioned that trade to Tau before the Takoo forts had been seized, and found that the Chinese expressed great indifference on the subject. Both the American and Russian draft treaties which had been com-

---

[1] Reed to Cass, 21 Oct. 1858 (Sen. Ex. Doc. 30, 1 Sess. 36 Cong., at p. 438).
[2] Reed to Cass, 15 June 1858 (ibid., at p. 349).
[3] Reed to Cass, 15 June 1858 (ibid., at p. 335).
[4] Reed to Cass, 9 Nov. 1858 (ibid., at p. 493); 30 June 1858 (ibid., at p. 351).

municated to Elgin included clauses specifying opium as a contraband article. In deference, however, to British objections, Poutiatine and Reed had promised to strike out the special reference to opium. The view taken by the former, Elgin thought 'perfectly consistent. He assured me that the Emperor of Russia disapproved of the trade and that he was prepared to punish those of his subjects who might engage in it.' The course which Reed proposed to follow did not, in Elgin's judgement, appear equally intelligible.

'He admitted that the government of the United States had not been in the habit of interfering to check or restrain those of the citizens of the Republic who might engage in the opium trade with China. He did not even deny the fact that until within a comparatively recent period the American consulates at Canton and Shanghai had been held by partners of a mercantile House which dealt largely in opium.'

Elgin informed his American colleague that he was in favour of the legalization of the trade because it was utterly impossible to put a stop to it and because by being contraband it became both privileged and demoralizing, though at the same time he had 'no intention of bringing any pressure to bear on the Chinese government to induce it to depart on such a point from its traditional policy, and that as far as the economic interests of Great Britain were concerned, nothing would be more advantageous than that the trade should continue on its present footing'.

Reed emphasized the view that the United States derived no revenue from opium or from tea, the commodity which in the main was paid for by opium imports, and that both he himself and the citizens of the United States were greatly impressed by the moral claim of the prohibitionists. On the other hand, he 'felt strongly that it was worse than a mockery to retain the specific prohibition' of an article which was being dealt in by Americans freely and unreservedly and to prosecute which an American-built but British-owned ship flying the American flag was 'plying regularly up and down the coast as a quick carrier of the poison'. He had to confess to Bruce that if the Chinese legalized the opium trade he could not interfere and, that they would take this step if the British Minister pressed it, he believed to be quite a probability.[1] Thus an understanding was arrived

[1] Elgin to Malmesbury (confidential), 10 June 1858 (F.O. 17/289).

at whereby Reed suppressed any specific mention of opium, and in return Elgin would not press for legalization of a trade for which he expressed a strong repugnance. Hence the treaty itself contained no reference to the opium trade and by the time the commercial regulations were discussed during the autumn at Shanghai, Reed had considerably modified his opinion on the question of legalization.

Just before the signature of the British Treaty Baron Gros sounded a warning note.

'I have come to the view that the concessions demanded are exorbitant and perhaps even dangerous for England. . . . The Treaty will indeed, I think, be difficult to execute and I have not left my honourable English colleague ignorant of my belief that his government will be obliged to use force to secure the execution of concessions obtained by force alone.'[1]

Though, before the treaties were ready for ratification, an important amendment had been introduced calculated to conciliate Chinese objections, Gros was none the less to prove only too true a prophet.

D. NEGOTIATIONS AT SHANGHAI

Upon the receipt on the 6th July of the Imperial approval of the treaties negotiated at Tientsin, Elgin moved down the river and arrived on the 12th in Shanghai, where Commissioners were to meet him to settle the tariff and kindred questions.[2] Though towards the end of the month he was complaining that he had received no information of the appointment by the Emperor of officers for the purpose of that negotiation, before his protest could have arrived in Peking an Imperial decree had in fact been issued by which no less exalted persons than the late Imperial Commissioners themselves had been nominated. As some time would necessarily elapse before their arrival, Elgin decided to go to Japan where he obtained without difficulty a favourable treaty. By the 3rd September he was back again in Shanghai,[3] but had to wait another month before the Imperial Commissioners arrived.[4] Having obtained satisfaction from them in regard to the conduct of the Viceroy of the two

[1] Gros to Walewski, 3 July 1858 (Chine 25).
[2] Elgin to Malmesbury, 5 July 1858 (P.P. 1859, Sess. 2, xxxiii, nos. 176–8).
[3] Elgin to Malmesbury, 3 Sept. 1858 (ibid., no. 201).
[4] Elgin to Malmesbury, 4 Oct. 1858 (ibid., no. 208).

Kwangs,[1] he appointed Oliphant and Wade to discuss the details of the new tariff arrangements with the Commissioners' deputies, Wang the Provincial Treasurer and Sieh the Provincial Judge.[2]

There were important differences between these negotiations at Shanghai and those at Tientsin. Now no military pressure was used, and not only was there no Russian Plenipotentiary, but also, since the British Treaty alone contained provisions for a modification of the tariff, 'as regards all these most important commercial transactions', as Elgin reported, 'I have to fight the battle of the western trading nations single-handed. I am endeavouring to construct an amended Tariff which all the Treaty Powers will accept, as otherwise great confusion and much injustice to China must be the result.'[3] Baron Gros, who knew that 'le commerce français en Chine y est presque nul'[4], did not hesitate to go to Japan while Elgin was negotiating with the Imperial Commissioners.[5] The meetings between the subordinates began on 12th October,[6] and although it was not until the 8th November[7] that the treaty was ready for signature, there was no point of serious conflict between the British and Chinese negotiators. New arrangements agreed upon included permission for foreigners to carry grain, with some specified exceptions, and copper cash between the various Chinese ports open to trade. The trade in rice was now legalized on payment of a 10 per cent. *ad valorem* duty. The Chinese pressed for the continuance of the existing duties on tea, and it was agreed that it and silk, the commodity which especially interested the French, should not be subject to the new *ad valorem* duties. Transit duties were now to be replaced by an extra duty payable at the port of entry. The proceeds of the tonnage duty were to be allocated to the provision of beacons to facilitate shipping, and to be controlled by the new maritime customs service. Thereby the Shanghai experiment was extended to all open ports under the control of a British Superintendent-General, who was empowered to recruit foreigners of any nationality to assist him. The Chinese promised to co-operate

[1] See page 284.   [2] Elgin to Malmesbury, 9 Oct. 1858 (ibid., no. 211).
[3] Elgin to Malmesbury, 21 Oct. 1858 (ibid., no. 212).
[4] Revue générale 1859 (Chine 29).
[5] Gros, to Min. Aff. Étr. 2 Sept. 1858 (ibid. 25).
[6] Elgin to Malmesbury, 22 Oct. 1858 (P.P. 1859, Sess. 2, xxxiii, no. 213).
[7] Elgin to Malmesbury, 8 Nov. 1858 (ibid., no. 222).

by supplying information in their possession concerning piracy and to use their preventive service actively to suppress that long-standing evil.[1]

With all these arrangements Reed was in general agreement. He would have liked, though he realized that it was impossible of attainment, to have seen the export duty abolished, and he doubted whether the substitution of an additional duty in lieu of the old transit duties levied in the interior at various octroi posts would work satisfactorily.[2] On one subject there might have been difficulties both with the Chinese and the American representatives—the vexed question of the opium trade. The Chinese negotiators stated that, while China retained her old dislike to the drug on moral grounds, they were convinced that the present method of toleration of a legally contraband article ought no longer to continue. To meet their susceptibilities the British made no objection to that commodity not being included in the tariff itself, but being dealt with in a separate declaration. After much bargaining both sides finally agreed to a duty of 30 taels a chest. The trade was thus recognized by the Emperor's Commissioners and placed on an unassailably legal basis. There was in fact no new situation created. For the last year and more the local authorities at Amoy and Foochow had exacted a regular tax, and at the two more northerly ports the Opium Guild had arranged a tax assessment to meet an exaction on their body.[3] Reed was equally emphatic that 'any course is better than that which is now pursued'. There were only two courses open. One possibility was that China should be urged to take active steps towards the suppression of the opium trade with an assurance that foreign governments would not interfere to protect their subjects and citizens guilty of commerce in the drug. At the same time Great Britain should pledge itself to stop the growth of the poppy in, and the export of opium from, India. Such a measure might now be possible, seeing that as a result of the Mutiny the privileges of the East India Company, including its receipts from, and the administration of, the opium revenue, were about to pass into the control of the Crown. As Reed did not believe that prohibition could be

[1] Elgin to Malmesbury, 22 Oct. 1858 (P.P. 1859, Sess. 2, xxxiii, no. 213).
[2] Elgin to Malmesbury, 21 Oct. 1858 (ibid., no. 212).
[3] J. K. Fairbank, 'The Legalization of the Opium Trade before the Treaties of 1858', *Chinese Social and Political Science Review*, vol. xvii, no. 2.

made effective he favoured the second alternative: the imposition of duties high enough to restrain the supply and low enough to prevent the encouragement of smuggling. He was quite prepared to take his full share of responsibility for either of these two courses.[1] Explaining to Washington his changed attitude Reed urged that both missionaries and merchants agreed that legalization was better than the existing state of affairs. 'Most honest men concur, that nominal prohibition is, in point of fact, encouragement; and that the only remaining chance of restraint is making the trade dutiable, and placing it under direct custom-house control.'[2] Elgin reminded Reed that he had refrained from urging the legalization of the opium trade at Tientsin 'because I could not reconcile it to my sense of right to urge the Imperial Government to abandon its traditional policy in this respect, under the kind of pressure which we were bringing to bear upon it at Tientsin'[1]. To the British Government he emphasized the futility of the 'barren announcement by a foreign government of its assent to the principle that the trade in opium is illegal'. The opium clause in the American Treaty of Wanghia had been a delusion and a snare both to the Chinese and to those who had commercial dealings with them. 'I have merely sought to bring the trade in opium from the region of fiction into that of fact, and to place within the pale of law, and therefore under its control, an article which is now openly bought, sold and taxed by them beyond that pale.'[3]

Thus was removed a cause of antagonism between the British on the one side and their American competitors and the Chinese authorities on the other. Indeed, not until the British Government's control over India, including the native States, was much more complete than it was in 1858 could any other solution have been contemplated. If the Government would not or could not effectively prohibit Indian production for Chinese export, prohibition of the import of opium into China, in view of its widespread consumption, was as futile and as dangerous to good order as the prohibition of alcoholic liquor was to prove in the United States some sixty-five years later. When Gros had to complain that the delay in transcribing his treaty into Chinese was due to the fact that the scribes, who

---

[1] Elgin to Malmesbury, 21 Oct. 1858 (P.P. 1859, Sess. 2, xxxiii, no. 212).
[2] Reed to Cass, 9 Nov. 1858 (Sen. Ex. Doc. 30, 36 Cong. 1 Sess. at p. 493).
[3] Elgin to Malmesbury (P.P., ibid., no. 236).

had been lent to him by the Imperial Commissioners themselves, 'habitués à s'enivrer par les vapeurs de l'opium, ne
voulaient pas se priver de leurs extases pendant un seul jour
pour s'occuper d'intérêts matériels'[1], it could be said that the
law was beyond or out of touch with the moral and social
conditions of the age. To the legalistic mind of a British representative such a clash seemed particularly harmful, and to the
practical common sense of a man like Elgin both harmful and
stupid.

During the discussions Elgin received on the 16th October a
formal visit from the Imperial Commissioners attended by a
large retinue. He made it his business to do what he could to
put them at their ease and to remove the painful impressions
which the interviews at Tientsin might have left upon their
minds.[2] It soon became apparent why officers of such high
dignity had been sent to discuss what were after all matters of
secondary importance; they had come to renew their efforts,
which had proved fruitless at Tientsin, to persuade Elgin to
drop the right of maintaining constantly a British Minister in
the capital, which, under Lay's threat of a resumption of
active hostilities, they had conceded to Great Britain. On the
22nd October Elgin received a long letter from them expressing
their hope that Her Majesty would make use of the option in
Article III of sending her representative only occasionally to
Peking. They urged that little would be gained by the residence of foreign envoys at the Emperor's court, as the official
establishments there were purely concerned with metropolitan
affairs and had no knowledge of the situation in the provinces.[3]
Elgin thought that they had some grounds for dreading the
presence of foreigners in Peking: they had suggested that if the
ministers were thoroughly wise and discreet the objections
would not be so strong, but they feared that if certain persons
were sent quarrels might be provoked within a month.

The British Plenipotentiary, thinking perhaps of Sir John
Bowring, was as aware as many of his predecessors that there
were foreigners who took the view 'that every Chinese was a
knave, manageable only by bullying and bravado, and that such
a doctrine had sometimes been pushed a little too far in our

---

[1] Gros to Walewski, 3 July 1858 (Chine 25, no. 55).
[2] Elgin to Malmesbury, 22 Oct. 1858 (P.P. 1859, Sess. 2, xxxiii, no. 214).
[3] Elgin to Malmesbury, 22 Oct. 1858 (ibid., no. 215).

dealings with this people'. The Chinese Commissioners, who had been eminently reasonable, would be degraded and punished if they secured no modification of Article III, and on the other hand there were reasons from the British point of view for meeting their objections. Elgin was very anxious before he left China to visit Hankow, and until the treaty was ratified he had no right to do so. And he had gathered from incidental expressions in the dispatches from the Foreign Office that it was at least doubtful whether, apart from the feelings of the Chinese, Her Majesty's Government would not decide against the establishment of a British Mission in Peking on the ground of practical inconvenience. The only result of an adamant refusal to consider modification might be making a present to the Chinese of something for which they were willing to pay. Malmesbury, as he minuted on Elgin's dispatch, had indeed suggested that, so far from the sea and the protection of our ships, the British envoy at Peking might find himself in a trap.[1] Elgin therefore agreed to refer the question home, and urged that if the British Government decided to keep the right secured in the treaty, but to waive the exercise of it in their discretion, they would have in their hands, 'to be wielded at their will, a moral lever of the most powerful description, to secure the faithful observance of the Treaty by the Chinese government in all time to come'[2].

The immediate result of Elgin's promise to refer the question home was the granting of permission for his Yangtse journey,[3] which, after informing Gros and Reed of his intention, he began on the 8th November. On the way up he was obliged to silence the fire from the Taiping batteries at Nanking and, after various incidents due to the difficult navigation through the sand-banks which abounded in the river, he arrived at Hankow on the 6th December. There in spite of a somewhat frigid start the Governor-General received the British officers with a profusion of courtesies. Business activity seemed keen in the city, but it appeared to Elgin that British manufacturers would have to exert themselves to the utmost if they wished to supplant, to any considerable extent, in the native market, the fabrics produced in their leisure hours by the industrious, frugal,

[1] Elgin to Malmesbury, 5 Nov. 1858 (F.O. 17/291).
[2] Elgin to Malmesbury, 5 Nov. 1858 (P.P. 1859, Sess. 2, no. 216).
[3] Elgin to Malmesbury, 5 Nov. 1858 (ibid., no. 217).

and sober population. The expedition left Hankow on the 12th and all the ships were back before the end of the first week of January. On the journey Elgin, accompanied by Wade or Lay, took several walks some miles from the banks, unarmed and without difficulty. But it was impossible to gather any accurate impression from their conversations with the Chinese, as 'having been civilized for many generations, they carry politeness so far, that in answering a question, it is always their chief endeavour to say what they suppose their questioner will be best pleased to hear'[1].

As the British Government concurred in Elgin's suggestions with regard to the establishment of a legation in Peking, he was in a position, before sailing for Europe, to tell the Imperial Commissioners that his brother, Bruce, would be authorized, if properly received in the capital when he went to exchange ratifications, to choose a place of residence elsewhere. Yet the right was to remain inviolate and would be exercised if the action of the Chinese officials at the ports or in the interior made it, in the opinion of the British Government, essential to the continuance of peaceful relations between Great Britain and China.[2]

In one respect the British Government had shown from the beginning of its intercourse with China in 1833 a notable superiority over other Treaty Powers. It had established professional whole-time consuls who were stringently forbidden to engage in trade. Whatever other criticisms he may have passed on the British, Reed generously allowed that 'the English consuls have been able to execute the laws of their country upon the criminals who are brought before them, and their efforts tend to relieve the short-comings of others, as the mass of natives make no distinction' between foreigners of one nation and another.[3] The growing list of cases tried by summary jurisdiction in the consular courts annually forwarded to the Foreign Office testifies to a desire on the part of the British authorities to maintain a standard of discipline. But the subjects of States which were not in treaty relations with China could not be so controlled, and Elgin and the London Government recognized the cogency of the arguments of the Imperial Commissioners

---

[1] Elgin to Malmesbury, 5 Jan. 1859 (P.P. 1859, Sess. 2, xxxiii, no. 228).
[2] Elgin to Malmesbury, 7 Mar. 1859 (ibid., no. 246 and F.O. 17/328).
[3] Reed to Cass, 4 Sept. 1859 (Sen. Ex. Doc. 30, 36 Cong. 1 Sess. at p. 429).

that something should be done to ameliorate such a state of affairs. Some of these Powers employed as consuls, merchants, subjects or citizens, of Treaty Powers. These men were ready enough to protest at any action on the part of the Chinese authorities which they imagined hindered the commercial interests of those under their protection, whom, however, they were powerless to restrain from committing irregularities at the expense of the Chinese. The fact was that British subjects who wished to act wrongly in too many cases embarked their fortunes in vessels of non-Treaty Powers, and under the cover of foreign flags perpetrated with absolute impunity crimes of every description. Malmesbury agreed to represent to maritime non-Treaty Powers the importance of taking steps to prevent abuses of their flags and to provide for the control and punishment of their subjects in China who might commit crimes. 'If all powers could be induced to combine to do this, we should do more for promoting peace and commerce than by any isolated measures of the Treaty Powers alone.'[1] Reed thought China in her own interests should enlarge the number of Treaty Powers and refuse an exequatur, for example, to an American acting for another Power if he abused his position.[2]

Elgin agreed in the necessity of strict regulations for governing the issue of passports for internal travel, and that the privilege of carrying the British flag should be limited to ships of a certain tonnage, having on board a British master. He also agreed that, in future, if a consul became involved in a question which threatened peaceful relations, he should be forbidden to act locally in a high-handed manner and instructed to remit the case to his superiors.[1]

In these ways the goodwill of the London Government and their representative was abundantly testified. Before leaving Shanghai, in reply to an address of congratulation from the British community for his successful and 'honourable efforts for the extension of civilization and commerce', Elgin summed up the situation and the obligation of which he was conscious in the following words:

'Uninvited and by methods not always of the gentlest, we have broken down the barriers behind which these ancient nations sought to conceal from the world without, the mysteries, perhaps also, in

[1] Elgin to Malmesbury, 22 Jan. 1859 (P.P. 1859, Sess. 2, xxxiii, no. 238 and F.O. 17/328).   [2] Elgin to Malmesbury (confidential) 22 Jan. 1859 (F.O. 17/328).

the case of China at least, the rags and rottenness of their waning civilizations. Neither our own consciences nor the judgement of mankind will acquit us if, when we are asked to what use we have turned our opportunities, we can only say that we have filled our pockets from among the ruins we have found or made.'[1]

E. THE CANTON SITUATION (*February* 1858–*February* 1859)

While Elgin with the bulk of the British forces was fully occupied in the north, the situation in and around Canton looked serious. By the end of April 1858 the people of a village some ten to fifteen miles from the city issued a notice offering a reward of $100 for the capture of an English or French Barbarian and $5,000 for the head of one of their commanders. At Fatshan a spurious edict was circulated which purported to be an Imperial command to foreigners to leave the city. Individual Chinese were warning foreign friends of imminent danger: boatmen and pilots spoke of troubles ahead: it was said that large numbers of persons were leaving the city with their furniture and other effects. Pih-Kwei had heard rumours that the militia was being embodied; in an interview which the Commissioners had with him he appeared listless—whether that condition was due to illness or to hostility it was difficult to determine. But it was felt that no reliance could be placed on his view that the embodiment of the militia was a move against the rebels rather than directed at foreigners.[2] Sir John Bowring (whose conduct Elgin was later to criticize to Gros on the ground that both in Hong Kong and in London the Governor of the colony was behind attacks on the Plenipotentiary by the medium of the Press and in his correspondence,[3]) wrote to Malmesbury: 'I shall heartily rejoice if the Ambassadors direct that an end be put to the double (and not very intelligible) government existing there, and the supreme authority of the Allied powers established in all its ramifications.'[2] At the beginning of June money continued to be offered for the capture of foreigners and their servants, and, though there was some relaxation of the activities of the 'Anti-Barbarian Committee', foreigners were not safe outside the immediate neighbourhood of the city of Canton. Bowring thought that probably the Mandarins had for a time received violent instructions from

---

[1] Elgin to Malmesbury, 18 Jan. 1859 (P.P. 1859, Sess. 2, xxxiii, no. 236).
[2] Bowring to Clarendon, 27 April 1858 (F.O. 17/296).
[3] Gros to Walewski (private), 5 Sept. 1858 (Chine 25, f. 287).

the Emperor, though it was almost certain that the Chinese authorities at the other ports had no more desire then, than in the past, to compromise themselves with foreign Powers and that therefore they would be disposed to evade or delay in putting into force any measures of violence.[1] Towards the end of June the audacity of the 'braves' was increasing, and the city was being rapidly abandoned. The new Viceroy Hwang, whom the foreign representatives at Shanghai had been bidden to meet in Canton, issued a proclamation of a highly incendiary character. He called to mind that he had been a subordinate official in Canton when the citizens resisted the Barbarian entry inside their walls. All evils were due to the English, to whom his master might be willing to show clemency, if the knowledge of his arrival with troops by forced marches produced in them a changed disposition: for he had come by the Emperor's commands either to tame them or to execute his wrath upon them. 'Go forth in myriads, then, and take vengeance on the enemies of your Sovereign . . . imbued with public spirit and fertile in expedients.'[2] In face of such threats General Van Straubenzee decided to put the city under direct martial law and bring to an end this 'somewhat ambiguous and indefinable administration which has lately existed in Canton'. There was no possibility that the Chinese would be able to expel the foreign troops, but more natives might abandon the city, including the Chinese bankers, linguists, and merchants who were the intermediate agents of foreign trade.[3]

At the beginning of July Bowring moved the consulate to Whampoa, as the position of foreigners at Honan and Canton was becoming daily more precarious;[4] skirmishing was in progress in the eastern suburbs of the city and Chinese were firing at isolated parties of foreigners.[5] Though by the 20th July the signature of the Treaty of Tientsin was known, the Cantonese, menaced by the authorities, continued to leave the city and Hong Kong: the braves dragged a field-piece to a height outside Canton and fired several shots at head-quarters.[6] By the beginning of August there was a reign of terror in the colony:

[1] Bowring to Malmesbury, 1 June 1858 (F.O. 17/297).
[2] Bowring to Malmesbury, 13 June 1858 (F.O. 17/297).
[3] Bowring to Malmesbury, 26 June 1858 (F.O. 17/297).
[4] Bowring to Malmesbury, 3 July 1858 (F.O. 17/298).
[5] Bowring to Malmesbury, 19 July 1858 (F.O. 17/298).
[6] Bowring to Malmesbury, 20 July 1858 (F.O. 17/298).

20,000 Chinese, including all men of opulence, had fled to the mainland, most of the foreigners' servants had been summoned away, including those of Bowring himself,[1] who was earnestly looking forward to the arrival of British and French forces, now released from duty in the Gulf of Pechili.

At the very end of July the situation seemed somewhat improved: the Viceroy Hwang informed the Allied commanders that he had heard officially that peace had been made and was therefore instructing the general committee at Fa-yuen, who controlled the braves, to prevent them from entering the city.[2] By the middle of August the Chinese were returning to Macao and Hong Kong, where shops were being reopened.[3] But this movement towards a normal state of affairs did not continue; Bowring noticed that by the beginning of September there was considerable hesitation on the part of shopkeepers to return either to Macao or to Hong Kong, and that but few merchants were in Canton though the busy trading season had begun.[4] Alcock, who had recently been appointed Consul at Canton only to strike his flag, reported that, though the active hostilities of the braves had ceased, they had laid down their arms and dispersed—so far as that had in fact been done—with no sense of inferiority to the Allied forces. They and the gentry, except for a small affair at Nantao (where revenge had been taken and a fort destroyed in August as a result of a violation of a flag of truce[5]), had met with no signal check or humbling reverse. All the elements of hostile combination were still in vigorous though latent existence.[6] They were called into activity again by a fresh circular from Hwang to the gentry dated the 21st August, commanding the enrolment of the braves and the levying of contributions; mainly, it is true, to deal with the rebels, but also owing partly to the unsettled state of Barbarian affairs. By mid-September influential Chinese were saying that much yet remained to be settled before peace was really established,[7] for the animosity of the Cantonese had never been so intense.[8]

---

[1] Bowring to Malmesbury, 5 Aug. 1858 (F.O. 17/298).
[2] Bowring to Malmesbury, 20 Aug. 1858 (F.O. 17/299).
[3] Bowring to Malmesbury, 23 Aug. 1858 (F.O. 17/299).
[4] Bowring to Malmesbury, 9 Sept. 1858 (F.O. 17/299).
[5] Bowring to Malmesbury, 17 Aug. 1858 (F.O. 17/298).
[6] Bowring to Malmesbury, 10 Sept. 1858 (F.O. 17/299).
[7] Bowring to Malmesbury, 16 Sept. 1858 (F.O. 17/299).
[8] Bowring to Malmesbury, 25 Sept. 1858 (F.O. 17/299).

Hwang had received a secret Imperial edict issued on the 14th August, seven weeks after the signature of the Treaties of Tientsin, in which he was bidden to act in concert with Lo-tung, the leader of the braves, to prevent the spirit of opposition from dying out in the then state of affairs. Hwang accordingly communicated the Imperial commands to all the magistrates of his province. Bowring agreed with Alcock that the position of the Allies in Canton had failed to inspire proper respect for the authority of Great Britain and France. Before the end of October there was much native produce ready for market, though sellers were unwilling to bring it forward lest they should be exposed to extortions.[1]

Such was the situation which Elgin found on his return from Japan in the early days of September. At the same time he received dispatches from England and was pained at the spirit which dictated them and at the indirect censure, which he attributed to the influence of Bowring, on the setting up of the mixed government at Canton. Elgin's first thoughts were to give up his intention of waiting at Shanghai for the arrival of the Commissioners and the negotiation of the Tariff Treaty, to sail to Hong Kong, visit Canton, hand over the conduct of affairs to Bowring, and return to Europe. Two days later, however, he had changed his mind and decided to await the arrival of the Chinese representatives. This irresolution, wrote Gros privately to Count Walewski, was characteristic of one aspect of Elgin's character: and the reason of his change of plan was his surmise that Bowring, 'dont il ne peut pas prononcer le nom sans y ajouter quelque épithète mal sonnante', would profit by his departure to arrive quickly at Shanghai, treat with the Commissioners in order to put the finishing touches to the incomplete work, and throw blame on him.[2]

Elgin was impressed by the fact that there was a connexion clearly established between the Peking Government and the troubles in the region of Canton, and emphasized the wisdom of the British Government in insisting upon direct representation at the capital as a means of influencing the course of events in the ports.[3] Immediately on the arrival of the Imperial Commissioners in Shanghai and before he would consent to enter

[1] Bowring to Malmesbury, 20 Oct. 1858 (F.O. 17/300).
[2] Gros to Walewski (private), 5 Sept. 1858 (Chine, 25, f. 287).
[3] Elgin to Malmesbury, 20 Sept. 1858 (P.P. 1859, Sess. 2, xxxiii, no. 206).

into a discussion on tariff questions, the British Plenipotentiary
protested against the policy of Hwang, demanded his dismissal
by the Emperor and the withdrawal of the special powers given
to the gentry.[1] Kweiliang and Hwa-shana announced that
from the information which had reached them on their journey
south they had become convinced that Hwang had 'failed to
manage anything satisfactorily'; they had already denounced
him to the court, and had little doubt that the Emperor would
remove him. They would ask the sovereign to withdraw from
the gentry their powers, though as elsewhere, so in Canton,
they were enrolled against evil-doers and disturbers of the
peace.[2] The immediate result of Elgin's emphatic protest was
an official notification to the Kwantung provincial authorities
from the Imperial Commissioners at Shanghai of the restoration of friendly relations: a step which Bowring thought would
lead at once to a resumption of trade at the southern port.[3]
Alcock, who had been ordered by Elgin to resume his consular
functions, was received in the city by Pih-Kwei and the Hoppo
and was advised by the Governor of Canton to live at Whampoa
or on the island of Honan. Alcock carried away with him from
this interview 'a deep persuasion that they had learnt nothing
from the past',[4] and this impression was further strengthened
by a visit he paid subsequently to the Tartar General.[5] At the
beginning of the new year General Van Straubenzee made
several short excursions at the head of small contingents of
British and French troops. Advantage was taken of the colder
weather to show the armed forces of the Allies to the rural communities and their ability to punish the braves.[6] The first of
these expeditions to Shektsing was followed by a peaceful
demonstration at Fatshan,[7] and in February a column of 900
British and 130 French made a five-day tour to visit Fa-yuen,[8]
the head-quarters of the braves' organization. Elgin justified
these military parades, as a secret edict dispatched from Peking
on 7th November, which had been received at Fa-yuen on the

[1] See p. 273.
[2] Elgin to Malmesbury, 19 Oct. 1858 (P.P. 1859, Sess. 2, xxxiii, no. 209).
[3] Bowring to Malmesbury, 28 Oct. 1858 (F.O. 17/300).
[4] Bowring to Malmesbury, 10 Nov. 1858 (F.O. 17/300).
[5] Bowring to Malmesbury, 15 Nov. 1858 (F.O. 17/301).
[6] Elgin to Malmesbury, 20 Jan. 1859 (P.P. 1859, Sess. 2, xxxiii, no. 235).
[7] Elgin to Malmesbury, 6 Feb. 1859 (ibid., no. 241).
[8] Elgin to Malmesbury, 12 Feb. 1859 (ibid., no. 243).

22nd, and had fallen into the hands of Parkes, seemed to suggest that the Emperor was playing a double game. This document explained that the acceptance by the Emperor of the peace terms was dictated by the needs of the moment. In the north preparations for resistance were being made by fortifying the mouth of the Peiho with stakes, while in Kwantung, though it was important that the authorities should not appear hostile, the rural population should be marshalled in secret, and the train-bands established once more. The Imperial Commissioners assured Elgin that the document in question was a forgery and forwarded to him the Imperial reply, dated 20th October, to their request for the dismissal of Hwang. This was couched in ambiguous terms—'as to the question of Hwang-tsung-han—if he disobeyed our commands, after the peace was negotiated it is with us to give judgement, without waiting for the condemnation of Kweiliang and his colleagues'. As it therefore appeared to Elgin that the Emperor had refused to accept the advice of the Imperial Commissioners, he declined to hold any further correspondence with them, and decided to return to Europe, leaving a warning with the perturbed Chinese that when he or his successor should arrive in Peking for the ratification of the Treaty of Tientsin, he would make it his business to ascertain whether the disturbed condition of Canton was approved by the Emperor and shape his course accordingly.[1]

There still remained several points to be decided, mainly Canton questions, such as the allocation of a site for the foreign factories, the time and mode of payment of the indemnity, the conditions for the handing over of the city, and lastly the acquisition of Kowloon, which Elgin had been instructed by a dispatch from Malmesbury to secure. To settle some of these points Elgin was in need of more precise instructions—for instance could the cession of Kowloon be accepted as payment for part of the indemnity? Then the Chinese had asked for payment of duty arrears arising out of the condition of Shanghai in 1853. When he broke so brusquely with the Imperial Commissioners and left Shanghai for Canton he had informed them that either he or his successor would return to finish the discussion of these questions in a few weeks time. He had taken that step so as to avoid the danger of their being dismissed by the Emperor on the ground that they had shown themselves

[1] Elgin to Malmesbury, 22 Jan. 1859 (P.P. 1859, Sess. 2, xxxiii, no. 237).

incapable of 'pacifying the Barbarians'. Upon the whole he thought some time must inevitably elapse before he was in a position to resume these negotiations, and when he knew that Bruce, whom he had sent home from Tientsin with the Treaty, was leaving England early in February he decided to hand over to him the settlement of the outstanding questions.[1]

Elgin was certain that 'our difficulties in this (Canton) question are, in a great measure, the fruit of promptings from Peking, but in their turn they re-act upon Peking itself and supply food and strength to those retrograde and anti-foreign influences which are constantly at work in the councils of the Emperor'. The Allies had indeed, as Elgin informed Kweiliang, been so moderate that they had been misunderstood by both braves and officials.[2] His breaking off negotiations with them, together with the increased activity of the Allied troops, did, however, produce the desired result: the influence of Ho, the liberal Governor-General of the Two Kiangs, which the anti-foreign party at Peking and Canton had shaken, was restored, and while Hwang was left in his office as Viceroy of the Two Kwang provinces, Ho was entrusted with the management of foreign affairs.[3] Just before Elgin left Hong Kong, as he thought for ever, an Imperial Decree denouncing the captured Secret Decree as a forgery was not only issued, but was published without any request from the British representative in the *Peking Gazette*. As Elgin was sailing home he thought he could congratulate himself that such an action 'proclaims to the whole Empire the Emperor's intention to abide by the terms of the peace negotiated with the foreigners at Tientsin'[4].

[1] Elgin to Malmesbury, 7 Mar. 1859 (F.O. 17/328).
[2] Elgin to Malmesbury, 12 Feb. 1859 (P.P. 1859, Sess. 2, xxxiii, no. 242).
[3] Elgin to Malmesbury, 26 Feb. 1859 (ibid., no. 244).
[4] Elgin to Malmesbury, 19 Apr. 1859 (ibid., no. 253).

VII

BRUCE'S MISSION, 1859

A. THE FAILURE

O^{N} receiving the Treaty of Tientsin the British Government at first thought of establishing a full embassy in Peking, in order that the high rank of their diplomatic representative might 'impose not only unbounded respect on the part of the Chinese—but also obtain it from the great number of British Agents who will be submitted to his directions. It is the object of Her Majesty's Government to place the Ambassador at Peking in a position as regards the Consular and Commercial authorities analogous to that of Her Majesty's Ambassador at Constantinople'.[1] The French Government concurred and decided to offer Baron Gros the appointment as their first resident Ambassador. He declined partly on personal grounds, and partly because he was of opinion that the Emperor of China would not receive those who had forced him, at the point of the bayonet, to grant concessions so revolutionary.[2] When the news arrived in Europe that Elgin had promised to urge his Government not to exercise the right of permanent residence, both the London and Paris Cabinets agreed to accept Elgin's advice and decided in consequence to appoint merely Ministers Plenipotentiary and Envoys Extraordinary.[3]

By the middle of January 1859 the British Government had decided to send Bruce out to China to exchange the ratifications of the Elgin Treaty and assume thereafter the office of Minister Plenipotentiary accredited to the court of the Emperor.[4] They naturally hoped to have the benefit of Elgin's advice before his brother left England. The news of the intended Yangtse expedition, however, made it certain that if the ratifications were to be exchanged in Peking, as was stipulated, within one year of the signing of the treaty, Bruce would have to start before his brother's return. While waiting in London, Bruce drew up a memorandum on certain questions which he

---

[1] Malmesbury to Cowley, 22 Oct. 1858 (Cordier, *L'Expédition de Chine de 1860* [cited after as Cord. *L'Expéd.* ii], p. 35).
[2] Gros to Min. Aff. Étr. 28 Dec. 1858 (ibid., p. 37).
[3] Walewski to Pélissier, 21 Jan. 1859 (ibid., p. 40).
[4] Bruce to Hammond, 19 Jan. 1859 (F.O. 17/312).

foresaw were likely to be raised on his arrival. What should he do if a high officer were to meet him at the Peiho with the suggestion that the ratifications could well be exchanged there on the ground that the populace of the capital might be ill-disposed, or that the Emperor was out of the city? He himself thought that to omit a visit to Peking on the occasion of the exchange of ratifications would immensely increase the difficulty of gaining access there in the future and tend to the maintenance at Peking of 'its dogmas of universal supremacy and national superiority'. The Foreign Secretary (Malmesbury) and the Prime Minister minuted 'he must insist on going to Peking. The time of his stay may be limited by agreement.' Arrived in Peking, was he to be satisfied with a private audience of the Emperor rather than with a public reception? Neither Foreign Secretary nor Prime Minister objected to such a compromise, provided it was put on the ground that Bruce was an Envoy and not of the higher rank of Ambassador. Nor did they dissent from Bruce's proposition that as the exercise of the right to residence in Peking depended upon the reception given to the British Minister and the fulfilment of the stipulations of the treaty, it would be important to bring those conditions forward in all communications addressed by him to the Chinese Government, for such a course would materially assist a speedy settlement of matters of pressing moment connected with the opening of the new ports and the inauguration of the new passport system. On the other hand, the British statesmen were unwilling to commit themselves to the policy of acquiring a house as a permanent residence. Nor would they agree to the establishment in Peking forthwith of a College of Interpreters similar to the institution maintained there by Russia.[1]

Bruce received his instructions on 1 March: on arrival in Hong Kong he was to relieve Sir John Bowring of his superintendency of Trade. Bowring from the 2nd May was no longer an officer of the Foreign Office, though he continued for some time as Governor of Hong Kong to be responsible to the Secretary of State for the Colonies. Bruce was to establish the superintendency and his mission at Shanghai and to send from thence an intimation of his approach to the capital.

'The Admiral in command of Her Majesty's naval forces in China

---

[1] Bruce to Hammond (Memorandum), 5 Feb. 1859 (F.O. 17/312).

has been directed to send up with you to the mouth of the Peiho a sufficient naval force, and unless any unforeseen circumstances should appear to make another arrangement more advisable, it would seem desirable that you should reach Tientsin in a British ship of war. It is impossible for Her Majesty's government, and indeed it would not be wise, to lay down any definite rules to be rigidly adhered to, in regard to your approach to, and your communication with the Chinese Court. The acquaintance which you possess with the Chinese character will enable you to judge when you may give way and when you must stand firm, bearing in mind that your treatment on your first visit to Peking will always be appealed to on the occasion of future visits, as establishing precedents not to be departed from.'[1]

Bruce arrived in Hong Kong on 26th April and remained there until the beginning of June. His French colleague, de Bourboulon, to whom on the 8th April Baron Gros had handed over the Archives, was apparently not in a position to move until the 1st June.[2] Very soon after his arrival in Hong Kong Bruce seems to have come to the same conclusion at which Elgin had earlier arrived—that the Chinese Government did not intend to receive him and his colleague in full friendship. He noted that although Lay had urged the Imperial Commissioners to go to Peking to make arrangement for the arrival of the two Ministers, these high officers continued to stay in Soochow. Reports[3] were to hand of the construction of new forts and defences at the mouth of the Peiho.[4] Bruce, discussing the position with his colleague on his arrival, laid stress on the fact that they would be in much greater force at the mouth of the river than they could possibly be at Tientsin where gunboats only could accompany them, and stronger at Tientsin than at Peking where they would arrive without means of forcible action. The conclusion which he reached, as reported by de Bourboulon to the Quai d'Orsay, was a logical corollary from such a consideration: 'If there are going to be difficulties there—and we must expect them—it is better to meet them and

[1] Malmesbury to Bruce, 1 Mar. 1859 (P.P. 1860, lxix, no. 1).

[2] Bruce to Malmesbury, 1 June 1859 (ibid., no. 7).

[3] They were not unfounded. As early as the 4th August the previous year orders had been given to hasten the delivery of timber for the construction of fortifications along the water-way between Tung-chow and the sea. Batteries and camps were being erected along the Peiho and cannon cast at Tung-chow. (Erskine to Russell, 17 Sept. 1860 (F.O. 65/554)).

[4] Bruce to Malmesbury, 4 May 1859 (ibid., no. 2).

even in some sort to provoke them in advance, for thus . . . we shall be in a much better position to solve them.'[1]

In order to achieve his fixed resolution of reaching Tientsin in a British warship, it was necessary to collect an adequate force. The Admiral thought that the force should be nearly what it was the previous year.[2] This time, however, there would be but two French ships, as Admiral Rigaud was occupied with a force of 4,000 men in not very successful operations against Annam.[3] This did not, however, make Bruce less anxious to be prepared for hostile action. The Chinese, he wrote to Admiral Hope,

'are perfectly well informed as to the reduction of French force in China and looking to our future political position in this country, as well as to the immediate success of the Mission, it would be a great mistake to throw away this opportunity of showing that . . . we are sufficiently strong single-handed to compel the Chinese to fulfil their engagements'[4]. ·

A mere demonstration of force and of the unanimity of the Powers would, he hoped, prevail upon the court of Peking if it was, as he imagined, 'wavering, anxious to evade, but unwilling to risk a rupture'. There was not likely to be any obstacle in the way of co-operation with his French colleague. But with Ward, the new American envoy who arrived on the 14 May, Bruce felt there might be difficulties. To the representative of the United States he laid stress on the changed character of their position *vis-à-vis* the Peking Government— which, however unpalatable it was to China by its implication of equality, was to the Western governments 'the keystone of improvement in our future relations'. 'The maintenance of a neutral position between the absurd pretensions of the Chinese Government and the reasonable demands of France and Great Britain was founded upon the erroneous assumption that the interests of one commercial nation could be advanced separately.' If America adopted such an attitude, the Chinese might be encouraged to attempt a vain resistance, but she could gain nothing by it, unless prepared to accept the Chinese principle that foreigners were inaccessible to reason and unacquainted

[1] de Bourboulon to Walewski, May 1859 (Cord. *L'Expéd.* ii, p. 50).
[2] Bruce to Malmesbury, 14 June 1859 (P.P. 1860, lxix, no. 8).
[3] Bruce to Malmesbury, 1 June 1859 (F.O. 17/312).
[4] Bruce to Malmesbury, 21 May 1859 (F.O. 17/312).

with the science of civil polity. To these arguments Ward was amenable: he agreed to a joint advance to the Peiho. But as there was no stipulation that the American Treaty should be ratified in Peking, he would have to content himself with the exchange of ratifications, if the Chinese desired it, in Shanghai or elsewhere. 'But as soon as that formality is over, Mr. Ward will notify his intention of proceeding at once by ship to Tientsin and thence to Peking.' He entirely agreed in the policy of putting the diplomatic relations with Peking on a proper footing and was anxious to help in accomplishing the opening up of China rather than 'in carrying out an isolated and narrow policy'[1].

In the middle of May Bruce and de Bourboulon addressed notes to Kweiliang, not as Imperial Commissioner, but in his capacity as Secretary of State, informing him that they were bearers of autograph letters from their sovereigns to the Emperor, and that in accordance with the Treaty they were about to go to Tientsin, where they expected to find the necessary arrangements made for their conveyance to the capital.[2] On their arrival at Shanghai they found the Imperial Commissioners waiting for them and urging, as the reason why they had not gone to Peking, Elgin's statement on leaving Shanghai that he or his successor would return there to arrange some final details with the Emperor's representatives. They pressed for the exchange of ratifications at that port, as it would take them two months to arrive at the capital. Bruce and de Bourboulon refused to accept such a policy of evasion, and would not meet Kweiliang and his colleague. This firmness brought about the immediate departure on the 13th of the Imperial Commissioners. De Bourboulon hoped that this action looked well. 'There is no longer any doubt', he wrote to Paris on the 14th, 'that our journey to Peking will end peacefully and without obstacles . . .'[3]

Bruce allowed the Chinese Commissioners four days start of him, hoping that they would thus have time to get to Peking to arrange a friendly reception.[4] At the same time, however, the Minister learnt that a high Chinese official had given expression to his fears that there would be trouble in the north and that it

[1] Bruce to Malmesbury (confidential), 21 May 1859 (encl. 2) (F.O. 17/312).
[2] Bruce to Malmesbury, 21 May 1859 (P.P. 1860, lxix, no. 4).
[3] de Bourboulon to Min. des Aff. Étr., 14 June 1859 (Cord. *L'Expéd.* ii, p. 61).
[4] Bruce to Malmesbury, 13 July 1859 (F.O. 17/313).

would be necessary for the Powers to give China another lesson. It was clear that a war-party existed and that 'a probability of resistance is a contingency not to be lost sight of'[1].

On the 16th June at the Peiho the Admiral had sent a notification to the shore that the foreign representatives were about to arrive, and moved the gunboats over the bar as heavy seas were running outside. The rabble on the shore asserted that there were no officers in the forts, which were manned solely by militia, and had been reconstructed by the people as a protection against rebels, not by order of the Government for the purpose of keeping the Allied forces out of the river. The people offered to take a message to Tientsin and the Admiral therefore wrote asking for an unobstructed passage to be opened within three days. When Bruce arrived on the 20th, the Admiral found further obstacles had closed the passage into the river. De Bourboulon and Bruce agreed that they had a right to use the river as an access to the capital—had they met with a friendly reception Bruce had intended to take up to Tientsin only sufficient gunboats to convey himself and his staff. On the 21st de Bourboulon and Bruce handed over to the Admiral the task of forcing, if necessary, the obstacles at the mouth of the river: a task for which he regarded himself as fully equipped, as he had under his command a force almost equal in gun-power to the joint Anglo-French squadron of 1858. The Admiral in consequence gave the Chinese on shore notice of his intention to remove the barrier in three days time unless they themselves had by that date prepared the way for the Ministers. On the 24th Ward was refused a passage and that night the obstacles at the river-mouth were partially blown up. At 9 a.m. on the 25th a petty Mandarin came to ask Bruce to proceed to the Pehtangho where Hengfu, the Governor-General of Chihli was waiting, until obstructions there had been removed, to come outside, welcome Her Majesty's Minister and conduct him overland to Peking. But it was too late. Even if Bruce had been disposed to acquiesce in this change of policy—for change it was, as there had never been mention of any place other than the Peiho in Kweiliang's correspondence—the operations could not be delayed. Admiral Hope was nine miles off and intended to start forcing a passage at 10 a.m.

Fire from the Chinese batteries made his attempt, which was

[1] Bruce to Malmesbury, 14 June 1859 (P.P. 1860, lxix, no. 8).

not begun in fact until 2.30 p.m., unsuccessful. Four gunboats were sunk. After three and a half hours' bombardment a landing-party made heroic endeavours, struggling through deep mud, to capture the forts. They were mown down; the Admiral, himself wounded, had lost 432 men and was unable to open the river. The Chinese had shown a vigorous and unexpected bravery. There was nothing for it but ignominious withdrawal without addressing any note to the Chinese Government so that the hands of Her Majesty's Government should be free. Bruce left the Gulf of Pechili with his French colleague, defeated and frustrated, for Shanghai.[1]

The incident of the 25th June 1859 was the most striking of a series of events which showed that when the sudden panic which the capture of Tientsin the previous summer had produced was over, the Chinese Government was still determined to preserve its old maxims on the right intercourse with foreigners. International relations with the barbarian tribes, living by trade—of all occupations that one in least repute among the Chinese—were to be studiously avoided. Devoid of civilization, ignorant of the rules of reason, the foreigners were still to be confined to the outskirts of the country. In its grant to the Minister of the right of access to the capital and to foreign merchants of the right of travel in the interior, the British Treaty had asserted principles diametrically opposed to these traditions. Already on the 25th July 1858 an Imperial decree had spoken of 'the barbarians suddenly rushing up the river to Tientsin and retiring moved by the commands of Kweiliang and his colleague, signified with affectionate earnestness'. The return of the High Commissioners to meet Elgin in Shanghai had been expressly delayed until the season of active operations in the north was passed, and the only rational explanation of their appointment to discuss the tariff was that under the cover of commercial negotiations they were to attempt the abrogation of the treaty itself in so far as the residence question, the circulation of foreigners in the interior, and the opening of the Yangtse were concerned.

B. OPINION IN ENGLAND

Not all the members of Palmerston's Cabinet were of Bruce's opinion that 'we should make a mistake in approaching the

---

[1] Bruce to Malmesbury, 5 July 1859 (P.P. 1860, lxix, no. 9).

Capital otherwise than by its recognized highway'. Sir George Lewis on receipt of the earliest information wrote to the new Foreign Secretary, Lord John Russell:

'If the ascent of the Peiho was a right guaranteed by the treaty, the act of the ambassadors must be adopted—but, as far as one can judge from the telegram, it seems to have been rash and precipitate, and I see no reason why we should be in any hurry to express any approbation of it.'[1]

When he had read Bruce's dispatches, he believed that even if every step taken by the Chinese was marked by perfidy, even if the blockade of the Peiho was a breach of agreement, although the treaty had not been ratified, the

'proper course, when the execution of a treaty engagement is resisted or withheld, is, not to take immediate steps for compelling its execution by force, but to remonstrate with the government as to the non-fulfilment of the engagement. If the government after this remonstrance does not give satisfaction there is a legitimate ground for war. . . . When we come into contact with Barbarian nations we try their conduct to us by rules of European international law. It is therefore incumbent upon us that we should apply to our own conduct the strict rules of that law.'[2]

Though Charles Wood's immediate reaction was expressed in the words 'we cannot submit to be repulsed by these Chinese'[3], it was not long before he thought that Bruce and Hope were both wrong. By the 19th September he was confessing 'what disturbs me most is that I doubt our being right in what has taken place in China. That the admiral was rash in his operations no one can doubt, but I doubt our right to force an entry up the river.'[4] He thought the Ministers should have ascertained whether the offer of the Governor to receive them at Pehtang on their way to Peking was genuine before having recourse to violence. An expedition to Peking and the occupation of Chusan might be necessary, but he begged his colleagues not to be in too great a hurry, for the Chinese Government might act honestly and 'then we should have incurred great expense and probably entangled ourselves in further operations unnecessarily'[5]. The First Lord of the Admiralty, the Duke of

[1] Lewis to Russell, 12 Sept. 1859 (G.D. 22/25).
[2] Lewis to Russell, 15 Sept. 1859 (G.D. 22/25).
[3] Wood to Granville, 13 Sept. 1859 (G.D. 29/18).
[4] Wood to Russell, 17 Sept. 1859 (G.D. 22/25).
[5] Wood to Russell, 19 Sept. 1859 (G.D. 22/25).

Somerset, likewise thought that both naval and diplomatic authorities had not shown great judgement.

'It is unfortunate that our case for war with China is not so clear as could be wished, and yet we cannot be at peace after what has occurred. If we decide on immediate war there are some passages in the dispatches from which it may be argued that war is not to be justified according to the international law of Europe: if we decide for further negotiation it will be said we have allowed our embassy to be insulted and our flag dishonoured.'[1]

Gladstone, in criticizing a draft of instructions to Bruce prepared by Hammond, took strong exception to a statement therein that

'the determination to proceed to Peking by the Peiho . . . was a "very proper" one. . . . It implies that we were authorized not only to go to the capital to exchange ratifications which is beyond all doubts but to choose our own route thither, and to take that route by force even in the event of any other being offered.

'In order to be very proper this decision must be 1. just and 2. prudent.

'For one I am not clear on either point. On the point of justice, our route to Peking is not stipulated in the Treaty.

'Mr. Bruce terms it the natural highway; but I suppose it to be open to question whether the inland waters of a country are the natural highway for ships of war at a period which was at least equivalent to one of armistice, if not of peace?

'If we can import into a Treaty or attach to its execution what it does not itself contain do we mean to allow the Chinese to do the same? It is surely difficult to teach them European manners by Asiatic methods?

'With regard to the prudence of deciding to force a passage up the Peiho, . . .

'I would submit . . . That it is doubtful whether the Emperor of China meant to resist by force our claim to proceed with a ship of war to Tien-Tsin—a claim which it is also doubtful whether we were authorized to make. . . . Even if access were absolutely refused a doubt could still remain whether a resort to force without a previous complaint could be justified. That the instructions of Lord Malmesbury, which approved of going to Tientsin in a man of war, still left a discretion in regard to that mode of proceeding. And it is still more important that these instructions'

bound Bruce, in the event of the Chinese Government throwing

[1] Somerset to Russell, 19 Sept. 1859 (G.D. 22/24).

obstacles in the way of his arrival in Peking, '*to say* "that H.M. Government will insist on the literal fulfilment of the Treaty" '[1].

On the other hand, the Prime Minister and the Foreign Secretary had no hesitation in urging that a strong line should be taken. On the receipt of the first telegraphed news Palmerston wrote from Broadlands to Lord John: 'This is a disagreeable Event in China, & we must in some way or other make the Chinese repent of the outrage' . . . 'We might send a military-naval Force to attack & occupy Peking & drive the Emperor out of it & put our Plenipotentiaries into it. This would be the most appropriate measure.' But it would require considerable forces. Perhaps the occupation of Chusan for which he thought from his experience in the forties the Chinese 'have a particular Regard & veneration' might serve the purpose, were it not that the French were likely to send 'an ample supply of Heroes from Italy', and 'in the end we might find this state of things inconvenient'. Thirdly, the occupation of an island in the Yangtse near the Grand Canal and a blockade of the Gulf of Pechili might exert sufficient pressure on the Emperor.[2] That would be the safest and easiest method. 'The only question will perhaps be whether that would be considered a sufficient Retribution', though national honour might be satisfied if the Emperor ratified the Treaty of 1858 and did 'some other things'[3]. After meeting Lewis and others of his colleagues Palmerston realized that the Cabinet would not give unqualified approval of Bruce's action. 'The only plausible ground of Doubt', in his mind, 'whether our People were or were not justified in having Recourse to violence to clear a Passage up the Peiho', seemed 'to rest on the offer made to send the Plenipotentiaries up by another road, . . . I think they were right in not consenting to go round by the Back Door and the servants Entrance, representing as they did the Two great Powers of the West'[4].

The Foreign Secretary was at Abergeldie when the first news of the disaster at the Peiho arrived, and he remained out of town from the 12th to the 24th September when the draft dispatch to Bruce was considered in the Cabinet. He confessed 'it seems strange that I who objected so much to Bowring's

---

[1] Gladstone, Memorandum, 22 Sept. 1859 (F.O. 17/311).
[2] Palmerston to Russell, 12 Sept. 1859 (G.D. 22/20).
[3] Palmerston to Russell, 14 Sept. 1859 (G.D. 22/20).
[4] Palmerston to Russell, 19 Sept. 1859 (G.D. 22/20).

proceedings about the lorcha should be so ready to support Bruce—but so it is'.[1] He wrote to Sir Charles Wood, who had, as we have seen, expressed his doubts on the justice of Bruce's conduct: 'I regret very much that we ever entered upon such a policy; but that was decided in the case of the Lorcha, & it is of no use to go back upon it—and indeed the position we then abandoned cannot be resumed.'[2] To Lewis's criticism he replied:

'Your argument in favour of the Chinese is very ingenious, but the case seems to stand thus—A gentleman has made an agreement with me which is to be confirmed on a certain day at his house—At the time named I go along the direct road to his house, finding stakes stuck up in the road I try to remove them, upon which he fires upon me from behind the hedge, and kills several of my servants—Query, was this murder or justifiable homicide? I should say murder and as such to be punished—Mine appears to be the general opinion. P.S. I have omitted all the lies which undoubtedly would only be urged in aggravation.'[3]

When he was informed by the Prime Minister that Grey was to consult the Lord Chancellor with a view to putting a case before the law officers,[4] Russell remonstrated on the ground that the question was one of policy rather than of law.

'If Bruce could have been sure that the Chinese would have ratified the Treaty had he gone alone to Peking, and without any degrading ceremony, he might be wrong to insist on going by the river. But this reliance he could not have had. Indeed the certainty was the other way. This appears to me his justification.'[5]

Russell's attitude was that of Hammond, his permanent Under-Secretary at the Foreign Office. Indeed, by the time Lord John had written his letters from which extracts have been quoted, he would have received a long review of the situation from Hammond, and it is possible that his position at the head of the Foreign Office is partly the explanation of his apparent change of attitude from that which he took up during the debate on the lorcha *Arrow* in 1857.

[1] Russell to Palmerston, 19 Sept. 1859 (G.D. 22/30).
[2] Russell to Wood, 21 Sept. 1859 (G.D. 22/29).
[3] Russell to Lewis, 19 Sept. 1859 (G.D. 22/29).
[4] Palmerston to Russell, 19 Sept. 1859 (G.D. 22/20).
[5] Russell to Ld. Chancellor, 21 Sept. 1859 (G.D. 22/31).

Hammond was emphatically of opinion that Bruce's course should be approved.

'After all, I cannot think in dealing with nations who do not recognize our code of international law we should bind ourselves to a strict and purely technical observance of it. The Treaty according to our technical rules was no Treaty, for the ratifications had not been *exchanged*; but . . . the Emperor's acceptance of the Treaty was formally signified to Lord Elgin, and . . . therefore he is morally bound by it.

'Now one of the Articles of the Treaty provides that the ratifications shall be exchanged at Peking, and it surely implies that the person charged with exchanging it may proceed by the most direct and easy road, and in that case such road was the Peiho. It would be absurd to say we do not prevent you going to Edinburgh, but you must go round by Glasgow; and instead of going at your ease in a carriage you must either walk or ride, and by the way we choose to point to you. . . .

'I think we must look at the question as raised by some of the members of the Cabinet not in the narrow point of view prescribed by technicalities, but by the light thrown upon it by all that has passed since the signature of the Treaty. . . .

. . . 'The allegation that the Peiho was barred as a protection against the rebels in that quarter was a clear falsehood. There are no rebels in that quarter, neither have the rebels ever attempted to move by water. . . . Bruce was, I think, fully justified in considering the conduct of the Chinese in barring the passage of the Peiho as an indication of the determination of the Chinese government to defeat the condition of the Treaty that its ratifications should be exchanged at Peking. . . .

'I think too that having gone so far and the Treaty being set at nought by the Chinese Bruce was fully justified in attempting to force a passage; and in fact if he had not done so would have been highly blameable. For his drawing back would have been a moral triumph to the Chinese as great and as influential upon our relations with them for the future as the material triumph which they have now obtained by the defeat of the attempt to force the passage of the Peiho.'[1]

It is probable that Clarendon summed up the general opinion fairly accurately when he wrote to Granville:

'If Bruce and the Admiral had succeeded people wd. have said they had done the right thing in the right way but having failed &

---

[1] Hammond to Russell, 18 Sept. 1859 (G.D. 22/28).

John Bull as usual wanting a victim they are generally blamed & there certainly are one or two pegs on wch. criticism may be hung, but I am glad to find that vigorous action is determined upon & that no one is more staunch than Ivan Ivanovitch.'[1]

Immediate steps were taken at a meeting held on the 16th September of the Duke of Cambridge, Palmerston, Sidney Herbert, and Charles Wood,[2] when it was agreed, as Russell had suggested,[3] that one European and one native regiment should be sent at once from India to Hong Kong.[4] Whatever any member of the British Cabinet might think, 'Napoleon is determined to send an expedition against the Chinese', and Palmerston concluded 'we cannot I think allow him to do so alone. It would be impossible for many reasons—we could not shrink from resenting an outrage offered mainly to us, and by which we were the main sufferers, when the French resented their lighter share both of the insult and the loss. Moreover, to let things alone would be to hand over to them our Position in the East'.[5]

A full Cabinet held on the 24th determined that the Chinese Government would have to yield the major point—residence in the capital—if not by diplomacy then by force, and this decision was embodied in a dispatch to Bruce dated the 26th September. The Government entirely approved his conduct up to the time of his leaving Shanghai. In insisting upon being received at Peking, and in proceeding to the mouth of the Peiho, Bruce had acted in strict conformity with his instructions. Upon his arrival at the Peiho he had to found his course mainly on presumptive evidence and Her Majesty's Government 'without being able in the present state of their information to judge precisely what measures it might have been most advisable for you to adopt at the moment, see nothing in your decision to diminish the confidence which they repose in you'[6]. Gladstone had told Russell that, however much he objected to the Foreign Secretary's draft dispatch, he was 'far from desiring that the Draft should now be drawn so as to pronounce blame upon any one'[7]. He

---

[1] Granville to Russell, 12 Sept. 1859 (G.D. 22/25).
[2] Wood to Russell, 17 Sept. 1859 (G.D. 22/25).
[3] Russell to Wood, 15 Sept. 1859 (G.D. 22/29).
[4] Palmerston to Russell, 17 Sept. 1859 (G.D. 22/20).
[5] Palmerston to Russell, 19 Sept. 1859 (G.D. 22/20).
[6] Russell to Bruce, 26 Sept. 1859 (P.P. 1860, lxix, no. 12).
[7] Gladstone to Russell, 22 Sept. 1859 (G.D. 22/19).

and his fellow critics had had their way. Hammond had been for sending an 'entire approval' to Bruce, but, as Sidney Herbert had hoped, 'that was at an end'[1]. The Cabinet refused to make their agent's act their own, and yet were at the same time unwilling to censure and recall him.

Already steps were being taken with Paris to send out an expedition. The measures which the British Government recommended to the French as necessary to the re-establishment of the just influence of Great Britain and France in China were communicated to Lord Cowley in a dispatch from Russell on the 26th September. A naval and military force should be assembled in the spring in Chinese waters, the terms upon which peace could be maintained were to be made known at Shanghai by the Western Plenipotentiaries, the indispensable condition of which should be the ratification of the Treaty of Tientsin at Peking. The two Governments should resume the right of maintaining permanent establishments in the capital, the Plenipotentiaries should proceed from the mouth of the Peiho to Tientsin in such vessels only as were required for the transport of themselves and their suites, and that thence they should be escorted in a suitable manner to Peking. Finally, no indemnity beyond that stipulated in the Treaty of Tientsin should be exacted:[2] on this point Elgin was particularly insistent as he feared that to exact an indemnity would entail a great loss of dignity to the Emperor, who would appear to be paying tribute to foreigners.[3]

The news which reached England at the end of October of the treatment of the American representative Ward justified, at least to Palmerston, the course pursued by Bruce and Hope.[4] It caused the Duke of Argyll to exclaim: 'I am all against submitting to any nonsense such as they seem to have practised on the Yankee Minister—who was sent up to Peking caged in a Van—like one of Wombwell's Wild Beasts.'[5]

Ward had intended to have entered the Peiho when the booms were removed. On the retirement of the Anglo-French force he went to the Pehtangho, where after some difficulty he got into communication with the Governor-General of the Province,

[1] Herbert to Granville, 20 Sept. 1859 (G.D. 29/18).
[2] Russell to Cowley, 26 Sept. 1859 (Cord. *L'Expéd.* ii, p. 101).
[3] Persigny to Walewski, 15 Oct. 1859 (Cord. *L'Expéd.* ii, p. 103).
[4] Palmerston to Russell, 31 Oct. 1859 (G.D. 22/20).
[5] Argyll to Granville, no date, 1859 (G.D. 29/29).

landed in the mud and was conveyed by closed springless carts
—a sign of inferiority—instead of on horseback or better still in
a sedan chair—to the capital. Bruce had thought that Ward
was likely to have been well treated, as the American Treaty
was far less exacting than the British. It gave no right to
continuous residence in Peking nor to travel in the interior, and
it opened no port north of Shanghai.[1] The political atmosphere,
too, was excellent for him. But he was treated without courtesy
and with a 'studied intention of making the visit so physically
exhausting and so morally irksome as to render its renewal
improbable'. A Roman Catholic missionary reported Ward's
arrival in the words 'Humillime intravit'. In Peking he was
hedged about with guards who were themselves reprimanded
for supplying him with fans on which a plan of the city was
depicted. He remained firm, however, on the question of
ceremonial and was thereby prevented from having an audience
with the Emperor. When he expressed his desire to treat the
Emperor with great respect, the Chinese seized upon his words,
which could be taken to suggest self-abasement as a justification
for solemnly receiving the letter of the President to their master.
There is little doubt that the whole proceedings were calculated
to impress the native population that Ward arrived in the capital
in a manner similar to the tribute bearers from the neighbouring
Asiatic States. It is not surprising, therefore, that on his return
to Shanghai, having exchanged the ratifications of his treaty at
Pehtang on his homeward journey, he was 'more convinced
than ever of the soundness of our determination to proceed to
Tientsin under our own flags'. In Peking all was confidence.
The British were thought of as 'rocky islanders', formidable
only at sea; and it was clear to Bruce at least that 'unless enlightened on the hopelessness of resistance the Imperial government will not establish relations on the basis I am instructed to
demand'[2].

---

[1] Bruce to Russell, 15 July 1859 (P.P. 1860, lxix, no. 11).
[2] Bruce to Russell, 3 Sept. 1859 (ibid. no. 18).

VIII

LORD ELGIN'S SECOND MISSION, 1860 [1]

A. THE PREPARATIONS

1. At Home

WHILE the British and French Governments were considering the policy they should adopt, a state of quiet expectation reigned in China. Ho characterized the incident at Takoo as 'an untoward accident', but Bruce could fairly comment that it was significant that neither in private conversation with Lay nor by official correspondence had he ever been given to understand that the Governor of Chihli Province intended to receive the foreign ministers at Pehtang nor that they should avoid what in an Imperial decree had been described as the highway to Peking. He was convinced that the intention of the Chinese authorities, when they could not retain him and his colleagues in Shanghai, was to put him on the footing of an agent for the transaction of business and so to avoid the essential point gained by the Treaty of Tientsin, the recognition of the political equality of Sovereign States.[2] This impression was confirmed by Ho's statement that, as the exchange of ratifications was really a question of trade, he as Superintendent of Trade was entitled to enter into a discussion of that question with Bruce.[3]

Three problems engaged Bruce's attention during the autumn and winter of 1859–60: the renewed activity of the Chinese crimps in kidnapping their countrymen for emigration in foreign ships to foreign colonies; the difficulties that arose over the system of convoying Chinese junks—a system which seemed but little removed from piracy; and thirdly, the extension to ports other than Shanghai of the Foreign Inspectorate of the Customs. A mob of Chinese on the 29th July beat Lay and the Rev. W. Hobson in the course of a riot caused by the kidnapping of coolies for a French ship at Woosung. Bruce, who strongly objected to such a trade, especially at Shanghai, thought the mob had some justification for their violent attitude towards the Ningpo crimps in question and some foreign sailors.[4] De

---

[1] Throughout this chapter use has been made of S. L. Poole, *Life of Sir Harry Parkes*, vol. i, cc. xvi and xvii, and of H. B. Loch, *Narrative of Events in China*.

[2] Bruce to Russell, 31 July 1859 (P.P. 1860, lxix, no. 13).

[3] Bruce to Russell, 2 Sept. 1859 (ibid., no. 17).

[4] Bruce to Russell, 1 Aug. 1859 (F.O. 17/313).

Bourboulon and Ho both assisted in the restoration of quiet conditions, the former by ordering the French ship concerned up to the port and securing the release of any coolies who wished to depart,[1] the latter by executing some native crimps. But Bruce met with great difficulty in persuading Ho to punish the Chinese who were guilty of the assault upon innocent British subjects, and thought him unwilling rather than unable to do justice in this matter.[2] If those guilty of the assault remained unpunished he thought the matter should be made an international question to be settled at Peking.[3] But Shanghai and Woosung were not the only places where the coolie trade was causing great anxiety: a disgraceful state of affairs continued to exist at Amoy, Ningpo, and Chinhai. At Ningpo riots broke out, and there also difficulty was experienced in obtaining the punishment of certain Chinese for assault on innocent Englishmen.[4] In Canton the violent and fraudulent activities of the native crimps, of which foreign agents were well aware, but which, from private greed they were not all prepared to discountenance, had the particularly unfortunate result of checking 'the kindly feeling, which the Missionaries are unanimous in declaring has been produced by the honest administration of justice and by the excellent conduct of the military police and of the troops in general since our occupation of Canton . . . because the Chinese cannot understand how they can be carried on without the permission of those who are virtually the masters of the country'[5]. Ward had censured the American Consul, and Bruce hoped that the King of Prussia would likewise call the Oldenburg Consul to book for tolerating such abuses. The Allied commanders were able to put a stop to kidnapping in the city, but the only permanent solution of the problem lay in the prohibition of private speculation in the trade and confining it to Government agents of the Colonial Powers. If this were done in co-operation with a Chinese customs service invigorated by foreigners, the disgrace of unwilling, almost slave, labour would be at an end.[6] By the end of March 1860 after initial difficulties the Allied commanders in Canton with the help of Parkes

[1] Bruce to Russell, 15 Aug. 1859 (F.O. 17/313).
[2] Bruce to Russell, 2 Sept. 1859 (F.O. 17/314).
[3] Bruce to Russell, 3 Sept. 1859 (F.O. 17/314).
[4] Bruce to Russell, 2 Dec. 1859 (F.O. 17/315).
[5] Bruce to Russell, 22 Jan. 1860 (F.O. 17/335).
[6] Bruce to Russell, 26 Feb. 1860 (F.O. 17/336).

prevailed upon the local authorities to agree to a legalized and properly controlled system of emigration, which was to be extended to Swatow:[1] such an outcome was the most hopeful for those who, like Bruce, were concerned not only with the economic but with the humanitarian aspect of the problem.[2]

The convoy system, which had sprung up because Chinese pirates paid more respect to foreign managed and foreign armed vessels than to Chinese junks, had already brought about considerable difficulty in Ningpo where Portuguese lorchas were chiefly concerned. An Englishman Schofield had got into trouble in the past with a Chinese piratical fleet under the control of one A Pak. A Pak had, as was customary, made himself respectable by being bought for service by the Imperial Government. When, however, this man organized a Canton Convoying Company to enter into competition with his erstwhile antagonist, Bruce withdrew Schofield's licence in order to avoid any difficulties with the Chinese authorities of Kwantung, for A Pak and Schofield treated each other's convoying vessels as pirates.[3]

Lay was in Canton making arrangements to bring into being there the Foreign Inspectorate system which had already proved of such value to the customs administration in Shanghai. Among the chief opponents of this measure were the American merchants whose enmity Lay, in his effort to organize a purer system of custom-house administration, had not unnaturally incurred, partly from national prejudice and partly because the Americans in particular and some British traders wanted big profits quickly and a speedy return home. The European element in the customs administration, in Bruce's opinion, was acting as usefully in teaching the Chinese to resist when right as in counselling them to yield when wrong; a result that was not always palatable to foreigners or to their national authorities.[4] When, therefore, Ward returned from his humiliating experiences in the north, apprehensive that he might be criticized for acquiescence without protest in treatment, the impropriety of which did not escape the notice of the United States naval officers, and disturbed in consequence at the effect on his sub-

[1] Bruce to Russell, 21 Mar. 1860 (F.O. 17/336).
[2] Bruce to Russell, 5 Dec. 1859 (F.O. 17/315).
[3] Bruce to Russell, 29 Nov. 1859 (F.O. 17/315).
[4] Bruce to Russell (secret and confidential), 28 Apr. 1860 (G.D. 22/49).

sequent political career of a possible loss of reputation with the American public, it became his urgent interest to support the wishes of the American merchants. His fellow countrymen in Shanghai tactfully presented him with an address of congratulation on his work in the north but at the same time pointed out what they expected him to do in regard to the customs arrangements in the south. As Ward was not a diplomat by career, 'as is unfortunately the case with most American appointments in China', commented Bruce, 'the disapprobation of his government will have much less effect on his prospects in his future career than the support he will gain by lending his aid to the lawless spirit which has always characterized American commerce and to the anti-English prejudices which flourish vigorously among the American community and which will be gratified by the overthrow of a system supposed to be English in its conception and in its elements'. Owing to the absence of any general interest in Chinese affairs in the United States, Americans were precluded from taking an active part in the settlement of questions at issue between Eastern and Western civilizations, and a participation in the material advantages failed to reconcile them to the reputation and influence naturally belonging to those whose sacrifices were crowned with success. Yet though 'no where is the tone of the American community more anti-British, and more jealous of her power and influence than in China', and though the privileges enjoyed by them were due to the efforts of Great Britain 'and would be speedily lost if she withdrew from the arena', the United States was still a Treaty Power, whose consent was necessary to carry out the stipulations of the Treaty and as such could be the cause of a great deal of embarrassment. Bruce fortunately had to deal with a minister in Ward who, whatever his temptations, was not likely 'to adopt blindly the prejudices of his countrymen and who will check the violence and recklessness in which their consuls too frequently indulge'.

Bruce did his best to make Ward's action easy. He used his influence with the British newspaper, the *North China Herald*, to prevent Ward's Peking visit being made the subject of discussion, and urged Lay to make such concessions as he could to satisfy Ward and enable him to get some credit with his countrymen.[1] The result was that the system of Foreign Inspectorate was duly

---

[1] Bruce to Russell (confidential), 22 Nov. 1859 (F.O. 17/315).

extended to and survived at Canton. Ward, satisfied with Lay's explanations and modifications agreed to instruct the United States Consuls to put into force the new arrangements. Bruce had acted with the utmost tact. He had shown that he was content with the assurances Ward had given at Shanghai by refraining from going down to Hong Kong and Canton and thus perhaps creating an impression that he thought it necessary to watch his American colleague. He got his reward—doubly: in the salvation of the new system and in the high compliment which Ward paid him by writing to the Washington Government, 'that, coming to China with strong anti-English prejudices it was natural that I should sometimes have imagined that an effort existed to thwart our views, and a reluctance to concede to us that to which we were justly entitled. Investigation and experience have alone been required to remove all such erroneous impressions on my part.' Were he remaining in the East, he added, he would have liked to help to carry out the British Minister's policy, 'which as expressed to me is as judicious and humane to China as it is wise and liberal to other governments'[1].

While Bruce was thus busy in Shanghai waiting for the policy of the British and French Governments to be defined, the Emperor Napoleon was negotiating the Treaty of Zürich, winning back the natural frontier of the Alps and making inevitable the Italian Kingdom. In spite of this work of major importance he found time and means to contemplate sending to China a large expedition consisting of 12,000 infantry, 2 squadrons of cavalry, and 8 batteries of artillery, accompanied by 20 gunboats drawing less than 3 feet of water. Palmerston seems to have been considerably taken aback by this news. 'Surely it is essential for our Standing and Reputation in Asia that our contribution should not be inferior to that of the French', he commented to his Foreign Secretary.[2] Newcastle from Balmoral urged the same consideration, adding that 'it is sufficiently unfortunate that we have any Ally at all in our Chinese quarrel'[3]. The French had suggested that if Great Britain did not see fit to send so many troops, she might furnish transport for them as in the Crimean War. Russell, who 'decidedly objected to being again beasts of burden for the French', thought the size of the

---

[1] Bruce to Russell (secret and confidential), 6 Dec. 1859 (F.O. 17/315).
[2] Palmerston to Russell, 5 Oct. 1859 (G.D. 22/20).
[3] Newcastle to Russell, 8 Oct. 1859 (G.D. 22/25).

expedition was too large, but as the French would not reduce
their numbers there was nothing left for it.[1] Sidney Herbert
concurred on the ground that 'our danger lies nearer home and
it is not our interest to upset the Chinese dynasty which there
is great fear of our doing if we march on Peking. If anarchy
should ensue, our trade and our tea will be nil, and after all they
constitute the two objects for the sake of which we go to China
at all.'[2]

The French objected to making any demand on the Chinese
Government before military operations had begun. The Prime
Minister, however, argued 'that what we want is not to kill
some hundred Chinese soldiers, which would do us no good,
but to bring the Emperor to Book and make him do what he
has failed to do'. If this could be done without war, 'we shall
stand better with the world by having accomplished our real
Purpose without being led away by an unworthy thirst for
Revenge'. If the Chinese, as was probable, refused to comply
with the Allied demands, 'the French would still have an opportunity of showing their military superiority over the Chinese,
if they think practical evidence necessary to prove it'. But above
all he feared that the Emperor might 'retire to the North and
wait till winter drives us away, & then all we can do is to
destroy the Imperial Palace, and go back to our Ships'[3].

The British Government decided to make its demands before
naval and military action began. Accordingly Bruce was instructed, if asked to proceed to Peking, not to accede to such a
request without a formal apology from the Emperor for the
events of the previous summer and without obtaining permission to proceed to Tientsin in a British vessel and with due
honour thence to the capital. The Chinese authorities were to
be informed that Elgin's promise that a British Minister would
not be ordered to reside in Peking was in abeyance. If he had
not been invited, before the receipt of the dispatch, with honour
to the capital, the above conditions were to be made into an
ultimatum to expire in thirty days. After that time the naval
and military commanders would be instructed to act, though
until reinforcements arrived action was to be limited to the
seizure of grain junks destined for Peking and the occupation of

[1] Russell to Herbert, 11 Oct. 1859 (G.D. 22/31).
[2] Herbert to Russell, 13 Oct. 1859 (G.D. 22/25).
[3] Palmerston to Russell, 29 Oct. 1859 (G.D. 22/20).

one of the Miatow islands in the Pechili Strait as a basis for operations. The British Government hoped on grounds of humanity that hostilities would not be necessary, but they were determined, without insisting on a personal interview between Bruce and the Emperor, that he must correspond personally with the chief officers of the Empire on terms of equality.[1]

The French informed the British Government that they intended to ask for an indemnity. Palmerston saw no reason why his Government should not join them in that demand, as 'those semi-barbarous governments have generally a Treasure hoarded up'. 'Moreover the French say they will occupy Territory, probably Chusan, as security for Payment and we might as well have a joint occupation with them as leave them in sole possession of an Island very much commanding Shanghai.'[2] This French initiative was accepted, and Bruce was instructed on the 10th November to notify the Chinese that unless an ample apology was made a large pecuniary indemnity would be demanded. The sum of half a million pounds in Russell's first draft gave place to this vague expression. But the French demand was for the payment by China of the whole costs of the expedition. The British Cabinet hoped that their Ally would agree to reduce this to a sum which the Chinese could pay in a few months. They were prepared to compromise to the extent of agreeing to 4 or if necessary 5 million pounds.[3] Not until the 8th February did the two Governments arrive at an agreed figure—60 million francs—which was to include both what the Chinese had already undertaken to pay and the contribution to be exacted towards the expenses of the new expedition.[4] At the beginning of 1860 the military and naval instructions were issued. The forces were to rendezvous in Hong Kong, an Anglo-French occupation of Chusan was to be effected, grain junks to be stopped, such points on the Gulf of Pechili as the Admirals might desire for bases were to be seized and the Takoo forts attacked. There was to be no blockade south of the Yangtse, but on that river, its mouths, and the coast northwards.[5] Public proclamation was to be made that

[1] Russell to Bruce, 29 Oct. 1859 (P.P. 1860, lxix, further correspondence no. 2, and F.O. 17/311).
[2] Palmerston to Russell, 29 Oct. 1859 (G.D. 22/20).
[3] Palmerston to Russell, 13 Dec. 1859 (G.D. 22/24).
[4] Russell to Bruce, 8 Feb. 1860 (P.P. 1861, lxvi, no. 10).
[5] Russell to Lds. of Admiralty, 7 Jan. 1860 (ibid., no. 8).

the war was undertaken against the Emperor and it was hoped that commerce would continue in spite of the hostile activities in the north.[1]

In explaining Ward's acquiescence in his undignified treatment, Bruce had emphasized the fact 'that a Minister freshly arrived from the West is entirely in the hands of those who have made the language and customs of China a study. It may be, as has been asserted, that those gentlemen are sometimes unnecessarily touchy on points of etiquette, but . . . in other instances' they are inclined 'to consult Chinese prejudices rather than to insist on what their own national dignity requires'[2]. Russell might have been afraid that Bruce's experts were of the touchy variety, for he warned the British Minister against 'too nice and minute an attention to Chinese distinctions and pedantic pretensions . . . you will therefore always keep in view both substance and form, but where one is to yield, let it be form rather than substance'[1].

2. In China

Though Bruce had received by the 6th January 1860 the Foreign Secretary's dispatch directing him to send the ultimatum, he stayed his hand, since de Bourboulon was not yet instructed by the French Government,[3] nor was Admiral Hope in a condition to act if the ultimatum was rejected.[4] But an informal channel of communication presented itself in the person of Wade's former teacher Chang, who had recently come from Peking. As Lay, through whom such private information had been given in the past, was in Canton, it was valuable to have this opportunity of letting the high Chinese authorities know what the British Government required in order that hostilities might be averted.[5] Shortly afterwards a young Chinese named Hwang, who, after an American mission education, had emigrated to Demerara, and had likewise been employed by Wade before entering the service of Sang-ko-lin-sin, arrived in Shanghai on a mission from the Chinese commander-in-chief to size

[1] Russell to Lds. of the Admiralty, 3 Jan. 1860 (ibid., no. 5).
[2] Bruce to Russell, 3 Sept. 1859 (F.O. 17/314).
[3] Bruce to Russell, 6 Jan. 1860 (P.P. 1861, lxvi, no. 12).
[4] Bruce to Russell, 21 Jan. 1860 (ibid., no. 14).
[5] Bruce to Russell, 6 Jan. 1860 (F.O. 17/335).

up the situation. To him also was given an inkling of the demands which Bruce was instructed to make.[1]

Bruce disliked the idea of intercepting the grain supplies—an action which he thought in itself would not be a very heavy blow to the Chinese Government as they were believed to have large reserves in the capital.[2] Such action would but hurt the best friends of the Maritime Powers, as the trade to the north was controlled by Shanghai and Ningpo capital worth £7 millions, and employed 3,000 junks and 100,000 men.[3]

When the instructions of the Quai d'Orsay arrived they were found to differ on one important point from those which Bruce had received from Downing Street: de Bourboulon was ordered to demand an indemnity, whereas the British required an indemnity only if the ultimatum were rejected. Impressed by the vital necessity of acting in concert with his French colleague, and of giving the war-party in Peking a lesson, Bruce decided to act in conformity with his colleague's instructions. 'If there is one art of diplomacy understood by the Chinese it is that of separating interests which ought to be identical.'[4] In a private letter to Hammond, Bruce urged the desirability of a similar ultimatum from the point of view of Anglo-French relations. 'If our ultimatum is accepted and that of the French refused, we shall lose all hold of French action in these seas. They will seize places as the Russians have without any title, & leave it to the Chinese to turn them out. Anyone can do this. As long as we act together we can check them to a certain extent.' Besides 'an apology from the Chinese for what they have done is not worth the paper it is written on—The only substantial apology is their consenting to pay for the mischief they have done—that is an apology for the past and some security for the future'.[5]

Before, however, formally handing over the ultimatum the British and French Plenipotentiaries awaited the return to Shanghai from the capital of Sieh, the officer associated with Ho in the government of the Kiang Provinces and in the commission for trade affairs.[6] In the meanwhile Bruce used another channel

[1] Bruce to Russell (secret and confidential), 21 Jan. 1860 (F.O. 17/335).
[2] Bruce to Russell, 6 Feb. 1860 (P.P. 1861, lxvi, no. 15).
[3] Bruce to Russell, 7 Apr. 1860 (ibid., no. 25).
[4] Bruce to Russell, 6 Feb. 1860 (P.P. 1860, lxix, further correspondence, no. 1).
[5] Bruce to Hammond (private), 6 Feb. 1860 (F.O. 17/336).
[6] Bruce to Hammond (secret and confidential), 21 Jan. 1860 (F.O. 17/335).

to make known in advance the moderate terms of the British demands. This means was the manager of Messrs. Jardine, Matheson and Company in Shanghai, to whom an influential Chinese paid repeated visits in the hopes of finding grounds for an accommodation. Through him it was suggested that if the Chinese Government frankly and spontaneously showed that it was anxious to make full satisfaction for the past by welcoming the Allies as friends, peace could be preserved.[1]

Nothing, however, as de Bourboulon had rightly surmised, came of these informal talks, and Sieh, now returned from Peking, seemed charged with no overture by the Imperial Government. Admiral Hope, too, would be in sufficient strength during March to protect Shanghai and occupy Chusan if the Chinese Emperor refused to comply with the British and French ultimata. Bruce at first hesitated to bring his demands into line with those of the French Government, but finally, unauthorized by his instructions, he demanded in the name of the British Cabinet, in case of a refusal of compliance, 'a large pecuniary indemnity'[2]. These vague words could be translated into a more or less number of pounds as the British Government might decide, with their eyes on both Chinese capacity and ulterior French aims. For Bruce was certain that 'in the present condition of the Chinese Exchequer an immediate payment of even a moderate indemnity is not to be looked for'. And if it were not forthcoming there was always the danger that the French would 'require a guarantee, and I incline to believe that they will prefer relinquishing Canton, a position not without its inconveniences and retaining possession of Chusan, which Island they are about in common with ourselves to occupy in force'[3].

The reply to these ultimata, as thus finally settled, was received within the month and was categorical in its refusal to comply. No apology or expression of regret would be given for the Takoo affair; permission to ascend the Peiho was refused; the abandoned guns and ships would not be restored; and the French and British Ministers were referred generally to the regulations which had governed the reception of their American colleague, which, however, Ho was empowered to vary. Ho

[1] Bruce to Hammond, 19 Feb. 1860 (F.O. 17/336).
[2] Bruce to Hammond, 7 and 8 Mar. 1860 (P.P. 1861, lxvi, nos. 19 and 20).
[3] Bruce to Hammond, 7 Mar. 1860 (F.O. 17/336).

had also been instructed to consider what parts of the Elgin Treaty could be confirmed and what parts modified.[1]

In transmitting this reply Sieh's 'language was that of menace; he stated that while we were only half prepared, the Chinese were quite ready for action; that they would be able to excite the population against us at the Ports, and do us serious injury. . . . This tone of bravado and menace is no doubt assumed in compliance with instructions received from the Court of Peking'. For Sieh, like Ho, doubtful of the wisdom of such intransigence, had delayed forwarding the Emperor's answer to the ultimata for several days, hoping that his representations to Peking might have enabled him to alter its terms. But Pang, the Secretary of State, had warned him that he would be held responsible for any alteration. The real trouble was that the influence of Sang-ko-lin-sin was paramount in the capital. He had been the author of the resistance in 1859, and so long as he retained his position the Emperor could not without loss of dignity accept the ultimatum.[2] The real views of Sieh were known to Bruce through the channel of Lay. Lay's account of his discussions with the Chinese officer was given in great confidence to the British Minister on condition that it should not appear in the public archives, for his position would be seriously jeopardized if the terms of confidence in which he was with the provincial authorities were realized. It was clear that 'the same process of enlightenment' which had already done so much in teaching the Chinese in the restricted and local sphere of customs administration,

'will have to be gone through, should international relations be fairly established at Peking, and it is only by its means that China will be brought gradually to understand her position and rights among other nations, and will discover that her own safety and security are better consulted by taking this middle and reasonable course than by persisting in a blind and indiscriminating antagonism, which is certain to create fresh embarrassments, and tends to separate her from the interests and sympathy of that large and increasing part of her population which both in China and abroad is brought daily more and more in contact with foreigners and foreign ideas, and over which her old system is gradually losing all hold'.

Lay thought it was in the common interest of Great Britain

[1] Bruce to Hammond, 9 Apr. 1860 (P.P. 1861, lxvi, no. 24).
[2] Bruce to Hammond, 17 April 1860 (F.O. 17/337).

and China, for which he had always tried to act, that he should send Bruce a memorandum of his conversations with Sieh. To Sieh's initial bravado Lay replied that the only advice he could offer was the unconditional acceptance of the British demands, not one single one of which he was sure would be abated. At his last interview, before Sieh repaired to the residence of the Governor-General Ho at Changchow, some 130 miles from Shanghai, Lay emphasized the fact that the recent parliamentary debates in England had shown that the British Government and people believed that China had behaved treacherously and demanded reparation. They discussed the feature of the Elgin Treaty most obnoxious to the Chinese:

'The only reason he could give me against our having a Minister permanently residing in the capital was that we should find relations with the officials there impossible. I asked whether the real objection was not the abrogation of the Commissionership at a port, the breakwater the old foreign policy interposed between the government and the barbarians. . . . With the foreign Minister at Peking, the Court would have to entertain and deal with foreign questions and complaints. It could not as heretofore throw them aside or refer them to a Yeh, for consideration. Our experience of the past year, I said, proves that we can have no satisfactory relations with you unless we have a representative stationed at the Capital; that without one we should have no security for peace. The Chinese would violate the treaties as before and make it necessary for us to dispatch expeditions from time to time to insist on their fulfilment. The occasional visit of a Minister unless supported by a force strong enough to march on Peking would procure him nothing better than a reception such as was vouchsafed to Mr. Ward; to whom, I said, you behaved as you would to a tribute bearer from Siam. . . . And would not this have been precisely the way in which you would have attempted to treat Mr. Bruce had he gone up last year via Pehtang? And the moment ratifications had been exchanged would he not have been dismissed from the capital? And would one word about the carrying out of the Passport or Transit duty clauses ever have been listened to? No; as you know very well, this would have been the result of a "gentle" method of proceeding.'

Sieh in reply to Lay's criticism of the reception of Mr. Ward acknowledged:

'The fact was you see that I did not dare to show them the slightest good will. If I had I should have been denounced as a traitor. I was obliged to snub them. I could not help myself.'

'Exactly', I exclaimed, 'what does this prove, but that relations are impossible until these arrogant fellows in the North have been well chastised?' 'Yes', he answered, 'if you would only administer the thrashing, all would be set right soon enough: but without a thrashing I don't think they will yield'. China, Lay complained, was always in extremes; now she was arrogant at Peking and in Canton all submission. We would not have the one and do not want the other. They must take a middle course which might easily be found, and which would be productive of no injury to China.'

Sieh, much struck by Lay's remark that they must have a foreign office at Peking of men of experience of foreigners, observed 'with you by our side we should get along capitally. With you a go-between on your side, and me on ours, what great things we should accomplish!'[1] Already the close contact of a Westerner with an Easterner through the common work in the customs had produced a mutual understanding which pointed to an era of mutually helpful co-operation provided the extreme conservatism and antagonism at the capital could be successfully broken down.

The sole warlike act accomplished by the Allied forces before the end of June 1860 was the occupation of Chusan which was surrendered by the authorities and whose inhabitants eagerly looked forward to a golden harvest, showing by their whole attitude of complete indifference 'how obsolete and ill-adapted to the actual condition of China is the isolated and anti-foreign feeling of Peking'[2]. In contrast to the relatively pacific activity of the foreigners was the fresh move of the native rebels. Nanking had been closely invested by the Imperial troops at the beginning of March, and there seemed a reasonable prospect that the capital seat of the Governor-General of the Kiang Provinces might be recaptured from the Taipings,[3] when the rebels attacked and held for a time the great city of Hangchow,[4] and the siege of Nanking had, in consequence, to be raised. At the end of May Shanghai itself was threatened while Soochow had been captured by the Taiping forces on the 24th May.[5] The French general was anxious to send a column to Soochow to relieve the Imperialists, as there were there some 13,000

---

[1] Bruce to Hammond (secret and confidential), 28 April 1860 (G.D. 22/49).
[2] Bruce to Hammond, 28 April 1860 (P.P. 1861, lxvi, no. 30).
[3] Bruce to Hammond, 8 Mar. 1860 (F.O. 17/336).
[4] Bruce to Hammond, 30 Mar. 1860 (F.O. 17/337, no. 78).
[5] Bruce to Russell, 30 May 1860 (P.P. 1861, lxvi, no. 33).

Roman Catholic converts. Bruce refused to venture so far afield, though he and his French colleague publicly declared that they would protect the Chinese city of Shanghai, two gates of which were entrusted to the Allies, and a zone of four miles beyond it.[1] It is a curious commentary on the state of affairs in China in 1860 that the Allies should be safeguarding the interests of the Chinese Government while at the same time levying war on that Government by the occupation of Chusan and the move to Shantung. These operations began at the end of June when Elgin and Gros arrived to make another attempt to achieve recognition of equality of status.

B. TO PEKING

1. *Elgin lands*

Though the Prime Minister and the Foreign Secretary had had full confidence throughout in Bruce—a confidence shared by the Foreign Office and apparently by the Queen whose message of encouragement was gratefully acknowledged by her Minister early in December 1859[2]—there gradually became manifest a desire that Elgin should be sent out again to secure the ratification of the Treaty he had negotiated in 1858. Hammond was afraid lest Bruce should regard such a decision as a grave censure upon his competence and 'the heart-burning will not be less because Elgin and Bruce are brothers'[3]. Early in February Palmerston, however, sounded Elgin and found that 'he will go to China if he is desired to do so, but that he had much rather not do so'. In favour of his appointment it could be said that

'His going would no doubt be pleasing to the Public who are not aware how little there is for a Diplomat to do and it is just possible that the Chinese Emperor might be more willing to yield to an Ambassador who had come all the way from Europe to exchange Ratifications than to an Envoy who had had a conflict at the Peiho', but 'on the other hand that which is really to be done is a military and naval operation and it is the Fear and Pressure of Force and not the persuasive arguments of a Negotiator that will have an Effect upon the Chinese Government. . . . We do not want to negotiate a fresh Treaty, but to compel the Execution of a Treaty already concluded.

[1] Bruce to Russell, 10 June 1860 (P.P. 1861, lxvi, no. 34).
[2] Bruce to Russell, 5 Dec. 1859 (G.D. 22/49).
[3] Hammond to Russell, 3 Mar. 1860 (G.D. 22/49).

We cannot accept less, and we do not demand more, except in Regard to atonement, and Compensation, and those Demands must be enforced by Powder and Ball, and not by Pen and Ink.'

And it would be unfortunate to lose Elgin out of the Government, both from the point of view of the value of his counsel and the difficulties that would arise in filling his place of Post-master-General and providing for him on his return.[1] This last obstacle Palmerston thought could be met by appointing him, on the completion of his second China Mission, Governor-General of India.[2]

When the decision to send Elgin out to China again was finally made Bruce was immediately informed and on the 19th April he expressed his joy at the British Government's appointment.[3] Two days before, after negotiations with Napoleon III's Government had ended, Elgin was given his instructions similar to those of his French colleague Baron Gros. Though the British Government gave their envoy an indication of their policy, they wished him to have a free hand. They did not desire any occupation of Chinese territory when once ratifications had been exchanged and a method of liquidating the financial payments demanded of China had been satisfactorily arranged. They warned him of the danger which might result from a flight of the Emperor from Peking, and the still greater danger of widespread rebellion and anarchy. They insisted upon three conditions—a due apology for the Peiho affair, the ratification and execution of the Treaty of Tientsin, and an indemnity for payment of the naval and military expenses.[4] On the 18th April Russell informed Elgin that the Colonial Office were anxious to obtain the cession of the Peninsula of Kowloon, on the mainland opposite to Hong Kong, and he was instructed not to neglect any favourable opportunity for securing that cession.[5] A week later a secret dispatch from the Foreign Secretary warned Elgin that, however great the convenience to the colony of Hong Kong the cession of Kowloon might be for strategical and sanitary reasons and for the erection of ware-houses on its level ground, he was afraid lest a precedent might be set for demands by other Powers. In that case the convenience

[1] Palmerston to Russell, 5 Feb. 1860 (G.D. 22/49).
[2] Palmerston to Russell, 24 Feb. 1860 (G.D. 22/49).
[3] Bruce to Russell, 19 Apr. 1860 (P.P. 1861, lxvi, no. 29).
[4] Russell to Elgin, 17 Apr. 1860 (ibid., no. 16).
[5] Russell to Elgin, 18 Apr. 1860 (F.O. 17/329).

might be dearly purchased. Elgin was, therefore, left free to decide whether or not to abstain altogether from attempting to gain Kowloon if it was likely that other demands, injurious to China and unfavourable to British interests, might be put forward.[1]

Elgin did not delay his departure. He was in Alexandria on the 4th May, Aden on the 11th, and though the ship in which he was travelling with his French colleague was wrecked at the Point de Galle and an enforced delay in Ceylon resulted, he was in Singapore on the 14th June and in Shanghai on the 28th —almost exactly two years after the Treaty of Tientsin had been signed.[2] Shortly before, de Bourboulon and Bruce had been visited by Ho, Sieh, and the Taoutai Woo, who had received an edict couched in vague terms empowering them 'to concede what should be conceded and to refuse what should be refused'. They hoped to get the help of the Anglo-French forces against the rebels and urged that, if such help were given, the Emperor would understand that the Western nations were not always engaged in quarrels with the Chinese. They determined to wait on in Shanghai after the arrival of the Ambassadors, so as not to arrive in Peking until after the inevitable defeat of the Chinese forces should be known in the capital. Their position was an unfortunate one. For if disaster came they were likely to be degraded, and disaster could only be avoided if they told the truth and the court conceded the demands of the Allies. But in this case also they would be degraded.[3] Ho indeed urged his colleagues that a letter stressing the necessity of compliance should be sent immediately to the Emperor: he could well afford to do so as his position and even his life were in danger owing to the reverses of the Imperialists within his jurisdiction. He was, therefore, prepared to tell the truth to the Emperor. Sieh, however, whose credit and public career were not affected by the late events in the province, certain that the Emperor would not be sufficiently alarmed to shape his future course according to this unwelcome opinion, was naturally reluctant to take a step which would in all probability prove fatal to his prospects.[4] Ho was right in thinking he had already incurred

[1] Russell to Elgin (secret), 25 Apr. 1860 (F.O. 17/329).
[2] Elgin to Russell, various dates, 1860 (F.O. 17/330).
[3] Bruce to Russell, 12 June 1860 (P.P. 1861, lxvi, no. 35).
[4] Bruce to Russell, 12 June 1860 (F.O. 17/338).

the displeasure of his Master; shortly before Elgin's arrival his degradation and disgrace became known.[1]

Elgin entered into no negotiations at Shanghai, where he remained long enough to arrange to take with him Wade and the Canton Commissioner Parkes[2] and to meet Ignatieff, who had recently come from Peking. Gros had arrived on the 28th June, the day before himself, and the armed forces of the two Powers had since the 8th begun to concentrate (after considerable delay on the part of de Montauban, the French Commander-in-Chief, of which de Bourboulon complained to the Quai d'Orsay[3]), the British at Talienwan, the French at Chefoo on the northern and southern shores respectively of the Gulf of Pechili. On the 9th July Elgin joined the British contingent, which consisted of nearly 11,000 officers and men including about 500 sappers and 2,500 cavalry.[4] By that date General Sir Hope Grant, the commander of the British land force, was ready to move, somewhat before his French colleague who had hoped to have found a landing-place to the south of the Takoo forts, and to make thence a convergent attack in co-operation with the British who were to disembark at Pehtang. The French reconnaissance, undertaken surprisingly late,[5] proved, however, that this scheme was impossible. Final arrangements were made at a conference of the Allied commanders on the 19th for a conjoint move on Pehtang on the 31st, following a rendezvous of both forces to begin on the 26th.[6] Though the French had caused some anxiety and even annoyance to the British commanders by their dilatoriness, which was partly due to severe losses sustained by the wreck of several ships loaded with military stores, they raised no obstacle to Sir Hope Grant's taking into the field 11,000 men, instead of the 10,000 agreed upon by the two Governments. They themselves were after all only 6,700 strong. Elgin was gratified and perhaps somewhat surprised that Gros agreed that the weakness of one portion of the Allied forces was not a valid reason for reducing, but rather the reverse, the strength of the other.[7]

[1] Bruce to Russell, 29 June 1860 (P.P. 1861, lxvi, no. 37).
[2] Elgin to Russell, 2 July 1860 (ibid., no. 42).
[3] de Bourboulon to Thouvenel, 29 May 1860 (Chine 31).
[4] Elgin to Russell, 11 July 1860 (P.P. 1861, lxvi, no. 44). Hope Grant and H. Knollys, The China War of 1860, p. 49.
[5] Gros to Thouvenel, 24 July 1860 (Cord. L'Expéd. ii. 231).
[6] Col. Foley to Russell, 23 July 1860 (P.P. 1861, lxvi, no. 52).
[7] Elgin to Russell, 10 and 19 July 1860 (F.O. 17/330).

Already is obvious a certain suspicion and reserve between the heads of the two missions. As early as June Gros confessed that he was not on such cordial terms with Elgin as he had been on the former mission.[1] This was doubtless caused largely by the strained nature of Anglo-French relations in 1860—the year of the annexation by France of Savoy and Nice. 'The State of Europe', Elgin commented, 'is very awkward, and an additional reason for finishing this affair. For if Russia and France united against us, not only will they have a pretty large force here, but they will get news via Russia sooner than we do, which may be inconvenient.'[2] Personal factors also had their influence. General de Montaubon, an ambitious, domineering man, had been greatly upset at seeing first the command of the French naval forces removed from him and secondly the nomination of an Ambassador—a personage of a rank so high upon whom he could not expect to impose his views. 'Aujourd'hui', he complained to the Minister of War, 'je ne puis plus que demander, presser; mais commander, non.'[3] He was frequently in disagreement not only with Sir Hope Grant and his own subordinates and his Admiral but also with Baron Gros.

On the morning of the 1st August a landing was successfully made about 2,000 yards south of the town of Pehtang, and, struggling through the mud and marshy ground, the advance party reached the causeway leading in a south-westerly direction from Pehtang to Sin-ho. In the evening a drawbridge on the causeway over a canal just outside the town was occupied, and that night Parkes led by a native entered the deserted fort and noted the position of the infernal machines left by the absent defenders. During the following days the remainder of the troops and stores were successfully landed from the river, or north, side of the town, whole streets of which had to be demolished for the purpose of constructing quays and wharves. The inhabitants suffered considerably in other ways—most of them fled, while some forty or fifty committed suicide. Pillage and looting and rape were indulged in by members of both forces and most of all by the corps of Cantonese coolies. The French did not attempt to check the depredations of their men, though the British Provost Marshal flogged thirty of his men in one day

[1] Gros to Thouvenel, 30 June 1860 (Cord. *L'Expéd.* ii. 218).
[2] T. Walrond, *Letters and Journals*, p. 337.
[3] de Montaubon to Min. de la Guerre, 27 June 1860 (Cord. *L'Expéd.* ii. 217).

for looting. It was essential if the Allies were to have an easy task that these malpractices should cease.

2. *Capture of Takoo Forts*

On the 7th it was decided in a council of war to move forward in three days' time. Elgin was anxious to get on, 'for at this advanced period of the year the objects of the expedition might be compromised by delay';[1] which would also involve serious danger to the health of the troops. Pehtang, wrote a Catholic missionary to the Procureur of his Society at Hong Kong that August, was 'une ville construite avec de la terre, des rues qui sont plutôt des marais fongueux avec des centaines de corps d'animaux en putréfaction, figurez un peu ce que c'est'.[2] On the 9th, however, heavy rain fell and the advance was perforce postponed until the 12th. Shortly after noon of that day following a sharp brush with Mongolian cavalry, the town of Sin-ho fell to the Allies; on the 14th Tangku was seized and the Allies were at the back-door of the series of forts which guarded the entrance to the Peiho. Six days were required by the engineers to bridge the numerous canals and creeks and to make a road passable for the siege-guns, and it was not until the morning of the 21st that fire could be opened on the forts on the north, or left, bank of the river. Three days before, de Montaubon had thrown 300 men across the river in junks. For a moment their safety was in jeopardy but pressure was relieved by the passage of a French battalion. He strongly urged the view that the southern forts were the key to the defence position of the Chinese. He would even have risked his communications with the fleet at Pehtang by crossing the river in force on the 15th. General Hope Grant dissented strongly from this course. In consenting to send a detachment of French troops to co-operate in an immediate attack on the northern forts, de Montaubon expressly disclaimed all responsibility for an operation which he thought violated the rules of the art of war, but when the event had proved the soundness of Hope Grant's judgement the French commander asked that his protest might be withdrawn.[3] After a gallant resistance the innermost fort was captured at 10.30 a.m., and at 2 p.m. the outer and greater

[1] Elgin to Russell, 8 Aug. 1860 (F.O. 17/330).
[2] Lazenave to Libois, 25 Aug. 1860 (M.E. vol. 316, f. 2067).
[3] de Montaubon to Grant, and Grant to de Montaubon, 20 Aug. 1860 (Cord. *L'Expéd.* ii. 259, 260).

north fort, which had been flying a white flag, was entered without further struggle.

In the afternoon Parkes, Loch, and a small party including three French officers were dispatched to the south bank to ascertain whether the white flags there displayed meant that those forts had decided not to resist. As it was impossible to get into communication with the Chinese officer in command, they made their way in heavy rain over the slippery muddy road to Takoo where they met Hengfu, the Governor-General. From him, after a considerable delay and much prevarication, they eventually extracted an order to the officers in charge of all the fortifications on the south side to hand over those strongholds to the Allies. His order had, however, been anticipated by the withdrawal of the garrisons, and on arrival back Parkes and his party found that Sir Hope Grant had sent a small force across the river to occupy the forts and disconnect the fuses left lighted. By the 23rd August no Chinese soldiery remained to block the entrance to the Peiho, which had been cleared by the Allied naval forces of all obstructions on the water-line.

During the advance from Pehtang the Governor-General had fruitlessly attempted to enter into communication with Lord Elgin by means of the American Minister. Subsequently Hengfu, who had assumed that a flag of truce hoisted by a watering party in the Pehtang river had been flown at Elgin's express commands, was sharply disabused by the British Plenipotentiary, who roundly refused to meet any Chinese diplomatic officer until the Peiho forts were in Allied hands and until a satisfactory answer had been given to Bruce's ultimatum. After the capture of Tangku the Governor-General plied Elgin with letters, in an endeavour to delay the advance of the armies—for even a short delay might, as the season was already late, have warded off the blow at least for that year.[1] Before the forts were taken Hengfu announced the appointment of Imperial Commissioners, who shortly afterwards notified their arrival and offered to conduct Elgin and Gros to Peking. Among the papers found at Sin-ho were letters which, although they gave no hint of the Emperor's yielding to the British demands, proved him anxious to avoid war.[2] Gros had also, naturally, received similar overtures and given similar replies.

[1] Elgin to Russell, 8, 20 Aug. 1860 (P.P. 1861, lxvi, nos. 57 and 61).
[2] Elgin to Russell, 20 Aug. 1860 (ibid., no. 64).

The ambassadors and the commanders-in-chief desired to exploit their success at the mouth of the river to the full. Three gunboats and the *Coromandel* with Admiral Hope on board went on the 23rd to within ten miles of the city where they were met by officials from Tientsin who informed the Admiral that the city would not be defended. Having remained there for the night, the Admiral next morning seized two large and newly built fortifications, admirably sited, and anchored at the junction of the river and the Grand Canal. Hangki, the Assistant Imperial Commissioner, came on board and expressed his wish that the Admiral would consider himself the guest of the Government—but in reply was told that the Allies, masters of Tientsin by right of Conquest, had no need of hosts. Leaving a small force with Parkes to arrange for supplies and to 'hold' the east gate of the city, the Admiral returned to Takoo and with his colleagues arranged for the transport of the army inland. The Infantry went up in gunboats, the other arms by land. To Elgin, whose ship the *Granada* ran aground at one of the innumerable twists in the river, and who arrived just before dawn on the 26th, Parkes was able to give a reassuring account of the temper of the population: he had ridden about the city unguarded and unmolested, the committee of gentry formed by the Chinese commander-in-chief had agreed to supply the Allies with the provisions destined for their own countrymen and with suitable residences for the ambassadors. The Governor-General had caused the removal from the streets of hostile proclamations, and Sang-ko-lin-sin, the Chinese commander-in-chief, had passed beyond Tientsin in a state of dejection, deprived by the Emperor of his three-eyed peacock feather and other decorations.

3. *Negotiations at Tientsin and Tung-chow*

The new Imperial Commissioner, with whom the Governor-General Hengfu was associated, was Elgin's former Tientsin negotiator, Kweiliang. He arrived on the 31st, in possession of the 'Kwang-fang' seal, and announced that there was no proposition of the British Government which he was not empowered to discuss and dispose of. Kweiliang was told that as the ultimatum of March had not been accepted, the British Government demanded an extra four millions and the opening of Tientsin for trade. If these terms together with those in the ultimatum were accepted, the Allied troops would retire to

Takoo but remain there until the indemnity was paid. In accepting these terms on the 2nd September the Imperial Commissioners asked for a conference to discuss how the indemnity was to be raised from the various ports, and the arrangements for the ambassadors' entry into Peking. Elgin and Gros had drawn up draft conventions which they submitted confidentially to each other. Elgin, anxious to avoid giving the Chinese any occasion for not finishing the business by the introduction of demands not included in the Treaty or the Ultimatum of March, demurred to some of Gros's proposed clauses. In Gros's draft convention the scope of religious freedom recognized in the Treaty was enlarged by two new stipulations, one for the repeal of the clauses in the Penal Code which discriminated against the exercise of the Christian religion and the other for the restitution to the missionaries of religious and charitable establishments confiscated during the period of Christian persecution. Other fresh clauses defined the equivalence of rank of foreign consular agents and Chinese Mandarins, invited the Emperor to send an embassy to Paris, and authorized a controlled system of emigration. Elgin objected that he would be unable to continue warlike activity for the sake of these clauses, and in face of such an attitude Gros had to content himself with the hope that, when the restricted convention, on similar lines to Elgin's project, had been accepted and the treaty ratified in Peking, he might by an exchange of notes or a protocol obtain these points from the Chinese Government.[1] The draft convention was transmitted to the Imperial Commissioners whom Wade and Parkes supposed to be prepared to sign it on the 8th. They made some difficulty about the payment of the first million taels at Tientsin and finally refused to sign without reference to Peking.[2] Parkes was fully prepared for this denouement, for

'just half an hour before the time fixed for the formal interview at which Mr. Wade and myself as Lord Elgin's Deputies were to deliver to the Assistant Imperial Commissioner Hangki, the draft of the proposed Convention, I received word from the latter that he was anxious to speak to me. I went at once to his residence and on meeting him there he produced a copy of the incomplete draft of

---

[1] Gros to Thouvenel, 6 Sept. 1860 (Cord. *L'Expéd.* ii. 294).
[2] Elgin to Russell, 8 Sept. 1860 (P.P. 1861, lxvi, no. 78).

the above document which Mr. Wade had given him to read in the course of the private visit we had paid to him the previous evening.'

The chief difficulty was the necessity of finding two million pounds in two months to pay the first instalment to the British and French Governments. With that exception Parkes thought there was nothing serious in the amendments which Hangki wished to propose or which would prevent the convention being duly signed on the 8th.[1] But that was in fact not all. In the strictest confidence, having dismissed all his attendants Hangki then said

' As we are old friends, I can be frank with you. I want you to know that although we may be able to sign on Saturday, we cannot positively name that day, as we must first receive the Emperor's approval of the Convention before we can put our seals to it. . . . Of ourselves we can enter upon no responsible course with the feeling that we shall be supported in it. The parties who can take a decision on all points are in Peking, and these men (naming five personages) can upset any arrangements that we may make, if they do not concur in the necessity or expediency of them. It is a pity that you cannot negotiate your business with these men or the Great Council direct, as whatever they do must be decisive. They are ever ready to raise objections to the arrangements of their Comm[rs] but will never come to the front and do Comm[rs]'s work themselves. When they sent off Kweiliang on this occasion, one of them making a play upon Kweiliang's title of Tsai-tseang (Minister of State) observed that he, Kweiliang was the Seang (elephant) to whom they trusted to drag them out of their present difficulties, but they have imposed upon him a heavier burden than he or any other single "elephant" can pull along. . . . It is of no avail for you to maintain that we as Imperial Commissioners can do anything, for we cannot. The parties with whom you might discuss matters to some purpose, if it were possible to get into touch with them, are the Great Council or the personages named. '

He was, however, far from meaning that the Allies should employ any hostile advance as a means of gaining such access, and he begged Parkes to be very careful not to repeat his remarks, as if they became known the fate of a traitor would await him. In accordance with this last suggestion, Elgin forwarding the report to the British Foreign Secretary begged that the report should not be published, and it was not.[2]

[1] Elgin to Russell, 8 Sept. 1860 (P.P. 1861, lxvi, no. 124).
[2] Elgin to Russell (secret), 8 Sept. 1860 (F.O. 17/331).

It was clear, therefore, that Elgin was not likely to gain satisfaction at Tientsin, and he could not afford to wait there indefinitely. Gros and he, therefore, agreed to move directly on Tung-chow, a town twelve miles from the capital, and some sixty from Tientsin. Sir Hope Grant had already been informed that if peace were signed, Elgin desired to be escorted on from Tientsin by a force of some 1,000 men: he was, therefore, ready for an immediate advance. British forces began to leave on the 9th, the French on the following day. By the 11th the British were beyond Yang-tsun, having met with no resistance, but here they had to halt for a day partly because the coolies had decamped with many of the mules, partly by reason of the heavy rains. By the 13th they were in Ho-se-woo—two-thirds of the distance between Tientsin and Tung-chow.

Meanwhile in Peking consternation ruled. In reporting the loss of the Takoo forts Sang-ko-lin-sin had on the 26th August prayed the Emperor to go on a hunting tour in Jehol, for the Chinese commander-in-chief 'would then be at liberty to choose his own time and mode of attack and might advance or retire as events should make necessary'. On the day when the British forces advanced beyond Tientsin the Emperor had proposed to command the army in person and 'at Tung-chow exterminate the vile brood of barbarians'. One of the Principal Secretaries of State and twenty-five other officers protested that such a course would not best conduce to the interests of the State and was 'not lightly to be adopted'. Sang-ko-lin-sin's project of a hunting tour was even worse, for if a walled city was not secure, a fortiori open hunting fields were highly dangerous. It were best to issue an edict to reassure the people and promise high rewards for distinguished conduct, and to pay special attention to placing the army in a state of perfect efficiency. By the 12th the Emperor had apparently decided to go on the hunting tour. He received an outspoken protest in several memorials which later fell into the Allies' hands. 'For Your Majesty to undertake so unusual a journey'—last made by the Emperor Taoukwang forty years ago—'at the very moment when the approach of the outside barbarians is imminent, is a thing which must cause extreme alarm and confusion'. 'This sudden departure without any apparent reason although called a hunting-tour will bear the aspect of a flight,' and would cause 'a great disturbance of the ancestral and tutelary spirits, shake the confidence of the troops, and entail an escort of 10,000 men and great expenditure of money which the Treasury could hardly meet'. The President of the Board of Civil Office reminded the quaking Emperor that at periods of public distress, the man of heroic character should be prepared to die at his post. 'Your Majesty is well familiar with the maxim that the Prince is bound to sacrifice himself for his country.' Nobody would believe the Emperor was going to fight the enemy if he made great preparations at the north of the city when the Allies were at the south-east. The confusion in the city would become intolerable, and only an immediate denial of the rumours of the Emperor's intended evacuation could restore confidence. The Emperor was, however, not to be deterred from seeking his own safety. He left the capital, not to return until after the Allied troops were away back in Tientsin.[1]

While these deliberations were proceeding in Peking and the Emperor was meditating flight, two new Imperial Commissioners had been appointed, Tsai, Prince of I, President of the Court of the Imperial Clan, and Muh-yin, President of the Board of War.[2] On the 12th they sent Elgin an imperious communication, requiring him to return to Tientsin; this was followed on the next day by another note more modest in tone 'conceding unconditionally almost all points in controversy between us', and desiring the Allies not to advance beyond Ho-se-woo.[3] Elgin consulted Sir Hope Grant on the military situation, and learnt from him that it would be necessary to halt the armies at Ho-se-woo for eight to ten days, in order to create a depot of stores and heavy guns. Elgin thought he could not during so long a time turn a deaf ear to the Chinese officers without justifying the view that he had come not to secure the execution of the treaty but to conquer an empire. In the hope of bringing matters to a speedier issue, he informed the Prince, therefore, that the British army would continue its march towards, but halt short, of Tung-chow. He would then proceed with an escort of 1,000 men into that city where the convention presented to Kweiliang could be signed, and whence he would move forward with his escort to Peking for the exchange of

[1] Elgin to Russell, 15 Nov. 1860 (P.P. 1861, lxvi, no. 122).
[2] Elgin to Russell, 11 Sept. 1860 (P.P. 1861, lxvi, no. 82).
[3] Elgin to Russell 16 Sept. 1860 (P.P. 1861, lxvi, no. 83).

ratifications. These proposals were agreed to by the French Ambassador and by the commanders of both armies.

On the 14th, therefore, Wade and Parkes went forward with the intention of meeting these high Chinese officers in Matow, but finding they had gone back to Tung-chow pushed on to that city. After a discussion of eight hours the convention was accepted, and it was agreed that the Allied armies were to be halted five li[1] south of Chang-kia-wan—some eight miles short of Tung-chow. Parkes was to return on the 17th to make the final arrangements. Seeing that peace was likely to be made General Sir Hope Grant arranged to move the army from Ho-se-woo to the agreed halting-place—a two days' march—on the 17th.[2]

At daylight on the 17th there set out for Tung-chow, Parkes accompanied by Loch, de Normann (an attaché of Bruce's), and Bowlby of *The Times*, with an escort of six Dragoon Guards and twenty Indian cavalrymen under Lieutenant Anderson. With them rode the Quartermaster-General Walker who, with Thompson of the Commissariat, was to arrange the camping ground. They observed some small parties of Chinese soldiers on the way and met the general who had commanded the Chinese forces at Sin-ho, whose manner appeared cordial. Arrived in Tung-chow at 10.30 a.m. they were received by the Imperial Commissioners at one o'clock. To their surprise the Chinese Plenipotentiaries raised objections to and refused to discuss the Convention until the demand for the presentation of Elgin's letter of credence to the Emperor had been withdrawn. Their tone was offensive in spite of Parkes's reiterated statement that a *casus belli* could not arise from the question of the presentation of the Queen's letter. At last about six o'clock they settled the arrangements for the encampment and provisioning of the army, for which services the Imperial Commissioners actually detailed certain Chinese officers to assist the Allies.

4. *The Capture of the Allied Officers*

At daybreak next morning, Parkes and Loch with the Quartermaster-General and Thompson, accompanied by a small escort of the Dragoon Guards and three Sikhs left to make arrangements at the halting-place of the army. As it was Parkes's

---

[1] A 'li' is approximately ⅓ English mile.
[2] Elgin to Russell, 16 Sept. 1860 (P.P. 1861, lxvi, no. 83)

intention to return to Tung-chow when the encampment had been settled in order to provide accommodation for Elgin, most unfortunately de Normann, Bowlby, with Lieutenant Anderson and the remainder of the escort decided to stay behind in Tung-chow. On his way back Parkes observed large bodies of Chinese troops, masked batteries, infantry, and cavalry concealed behind high millet and in nullahs. It was apparent that treachery was at hand and the Allied armies might arrive at any moment. Colonel Walker and Thompson with five of the Dragoon Guards remained on the ground to be occupied, in accordance with the agreement, by the British troops; Loch with two Sikhs pushed on to the advancing British forces; while Parkes decided to return to Tung-chow with one Dragoon Guardsman and one Sikh to inquire of the Prince of I the meaning of the apparent hostility.

Very soon Loch came upon the commander of the British advance guard with whom he galloped back to the General. Sir Hope Grant had himself observed large masses of cavalry threatening his flank and was preparing for a possible surprise attack. Loch obtained his promise to keep off an attack if possible for two hours while he returned as speedily as possible to Tung-chow. Meanwhile, on his return to that city Parkes had set out in search of the Imperial Commissioners, and found them after considerable difficulty. 'They told me that they would not withdraw the troops, and in such a tone that I soon saw that the sooner I withdrew myself from them the better. . . . I made them give me, however, categorical replies to two categorical questions, which to prevent mistakes I took down before them in writing.' These replies were (1) that the Imperial Commissioners would *not* direct the troops to retire, because (2) peace had *not* been determined upon, in consequence of the audience question remaining still unsettled. When Parkes repeated that he could only refer this question to Lord Elgin, they said, 'You can do much more if you like. You can settle the point at once yourself; but you won't.'

The English and French who had stayed behind, as the French interpreter wrote subsequently of the fate of one of them, the Abbé Deluc, 'étaient restés deux heures de trop à dormir. S'ils avaient voulu partir avec nous ils étaient sauvés.'[1] By the time Parkes had returned from his visit to the Prince, they were back

---

[1] de Meritens to Mgr. Guillemin, 5 Dec. 1860 (M.E., vol. 550, f. 1401).

from an inspection of curiosity shops, and Loch had already joined them. They made their way towards the Allied lines with their Sikh escort as quickly as possible. Scarcely had they cleared Chang-kia-wan than batteries opened on both sides: the battle had begun and the whole of Parkes's party were on the Chinese side of the line. A Mandarin approached the party and suggested they should obtain a pass from the commander-in-chief which would enable them to go round the flank. Parkes and Loch with one Sikh bearing a flag of truce went with this officer and were ushered into the presence of no less a person than Sang-ko-lin-sin himself. The Chinese commander-in-chief derided and abused Parkes whom he regarded as the cause of all the troubles and difficulties that had arisen. Parkes and Loch were dismounted and thrown on their knees in presence of their captor, who ordered them to be taken before the Prince of I. Then, huddled into a common springless country cart, they were driven two miles beyond Tung-chow, where they were taken out and further examined by another Minister of State Juilin— kneeling with their arms twisted behind them and their beards pulled by the Chinese soldiery. They imagined that they were to be put to death, but instead were again placed in a cart and driven on into Peking and lodged in the prison of the Board of Punishments. Here with chains fastened to their ankles and necks they were thrust into different chambers which contained some fifty criminals, verminous, half-naked, murderers and the like—placed on boards and attached to a chain hung from a beam so that they were unable to walk. There with their elbows pinioned they were given tea and bread and left to their own devices and the company of the worst kind of Chinese.

Meanwhile, the Allies had experienced no difficulty in driving their enemy off the ground on which it had been agreed that they should camp, and the British cavalry made a reconnaissance up to the walls of Tung-chow. While attempting under cover of a flag of truce to carry into the town a message threatening that, unless the captives were immediately returned, Peking would be attacked and taken, Wade was fired upon. On the 20th news was received from an intelligent Chinese that the foreigners had been seen in a cart making towards the capital. On the 21st a large body of Tartar cavalry at Pa-li-chiau, between Tung-chow and Peking, was attacked and routed, and their camps extending for several miles destroyed. This—the final stand of Sang-ko-lin-sin—had been made at a cost of three French killed and seventeen wounded and about the same number of British casualties.

On the following day Elgin received a note from Prince Kung, the younger brother of the Emperor, aged twenty-eight, stating that the Prince of I and Muh had been deposed from their office for mismanagement, and that he had been appointed Pleni-potentiary in their stead. The Ambassadors refused to entertain his request for an armistice so long as the prisoners remained in captivity.[1] The halt which Sir Hope Grant had intended to make at Ho-se-woo was now made at Pa-li-chiau, eleven miles distant from Peking. It was vitally necessary to receive, besides reinforcements, fresh supplies and ammunition which would have to come up from Tientsin by junk, and to establish an advanced base at Tung-chow.[2] The interval, partly to disguise the temporary military weakness of the Allies, was occupied by an exchange of diplomatic correspondence between Prince Kung and Elgin and Gros. At first Kung, claiming Parkes and his party as proper prisoners of war captured after firing had commenced, agreed to free them as soon as the Allied armies and fleets had left Takoo. After conferring with the General, Elgin rejoined that if within three days—that was to say by the morning of the 29th—the British and French prisoners were released, and Kung agreed to sign the convention, the Allied armies would not advance further: the convention would be signed in Tung-chow, whence the British Plenipotentiary would go to Peking with an armed escort, and, the Treaty duly ratified, the armies would winter in Tientsin. If these conditions were not accepted by the time given, the Franco-British force would move on the capital.

Instead of handing over his prisoners on the 29th Kung on that day asked that the Allied armies should retire to Chang-kia-wan: that movement effected, the convention could be signed between that place and Tung-chow. The following day, for reply, the Prince was informed that the commanders-in-chief had been instructed to take such measures as they deemed necessary to obtain by force what diplomacy had been unable to secure.[3] To this threat Kung replied on the 1st October, agreeing to accept both convention and treaty; whereupon

[1] Elgin to Russell, 23 Sept. 1860 (P.P. 1861, lxvi, no. 84).
[2] Col. Foley to Russell, 22 Sept. 1860 (P.P. 1861, lxvi, no. 86).
[3] Gros to Kung, 30 Sept. 1860 (Cord. *L'Expéd.* ii. 342).

Elgin requested him to send a duly qualified officer with the foreign prisoners to the advanced posts of the army which was already on the move towards the capital.[1] As no reply was received to this reiterated demand for the return of the captives, Gros apparently became very despondent. On the 3rd October in a private letter to the French Foreign Minister, Thouvenel, he expressed his fears that there might be no one with whom the Allies could treat, and that the commanders-in-chief might be called upon to decide whether to winter in Peking or Tientsin.[2] Gros was considerably older than Elgin who, an active man, rode in the saddle by the side of his General, while his French colleague was obliged to travel in a litter. Gros frequently complained of the hardships to which he was necessarily subjected. He would have preferred to have waited in Tientsin until the Allied armies had taken possession of Peking—'this singular diplomatic campaign' as he called it, was for him *rude et pénible*.[3]

Meanwhile, on the 22nd September Parkes had been transferred from the filthy common jail to a special room eight foot square which he shared with four picked jailers, and thither Hangki was sent by Prince Kung in an attempt to urge Parkes to arrange a suspension of hostilities, and held with his prisoner long but fruitless conversations on the 22nd and 26th. At a third interview Hangki informed Parkes that the Prince disapproved of the ill treatment to which the captives had been subjected, and promised that Parkes should have no further cause of complaint. The chains and the iron collar were removed after eleven days of torture, and on the 29th at Parkes's express wish he and Loch again met and were housed comfortably in a temple outside the prison. Time and again the Mandarins tried to induce Parkes to take some step which might have hampered Elgin's freedom of action. He was induced to write that he was now being well treated, and trusted that hostilities would be suspended in favour of negotiations, though Loch was able to add in Hindustani that the letter was written to order. They were secretly informed in a package of clothes sent to them from British Headquarters that an ultimatum threatening to bombard the city in three days had been delivered. The first shot, Hangki told them, would be the

[1] Elgin to Russell, 8 Oct. 1860 (P.P. 1861, lxvi, no. 88).
[2] Gros to Thouvenel, 3 Oct. 1860 (Chine 34).
[3] Gros to Thouvenel, 19 Sept. 1860 (Cord. *L'Expéd.* ii. 321).

signal for their execution: nor is it to be supposed that they were greatly comforted by a letter from Wade which told them that their death would entail the burning of Peking from one end to another. They were to be executed on the evening of the 5th— then a reprieve to the next morning was announced, and finally Hangki came to say that the Prince had agreed to Elgin's terms.

On the 7th sound of heavy firing was heard. It was a salute Hope Grant had ordered to be fired to inform the British Cavalry and the French of his position. The Allies had moved round to the north-east angle of the city wall, where there were no suburbs between it and the open country. The French on the right had on 6th October seized the Summer Palace from which Prince Kung and the Empress had just managed to make good their escape. During the 7th and 8th a position was taken up on the north wall with a special concentration opposite the Anting Gate. On the 8th Hangki returned to the prisoners having seen the Prince and Wade, who had demanded the surrender of one of the city gates before operations would be stayed. Parkes and Hangki with other Mandarins discussed astronomical problems until close on midday when an officer arrived and had a long conversation with Hangki. Kung had decided forthwith to release his prisoners. At 2 p.m. they were driven out of the city in covered carts into the safety of the British lines—the party consisted of Parkes, Loch, the old Sikh who had been captured with them, M. d'Escayrac de Lanture, and four French soldiers.

5. *The Destruction of the Summer Palace*

Elgin had wisely decided to turn a deaf ear to the Chinese suggestions that the prisoners could be saved at the expense of a retrograde move by the army and the sacrifice of the public interests which such a step would have entailed. Unfortunately some of the prisoners had died. Lieutenant Anderson's arms had been so tightly bound that two days before his death his nails and fingers burst and mortification set in; while he was yet alive, worms were generated in his wounds, crawled over and ate into his body. Captain Brabazon and the Abbé Deluc had been, it was feared, decapitated. The bodies of others including Bowlby of *The Times* and de Normann were returned between the 14th and the 18th. Out of 26 English prisoners 13 were dead, of 13 French 7 were dead.[1]

[1] Elgin to Russell, 13 Oct. 1860 (P.P. 1861, lxvi, no. 91).

It was on the 12th October that the cruel fate of Lieutenant Anderson and de Normann became known, and when the mutilated bodies were brought into the camp, the sight of them, wrote Loch, 'excited general indignation'. Baron Gros in a private letter to his chief described the feelings of the Allied forces thus: 'You can well imagine that extreme indignation and rage reigns in the allied camps and that we shall need all the prudence and calm we can command to prevent horrible reprisals from spoiling our cause. There are people who would like to burn Peking and to torture every Chinese mandarin. . . .'[1]

Elgin decided that in spite of the surrender to the Allies on the 13th of the Anting Gate, before the expiration of an ultimatum,[2] Prince Kung could not regard himself as at peace with the British until 'this foul deed shall have been expiated'. It was necessary, he thought, to mark by a solemn act of retribution his government's indignation at such perfidy and gross brutality on the part of the Chinese officers. It was useless to ask that those chiefly guilty should be handed over for punishment by a court martial—for miserable subordinates alone would be given up: Prince Kung would never surrender Sang-ko-lin-sin. A money payment to the British Government did not in itself seem a suitable punishment and already 40 per cent. of the customs of four years would be required to meet the bill for indemnities.[3] He drew up a draft of a dispatch to Kung and transmitted it to Gros for the comments of his French colleague. They both agreed that compensation should be paid to the living sufferers of the treachery of the 18th September and to the relatives of those who had died or been put to death. But Gros demurred strongly to three other demands which Elgin made. Elgin concurred in his objection to one of these: that Chinese officers should be deputed to accompany the remains of the deceased to Tientsin, where at the expense of the Chinese Government a memorial was to be erected setting forth the circumstances in which they had met their deaths. Elgin apparently had suggested—though it does not appear in the draft note to Kung—that, if the Imperial Commissioner failed to meet all his liabilities within three days, the Allies would enter

---

[1] Gros to Thouvenel (particulière), 19 Oct. 1860 (Chine 34).
[2] Elgin to Russell, 13 Oct. 1860 (P.P. 1861, lxvi, no. 90).
[3] Elgin to Russell, 26 Oct. 1860 (F.O. 17/332).

the city and burn the Imperial Palace. Gros would have been prepared, if Kung had ultimately refused to agree to the Allies' terms, to advise the French commanders to take that course, but he objected to the propriety of playing at that stage the final card in the hands of the Allies: for a final card it was as it would in all probability have brought about the collapse of the Manchu dynasty.[1] But Elgin refused to forgo his third demand: the final destruction of the Summer Palace. To this Prince Kung's assent was not necessary, though Elgin meant to notify him of his decision. On this point the British and French Plenipotentiaries and military commanders remained divided.

Elgin demanded, therefore, an immediate payment to the British (from whom had been taken captive twice as many as from the French) of 300,000 taels and to the French of 200,000 taels as compensation for the sufferings of the prisoners and deceased. The military occupation of Tientsin would now continue until the whole indemnity, instead of the first million taels stipulated in the convention, had been paid. If the Prince was not willing to agree by 10 a.m. on the 20th to pay the compensation by the 22nd, to sign the convention as modified and to ratify the Treaty of 1858, Elgin threatened to seize the Imperial Palace in Peking. Besides this,

'What remains of the Palace of Yuen-ming-yuen,' he wrote, 'which appears to be the place at which several of the British captives were subjected to the grossest indignities, will be immediately levelled with the ground. This condition requires no assent on the part of His Highness because it will be at once carried into effect by the Commander-in-Chief.'[2]

While the Summer Palace was burning on the 18th and 19th October, Gros was writing an agonized private letter to Thouvenel. 'I must keep you in touch with the situation, certainly very serious, in which we are, and of the delicate position in which I am placed, vis-à-vis my English colleague. He wants to go too far and, torch in hand, to follow a course on which I cannot and will not accompany him.' He was afraid of the effect of Elgin's measures on the already terrified Prince Kung. 'Prince Kung does not sleep in the city; he spends each night in a different house in the country, so afraid is he of the Allies

---

[1] Elgin, 'Projet de Note'; Gros to Elgin, Elgin to Gros, 16 Oct. 1860; Gros to Elgin, 17 Oct. 1860 (Cord. L'Expéd. ii. 368–74).

[2] Elgin to Russell, 25 Oct. 1860 (P.P. 1861, lxvi, no. 103).

seizing him and making him expiate by torture the terrible *attentat* of which I have just told you.' Ignatieff was in touch with Gros. He had entered the city whence Kung had departed, and was trying his best to urge the Chinese who were there to come speedily to terms. He asked Gros to give him an inkling of his intentions especially in regard to Peking so that he could look after Russian interests. Gros hoped fervently that the Russian Minister's advice would be followed. If Elgin's policy were to jeopardize French interests, he hinted to Thouvenel that he might turn to Russian advice and help. 'I shall not hesitate to ask his help if necessary. The savage, I might even say, Chinese, burning of the Summer Palace by the English will perhaps strike Prince Kung with terror, and if he leaves Peking, where shall we go? I confess I am afraid lest tomorrow go by without an answer.' 'Ce qui serait mon désespoir réjouirait Lord Elgin, il veut tout brûler, tout détruire, et il cherche évidemment à faire disparaître la Dynastie actuelle.' Gros, in fact, in his despair wrote to Ignatieff 'in the greatest secrecy to engage him to make Prince Kung understand that the fate of the dynasty was in his hands and if he yielded this morning before 10 o'clock (it was then 6.30 a.m. on the 20th) to all our requests without conditions peace would be made and Peking saved'. He gathered from Ignatieff that Kung had agreed to degrade Sang-ko-lin-sin and Juilin, the two men chiefly responsible for the affair of the 18th September. This had been obtained in spite of or without English influence, 'de concert avec le général Ignatieff qui s'est conduit dans toute cette affaire avec un tact que je ne saurais trop louer'[1].

Elgin also gave in a private letter to his chief his account of the difference between the Allies. He too had had private conversations with Ignatieff, who would not perhaps have been so unreservedly praised by the French Ambassador if he had known that the Russian rather suspected the purity of his motives in protesting so energetically against the burning of Yuen-ming-Yuen. Elgin reported to Russell that 'Gros got into a maudlin state about the existing Dynasty. He wishes to avoid inflicting a penalty on China for the treatment of the British and French prisoners. I suspect (and Ignatieff agrees) Jesuit influence',—for this body wanted the revival of the former edict of two hundred years ago in their favour, and hated the rebels

[1] Gros to Thouvenel (particulière), 19 Oct. 1860 (Chine 34).

for their iconoclasm. Gossip had it, wrote Elgin, that de Montauban had made much money by the loot of the Summer Palace and wanted to get home as quickly as possible to enjoy it.[1] The gossip which Elgin heard was not idle talk. Gros confessed later in a private letter to Thouvenel that there was one fatal element in so much that was satisfactory: the demoralization of the army,

'as a consequence of pillaging culminating in the looting of the Yuen-ming-Yuen Palace. What is the use of a soldier who has 20, 30, 50 and even 100 thousand francs in his pack? One Corps commander is said to have in his baggage pearls and diamonds worth more than 800,000 francs. Tientsin at this moment presents the distressing sight of soldiers selling at every cross road, rolls of silk, jewels, jade vases, and thousands of precious objects coming from Yuen-ming-Yuen worth at least thirty million francs. . . . As for our allies they are perhaps in an even worse condition than our army.'[2]

This last statement was fortunately entirely without foundation. Fearful of the demoralizing influence of indiscriminate plunder, General Hope Grant had confined his troops to their bivouacs in front of Peking, and appointed officers to collect the British share of the booty. The property handed to them was sold by auction, realizing about £8,000. This, together with £18,000 in specie, was divided among the Army on the spot, one-third to the officers and two-thirds to the men who received about £4 each. The major-generals and Hope Grant himself resigned all claim to their share in the prize.[3] On the other hand,

'Montauban's virtue which allowed him to plunder the Palace in question' with no special object except that 'of putting the contents into his own pocket and that of the army', but 'compelled him to protest against the act of burning it when that act suggested itself as the only practicable mode of marking our abhorrence of a great crime, and of proving to the Emperor and his entourage that such crimes could not be committed with impunity is of a somewhat questionable complexion. The burning of the Palace was not a proceeding to my taste—but it was a necessary act—and has proved, I think, quite successful in its results.'[1]

This act of revenge was fully endorsed by the British Prime Minister, who wrote on Boxing Day to his Foreign Secretary:

[1] Elgin to Russell (private), 27 Oct. 1860 (G.D. 22/49).
[2] Gros to Thouvenel (particulière), 17 Nov. 1860 (Chine 34).
[3] Hope Grant to Herbert, 21 Oct. 1860; Hope Grant and H. Knollys, *The China War of 1860*, p. 226.

'This Alexandria Telegram about Events in China makes one's Blood boil with Indignation. . . . I am delighted that the Emperor's Palaces have been burnt to the ground, and that the Money Payment has been doubled. I only wish we had been able to make the Emperor a Present of the Head of Singolinsin in a charger.'[1]

He must have been all the more pleased as he had written in November: 'I am afraid Elgin is disposed to be too soft with the Chinese.'[2]

6. *Peking and Peace*

The results certainly were not as the French General had feared, for on the 20th Kung asked Elgin to fix an hour on the 23rd at which the convention could be signed and the Treaty of 1858 ratified. Two days later he made arrangements for the payment demanded as compensation for the sufferings and losses of the British officers and soldiers who had been made prisoners. It was agreed that the ceremonies should take place at 2 p.m. on the 24th,[3] when Elgin would be accompanied by an escort of 100 cavalry and 400 infantrymen to the court of the Board of Ceremonies,[4] a place chosen by Parkes and Loch after a personal inspection of the Public Offices.

On that day at long last the convention was duly signed. Elgin inserted two new articles—emigration was to be legalized, and the cession of Kowloon leased to Parkes by the Governor-General of the Two Kwangs was made in full sovereignty to Great Britain. Baron Gros had been dissuaded by Elgin during the Tientsin negotiations from adding clauses to legitimize the emigration of coolies and in favour of Christianity. But as the French Ambassador thought that his and Elgin's liberty of action was restored by subsequent events he had added to his ultimatum to Kung a demand for an indemnity for the victims and for the restitution of the Catholic churches closed by the Emperor's predecessors. He now agreed, at Elgin's request, to add, but declined to insist upon, the legalization of emigration.[5]

Nothing was lacking in the ceremony to mark the significance of the occasion. A body of cavalry headed the procession, then

[1] Palmerston to Russell, 26 Dec. 1860 (G.D. 22/21).
[2] Palmerston to Russell, 8 Nov. 1860 (G.D. 22/21).
[3] Elgin to Russell, 23 Oct. 1860 (P.P. 1861, lxvi, no. 99).
[4] Elgin to Russell, 23 Oct. 1860 (P.P. 1861, lxvi, no. 102).
[5] Elgin to Russell, 25 Oct. 1860 (F.O. 17/331).

came the officers detailed to attend the signature of the instruments, followed by the Head-quarter Staff and the General with his personal staff. At an interval of thirty yards behind Sir Hope Grant, Lord Elgin was borne in a chair of State carried by sixteen Chinese dressed in royal crimson liveries. The diplomatic staff were on either side of the Ambassador, who was followed by a detachment of infantry. Important points on the three-mile route from the Anting Gate to the Hall of the Board of Ceremonies were guarded by detachments of Sir Robert Napier's division. Crowds of Chinese gazed in a well-behaved way at the strange sight. On arrival at the hall Prince Kung came forward to meet Lord Elgin à la chinoise with clasped hands. The British Ambassador with a proud and haughty look responded by making a slight bow: an act which must have frozen the blood in the veins of Prince Kung.[1] In the hall itself two chairs of State were placed for Lord Elgin and Prince Kung. Elgin's full powers were duly communicated in translation by Wade to His Highness, and in return the Emperor's decree wrapped in yellow silk was reverentially produced and read. It granted Kung full powers to negotiate and conclude a peace and to affix an Imperial seal to the treaty. The conventions were then signed, and the ratified treaties exchanged, and in addition Prince Kung signed a document which expressed the acceptance by the Emperor of all its terms and conditions. After a few complimentary remarks had been exchanged Elgin rose to leave. For a moment Kung hesitated to accompany him to the edge of the steps leading to the courtyard—a momentary desire perhaps at the last to mark in some way the superiority of his Sovereign and people. But at the urgent signs of some of the principal Mandarins he desisted and accompanied Her Britannic Majesty's Ambassador to the threshold of the Hall.

On the following day the French Convention and Treaty were duly signed and ratified. At the ceremony Baron Gros was at pains to mark by his manner that he did not approve of the cold attitude assumed by Elgin. In a private letter to Thouvenel he gave an account of his reception and explained his attitude: 'I meant to be as agreeable and respectful towards him as, from what I have been told, Elgin had been cold and severe.' He was much pleased with a remark of the Prince's after the documents had been signed and sealed: that if Gros were to stay in

[1] Grant and Knollys, *Incidents in the China War*, p. 209.

Peking it would not be as a Plenipotentiary but as a friend—
a remark which drew upon the Baron the friendly smiles of
the 200 Mandarins who were present at the ceremony. After
his return, Gros received a visit from Ignatieff and reported to
Paris: 'I understood from General Ignatieff that Prince Kung
was very pleased by the respectful appearance with which
I presented myself before him.' Already Peking was becoming
a stage on which the by-plot of Anglo-French rivalry could be
enacted. Gros suspected Elgin of desiring to upset the Dynasty
'and to stretch out a hand to the bandits of Nanking',—to
counter this possibility 'I have had confidentially to call
General Ignatieff into play, and he has lent a hand with the
best grace in the world'[1]. If the Manchus were overthrown
by the rebels, 'would it not be a triumph for England if Nanking,
before which ships can be brought to bear broadside on, became
the capital of the Empire?'. On the 30th Gros heard from the
Roman Catholic Bishop of Chih-li and his coadjutor that they
had been handsomely received by Prince Kung. Upon the
Prince's recommendation they had called upon Chang-Pao, the
new commander-in-chief, who had asked them whether in
the event of a formal request for French aid against the rebels,
the Chinese Government would receive a negative answer.
Only of the French would he make such a request, for they were
'a loyal and generous nation, and never of our Allies who were
known to be much more inclined to protect the rebels than to
uphold the reigning dynasty'. Gros could of course make no
certain answer to these informal suggestions without instructions from Paris. For the moment he put the Chinese off by
observing that it would be difficult for him to press his Government to aid the Emperor when His Imperial Majesty refused to
come to Peking to receive the letters of which Gros was the
bearer from Napoleon III. Yet he suggested to Thouvenel that
the French Government would enjoy a magnificent position in
China if through their efforts the dynasty was saved; and there
was not lacking an adequate pretext for such action as the
Shanghai rebels had strangled twenty-three children and a
missionary protected by France. Nor would it be difficult to go
to Nanking for redress for that outrage, seize the city, and hand
it over to the Imperialists.[2]

---

[1] Gros to Thouvenel (particulière), 26 Oct. 1860 (Chine 34).
[2] Gros to Thouvenel (particulière), 1 Nov. 1860 (Chine 34).

Though the conventions and treaties of both Allies were now fully executed, Elgin decided after consulting with Sir Hope Grant, not to begin the withdrawal of the troops until an Imperial decree had been received authorizing the publication of the ratified Treaty and the Convention in all the provinces of the Empire. As soon as the announcement, according to Article VIII, had been made, Elgin promised to evacuate Chusan. The troops would be confined to Tientsin, Takoo, and north Shantung and Canton. Elgin himself would have liked to have agreed to evacuate Canton, thinking that the northern places would be healthier for the troops, but as Gros was unwilling to concur without instructions from home, he had to content himself with urging his Government to persuade Napoleon III to adopt that course.[1]

On the 4th November Prince Kung paid a visit to Elgin, which the British Ambassador duly returned. Elgin was pleased to hear his repeated admission that advantages would accrue from the more direct intercourse between foreign ministers and the Government of Peking, now about to be established under the new treaties.[2] The Imperial edict on the publication of the Treaty and Convention had arrived in the capital on the 2nd November, couched in very full and satisfactory language, printed in the *Peking Gazette* and placarded in the city. On the 7th Bruce arrived from Shanghai, and was formally introduced by Elgin to the Prince. As Bruce was now the Queen's representative Elgin took care to put him in the seat of honour and on the following day to absent himself when Kung returned the call. Bruce 'had a long and somewhat interesting conversation, in which, as in several interviews which he had previously had with me', reported Elgin, 'the Prince showed much less reserve than the provincial functionaries, with whom we have formerly dealt, ever dared to do, in discussing delicate questions, such as the advisability of the mission of a Chinese Ambassador to England'[3].

As Ignatieff had decided to leave Peking, and Gros was anxious to give the Emperor the opportunity of returning to his capital and accommodating himself to the changed position before the French Minister took up his residence in the city,

[1] Elgin to Russell, 27 and 31 Oct. 1860 (F.O. 17/332).
[2] Elgin to Russell 4 Nov. 1860 (P.P. 1861, lxvi, no. 118).
[3] Elgin to Russell 13 Nov. 1860 (P.P. 1861, lxvi, no. 119).

Elgin and Bruce agreed that the latter should retire to Tientsin until the following April. Gros had pointed out that the position of Bruce, who was regarded by the Chinese as the primary cause of their recent catastrophes, was personally one of some delicacy. 'Pour faire arriver officiellement et sûrement Mr. votre frère dans les yamuns des hautes fonctionnaires de l'Empire il faut peut-être applanir d'avance la route qu'il a à parcourir.'[1] During the winter, therefore, Bruce remained in Tientsin while the house in which he was to reside was being prepared. But he took pains to emphasize to Prince Kung that he would not correspond with any Provincial High Commissioner, but only with himself or other Foreign Minister.[2]

It is needless to say that the British Government were warm in their approval of what had at last been effected. In the thirty years since the adoption of the policy of free trade and commencement of relations between the Sovereign of Great Britain and China a profound revolution had taken place. Bruce in sending new-year greetings to the Foreign Office from Tientsin on the last day of 1860 summed up the meaning of what had just been effected and the hopes he cherished.

'You must recollect in dealing with questions here that it is as difficult to induce our people to respect the rights and authority of the Chinese as it is to lead the Chinese to recognize our privileges—this is perfectly intelligible—as the bigotry and arrogance of the Chinese for a long time made the satisfactory solution of every question to depend on force—they made a great mistake—for the balance of force is against them, and they have taught foreigners on their part to think anything justifiable than can be carried through by violence. Our great difficulty is to substitute for this state of chronic war, pacific discussion—and the possibility of pacific discussion depends on our being able to induce them to admit those general principles of mutual fair dealing which form the basis of international intercourse—I see no means of effecting this change, short of being alongside the Central Government. If we are fortunate enough to come into contact with an influential man of reasonable views, I do not despair of proving that our objects are essentially pacific, that our demands are reasonable, and that we are inclined to be moderate and conciliatory, if we are met in a corresponding spirit. In that case there are no questions likely to arise of difficult solution, and we might be able eventually to reduce materially the large and

[1] Elgin to Russell (confidential), 13 Nov. 1860 (F.O. 17/332).
[2] Bruce to Russell (confidential), 16 Nov. 1860 (P.P. 1861, lxvi, no. 125).

expensive naval force we keep in these seas. But the first step is to be up at Peking.'

Doubtless the Chinese Government were still very sore at the thought of receiving foreign ministers on a footing of equality, but experience Bruce hoped would reconcile them to the change. 'I have set my heart on effecting this change, and I am persuaded that the interests of our trade, and of China herself, require that it should be made without more delay.'[1] Elgin expressed similar views in a private letter to Russell:

'If the party now in power which seems to have caught some glimpse of the truth that the interests of China and of peace will be promoted by the arrangements remains at the head of affairs the benefit will be great. The disputes which constantly arise between the subordinate agents of the two governments at the Ports will be settled by the authority of the English Minister and the Imperial government at the capital instead of by acts of war—the short cuts to a settlement too frequently adopted under existing conditions. The mere fact that we shall be able to make the truth of the case known to the government when such disputes arise will effect a marvellous change.'[2]

[1] Bruce to Alston, 31 Dec. 1860 (F.O. 17/339).
[2] Elgin to Russell (private), 31 Oct. 1860 (G.D. 22/49).

EPILOGUE

'A MARVELLOUS change.' For the short space of thirty years the British Government had been striving to effect a radical change from Peking's policy of rigid exclusiveness to a recognition by the officials and Emperor of China that they were not the sole possessors of right reason and of the virtues of civilization. The inventions and discoveries which since the end of the fifteenth century had transformed the intellectual and material surroundings of the men of western Europe had loosed unexampled energies. No Wall could shelter the inhabitants of China from their restless activity. They had caused the earth to shrink both geographically and spiritually. These prosperous middle classes living at home in freedom and comfort were filled with the universal humanitarianism of Christianity and nineteenth-century Liberalism. Though the French Catholic missionaries and the fewer Protestants from America and Britain were fulfilling a mission directly of a spiritual order, working in the cause not only of the Church but of *la civilisation européenne*, and though the impulse which had at the start brought most of the Anglo-Saxons to China was trade and commerce, it is none the less true that to men like Bowring commercial progress was a sign and a pledge of ethical and cultural advance. The old colonial policy of the eighteenth century which aimed at isolation and monopoly had given place before the beginning of our story to the new idea of free trade and the principle of the open door. The humanitarian voices, which had spoken at the Vienna Congress against the slave trade, are heard as loudly protesting against the exploitation of the defenceless coolies of Amoy, in the name of a humanity which is all-embracing. The expression of the dynamic spirit of the West which we have been studying is not in any proper sense 'imperialistic'. The pushing and grasping merchant in China—often a hot-blooded young man desirous of a quick fortune and expecting to make it before he was much over thirty—seemed indeed to have no time and little inclination for matters of eternal moment. And indeed the vanguard overseas was not, as a body, representative of the highest of Western society. But it is a matter worthy of note that the British Government was as deeply conscious of its responsibility as it was of its power. From the beginning it sought to control and govern its unruly subjects. A man like Palmerston was not only steeped in the conception of the Rule of Law, but was by temperament a grand hater of injustice and by instinct a member of a class whose right and duty it was to govern.

If in his conduct the individual Englishman was sometimes harsh and even brutal, such as was Compton beating a paltry huckster, it may be thought that Palmerston was not essentially different when he used his Big Stick of a naval demonstration or a small punitive force. But it would appear that the British Government was unwilling to use that Stick save as an instrument of what it considered justice in a legally ordered international society. It is not difficult for it to plead at the bar of international law that the Stick was not brandished for the sake of mere expediency. Both in the question of the exchange of ports and in the regulation of the opium trade in 1858, two matters which deeply concerned British interests, the Government and its representative were careful not to arrive at their ends by forceful means. When they used force it was to meet the duplicity, evasion, cunning, and cruelty of the Chinese officials.

As the British were so much the most influential in numbers, wealth, and power, it was, no doubt, the especial duty of their Government to introduce order and harmony both among its own subjects and into its relations with the Chinese authorities. Throughout the story from 1833 to 1860 it did much, in marked contrast to the American Government, to achieve this purpose. From 1833 onwards a growing body of civil servants, divorced from trade, battled manfully with the problems of disorder and lack of governance. The Washington authorities were content to grant consular status to the principal American merchants, and, unlike their British colleagues, the diplomatic representatives of the United States were not 'hommes de carrière'. Inheriting a legacy of suspicion and influenced by a desire to court popularity at home they were prevented at times from working in friendly harmony with the British representatives who on their side evinced a contempt and impatience born of a proud feeling of superiority. It is important to remember that in this age the United States, by tradition and interest, were primarily occupied with the consolidation of their domestic economy and the pressing problems of expansion towards the west. Not until 1846 was California ceded to them by Mexico, and at the end of our period the route from Washington to Canton lay through London. However impressed some of their representatives became on closer acquaintance with the situation by the essential soundness of British policy, their powerlessness, irritating to themselves, compelled them to act in a way which at times seemed likely to thwart the fulfilment of aims with which they were fundamentally in agreement. Men who have to reap where they have not been able to do much of the sowing themselves are not likely to be enthusiastic admirers of the sowers.

Before our story closes, the shadow of European and world rivalries is clearly being cast over the Chinese landscape. In the minds of Russians, Frenchmen, and British China is becoming another Turkey, fit only for Partition or Protection. This development, hastened by the Crimean War, is one at least of the factors which explain the desire of the Western Powers to establish missions in Peking. Another factor was the impossible situation in which these Powers, and Great Britain in particular, found themselves when face to face with the Chinese authorities at the ports.

The Chinese did not adopt a rigidly isolationist policy. They had no objection to the commercial activities of the Barbarians at the limits of the Empire. But the toleration of that amount of contact necessitated a much closer intercourse. To prevent the distortion of their grievances by the Hong merchants, Lord Palmerston, advised and influenced by the powerful trading interests in England, had insisted upon direct communication between the representative of the British Crown and the Viceroy at Canton. But, when once that had been obtained, it became necessary to approach the Dragon Throne itself. For experience showed that the Viceroy himself, no less than the Hong merchants, might either deliberately misrepresent, or turn a deaf ear to, the remonstrances which the British and other Governments saw fit to make.

There were thus face to face two communities which differed so radically in their organization and conception of life that a clash could not be avoided unless the Chinese had shown that they were not unwilling to absorb the new influences, and unless the Western peoples had been content to allow their new ideas to permeate gradually into the strange society with which they were in contact. It is abundantly clear that, when the first shock of the defeat in 1842 had passed away, the Chinese tried to preserve as far as possible their isolationist past. Had the early promise of the Pottinger-Keying days been fulfilled it is not certain that the British would have been content to await a slow absorption of the new ideas which they were bringing with them. But it is clear that they never were put to the test. In Japan in a later generation they survived the ordeal.

It would indeed have been an act of faith to expect the Chinese Government to change its suspicious attitude to impending economic changes and freely to treat foreign States on a footing of equality. For there was a momentous internal limitation of sovereignty to be overcome. Just as the Sultan of Turkey would have ceased to be Sultan if he had abandoned Mohammedanism for Christianity, so the Son of Heaven would have denied himself by recognizing the Queen of England as his equal. It was not just arrogance that led the Chinese scribes continually to place the name of their master in a more honourable position than that of Victoria or the President of the United States. And so it was that the change was never morally complete until the Empire collapsed. There can be little doubt that the military and diplomatic defeats of the Empire seriously imperilled the stability of the régime, even when later the Westerners lent it military and financial support. The collapse was inevitable if there was to be a full recognition of that equality of status and common humanity which was the real demand of the British and other foreign Governments. It is certain that the modern Chinese with his strong nationalist feeling is the abiding result of the contact between the European Governments and the Ruler of Peking. Whether the young nationalist educated in and by the West is as alien in the land of his birth as were the British in China in the middle of the last century, or whether through him the horizon of his fellows, still for the most part living the life of the Middle Ages, in the innumerable villages and cities of the interior, will be lifted beyond their immediate vision, so that in due time they may reach out into the full and free life of a positive common citizenship and a collective partnership with other peoples, is the question which any Englishman who contemplates the first step in such a possible development is bound to ask himself in all humility and reverence.

SHORT BIBLIOGRAPHY

A. MANUSCRIPTS

1. *British Museum:* Aberdeen Papers: correspondence with Ellenborough: Add. MSS. 43198. Auckland Papers: Add. MSS. 37715 and 37717. Peel Papers: General Correspondence: Add. MSS. 40428.
—— ——: correspondence with Stanley: Add. MSS. 40467; 40468.
—— ——: correspondence with Aberdeen: Add. MSS. 40453; 40454; 40455.
2. *Church Missionary Society:* Salisbury Square, London—some few missionaries' letters of little political importance—cited as 'C.M.S.'
3. *Missions Étrangères:* Rue du Bac, Paris. Well indexed, calendared, and bound, the correspondence of the fathers of this Society is of considerable political interest—cited as 'M.E.'
4. *Public Record Office:* China dispatches to and from the Foreign Office, and domestic correspondence. For this period they are contained in 343 volumes, numbered 4 to 347, listed and cited as F.O. 17/. Occasional reports on Chinese affairs in the diplomatic correspondence of British representatives at other courts can be found by references to them in dispatches from the Foreign Office to British representatives in China: for example Russia F.O. 65/. Granville Papers: listed and cited as G.D. 29/. Russell Papers: listed and cited as G.D. 22/. These contain, as the text will show, some interesting comments on China affairs. These collections uncalendared and unbound were recently deposited in the Record Office.
5. *Quai d'Orsay:* China dispatches to and from the Ministère des Affaires Étrangères, and other official correspondence. For this period they are contained in volumes numbered 4 to 34. It is a significant commentary of the relative unimportance of French interests in China at the time that these French documents are about one-tenth as numerous as the British. Cited as 'Chine'.

B. PUBLISHED OFFICIAL CORRESPONDENCE

1. *British Parliamentary Papers* (cited as P.P.):

1831–2	XXXI	East India Company Correspondence.
1840	XXXVI	Correspondence of Foreign Secretaries with the Superintendents from 1833–9.
1848	XLVIII	Murder of six Englishmen.
1851	XXI	Report on Steam Communication.
1852–3	LXIX	Civil War.
1852–3	LXVIII	
1854–5	XXXIX	Emigration.
1857	X	
1857–8	XLIII	
1857	XII, XLIII	Insults in China: and Opium.
1857–8	LX	Elgin and Yeh, December 1857.
1859	XXXIII	Elgin correspondence, 1857–9.

1860   LXVIII   Gunboats at Peiho.
1860   LXIX   Bruce correspondence, March 1859—April 1860.
1861   LXVI   Correspondence, October 1859—January 1861.
It appears that unless a dispatch is described as 'Extract' it is printed in full. An 'Extract' usually suppresses criticism of a foreign colleague and sometimes information which might be damaging to a Chinese informant.

2. *United States: Senate Executive Documents* (cited as Sen. Ex. Doc.):
28 Congress, 2nd Session, No. 67.
35   ,,   1st Session, No. 47.
35   ,,   2nd Session, No. 22.
36   ,,   1st Session, No. 30.
House Documents (cited as H. Doc.):
33 Congress, 1st Session, No. 123.

3. *France:* H. CORDIER in *L'Expédition de Chine de 1857-8*, (cited as Cord. *L'Expéd.* i) and in *L'Expédition de Chine de 1860*, (cited as Cord. *L'Expéd.* ii) gives sometimes in full, more often extracts of, many dispatches to and from de Courcy, de Bourboulon, and Baron Gros.

4. *Hansard:* especially Second Series, xxiii, xxv; Third Series, xliv, lii, liii, cxliv.

C. SOME SELECT BOOKS AND ARTICLES

ABEEL, D.   *Journal of Residence in China.*   1835.
ABEL, C.   *Narrative of Journey in the Interior.*   1819.
ALLEN, N.   *The Opium Trade.*   1853.
ASHLEY, E.   *Life of Lord Palmerston.*   1879.
BEAUMONT, J.   *What is Lord Elgin to do?*   1857.
—— *The New Slavery.*   1871.
BERNARD, W. D.   *Narrative of the Voyages and Services of the 'Nemesis'.*   1844.
BOWRING, J. B.   *Autobiographical Recollections.*   1877.
CHINESE REPOSITORY.   Canton, 1833–51.
CORDIER, H.   *L'Expédition de Chine de 1857-8.*   1905.
—— *L'Expédition de Chine de 1860.*   1906.
DAVIS, J. F.   *The Chinese.*   1836.
—— *Sketches of China.*   1841.
—— *China during the War and since the Peace.*   1852.
—— *China Miscellanies.*   1865.
DE KAT ANGELINO, A. D.   *Colonial Policy.*   The Hague, 1931.
DOWNING, C. T.   *The Fan-qui in China in 1836, 7.*   1838.
EITEL, E. J.   *Europe in China. The History of Hong Kong.*   1895.
'EYEWITNESS.'   *Opium Trade in China.*   1858.
FAIRBANK, J. F.   'The Legalization of the Opium Trade' (*Chinese Social and Political Science Review*, vol. xvii).
—— 'The Provisional System at Shanghai' (ibid., vols. xviii, xix).
—— 'The Creation of the Foreign Inspectorate' (ibid., vols. xix, xx).
—— 'Definition of the Foreign Inspectors' Status' (*Nankai Social and Economic Quarterly*, vol. ix).
'FIELD OFFICER.'   *The Last Year in China.*   1843.

FISHBOURNE, E. G. *Impressions of China.* 1855.
FORTUNE, R. *Wanderings in China.* 1847.
GIRARD, O. *France et Chine.* Paris, 1869.
GRANT, H., and KNOLLYS, H. *The China War of 1860.* 1875.
HART, R. *These from the Land of Sinim.* 1901.
HUC, E. *Souvenirs d'un Voyage.* Paris, 1850.
HUNTER, W. C. *Bits of Old China.* 1885.
JAMES, J. A. *God's Voice from China.* 1858.
JONES-PARRY, E. 'Under-Secretaries of State for Foreign Affairs, 1782–1885' (*English Historical Review*, vol. xlix).
K'AIMING CH'IU, A. 'Chinese Historical Documents' (*Pacific History Review*, vol. ii).
KEETON, G. W. *Development of Extraterritoriality in China.* 1928.
KRAUSSE, A. *Russia in Asia.* 1899.
LATOURETTE, K. S. *A History of Christian Missions in China.* 1929.
—— 'Chinese Historical Studies' (*American Historical Review*, vols. xxvi, xxxv).
LEONG, Y. K. *Village and Town Life in China.* 1915.
LIN, T. C. 'The Amur Frontier Question' (*Pacific Historical Review*, vols. iii, iv).
LOCH, H. B. *Personal Narrative of Occurrences during Lord Elgin's Second Embassy to China.* 1869.
MAXWELL, H. *Life of Lord Clarendon.* 1913.
MEADOWS, T. T. *Desultory Notes.* 1847.
—— *The Chinese and their Rebellions.* 1856.
MEDHURST, W. H. *China: Its State and Prospects.* 1838.
MICHIE, A. *The Englishman in China.* 1900.
MOORE, J. B. *Digest of International Law.* Washington, 1906.
MORLEY, J. *Life of Gladstone.* 1903.
MORSE, H. B. *The International Relations of the Chinese Empire.* 1910.
—— *Trade and Administration of China.* Third Edition, 1920.
—— *Chronicles of the East India Company.* Oxford, 1926, 1929.
—— *The Gilds of China.* 1909.
MURRAY, H. *Historical and Descriptive Account of China.* Edinburgh, 1836.
OLIPHANT, L. *Narrative of the Earl of Elgin's Mission.* 1859.
OUCHTERLONY, J. *The Chinese War.* 1844.
OWEN, D. E. *British Opium Policy.* New Haven, 1934.
PEAKE, C. H. 'Documents on Modern China' (*American Historical Review*, vol. xxxviii).
POOLE, S. L. *The Life of Sir Harry Parkes.* 1894.
RAVENSTEIN, E. G. *The Russians on the Amur.* 1861.
SANDERS, L. C. *Lord Melbourne's Papers.* 1889.
San Kuo. Translated by C. H. Brewitt-Taylor. 1925.
SCARTH, J. *Twelve Years in China.* Edinburgh, 1860.
SMITH, A. H. *Village Life in China.* 1899.
STAUNTON, G. T. *Memoirs.* 1856.
—— *Ta Tsing Leu Lee.* 1810.
TAYLOR, H. *Autobiography.* 1874.
TILLEY, J., and GASELEE, S. *The Foreign Office.* 1933.
TSIANG, T. F. 'China after the Victory of Taku' (*American Historical Review*, vol. xxxviii).

TSIANG, T. F. 'China, England, and Russia in 1860 (*Cambridge Historical Journal*, vol. iii).
—— 'Extension of Equal Commercial Privileges' (*Chinese Social and Political Science Review*, vol. xv).
—— 'The Government and the Co-Hing' (ibid., vol. xv).
WADE, T. F. 'Note on Chinese Empire in 1849' (*Bombay Quarterly Review*, October 1855 and April 1856).
WALROND, T. *Letters and Journals of James, eighth Earl of Elgin.* 1872.
WEBSTER, C. K. Lord Palmerston (*Politica*, No. 2).
WEST, A. *Memoirs of Sir Henry Keppel.* 1905.
WILLIAMS, S. W. *The Journal of S. Wells Williams*, edited by F. W. Williams. Shanghai, 1911.
WINGROVE COOKE, G. *China, 1857–8.* 1858.

INDEX

A a

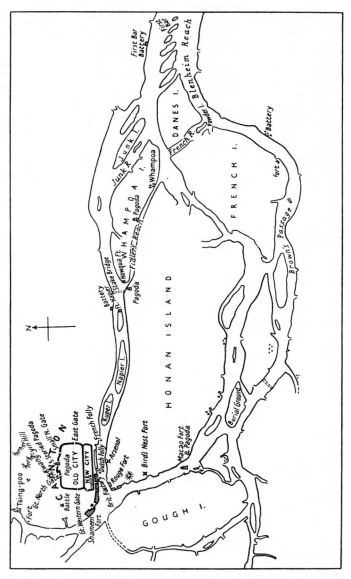

WHAMPOA AND CANTON

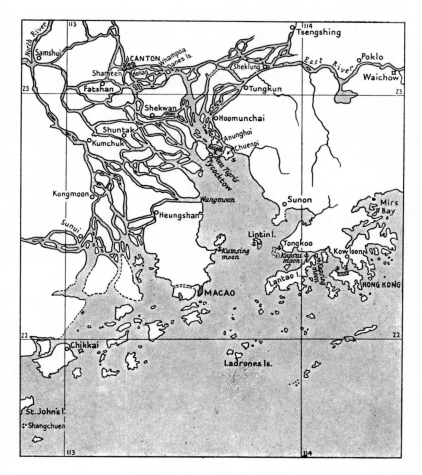

HONG KONG AND CANTON